Reason, Faith, and Tradition

and Tradition

Explorations in Catholic Theology

D0910996

Author Acknowledgments

No book is written in complete isolation. For this one, I am indebted to the help of many people. Interaction with students at Marquette University, Mount Marty College, and Presentation College have helped me to sharpen my own thinking and understanding of these theological issues, as has my interaction with many colleagues at those institutions.

I wish to acknowledge the publishing team at Anselm Academic, especially Leslie Ortiz for first accepting this book for publication, and my editor Jerry Ruff for his critical insights and sensitivity to reader perceptions.

Through the process of writing, my wife, Judy, and son, Daniel, supported a too often distracted, tired, or unavailable husband and father. I am grateful for their patience.

My final debt of gratitude is to my own father, Ludwig Albl. His love of learning and culture, his ethic of hard work, and his openness to ecumenical understanding have shaped not only my thoughts but, more essentially, who I am. I dedicate this book to his memory.

Publisher Acknowledgments

Our thanks to the following individuals who advised the publishing team or reviewed this work in progress:

Professor Mara Kelly-Zukowski, PhD, Felician College, Lodi,
    New Jersey
Susie Paulik Babka, PhD, University of San Diego, California

Reason, Faith, and Tradition

Explorations in Catholic Theology

Martin Albl

ANSELM ACADEMIC

Created by the publishing team of Anselm Academic.

Cover and interior images royalty free from iStock and Shutterstock.

Printed in the United States of America

7009

ISBN 978-0-88489-982-2

Library of Congress Cataloging-in-Publication Data

Albl, Martin C.
Reason, faith, and tradition : explorations in Catholic theology / Martin Albl.
      p. cm.
Includes index.
ISBN 978-0-88489-982-2 (pbk.)
      1. Christian education—Catholic. 2. Faith and reason—Christianity—Textbooks. 3. Catholic Church—Doctrines. I. Title.
BX930.A38 2009
231'.042—dc22

2008044912

Contents

Introduction

One of the tragedies of our modern world is the widespread belief that faith and reason are opposites. In more than ten years of teaching theology at the college level, I have encountered numerous students who assume that a person must choose between a rational, scientific view of the world, and a worldview based on faith. The message of this book is that we need not choose. In the Christian understanding of reality, these two views, properly understood, are in perfect harmony. The ultimate goal of Christian theology is to demonstrate that harmony, and this book, I hope, makes a small contribution toward achieving that goal.

This book is not intended as a comprehensive introduction to all aspects of Christian or Catholic theology. Rather, I hope to introduce students to the Christian and Catholic theological tradition by exploring some key questions involving the relationship between faith and reason. This approach allows us to go straight to the heart of Christian theology: the deep conviction that faith and reason are harmonious.

To help illustrate the organic nature of the centuries-old Christian theological tradition, I include a fair amount of cross-referencing within the text. Students need not look up each cross-reference to understand any particular topic, however. Rather, the references serve as a reminder that Christian theology is best understood as a whole, and as an aid to studying a specific topic in further depth if the student so desires.

Key theological terms are defined within the text; some of them also are defined in a brief glossary. Terms included in the glossary are highlighted in bold at first use in the text. Also following this introduction you will find listed some abbreviations used in this text.

An introductory book such as this one can only skim the surface of many deep and complex issues. But if it can help motivate students to continue their own efforts to recognize the deep harmony between faith and reason, it will have achieved its purpose.

Abbreviations

The following abbreviations are used in this text:

BCE = before the Common Era (dates before the birth of Jesus)

c. = *circa*. Means "approximately."

CCC = *Catechism of the Catholic Church* (2nd ed.; Vatican: Libreria Editrice Vaticana, 1997)

CDF = Congregation for the Doctrine of the Faith

CE = Common Era (dates after the birth of Jesus)

NJBC = R. E. Brown, J. A. Fitzmyer, and R. E. Murphy, eds., *The New Jerome Biblical Commentary* (Englewood Cliffs, NJ: Prentice Hall, 1990)

par. = parallels. In references to the Gospels, this means that the cited passage has parallels in one or both of the other Synoptic Gospels.

PBC = Pontifical Biblical Commission

SCG = Thomas Aquinas's *Summa contra Gentiles*

ST = Thomas Aquinas's *Summa Theologica*

Vatican II documents

All references are to Austin Flannery, ed., *Vatican Council II,* vol. 1, *The Conciliar and Postconciliar Documents*, rev. ed. (Northport, NY: Costello Publishing Co., 1992).

DV = *Dei Verbum (Dogmatic Constitution on Divine Revelation)*

GS = *Gaudium et Spes (Pastoral Constitution on the Church in the Modern World)*

LG = *Lumen Gentium (Dogmatic Constitution on the Church)*

NA = *Nostra Aetate (Declaration on the Relation of the Church to Non-Christian Religions)*

UR = *Unitatis Redintegratio (Decree on Ecumenism)*

1

Faith and Reason I

Are Reason and Faith Contradictory?

The title of this book combines two terms that may seem incompatible: *reason* and *faith*. Many people assume that religious beliefs or faith can only be opinions and conjectures about the unknown and unknowable. The very fact that there are so many different religions (often with widely differing beliefs and practices) seems to prove that religious beliefs lie simply in the realm of opinion, and are not open to reasonable discussion and investigation.

The central aim in this book is to show that reason and Christian belief are in fact neither contradictory nor mutually exclusive. In fact, we'll argue that the two are inseparable. Reason, aided by Christian faith, reveals truths about the universe and about humans that could never have been reached by reason alone. Conversely, Christian faith needs reason in order to communicate its beliefs clearly, to arrange those beliefs in a more systematic form, to guard it from straying into fanaticism or error, and to provide answers to reasonable objections to those beliefs.

Specifically we will be considering Christian **theology**—the reasonable study of the Christian faith. Studies of this type have sometimes been mocked as useless theoretical debates about such topics as "how many angels can dance on the head of a pin." The argument of this book is that, on the contrary, theology is intensely practical, because our religious beliefs (or lack of beliefs) profoundly shape the way in which we understand the world, and thus how we act in the world. Theology helps us to clarify what our basic religious beliefs are (or are not), and how these beliefs influence all aspects of our daily life and world.

The third word in our title, *tradition*, essentially means "a way of life" or "customs" that are passed down through the generations. We hear the word used in many ways: a family has certain holiday traditions; different nations and peoples have "traditional" music, dances, or food.

In this book *tradition* will refer to the specific way of thinking that is the Roman Catholic theological tradition—a way of combining reason with religious faith that has been passed down from generation to generation for two thousand years.

In a world full of many different religious and theological traditions, isn't it rather narrow-minded, or even prejudiced, to focus on just the Catholic tradition? Wouldn't it be better to be more inclusive, and study a diverse range of theological ideas?

Although we'll discuss the reasons for focusing specifically on the Catholic tradition in more detail below (sec.s 1.11–1.13), we will here make three quick observations:

1. Any theological thinking must be thinking within a specific theological tradition: it is simply impossible to think theologically in general.

2. The Catholic theological tradition has a rich, two-thousand-year-old intellectual and spiritual heritage that has profoundly influenced Western culture (and, through Western culture, the rest of the world): anyone wishing to gain a true understanding of the broader culture must also consider this heritage.

3. While our study focuses on Roman Catholic thought, it does not exclude important contributions from non-Catholic thinkers (for example, C. S. Lewis and Hans-Georg Gadamer).

Our study will not be a technical one, explaining in detail what theology is, or how theology works. Rather, our approach will be to select certain basic theological issues and questions (for example: Can God's existence be proven? Do science and religion contradict one another?) and study how the Catholic tradition has combined faith and reason in an attempt to respond to these questions. We will also consider some basic Christian beliefs (for example: that God is a Trinity, that the Bible is God's word, that people spend eternity in either heaven or hell after death) and ask how faith and reason relate in these specific beliefs.

Before discussing Christian theology specifically, however, we must first explore how reason relates to human religious belief in general. So we begin by trying to gain a better understanding of that often-strange human activity that we call "religion."

Centrality of Religion   1.2

If we have any desire to understand human existence, we must consider the role of religion in people's lives. Billions of people throughout the world identify themselves as members of religious traditions: they are followers not only of the great religious traditions of Judaism, Christianity, Islam, Hinduism, and Buddhism but also of countless smaller or lesser-known traditions. We have only to watch the news on television or to read the newspaper to know that religion and religious beliefs play a central role in a variety of national and international issues: the conflicts in the Middle East, the discussion on teaching evolution in the public schools, the public policy debates on such issues as same-sex marriage or abortion.

At the personal, subjective level, the vast majority of humanity seems to experience some sense of the religious. Even if people do not regularly attend religious services or follow an organized religion, they will certainly have been confronted with what we call "religious" questions at some point. For example, when a close friend or family member passes away, a natural human response is to wonder, "What happened to my loved one? Is she in a better place? Will I see her again?" As young people consider which career to pursue, or which college major to choose, the question may arise (even if somewhat vaguely), "What is the purpose of my life?" or, more specifically, "Does God have a plan for my life?" Or perhaps as a couple considers marriage, each one may wonder, "Is this the person whom I was meant to marry?" These questions are "religious" to the extent that they all imply the existence of a supernatural reality—a reality completely different from our everyday experience in this world.

People who do not identify themselves as "religious" often still consider themselves "spiritual"—they believe in a "higher power" that exists beyond the visible and tangible world, and they believe that this "higher power" gives sense and purpose to their lives.[1]

From both these general and individual considerations, it is clear that religion is a central dimension of human life, and thus an important subject of study.

Religion: Encounter with the Transcendent   1.3

We will try now to define the term *religion* a little more closely. We commonly refer to Buddhism, Hinduism, Judaism, Christianity, and Islam as religions; we can also refer to Lakota religion, Hopi religion, or the religious traditions of various indigenous groups throughout the world. We speak, too, of ancient Greek, Roman, or Babylonian religions. But it is difficult to identify what it is, exactly, that makes all these religions. What do they all have in common?

Clearly it is not just a belief in God. While adherents of Judaism, Christianity, and Islam are monotheists (believers in one God), the ancient Greeks were polytheists (believers in many gods), and other traditions speak not of gods but of spirits or other supernatural beings. While Buddhism accepts the existence of gods and spirits, the Buddha himself focused not on these supernatural powers but on the ability of humans to achieve a state of being known as Nirvana. So once again we face the question, "Is there a common link that unites all these various beliefs?"

In his classic study *The Idea of the Holy*, Rudolf Otto claims to have found that common link.[2] Otto identifies the primary source of all religious feeling in the common human encounter with what he calls "the numinous." The Christian writer C. S. Lewis summarizes Otto's concept well:

> Suppose that you were told that there was a tiger in the next room: you would know that you were in danger and would probably feel fear. But if you were told "There is a ghost in the next room," and believed it, you would feel, indeed, what is often called fear, but

of a different kind. It would not be based on the knowledge of danger, for no one is primarily afraid of what a ghost may do to him, but of the mere fact that it is a ghost. . . . Now suppose that you were told simply, "There is a mighty spirit in the room," and believed it. Your feeling would then be even less like the mere feeling of danger; but the disturbance would be profound. You would feel wonder and a certain shrinking—a sense of inadequacy to cope with such a visitant and of prostration before it. . . . This feeling may be described as awe, and the object which excites it as the Numinous.[3]

Otto himself uses the Latin phrase *mysterium tremendum et fascinans* to sum up his understanding of the numinous. *Mysterium* refers to the "wholly other": something we experience as completely different from ordinary human knowledge and experience. *Tremendum* refers to the overwhelming power of the numinous presence: people become acutely aware of their human limitations and can only react by falling to their knees in worship. Otto illustrates this term with two biblical examples: When Moses encounters God in the burning bush, "Moses hid his face, for he was afraid to look at God" (Exod 3:6). After Jesus had performed a miracle, Simon Peter "fell at the knees of Jesus and said, 'Depart from me, Lord, for I am a sinful man'" (Luke 5:8).

But the numinous is also *fascinans*—it attracts a person in spite of the person's fear and dread. This double reaction can be illustrated in the fact that most people, even while experiencing some fear, are attracted to, and even fascinated by, ghost stories or other paranormal accounts. At more developed levels, Otto finds the *fascinans* in the Christian's desire for the beatific vision of God (seeing God "face-to-face") and in the Buddhist's desire for Nirvana—that state of pure peace and bliss that is beyond all human language and even conception.

Another scholar of world religions, Mircea Eliade, agrees that all religions share a common belief in a realm of otherworldly, numinous reality (a realm he calls the "sacred"), one that is distinct from the profane (everyday, visible reality).[4] Religions use this distinction to divide the world into sacred space (such as temples, altars, or sacred places in nature where the numinous may be encountered) and profane space (all other places of ordinary human activity); they divide time into sacred time (such as special times of year marked by festivals and religious rituals) and profane time (all other times of ordinary human activity).

As a general term to cover both Otto's concept of the numinous and Eliade's concept of the sacred, we shall use the word **transcendent** to refer to a reality that transcends natural, everyday human experience. The belief in the transcendent is at the heart of all religions.

The Transcendent Horizon of Human Nature 1.4

The Catholic theologian Karl Rahner argues that the experience of transcendence is found not only in special encounters with the numinous, but also in the very structure of the human person himself.[5] In every human experience, we are aware not only of our own human limitations but, at the same time, of the possibility of transcending those limitations. Our basic human experiences point beyond themselves to a "transcendent horizon." Let's consider a hypothetical example.

Jeff claims to be a complete skeptic: he denies that any absolute, objective truth exists. "Truth" is really only based on people's perceptions. Every society, he insists, has had its own subjective opinions about truth, and the stronger or more ruthless society usually imposes its own version of truth on the weaker.

But notice the logical problem in Jeff's analysis: if Jeff's statement, "There is no such thing as truth" is true, then there is at least one statement (Jeff's) that is in fact true. But if Jeff's statement is true, then Jeff's claim ("there is no truth") makes no sense. By the very act of denying truth, Jeff in fact shows that absolute truth must exist.

As humans, we realize that our own thinking and opinions will always be limited (whether because of our prejudices, lack of knowledge, or limited experiences). But at the same time, we are also aware that it is necessary for this absolute truth to exist, or we would never be able to think at all. How else would we know that our grasp of truth is limited, unless we had a sense of an absolute truth? With this intimation, this glimpse into absolute truth, a person transcends himself—he knows that there is an absolute horizon of truth that is infinitely beyond his (or any other human's) knowledge and control. He becomes aware of the transcendent.

Let's consider another example. In Clara's studies of social sciences such as psychology or sociology, she becomes aware of the great influence that outside forces have on human personality. Psychology, for example, shows her how profoundly a childhood trauma may affect an adult's experiences and choices. She learns from sociological and pedagogical studies that a child's capacity to learn may be severely limited if the child is raised in an impoverished or insecure environment.

Clara herself was raised in a poor neighborhood plagued by crime and violence, and she suffered childhood traumas. She knows that these experiences have influenced her deeply — yet at the same time, she knows that these factors, and any other outside factors, do not define her. The very fact that she can think about these experiences, analyze them, and learn from them shows that she has transcended them. Despite the very real difficulties, she is free to rise above these limitations. In Rahner's terms, she has realized that in her freedom to respond to these traumatic events, her life is open to a transcendent horizon.

Meaning and Transcendence   1.5

The personal religious questions that we mentioned in section 1.2 — "What is the purpose of my life?" or, "Is this the person whom I was meant to marry?" — are questions about *meaning*, and they are clearly transcendent questions. They presume that life has a meaning beyond itself.

Many common, everyday expressions also presuppose that life has a transcendent meaning. A common response to an unpleasant or even a tragic event may be, "Everything happens for a reason." An often heard response to a disappointment is, "I guess it wasn't meant to be." If it is true that a certain event "wasn't meant to be," it can only be true if some kind of transcendent plan exists that shapes whether events occur or not.

A more philosophically inclined individual might ask if life itself has a meaning, a purpose, or is human life simply a random collection of cells, tissues, and organs that, through blind chance, evolved the ability to think about itself? (We will discuss this question in chapter 4.)

Raising questions about meaning is an essential human characteristic, and a central function of any religious tradition is precisely to provide believers with a sense of meaning. Thus the person who encounters the numinous is not left with only fear and terror, but rather is given an orientation and a mission that help to make sense of daily life. To return to Otto's examples, after Moses' encounter with

God, Moses is sent to free his people from Egypt; after his encounter with Jesus, Peter is sent out as an apostle. Eliade describes how sacred space and time give structure and meaning to the basic worldview of a religious people. The discovery of a sacred space, for example, can be conceived as the fixed reference point that "is equivalent to the creation of the world."[6]

All societies have asked questions about the basic meaning of life; countless millions have asked and continue to ask questions about the meaning of their individual lives. The question is a transcendent one, since it is oriented toward ultimate meaning, a meaning transcending the meaning any individual person or group can give to human life. For the religious person, this transcendent realm gives everyday life its meaning.

Right, Wrong, and Transcendence   1.6

The first part of C. S. Lewis's book *Mere Christianity* is entitled, "Right and Wrong as a Clue to the Meaning of the Universe."[7] Lewis points out that all humans of every culture have the same basic sense of right and wrong. Of course some details vary, but all cultures share the basic sense that such things as lying, stealing, and committing adultery are truly wrong, not just wrong in the opinion of some people. Even when people do lie or steal, they almost always try to rationalize or justify their behavior — thus proving that they accept the common standards of right and wrong, but are simply arguing that their particular behavior qualifies as an exception. Lewis calls this common set of ethical standards the "Moral Law."

What is the ultimate source of this Moral Law? Lewis shows that individual societies could not simply have invented it — or else how could we explain why the basic ethical standards of the ancient Egyptians, ancient Chinese, medieval Europeans, and modern Americans are essentially the same? Nor can the Moral Law simply be based on instinct, because our natural instincts are often contradictory. When another person is in danger, for example, we have a natural instinct to help a fellow human being, but we also have a natural instinct for self-preservation that functions to prevent us from helping. Some would argue that the rules of the Moral Law were simply invented in order to prevent chaos in society. But if this was so, why would anyone follow them, unless they happened to benefit that individual personally? Why should the individual care about society as a whole?

The Moral Law, Lewis concludes, can only come from a transcendent source. We did not invent it, but we feel obligated to obey it. Even when we break the Law, we feel obligated to rationalize or justify our behavior.

Experiences of Transcendence 1.7

Perhaps you have stood outside in the evening, watching a sunset. The air is still and cool, the light on the distant horizon is streaked with a palette of soft colors. A feeling of infinite peace comes over you. But the feeling only lasts a moment—a child asks you a question, you hear the sound of an airplane overhead, you recall a bill you forgot to pay, and the spell is broken. But you have had an experience of the transcendent—a sense of peace and beauty that does not seem to belong to everyday reality, but rather seems to point beyond it.

Or perhaps you have held your newborn baby in your arms for the first time. As you first gaze upon his little face, you are overwhelmed by a feeling of unlimited love and a sense of responsibility for this new life. Of course you are familiar with the biological facts of how this baby was conceived and born, and yet biology cannot describe or even begin to explain the experience of first seeing and holding your child. You are overcome with the wonder of a new life that you did not create but that was given to you as a gift. Babies are commonly described as "small miracles"—an expression that is simply one way of trying to define realities that touch on the transcendent, beyond our normal reality.

At times the experience of the transcendent can take the form of dissatisfaction with this world, restlessness, a longing for something more, something better. We are often frustrated with our lack of ability to communicate with others, to find meaning in our schooling or work, to find peace in our family life. Nor does this dissatisfaction come only when we are frustrated or unhappy. It also comes precisely when we are content, when life is good. It is after those moments when we experience the best of what life can offer us—love, beauty, peace, deep joy—that we often find ourselves longing for more. These brief experiences of happiness seem to awaken within us a desire for something on a completely different scale: perfect, lasting love; perfect, eternal peace.

The great Christian theologian Augustine (354–430) describes that experience of longing and desire with these words, "Our hearts

Transcendence and Death

1.7.1

An elderly man wakes up suddenly in the middle of the night, thinking about an old friend with whom he has lost contact. He cannot get back to sleep, so he reads some magazines, gets a drink, and finally goes back to bed—all the while still thinking of his friend and wondering how he is doing. In the morning, he calls his friend's sister. "I'm so glad you called," she tells him, "John just passed away last night."

Over the course of two years during World War II, a woman lost three sons who were serving as soldiers. On each occasion, she had a vivid dream and knew even before she received the news that one of her sons had fallen.

I have heard these stories through reliable sources; you may know of similar accounts. We can certainly dismiss these and similar stories as coincidence or exaggeration, but is that the most reasonable reaction? When faced with events that have no natural explanation, perhaps the most sensible response is to admit that our reason is limited and to leave open the possibility of an explanation that transcends nature. o

are restless until they rest in thee, O Lord" (*Confessions* 1.1.1). Even the atheist philosopher Friedrich Nietzsche (1844–1900) knew this longing; in his most famous work, *Thus Spoke Zarathustra*, the line "All joy wants eternity—wants deep, deep eternity" is repeated several times.

The Reality of the Transcendent

1.8

Let's review our discussion so far. All recorded societies have believed in the reality of a transcendent realm. They have described this realm in different ways: as Nirvana, heaven, the gods of Mount Olympus. But in every case, these societies have agreed that a realm beyond everyday, visible, tangible reality does exist, and that this transcendent realm is absolutely crucial for giving everyday life its meaning.

We have identified that same drive toward the transcendent in our experiences of truth and freedom, beauty and love, and in certain mysterious experiences that defy rational explanation. That same drive is apparent in our experience of an ethical law demanding right behavior, and in our restless desire for deep, lasting peace and perfect joy.

How can we explain this universal thirst for the transcendent? Various sociological or psychological reasons have been suggested. Karl Marx (1818–1883) believed that religion was a man-made illusion that functioned to keep the oppressed working classes in a passive state: religion, said Marx, was "the opium of the people."[8] Sigmund Freud (1856–1939) argued that religious beliefs arose as civilizations projected their need for a protective father-figure onto the supernatural realm.[9]

But such explanations are far too simplistic. Neither Marx nor Freud addressed a basic question: *why do humans insistently seek meaning beyond the boundaries of this world*? We can agree with Marx that humans can become alienated because of oppressive economic conditions, but why would they seek escape from these conditions in a transcendent realm? We can agree with Freud that humans have a deep desire for security, but why seek that security in an unseen transcendent realm?

Commenting on the unquenchable desire for the transcendent, Lewis concludes, "Creatures are not born with desires unless satisfaction for those desires exists. A baby feels hunger: well, there is such a thing as food. A duckling wants to swim: well, there is such a thing as water. Men feel sexual desire: well, there is such a thing as sex. If I find in myself a desire which no experience in this world can satisfy, the most probable explanation is that I was made for another world."[10]

We have good reason, then, to take the world of the transcendent seriously as an object of study.

Religious Studies and Theology   1.9

We may identify two general approaches to the study of the transcendent or of beliefs in the transcendent. The first approach has many labels: *history of religions*, *philosophy of religions*, *comparative religions*, or simply *religious studies* (the term we will use). The religious studies scholar focuses on the human religious experience as a specific field of academic study. A common procedure is to gather data on as many religions as possible throughout history and the world and then study and interpret this data, focusing especially on beliefs and practices shared by all religious traditions. Eliade's *The Sacred and the Profane* is a classic work in this discipline: from his studies of a variety of religions, Eliade identifies common beliefs (such as the division of the world into the sacred and profane) and common practices (such as rituals marking sacred times) that provide us with great insight into the nature of religion as a human activity.

In religious studies, however, the question of the truth or the reality of the transcendent is generally not allowed to arise. The religious studies scholar may either (explicitly or implicitly) deny the reality of the transcendent realm, or may simply "bracket out" the question of its existence as irrelevant. In general it would be understood as a serious fault if religious studies scholars were to let personal convictions intrude into their work: the goal of the discipline is to describe religious phenomena as objectively as possible.[11]

The theologian, however, takes seriously the reality of the transcendent—we have already discussed some of the reasons for doing so. From the theological point of view, persons who study the nature of reality in general, or of human nature in particular, while denying or ignoring the transcendent dimension can achieve only a very limited, if not distorted, view of reality and humanity. The vast majority of humanity has believed that a grasp of the transcendent dimension of reality is essential for correct understanding.

Persons who take the theological approach, however, obviously must operate from within a specific faith tradition. We have already pointed out that different religions conceive of the transcendent realm differently: the realm of the gods, the spirits, of the one God, of Nirvana. By definition, then, a particular theologian must work within the belief system of one of the traditions.

The Role of Reason in Theology   1.10

It would be a serious error, however, to conclude from our comparison that the religious studies scholar is working in an objective academic discipline, while the theologian is working with subjective religious beliefs and opinions. The theologian insists that in taking seriously the truth of the transcendent realm he is working with a broader and truer vision of reality than those who deny or ignore this realm.

The very word *theology* gives us further insight into the task of this discipline. In Greek, *theos* means God or a god; the related adjective *theios* refers to divine things. The root word **logos** means essentially a "study" or "disciplined use of reason." This sense should be familiar from such English words as *biology*: the study of life.

Thus theology is the reasonable, or rational, study of the divine. As an academic discipline, theology insists on the disciplined, rigorous use of reason. The essential difference between it and other academic disciplines thus lies not so much in its methodology as in its subject matter. Theology insists on the reasonable examination of *all* reality—both this-worldly and transcendent.

Access to the transcendent, however, cannot come directly through reason. It can come only through faith, but through a faith that is reasonable. Clarifying just what faith is, and showing how faith is related to reason, are two topics central to our book.

Thinking within a Faith Tradition   1.11

Is religious studies a more objective and scientific discipline than theology, since theology limits itself to one particular faith tradition, while religious studies seeks to include all religious traditions in its study?

In his book *Truth and Method*, the philosopher Hans-Georg Gadamer argues that while the scientific method (observation, hypothesis formation, testing) is appropriate for understanding and attaining truth in the natural sciences, truth and understanding are attained in a fundamentally different way in fields of study such as art, history, or philosophy.[12] Gadamer insists that real truth and true understanding (not just opinions) could be attained in these latter fields—it simply couldn't be attained by employing methods appropriate to the natural sciences.

Let's consider the discipline of history, for example. A historical event, by definition, cannot be replicated in the laboratory and scientifically tested by the historian. We can know about a historical event only through the testimony of eyewitnesses, written documents, or perhaps through archaeological evidence. But even these resources cannot be understood directly. They can only be interpreted, and interpretations are not privatized, but are based on a *tradition* of understanding. Each nation, each social group, has developed certain ways of understanding history that shape the understanding of each member of that nation or group.

The same type of understanding applies also to philosophical texts. The Western philosophical tradition, for example, shapes the very way that people within Western cultures think about the world: the way in which Westerners think about good and evil, cause and effect, and even science and religion have been shaped by thinkers such as Plato, Aristotle, Thomas Aquinas, or Descartes. When people study a philosophical text, for example, they cannot pretend to be scientifically objective and neutral observers. They must be aware of the fact that the way in which they perceive and understand reality has already been fundamentally shaped by a particular tradition.

Let us use a hypothetical example to show how Gadamer's insights might apply to understanding within the Christian theological tradition. Jane, a college freshman, comes from a Christian background, but she isn't a churchgoer and does not consider herself to be particularly religious. One Friday night she receives a phone call telling her that her best friend Maureen has been killed in a car crash. A thousand thoughts and emotions begin to race through Jane's mind: shock, disbelief, confusion, anger, perhaps guilt. Some of her thoughts take a theological turn: Where was God when the accident happened? How could God take Maureen's life when she was still so young? Why does God allow such terrible things to happen? She is angry with God, but at the same time feels guilty about her anger. She feels that she should pray, but can't think what to say.

Jane's questions and emotions are complex—but the first point to notice is that simply by asking these questions, Jane already takes for granted several fundamental theological beliefs. She assumes, first of all, that there is one God, rather than many gods or other spiritual powers. Further, she assumes some knowledge about this God's characteristics. When she wonders why God did not prevent the accident, she seems to assume that God is all powerful, that God can control all events in the world.

Jane also seems to assume that God is generally kind and caring toward humans, because some of her confusion and anger arises from the apparent contradiction between God's goodness and the fact that a tragic event occurred in a world she assumes is controlled by a good, all-powerful God.

Where do Jane's assumptions originate? As we said, Jane does not attend church regularly and does not have a formal religious education. She may have received some religious ideas from her parents or other close family members. As she grew older, she was also no doubt influenced by ideas she picked up in school, from her own reading, or simply from everyday interactions with friends and other peers.

But where did her family, peers, and teachers pick up their religious ideas? The short answer is: from the Christian tradition, or, more precisely, the Judeo-Christian tradition.[13] Through thousands of years of history, Jewish and Christian theological ideas have spread in myriad ways through many nations in the world and have shaped the thinking, directly or indirectly, of billions of people, including Jane's family, peers, teachers, community, culture—and thus Jane herself.

If Jane had been raised in a different tradition, she would have found different answers; in fact, she would have asked different questions. If she had been raised in a Buddhist tradition, for example, she would not have raised the same questions and assumptions about the role of the one God in the accident. Of course she would have experienced the same basic human emotions of shock and sadness, but the way in which she reflected on her friend's death would have been shaped by such traditional Buddhist concepts as reincarnation (the idea of rebirth into another life) and Nirvana.

Our conclusion, then, is that all thinking in fields such as theology *must* be guided by a particular tradition—Jane cannot, at the same time, accept the Christian belief that Maureen is in heaven and the Buddhist belief that Maureen will be reborn in another life-form according to her level of karma.

Gadamer of course realizes that individuals are not shaped completely by a tradition but also have the freedom to think critically about their own tradition. Based on their personal experiences or on knowledge from outside a particular tradition, individuals might question certain aspects of the particular tradition that shaped them. Jane, for example, might question the traditional view that God is all good in the light of her friend's seemingly senseless death. In this situation Gadamer speaks of a "fusion of horizons"—Jane allows the viewpoint (horizon) of the traditional views to interact with the understanding of her own horizon (her own personal point of view). Deeper and truer understanding arises through the merging of the horizons.

But Gadamer's point is that even in questioning a tradition a person should be aware that the very questions and the way in which these questions are asked have already been deeply influenced by that tradition. A person simply cannot approach the basic questions of the meaning of life except by means of a particular tradition.

Christian Tradition in a Pluralistic World 1.12

In this chapter, we have examined compelling reasons to take the reality of the transcendent realm seriously, and we have seen that the only way to understand that realm is to approach it through a specific theological tradition.

Thus the study of any religious tradition—especially the study of the major religious traditions (like Judaism, Islam, or Hinduism) that have influenced and shaped the thoughts and actions of countless millions of people—would be of enormous benefit for enlarging our understanding of the human being and indeed of reality itself.

Why then choose the Christian theological tradition? The reasons are many. The tradition itself is two thousand years old (not counting its deep roots in the **Jewish** tradition) and has produced, and continues to produce, a rich theological reflection on the transcendent. Christian theological ideas have deeply influenced every aspect of Western culture, and many non-Western cultures as well. Because the Christian tradition is closely related, historically and theologically, to the Jewish and Muslim traditions, the study of Christian theology can shed light on these other traditions as well.

Catholic Christian Tradition   1.13

Yet the Christian tradition includes within itself a vast variety of more specific traditions. There are various Orthodox traditions, the Roman Catholic tradition, traditions arising from the Protestant Reformation, and many more. Gadamer's point about tradition applies here as well: on many basic theological questions, it is not possible to think theologically in a generically Christian way. Theologians, in the questions they ask and in the way they ask them, will always be shaped by a particular Christian tradition. This book, then, looks at Christian theology primarily through the lens of the Roman Catholic tradition, since that is the tradition of the author. Of course Roman Catholic theology itself is varied and vast, and I am painfully aware of my own limitations of knowledge and understanding in trying to present even an outline of it. My best hope is that this book will encourage readers to their own deeper study of the tradition.

The book, however, is not limited to the specifically Roman Catholic theological tradition—already in this chapter we have referred several times to C. S. Lewis, an Anglican. In this sense, the book's approach is also "catholic" (note the lowercase *c*)—taking the word *catholic* in its basic sense of describing what is "general" or "universal" in the Christian tradition.

Since it is impossible to cover the entire Catholic Christian tradition, I have chosen to focus on a central theme of the tradition: the relationship between reason and faith. I hope to show that serious study of the relationship between faith and reason within the Catholic (and catholic) tradition leads not to pointless pseudoknowledge about angels dancing on pins, but to a deeper, truer, more beautiful, and more satisfying view of the world than can be obtained through reason alone.

Questions about the Text

1. What is meant by *transcendent*?

2. How can religion be understood as the human encounter with the transcendent?

3. What is meant by *theology*?

4. How does the academic discipline of religious studies differ from the academic discipline of theology?

5. Describe Otto's concept of the numinous and Eliade's concept of the sacred.

6. What does Rahner mean by the "transcendent horizon of human nature"?

7. What does Lewis mean by the "Moral Law," and why does he say that it is a signal of the transcendent?

8. Explain how the universal experience of transcendence in human culture and in human nature suggests the actual existence of a transcendent realm.

9. Explain Gadamer's claim that truth in artistic, historical, philosophical, or religious experience can only be attained by following a certain tradition.

Discussion Questions

1. Have you had a personal experience of the transcendent?

2. Do you think that all people ask religious (or spiritual) questions at some point in their lives?

3. Do you agree that it is reasonable to believe in a transcendent reality?

4. What are some characteristics that all religions seem to share?

Endnotes

1. For the sake of simplicity, we will use the broad term *religious* to refer both to people who follow an organized religion and to those who simply consider themselves to be "spiritual."

2. Rudolf Otto, *The Idea of the Holy* (London: Oxford University Press, 1923).

3. C. S. Lewis, *The Problem of Pain* (New York: Macmillan, 1978), 17.

4. Mircea Eliade, *The Sacred and the Profane: The Nature of Religion* (New York: Harcourt, Brace 1959).

5. See Karl Rahner, *Foundations of Christian Faith: An Introduction to the Idea of Christianity* (New York: Seabury Press, 1978), 14–35.

6. Eliade, *Sacred and Profane*, 20–22.

7. C. S. Lewis, *Mere Christianity* (London: HarperCollins, 2001; orig. pub. 1952), 1–32.

8. Karl Marx, "Introduction" to *Critique of Hegel's Philosophy of Right*, trans. A. Jolin and J. O'Malley, Cambridge Studies in the History and Theory of Politics (Cambridge: Cambridge University Press, 1977; orig. pub. 1844).

9. See, for example, Freud's book, *The Future of an Illusion* (New York: Norton, 1989; orig. pub. 1927).

10. Lewis, *Mere Christianity*, 136–37.

11. Two classics in the field illustrate this procedure: William James, *The Varieties of Religious Experience* (Great Books in Philosophy; Amherst, NY: Prometheus Books, 2002; orig. pub. 1902), analyzes various religious experiences from a psychological point of view without raising the question of their objective reality; G. Van der Leeuw, *Religion in Essence and Manifestation*, trans. J. E. Turner (Princeton: Princeton University Press, 1986; orig. pub. 1933), uses a "phenomenological" approach—a method that attempts to give an exact description of the data without imposing value judgments on it.

12. Hans-Georg Gadamer, *Truth and Method*, 2nd rev. ed. (New York: Continuum, 1994).

13. The Christian theological tradition is founded upon Jewish conceptions of God and God's relationship with humans. But as it developed, the Christian theological tradition quickly took on a distinctive shape (e.g., in conceiving of God as a Trinity) and this fact justifies reference to the "Christian theological tradition" throughout the book.

2

Faith and Reason II

What Is Reason? What Is Faith? 2.1

The relationship between faith and reason is the theme of our entire book; this chapter has the specific task of further defining the terms. Though it may seem at first glance that the meanings of *reason* and *faith* are obvious, we'll find that this is not at all the case.

In the first chapter (sec. 1.11), we saw how influential a tradition is in framing how people look at reality—what basic questions they ask and what assumptions they make about the world. In this chapter we will see that our very understanding of the terms *reason* and *faith* is profoundly influenced by particular traditions. We will compare two broad types of tradition as we consider the meanings of *reason* and *faith*: (1) traditions that are open to the transcendent, and (2) traditions that are closed to it. I shall try to show how traditions that are closed to the transcendent produce a narrow view of both reason and faith that actually distorts the meanings of both. A fuller, more accurate understanding of these concepts can only be regained by viewing the world from traditions open to the transcendent.

As we proceed in our discussion, we will at times use the word *worldview*, meaning the basic way one looks at the world. Thus we might say that some people have an optimistic worldview, others a pessimistic or cynical one.

We can also see how closely worldview and tradition are related. The tradition in which one is raised profoundly influences one's worldview, and so we can speak of a Christian or a Buddhist worldview (worldviews open to the transcendent), but we can also speak of a rationalist or determinist worldview (worldviews closed to the transcendent).

Traditions Closed to the Transcendent: Rationalism, Materialism, and Determinism   2.2

The following description of traditions closed to the transcendent are necessarily simplistic. Intellectual traditions are complex, and so the labels that I will be using—*rationalism*, *materialism*, and *determinism*, are too broad to describe actual historical movements of thought. Few individual thinkers, for example, are purely rationalistic, materialistic, or deterministic. Nevertheless, the terms do accurately describe a general and highly influential trend in modern thinking, and we need to be aware of how this general trend has powerfully influenced common modern understandings of both reason and faith.

Rationalism   2.2.1

The French philosopher René Descartes (1596–1650) is usually considered a primary catalyst in the development of the rationalist tradition. Dissatisfied with the conflicting philosophical opinions of his time, Descartes worked to establish true knowledge on a solid basis. His first step was a negative one: to "reject as absolutely false everything in which I could imagine the least doubt, in order to see whether, after this process, something in my beliefs remained that was entirely indubitable" [incapable of being doubted].[1] Descartes's method is sometimes called "methodological doubt"—the process of sweeping away all uncertain ideas, so that only solid knowledge remains. After doubting everything, including the trustworthiness of his own sense observations, Descartes found he was sure of only one thing: that he doubted! But if he could raise these doubts, he himself must exist as the conscious subject raising these doubts. This train of thought led to Descartes's famous conclusion: "I think, therefore I am."[2]

Since the truths of mathematics are the most obvious and sure truths (everyone agrees that 2 + 2 = 4), Descartes chose mathematical knowledge as his model for all knowing: "In seeking the correct path to truth we should be concerned with nothing about which we cannot have a certainty equal to that of the demonstration of arithmetic and geometry."[3] This paradigm is also evident in the title of a work by Descartes's contemporary, the Dutch Jewish philosopher Baruch Spinoza (1632–1677), *Ethics: Demonstrated in Geometric Order*.

True knowledge must be based on objects of which we can have certainty, rationalists argue. Following in the tradition of Descartes, rationalists thus tend to define "true knowledge" as scientific knowledge of the physical world, because this knowledge is based on the mathematically exact laws of physics and chemistry. Any other knowledge that does not measure up to this standard cannot be called true knowledge, only opinion. The rationalist thus dismisses any possibility of true transcendent religious knowledge—since true knowledge can only be grounded in observable, demonstrable facts. A variation of rationalism is what we might call *scientism*—the belief that the only sure knowledge is knowledge based on strict scientific evidence.

Descartes's thought was a precursor to the highly influential intellectual movement known as the **Enlightenment**. Partly in reaction to the bloody religious conflicts of the Thirty Years' War (1618–1648), Enlightenment rationalists such as David Hume (1711–1776) attacked belief in the supernatural as irrational, and thinkers such as Voltaire (1694–1778) criticized religious belief as blind obedience to church authority. Rationalists in the Enlightenment tradition thus associate the term *reason* with strictly logical, empirical, mathematically based thinking, and *faith* with a blind adherence to traditional doctrine.

Materialism and Determinism   2.2.2

The materialist worldview is one logical extension of the rationalist worldview. If one believes that the material, physical world is the only basis of true knowledge, then it is just one short step further to the conclusion that the material world is the only true reality. Variations of the materialist worldview occur in many fields of study. In psychology, a strict behaviorist rejects concepts such as *mind* and *thought* as ultimately meaningless and focuses strictly on the facts of observable behaviors that can be understood as responses to external stimuli. Karl Marx claimed that his economic philosophy was based on "scientific materialism"—a view of the world that rejects such vague notions as *spirit* and *soul* in favor of observable, physical realities that provide us with the real explanation of human behavior.

In neuroscience, research into genetics and brain function is increasingly revealing the physical foundations for mental processes in the brain and in our genetic makeup. For example, we can identify which parts of the brain control certain functions, and which specific genes are associated with specific character traits. For the materialist, the logical conclusion is that there is no difference between mind and thoughts and their physical foundation. Thoughts are simply electronic signals sent by the brain along the human nervous system. For Sir John Maddox, former editor of the premier scientific journal *Nature*, an explanation of what we mean by *mind* "must ultimately be an explanation in terms of the way neurons function."[4]

Similarly, emotions can be broken down to their "true" material basis: they are simply the result of certain chemical reactions that take place in the stomach or other bodily organs.

Francis Crick, one of the discoverers of DNA, nicely sums up the materialist conclusion. "'You,' your joys and your sorrows, your memories and your ambitions, your sense of personal identity and free will, are in fact no more than the behavior of a vast assembly of nerve cells and their associated molecules."[5]

The strict materialist view is closely allied to a determinist view. If the material world is all that exists, then it is obvious that everything that happens in the universe is a result of the strict laws of cause and effect that govern the physical world. If this is true, human free will must be an illusion. Again Crick illustrates this way of thinking: "What you're aware of is a decision, but you're not aware of what makes you do the decision. It seems free to you, but it's the result of things you are not aware of."[6] Our choices are determined by our genetic makeup and the influence of our environment, according to the determinist. If one takes away genetics and environmental stimuli, there is no "mind" or "will" left over to make a choice.

Implications of Worldviews Closed to Transcendence

2.2.3

Ethical relativism is one natural consequence of the rationalist, materialist, and determinist views. For the rationalist, ethical standards of "right" and "wrong" can have no certain objective value, since they are not based on certain physical knowledge. They must simply be matters of opinion. At most, "right" might be defined in a pragmatic way as that which leads to material comfort for the most people. For the strict materialist and determinist, of course, ethical "right" and "wrong" can have no meaning, since actions are not chosen, but determined by forces beyond human control.

A further implication of these modern trends of thought is that humans must make their own meaning, since no meaning is "given." Joseph Ratzinger (now Pope Benedict XVI) sees this implication working itself out in modern biotechnology (genetic manipulation, in vitro fertilization, cloning): since there is no "given" order in nature (that is, given by a transcendent reality), humans are free to manipulate nature in any way that is technologically possible.[7]

We noted earlier that although few people are pure rationalists, materialists, or determinists, the influence of these philosophies is everywhere apparent. Consider these examples of common statements, followed by the rationalist or determinist logic behind each.

- "It is inevitable that teenagers will be sexually active because of their 'raging hormones.'" *Translation*: Hormones determine the behavior of the teen.

- "I'm not a morning person." *Translation*: Certain genetic factors determine whether or not people function well in the morning.

- "It's all about the money." *Translation*: In business transactions, people may speak of ethical qualities such as honesty and integrity, but their real motivation will always be economic gain and material comfort.

- "I think abortion is wrong, but I can't judge anyone who thinks it is right." *Translation*: Transcendent or objective ethical standards do not exist: standards of right and wrong are matters of opinion.

While few people would see themselves as strict materialists or determinists, many think and act in ways that presume materialistic and deterministic principles, whether they recognize them as such or not. ●

Rationalist and Materialist Critiques of Faith   2.4

Let us now consider how traditions closed to the transcendent think about religious faith. Following is a general summary of some of the more common views.

The concept of a transcendent God who created the universe is meaningless. All things in the universe can be explained by material causes, so there is no need for God.[8] Religious knowledge is not true knowledge, since it is not based on observable, testable evidence. Thus "invisible" realities such as spirits, the soul, heaven, and hell can only be accepted by a blind faith that is the opposite of reason. British biologist Richard Dawkins speaks of the "overweening confidence with which the religious assert minute details for which they neither have, nor could have, evidence."[9]

There can be no ultimate meaning to the universe. Ultimate reality is matter, and matter can have no higher purpose or goals.

Religious thinking is based on a prescientific view of reality. Religion arose as a way of explaining natural phenomena. For example, with no scientific understanding of electrical charges, the ancients imagined that lightning was caused by Zeus hurling thunderbolts across the sky. As science advances, the need for "religious" explanations will shrink and eventually vanish.

Faith is an irrational way of thinking that can only be imposed on people by authoritarian churches. Again Dawkins illustrates this view, "Faith is an evil precisely because it requires no justification and brooks no argument."[10]

Faith and science are opposites. Scientific knowledge can only advance when it is free of religious restriction. A classic case was when the Roman Catholic Church forced Galileo to deny his scientific conclusion that the earth revolved around the sun, because this contradicted the literal meaning of some biblical passages. A contemporary example is when a strictly literal reading of Genesis causes people to reject the scientific theory of evolution.[11]

To sum up: in the traditions closed to the transcendent, faith and reason have specific meanings. *Reason* is defined as logical thinking based on sure, physical, and scientifically provable evidence. *Faith* is defined, at best, as unprovable opinions about highly speculative subjects. At worst, especially as it is embodied in organized religion, faith is narrow-minded, judgmental, resistant to scientific truth, and insists on blind obedience to its authority.

Critiques of Rationalism, Materialism, and Determinism   2.5

Yet the above definitions can themselves be critiqued as excessively narrow, distorting, and in the end, irrational. Regarding such narrow definitions of reason, the Jewish theologian Abraham Joshua Heschel wrote, "Extreme rationalism may be defined as the failure of reason to understand itself."[12] In the following sections, we will explore a broader understanding of reason.

Critique of Rationalism   2.5.1

The rationalist view that reason operates with strict logic on scientifically observable facts actually accounts for only a small percentage of human knowledge. Humans, in fact, gain knowledge in a variety of ways. We have already considered the point (sec. 1.11) that humans acquire aesthetic, historical, or philosophical knowledge in ways that cannot be based on strictly scientific methods, and yet such knowledge is accepted as reliable truth. Let us consider some other points.

Knowledge through Authority   2.5.1.1

The vast majority of anyone's knowledge is based not on personal, scientific observation, but rather on accepting the authority of someone else. C. S. Lewis writes, "Do not be scared by the word *authority*. Believing things on authority only means believing them because you have been told them by someone you think trustworthy. Ninety-nine percent of the things you believe are believed on authority. I believe there is such a place as New York. I have not seen it myself. I could not prove by abstract reasoning that there must be such a place. I believe it because reliable people have told me so. The ordinary man believes in the Solar System, atoms, evolution, and the circulation of the blood on authority—because the scientists say so. Every historical statement in the world is believed on authority. No one of us has seen the Norman Conquest or the defeat of the Armada. None of us could prove them by pure logic as you prove a thing in mathematics. We believe them simply because people who did see them have left writings that tell us about them: in fact, on authority."[13]

G. K. Chesterton, in typically humorous fashion, begins his autobiography by contrasting knowledge gained through authority with the rationalist's paradigm: "Bowing down in blind credulity, as is my custom, before mere authority and the tradition of the elders, superstitiously swallowing a story I could not test at the time by experiment or private judgment, I am firmly of the opinion that I was born on the 29th of May, 1874, on Campden Hill, Kensington."[14]

Knowledge through Tradition   2.5.1.2

In his reflections on human understanding, Hans-Georg Gadamer shows how much of human understanding is based not on one's own understanding, but on taking one's place in a certain tradition of understanding, whether artistic, philosophical, or theological (see sec. 1.11). The rationalist ideal is that of a completely independent thinker who has shed the chains of past authority and who dares to think for himself. While such a model is noble in many aspects, it hardly corresponds with reality. Every thinker has been profoundly shaped by tradition: he can no more leave tradition behind than he can jump out of his own skin.

The French philosopher Paul Ricoeur makes the same point in his analysis of language. Consider a philosopher who wishes to understand the human condition of guilt, suffering, and sin. The very fact that the philosopher thinks in a certain language (let us say, in English) already has shaped profoundly his understanding. The meaning of these English words cannot be separated from the influence of a centuries-old religious tradition that stretches back to the practices of ancient Greeks and Hebrews. Of course the philosopher is able to think critically about the meaning of these words, or to compare them with similar concepts in non-Christian traditions, but he can only begin to do so from within the horizon of a tradition shaped by a particular language.[15]

Knowledge Based On Probability   2.5.1.3

In everyday life our reasoning is constantly based on probabilities, not strict logical necessity. I make preparations to teach my class tomorrow based on the probability that I will have class, but I have no sure knowledge of that, since it is logically possible that the college may burn down in the night, or that all the students will be sick. I lend a close friend some money based on the probability that he will pay it back: he has always been trustworthy in the past, but it is logically possible that in this particular case he will be untrustworthy.

Any important life decision is based not on strict logic but on probabilities. Given what she knows about her interests, abilities, and talents, and after weighing practical considerations such as job opportunities, Jill believes that nursing would be a good career for her. But this is not logically certain. Given what he knows about Martha's good character, their common interests, and their five years of dating, Jeff feels certain that his marriage to Martha will be a happy one. But he has no logical guarantee.

The English theologian John Henry Newman shows that even when we do not have strict logical proof we can still be certain of our knowledge in various fields, based on an accumulation of sufficient probabilities.[16] Thus an Englishman, though he cannot personally prove it, is certain that Great Britain is an island based on a convergence of probabilities: he was taught this at school; Britain appears as an island on maps; he has never heard anyone deny the assertion.

Newman applies his insight to faith: the truth of Christianity also can never be based on strict logic — an argument for the truth of Christianity would necessarily take the form of an argument from a convergence of probabilities.[17]

Personal Reasoning   2.5.1.4

We often make decisions and judgments based on what Newman calls the *illative sense*.[18] The illative sense is a type of reasoning, Newman insists, but it is not a strictly logical one. It is often based on personal, implicit knowledge. Thus a farmer may be able to make highly accurate predictions about the weather based on his long years of observations, but he might not be able to articulate his reasons logically.

A cook, based on experience, may have a highly developed sense of just what seasonings to put in a soup and in what amounts, but would have difficulty in writing out an exact recipe.[19]

Many of our judgments cannot be based on precise rules: the judge instructs the jury that they should only deliver a guilty verdict if they find the defendant guilty "beyond a reasonable doubt" — but the judge cannot provide them with precise rules for determining what a "reasonable doubt" is. Yet a decision must be made, and is.[20]

Knowledge, Experience, and Emotions   2.5.1.5

Newman makes a distinction between what he calls "real assents" and "notional assents." In a notional assent, my mind accepts an abstract idea as true. But a real assent involves more: I accept something as true not merely abstractly and intellectually, but with my emotions, my imagination, my whole being.

Thus, for example, Roger might give a notional assent to the principle that one should wear a seat belt when driving: his mind accepts the abstract idea that wearing a seat belt makes one safer. It happens, however, that Roger is involved in a serious accident; the police officer tells him afterward that wearing his seat belt saved his life. Now Roger can give a real assent to the principle. When he agrees that people should wear seat belts, he thinks not of an abstract idea, but of his own personal experience—the slamming on the brakes, the shattering glass, the sudden jolt, and the immense relief of simply being alive and well after the accident.[21] With his experience, Roger now *knows* this principle in a much deeper, more experiential way.

Determinism, Materialism, and Reason   2.5.2

We considered in chapter 1 (sec. 1.4) the point that strict skepticism is self-contradictory since the person asserting that there is no truth in fact assumes that his own assertion is true. Strictly materialist and determinist points of view run into similar logical difficulties.

For example, how can the thought, "My thought is simply a firing of neurons, nothing more," itself be a firing of neurons? Logically, the person thinking this thought is (so to speak) standing apart from his neurons and thinking about them.

Similarly, a strict determinist cannot rationally say, "My every thought is determined by an outside force." If this is true, how would the person ever have become aware that his thought was determined? The fact that humans are self-aware shows that humans have the freedom to stand apart from themselves and consider the causes that influence, but do not fully determine their beliefs and behaviors.

Strict determinism destroys any possibility of true knowledge. C. S. Lewis quotes a Professor Haldane's critique:

> If my mental processes are determined wholly by the motion of atoms in my brain, I have no reason to believe that my beliefs are true . . . and hence I have no reason for supposing my brain to be composed of atoms.[22]

The materialist thus has difficulty in explaining self-awareness or self-consciousness. Admittedly, consciousness has a material basis in the physical functioning of the brain, but it cannot reasonably be reduced to this physical phenomenon and nothing more.

The newly developing science of neuroplasticity also challenges materialist thinking. Conventional neurology had assumed that adult brains in particular are "hardwired, fixed in form and function."[23] But recent research and practice is showing that carefully planned mental exercises can in fact change the structure of the brain in significant ways. This research has caught the attention of religious leaders such as the Dalai Lama, who finds in it confirmation of his belief that not only does the brain affect the mind, but "how people think really can change their brains."[24]

Stephen Barr has shown that the materialist belief that all reality is simply physical reality is itself an article of faith that cannot be proven. How does the materialist know that no reality exists beyond material reality? He simply makes the assumption and then uses the assumption to try to explain any evidence against it.[25]

The Madness of Rationalism and Materialism and the Sanity of Faith   2.5.3

G. K. Chesterton shows that the commonly accepted idea that the religious worldview is irrational and the rationalist worldview is reasonable has it exactly backwards. In fact, argues Chesterton, a rationalistic view of reason is more closely related to insanity than to healthy reason.

Chesterton uses the example of a paranoid man who is convinced that everyone is secretly plotting to kill him. It is impossible, using strict logic alone, to convince the man that he is wrong. If we point out that other people deny that they want to kill him, he answers that of course they deny it, because they are trying to conceal their plot. His version of reality explains the facts.

The real problem with his paranoid view of reality is not that it is irrational, but that it is *too narrowly* rational — it

continued

continued

takes a single idea and uses it in a strictly logical way to explain all events. The only way to restore the paranoid man — and indeed the strict rationalist and materialist — to sanity is to help him to see how cramped and narrow his worldview is.

Chesterton contrasts narrow rationalism with the imagination of the poet who knows that life is complex and full of mystery. The poet allows his mind to move beyond the visible facts and imagine a much larger reality. He is open to the transcendent. The rationalist, on the other hand, is convinced that every event must have a strictly logical explanation, and the materialist restricts his reality to what he can see and touch.

> The poet only desires exaltation and expansion, a world to stretch himself in. The poet only asks to get his head into the heavens. It is the logician who seeks to get the heavens into his head. And it is his head that splits.[26]

The determinist logically convinces himself that he has no free will, but the ordinary, less intellectually sophisticated person very sensibly takes it for granted that free will is real.

> The determinist makes the theory of causation quite clear, and then finds he cannot say "if you please" to the housemaid. The Christian permits free will to remain a sacred mystery; but because of this his relations with the housemaid become of a sparkling and crystal clearness.[27] ●

Reason and Faith in the Christian Worldview   2.6

Rationalism and materialism understand faith as, at best, a harmless opinion about matters that are not real. At its worst, religious faith is actively evil: it is intolerant of other beliefs, obstructs rational and scientific thinking, and demands slavish and blind obedience. Dawkins writes, "More generally (and this applies to Christianity no less than to Islam), what is really pernicious is the practice of teaching children that faith itself is a virtue. Faith is an evil precisely because it requires no justification and brooks no argument."[28]

How differently do faith and reason look when considered from a Christian worldview?

Reason Ultimately Based On Faith   2.6.1

Chesterton comments, "It is idle to talk always about the alternative of reason and faith. Reason is itself a matter of faith. It is an act of faith to assert that our thoughts have any relation to reality at all."[29] If complete skeptics are consistent, they must doubt even their own ability to reason: if there is no such thing as truth, how could their own skeptical reason make a true statement? But once we seriously question our ability to reason, then reasoning has come to an end. Chesterton labeled this trend toward complete skepticism in some strands of modern thought as the "suicide of thought."[30]

When scientists or investigators of any kind begin to research a question, they can only proceed on two articles of faith: (1) that their own reasoning ability is trustworthy and can achieve actual true results, and (2) that the world is governed by rational laws that will allow them to discover true and reliable information. Neither of these two statements could be logically proven: they are the presumptions of faith upon which all reason relies. These two assumptions can only be based on a radical and strictly unprovable confidence in the rationality of the universe.

Faith in the Rational Structure of the Universe   2.6.2

The Christian worldview does offer a rationale for its faith in human reason and in the rationality of the world. Both beliefs are grounded in the belief that God—understood as the ultimate source of all rationality and order—created both humans and the universe.

A classic expression of the belief in the rational order of creation is found at the beginning of the Gospel of John, "In the beginning was the Word, and the Word was with God, and the Word was God. He was in the beginning with God. All things came to be through him" (John 1:1–3). With this introduction, the Gospel writer echoes the first words of Genesis, "In the beginning, when God created the heavens and the earth" (Gen 1:1). With his reference to the "Word," John alludes to a theological tradition that described God creating the universe through God's own rational power.

The Greek for *word (logos)* was familiar in pre-Christian Greek philosophy. It referred not only to verbal or written communication, but more generally to rational order. The Stoic philosophers, for example, referred to the rational order present throughout the universe as the *logos*. Pre-Christian Jewish thought applied this concept to God's creation. The Book of Proverbs, for example, describes Wisdom as God's "first-born" who was with God when he established the heavens and fixed the foundations of the earth (Prov 8:22–31). The first-century Jewish philosopher Philo shows some striking parallels with the Gospel of John in his understanding of the *logos*. For Philo, the *logos* is the divine means by which God brought order and law into the universe, giving form and rationality to the original formlessness.

The universe is understandable because God created it through his *reason*. The rational order of nature—apparent when an object falls to the ground, when a seed grows into a plant, when spring follows winter, when the planets orbit the Sun in regular patterns—all of these orderly laws are the result of God's *logos* throughout the universe. God's order is seen not only in the physical realm but in what we call the ethical realm as well—in the laws of human nature. Just as nature has its laws, so too does human nature: if humans do not lie, steal, or commit adultery they will prosper; if they break these laws, disorder and chaos result.

The human mind can recognize and understand this order because it participates in the same divine *logos*. God created humans in his own image (Gen 1:26–27): one essential aspect of this image is the human mind's ability to participate in God's *logos*.

Faith's Openness to Wonder   2.6.3

For the materialist and determinist, the universe is a closed system, bound by inflexible and necessary natural laws. There can be no "meaning" outside of the necessary working out of these laws. The human being, for example, is simply a chance product of the laws of evolution guided by natural selection.

The beginning point of faith, in contrast, is fundamentally different. The person of faith recognizes the same material reality and the same laws of nature that the materialist observes. But the person of faith allows some fundamental questions that the materialist simply glosses over. Granted that laws of nature do exist, the person of faith wonders, "Why do they exist at all? Could they have been different?"

Chesterton describes the view of a person of faith: "He is pleased that snow is white on the strictly reasonable ground that it might have been black. Every color has in it a bold quality as of choice; the red of garden roses is not only decisive but dramatic, like suddenly spilt blood."[31] Persons of faith allow themselves the simple wonder of a child as they look above and ask, "Why is the sky blue?"

The faith perspective also asks the most fundamental question, "Why does anything exist at all?" Persons of faith do not simply take it for granted that the universe exists (as materialists do): they know that it is possible for it not to be at all.

Faith in the Goodness of Existence   2.6.4

Closely connected to the sense of wonder is a sense of gratitude. Persons of faith have a lively sense that their own existence, along with the existence of the entire universe, is a *gift*. It is not something that we humans have created for ourselves, and so is not something that we should take for granted. It is something that might not have been.

Again Chesterton captures this sense:

> The test of all happiness is gratitude; and I felt grateful, though I hardly knew to whom. Children are grateful when Santa Claus puts in their stockings gifts of toys or sweets. Could I not be grateful to Santa Claus when he put in my stockings the gift of two miraculous legs? We thank people for birthday presents of cigars and slippers. Can I thank no one for the birthday present of birth?[32]

The person of faith considers life and all existence a good gift. It is the faith of a child who has a natural instinct for the joy and goodness of life. In asking, "Why is the sky blue?" the child is not motivated simply by an intellectual curiosity. The child is delighted that the sky is blue, sure that it is a very good thing that the sky happens to be that color. The child's question is simply an attempt to understand better the basic, miraculous fact that the sky is blue. Chesterton sums up his own basic childhood convictions in this way, "The world was a shock, but it was not merely shocking; existence was a surprise, but it was a pleasant surprise."[33]

Hamlet reflects, "To be or not to be, that is the question." The basic orientation of the person of faith is to respond: To exist is good. Life is a wonderful gift that was given to me in a way beyond my understanding—I can only accept it with gratitude. This basic orientation can be upheld even when life is difficult, and even when doubts arise.

Once again, this confidence in the goodness of creation has a solid grounding in Christian faith: the belief that God, the ultimate source of goodness, created the universe. In the creation story in Genesis 1, the phrase, "God saw how good it was" is repeated throughout the account, culminating with, "God looked at everything he had made, and he found it very good" (Gen 1:31).

Faith In an Orderly Universe 2.6.5

Sociologist Peter Berger finds a basic faith in the orderliness of the universe in all religious societies. Throughout most of history, people have believed that the "created order of society, in one way or another, corresponds to an underlying order of the universe, a divine order that supports and justifies all human attempts at ordering."[34] Rituals marking sacred space and time (see sec. 1.3 above) are one way in which this belief in the correspondence of the natural and supernatural order is manifested.

Berger also illustrates this belief with an example from everyday life. A child awakens from a nightmare, alone, threatened by nameless terrors, and cries for his mother. The mother comes, comforts him, perhaps turns on a light, and assures him, "Everything is OK."

It is precisely the statement, "Everything is OK," that interests Berger. For it truly is a universal claim: an assurance to the child that there is fundamental goodness and order to the world that we can trust, in spite of temporary dangers or disruptions. Berger points out that the mother's assumption is a natural one, but that the assumption cannot be based merely on an empirical observation of the world as it is. After all, objective observation shows us that life is full of uncertainty, unfairness, suffering, and eventually death. The confident assertion that "everything is OK" can only be based on a faith in a transcendent reality that gives order and meaning to the world; the world seen in itself (characterized by uncertainty and death) would give us no ground for this confidence.[35]

Faith Begins with God's Grace 2.6.6

Let us now consider a more technical definition of faith from a well-known representative of the Catholic tradition, the medieval theologian Thomas Aquinas (1225–1274). "Now the act of believing is an act of the intellect assenting to the divine truth at the command of the will moved by the grace of God" (*ST* 2 – 2.2.9).[36] We'll consider each part of Aquinas's definition in turn.

Aquinas argues that faith, the act of belief, begins when the human will is "moved by the grace of God." The essential meaning of *grace* can be summed up by considering the idea of life as a gift, as we have suggested. Grace is a free gift given by God; by definition, one cannot earn this gift. God's primary, fundamental gift is simply the gift of existence.

Aquinas's definition describes God's grace as moving the human will; in other words, God's grace is operating in some sense within the human person. Aquinas speaks of an "inward instinct of the Divine invitation" (*ST* 2 – 2.2.9 ad. 3). Further, an act of faith is "related both to the object of the will, i.e., the good and the end, and to the object of the intellect, i.e., to the true" (2 – 2.4.1). Both the will and the intellect have a natural aptitude to be perfected (2 – 2.4.2).

We can connect Aquinas's teaching with our discussion in chapter 1 about how the human being is naturally oriented toward the transcendent. We have within us a natural orientation toward the truth, the good, and a transcendent meaning: in other words, we have a natural orientation toward God.

Karl Rahner understands this transcendent horizon as God's offer of grace to every human being; he calls this offer the "supernatural existential." In the very structure of the human person, in our built-in desire for truth, for goodness, and for meaning, God offers each person the opportunity to transcend his or her limitations. Each person is given the opportunity to respond to this offer from God and in faith open the self to the transcendent.[37] At the same time, each person is given the opportunity to reject this offer of grace and remain closed to the transcendent.

Human Cooperation with God's Grace   2.6.7

At the time of the Reformation in the sixteenth century, a great debate took place between the Reformers and the Catholic Church precisely on the issue of how truly free a person is to cooperate with God's offer of grace (see sec. 7.17.2). In recent dialogue, however, Catholic and Lutheran theologians have found basic common ground in their mutual belief that the initial offer of grace can only come from God, although they continue to differ in their description of how humans respond to that offer. (see sec. 7.17.4).

The Catholic imagination sees the classic example of this cooperation with God's grace in Mary's acceptance of God's will for her life. When the angel Gabriel told Mary that she would have a child, Mary was confused; she didn't understand how this would be possible. In the end, however, she agreed to cooperate with God's mysterious plan for her, proclaiming, "Behold, I am the handmaid of the Lord. May it be done to me according to your word" (Luke 1:38).

In the materialist/determinist view of the world, as Ratzinger notes, the question of the meaning of life is answered either by denying that life has any ultimate meaning or by insisting that humans create their own meaning by their actions. In contrast, the worldview of faith, following Mary's example, is open to accepting the meaning already present in the world.[38]

Faith as Conversion   2.6.8

The word *conversion* is derived from the Latin *converto*: "to turn around." In the Christian view, the fundamental "turnaround" is when a person turns from a worldview closed to the transcendent to one open to the transcendent. To believe, writes Ratzinger,

> means that man does not regard seeing, hearing and touching as the totality of what concerns him, that he does not view the area of his world as marked off by what he can see and touch but seeks a second mode of access to reality, a mode he calls in fact belief, and in such a way that he finds in it the decisive enlargement of his whole view of the world.

Yet because the human is still naturally oriented toward the physical world, the world of the senses, this conversion will be a lifelong process.[39]

But far from being an irrational turn from the world of the senses to a worldview of blind faith, the Catholic and catholic understanding of conversion includes a rational dimension. Jesuit theologian Bernard Lonergan speaks of three kinds of conversion: moral, religious, and intellectual. The movement toward intellectual conversion might well begin precisely with the kind of critique of the limitations of the rationalist, materialist, and determinist worldviews that we have been considering.[40] Such a critique would be the necessary prerequisite to accepting a viewpoint open to the transcendent.

In his *Confessions*, Augustine describes how his own intellectual conversion helped to prepare him for his later religious conversion to the Christian faith. As a follower of the materialist-oriented Manichean religion, Augustine relates that he had been unable to conceive of nonphysical existence; it was only when he began to read Platonist philosophy that he was "prompted to look for truth as something incorporeal" (*Confessions* 7.20).[41] C. S. Lewis, too, describes his intellectual conversion from an atheistic materialist view to an idealist philosophy as an important step in his eventual conversion to Christianity.[42]

Faith as Conversion of the Whole Person   2.6.9

Aquinas's teaching that the will commands the intellect to assent to the divine truth is one way of expressing the truth that faith is a response of the whole person, not merely their reason. "After all," writes Newman, "man is *not* a reasoning animal; he is a seeing, feeling, contemplating, acting animal. . . . Life is for action. If we insist on proofs for everything, we shall never come to action: to act you must assume, and that assumption is faith."[43] A person makes decisions based on his or her fundamental worldview, and this worldview is not chosen by strict reason alone.

Just as the decision to convert to Christianity is never based purely on reason, a movement away from Christian faith rarely involves merely an intellectual decision. Lewis writes that a Christian will experience times when he will find it difficult to hold to the strict ethical teachings of Christianity: he will feel pressure to conform to non-Christian standards, or he will be tempted to tell a lie to get out of trouble, or he will have an opportunity to make some money in a way that is slightly unethical. At these times, his emotions and feelings, not his intellect, will try to persuade him that Christianity—with its strict ethical standards—is untrue.

Or again, there will be times when attending church or praying will be difficult or bothersome, and the person may begin to drift away from faith.

To hold faith in these situations, according to Lewis, a person must "train the habit of Faith." This might involve a deliberate, daily effort to recall the basic articles of faith through attending services, saying prayers, or reading religious books.[44] A person would have to discipline his emotions and even his imagination in order to hold solidly the Christian worldview.

In the Catholic view, too, faith cannot be defined as a onetime decision in which a person chooses to believe in God or to "accept

Christ" as one's personal Savior. Rather, faith is an ongoing process requiring systematic discipline: Aquinas calls it a "habit of the mind" (*ST* 2 – 2.4.1). Faith (along with hope and love) is considered one of the "theological virtues"; as a virtue, it is defined as "an habitual and firm disposition to do the good" (*CCC* no. 1803).[45]

Faith and Objective Statements of Faith   2.6.10

Let us return to Aquinas's definition of faith as the assent of one's intellect to the divine truth. We must now ask, "How does a person know this divine truth?" In another passage of the *Summa*, Aquinas clarifies: "The formal object of faith is the First Truth as manifested in Holy Writ and the teaching of the Church, which proceeds from the First Truth" (*ST* 2 – 2.5.3).

The primary object of faith, in other words, is God himself, considered as the source of all truth. The person trusts God, and because God is trustworthy, he can believe in what God communicates.

For Aquinas, God communicates the specific content of faith through Scripture ("Holy Writ") and Church teachings. These teachings are expressed as articles of faith (for example: "God is a Trinity," or "the Second Person of the Trinity became human"); these articles in turn are expressed through the **creeds** of the Church (*ST* 2 – 2.1.6 – 10).

In the modern world, the idea that faith can be summed up in specific articles of belief is often challenged. Many argue that religion should be a matter of the heart, and that when theologians draw up precise definitions in creeds, they make religion too abstract and intellectual, and thus kill the true religious spirit.

In the Catholic view, however, the precise definitions of the articles of faith in no way contradict true religious devotion. Newman, for example, recognized the difference between accepting the theological proposition that God exists (by a notional assent) and worshipping God with a loving devotion (a real assent). But the theological propositions are necessary, because one cannot love what one doesn't know. Theological propositions are as necessary for the religious mind as language is for everyday communication.[46]

Lewis makes a similar point in his response to an air force officer who rejected theological ideas as "petty and pedantic and unreal" in comparison to his real experience of the tremendous mystery of God when he was out flying alone in the desert at night. Lewis agreed that such an experience was more real than a theological statement, just as the Atlantic is more real than a map of the Atlantic.[47]

But the map analogy supplied Lewis with a further point: theology in fact functions as a good map. First, maps, like theological statements, are based not on the experience of a single person, but on the combined experience of many thousands of people. Second, just as when one wishes to leave the beach and travel on the ocean, a map is necessary, so too if one wishes to make any progress in growing closer to God, then one cannot rely on personal feeling alone; one needs a more objective guide. The officer's experience of God in the desert may have been very real, but

> It leads nowhere. There is nothing to do about it. In fact, that is just why a vague religion—all about feeling God in nature, and so on—is so attractive. It is all thrills and no work: like watching the waves from the beach. But you will not get to Newfoundland by studying the Atlantic that way, and you will not get eternal life by simply feeling the presence of God in flowers and music.[48]

Lewis's last point is that theology is practical. In today's world, Lewis writes (and his point is even more true in our current Internet-centered culture), people have access to literally thousands of different—and often contradictory—theological ideas. Even if people do not make a disciplined study of theology, they will inevitably have some basic theological ideas. Without a disciplined theological study, however, the ideas are virtually certain to be muddled and confused.[49]

Returning to Aquinas' definition, is clear, too, that belief in the articles of faith is based not only on a trust in God as "first truth" but also on a fundamental trust in the authority of Scripture and of **Church** teachings as accurate reflections of God's communication. This should come as no surprise, however—we have seen that religious thinking is impossible unless it is done within a specific religious tradition (sec. 1.11), thus presuming a fundamental trust in the reliability of that tradition (sec. 2.5.1.2)

The Vatican II document *Dogmatic Constitution on Divine Revelation (Dei Verbum)* emphasizes this aspect of faith as an obedient acceptance of God's revelation:

> "The obedience of faith" (Rom 16:26, cf. Rom 1:5; 2 Cor 10:5–6) must be given to God as he reveals himself. By faith man freely commits his entire self to God, making "the full submission of his intellect and will to God who reveals" and willingly assenting to the Revelation given by him. (*DV* no. 5, citing Vatican I's *Dogmatic Constitution on the Catholic Faith*, ch. 3)

Theological statements of faith found in the creeds (such as "I believe in one God") or in the Bible (such as "Christ died for our sins") form the more objective aspect of Christian faith. They are necessary expressions of faith that all believers can use as a reference point to clarify the beliefs that they share. They sum up the centuries-old religious experience and insights of the Christian tradition. They are a fixed guideline so that believers do not stray off into their own subjective ideas and opinions.

Catholic Faith: Between Fideism and Rationalism   2.7

In responding to rationalism, the Catholic tradition emphasizes the compatibility of faith and reason. Not all Christian traditions have taken this approach, however. Some traditions subscribe to what we will broadly term *fideism*; that is, they tend to separate sharply the realm of faith from the realm of reason. In a fideistic belief, critical reason has its rightful place in the scientific or other practical realms, but not in the realm of religion, since religion is simply a matter of feeling and personal faith.[50] Ironically, even though fideistic persons are typically very pious and devout, they share with rationalists the same definition of faith (that it is simply a matter of personal feeling).

Dawkins cites a contemporary example of fideism in the American geologist Kurt Wise, director of the Center for Origins Research at Bryan College, Dayton, Tennessee. Dawkins quotes Wise,

> As I shared with my professors years ago when I was in college, if all the evidence in the universe turns against creationism, I would be the first to admit it, but I would still be a creationist because that is what the Word of God seems to indicate. Here I must stand.[51]

The Catholic Church, however, has insisted that fideism is an error. Obedient faith in God can never contradict natural human reason, since God himself created our human reason. In the words of the Vatican I Council (1870):

> Though faith is above reason, there can never be any real discrepancy between faith and reason. Since the same God who reveals mysteries and infuses faith has bestowed the light of reason on the human mind, God cannot deny himself, nor can truth ever contradict truth.[52]

The Catholic tradition teaches, for example, that the existence of God can be known with certainty without faith and without divine revelation by "the natural light of human reason" (see sec. 3.3.1).

Faith and reason are contradictory, or at least exclude one another, if the terms are defined within the rationalist tradition. But viewed from the Catholic tradition, they in fact work in harmony.

Scriptural View of Faith   2.8

Our focus in this chapter has been on the relationship between faith and reason, and so our discussion of faith has tended to be theoretical. In the world of Scripture, however, the concept of faith has a more personal meaning, essentially signifying a person's trust in God.

In the Old Testament, the concept of faith is primarily summed up in the Hebrew root word *amn*. The word has a variety of meanings: firmness, stability, belief, and truth.[53] The word is used to describe Abraham's relationship with God: "Abram put his faith in the Lord, who credited it to him as an act of righteousness" (Gen 15:6). The relationship is one of trust: in this context, it refers to Abraham's trust in the Lord's promise that he would make his descendants as numerous as the stars.

In this **Hebrew** Old Testament scriptural view, God is worthy of this trust because of God's own trustworthy, faithful nature, expressed by the same Hebrew root word: "The Lord's love for us is strong; the Lord is faithful forever" (Ps 117:2); "For your love towers to the heavens; your faithfulness, to the skies" (Ps 57:11).

Another passage brings out the relationship between the two aspects of the Hebrew concept, "Unless your faith is firm you shall not be firm" (Isa 7:9). We see here the connection between trust or faith in God and the idea of a person being firmly established, confident, and secure in his own life.

The same concept, expressed with the same root word, occurs in the scriptural image of God creating the universe through his Wisdom: "Then was I beside him as his craftsman" (*amon*; Prov 8:30). If the universal craftsman of the universe, Wisdom, is firm and sure in her work, then humans are justified in their confidence that the universe also makes sense and can be trusted (see sect. 2.6.2).

In his discussion of Isaiah 7:9, Joseph Ratzinger connects this Hebrew concept with the fundamental principle of a worldview based on faith: that humans cannot make their own meaning, but rather must be open to the meaning that comes from a transcendent source (see sec. 2.6.7). He shows further how the basic meanings of *amn* (firmness and trust) extend naturally into the concept of *understanding*: we trust what we can understand. Understanding gives us a "place to stand," a firm worldview that helps us to make sense of our existence.[54] So, far from being irrational, faith "is a movement toward the *logos*, the *ratio*, toward meaning and so toward the truth itself, for in the final analysis the ground on which man takes his stand cannot possibly be anything else but the truth revealing itself."[55]

Finally, there is Christian faith in Jesus Christ, the key to the Christian understanding of the meaning of life and of the universe. We shall touch on some aspects of this faith in chapter 10.

Questions about the Text

1. How would you define *rationalism, materialism,* and *determinism* as intellectual movements?

2. Why does a materialist or determinist reject the reality of free will?

3. How do the rationalist and determinist worldviews define *faith* and *reason*?

4. In what ways do people commonly accept information on authority without strict proof?

5. What are some examples of Newman's "illative sense"?

6. Why is a strictly determinist view self-contradictory?

7. In what way is reason itself ultimately based on a kind of faith in rationality?

8. Does it make sense to define faith as trust in the fundamental order, meaning, and goodness of the universe?

9. What are the different elements in Aquinas's definition of faith?

10. In what ways does a conversion to Christian faith involve an intellectual conversion?

11. What is meant by the objective aspect of faith, and why does the Christian tradition consider this aspect necessary?

12. What is meant by a fideistic approach to faith? How do rationalism and fideism share a common definition of faith?

13. How would you summarize the basic biblical attitude toward faith?

Discussion Questions

1. Can you think of some examples of the influence of rationalism, determinism, or materialism in your life experience?

2. To what extent do you think your own actions are determined by forces outside of yourself?

3. In your field of study, how much information do you accept on authority, without proving it for yourself?

4. How much of your own decision-making process is based on strict logic?

5. Do you have faith in the essential goodness and meaning of the universe?

6. Do religious people whom you know tend to be fideistic, or are they open to rational discussions of faith?

Endnotes

1. René Descartes, *A Discourse on the Method of Correctly Conducting One's Reason*, trans. I. Maclean, Oxford World's Classics (Oxford: Oxford University Press, 2006), 28.
2. Ibid.
3. René Descartes, *Rules for the Direction of the Mind*, in René Descartes, *Philosophical Essays: Discourse on Method; Meditations; Rules for the Direction of the Mind*, trans. L. J. Lafleur (Indianapolis: Bobbs-Merrill, 1964), 152.
4. John Maddox, *What Remains to be Discovered: Mapping the Secrets of the Universe, the Origins of Life, and the Future of the Human Race* (New York: Simon and Schuster, 1999, 281.
5. Francis Crick, *The Astonishing Hypothesis: The Scientific Search for the Soul* (New York: Scribner, 1994), 3.
6. Private conversation noted in John Horgan, *The Undiscovered Mind: How the Human Brain Defies Replication, Medication, and Explanation* (New York: Free Press, 1999), 247.
7. Joseph Ratzinger, *Introduction to Christianity* (San Francisco: Ignatius Press, 2000; orig. pub. 1968), 66.
8. When Napoleon asked the Enlightenment mathematician Pierre-Simon Laplace why he did not mention God in his five-volume study of heavenly bodies, LaPlace famously replied, "I have no need of that hypothesis."
9. Richard Dawkins, *The God Delusion* (Boston: Houghton Mifflin, 2006), 34.
10. Ibid., 308.
11. Ibid., 282–86.
12. Quoted in Rodney Stark, *For the Glory of God: How Monotheism Led to Reformations, Science, Witch-hunts, and the End of Slavery* (Princeton, NJ: Princeton University Press, 2003), 201.
13. C. S. Lewis, *Mere Christianity* (London: HarperCollins, 2001; orig. pub. 1952), 62.
14. G. K. Chesterton, *The Autobiography of G. K. Chesterton* (New York: Sheed and Ward, 1936), 1.
15. Paul Ricoeur, *The Symbolism of Evil*, Religious Perspectives 17 (New York: Harper & Row, 1967), 350.

16. John Henry Newman, *An Essay in Aid of a Grammar of Assent*, ed. I. T. Ker (Oxford: Clarendon Press, 1985), 187–95.

17. Ibid., 265.

18. Ibid., 222–47.

19. Kathleen Fischer and Thomas Hart, *Christian Foundations: An Introduction to Faith in Our Time*, rev. ed. (New York: Paulist Press, 1995), 19.

20. Newman, *Grammar of Assent*, 210–12.

21. For the contrast between notional and real assents, see ibid., 54–68.

22. C. S. Lewis, *Miracles* (New York: Macmillan, 1960), 15.

23. Sharon Begley, *Train Your Mind, Change Your Brain* (New York: Ballantine Books, 2007), 6.

24. Quoted in ibid., viii.

25. Stephen Barr, *Modern Physics and Ancient Faith* (Notre Dame, IN: University of Notre Dame Press, 2003), 15–18.

26. G. K. Chesterton, *Orthodoxy* (Peabody, MA: Hendrickson, 2006; orig. pub. 1908), 13.

27. Ibid., 23.

28. Dawkins, *God Delusion*, 307–8.

29. Chesterton, *Orthodoxy*, 28.

30. Ibid., 25–39.

31. Ibid., 53–54.

32. Ibid., 50.

33. Ibid., 50.

34. Peter Berger, *A Rumor of Angels: Modern Society and the Rediscovery of the Supernatural* (Garden City, NY: Doubleday, 1969), 66–67.

35. Ibid., 66–71.

36. St. Thomas Aquinas, *Summa Theologica*, trans. Fathers of the English Dominican Province, Christian Classics (Notre Dame: Ave Maria Press, 1981; orig. pub. 1911).

37. Karl Rahner, *Foundations of Christian Faith: An Introduction to the Idea of Christianity* (New York: Seabury Press, 1978), 152.

38. Ratzinger, *Introduction to Christianity*, 69–74.

39. Ibid., 50–51.

40. Bernard Lonergan, *Method in Theology* (Toronto: University of Toronto Press, 1990; orig. pub., 1971), 238.

41. Saint Augustine, *Confessions*, trans. R. S. Pine-Coffin (New York: Penguin 1961).

42. C. S. Lewis, *Surprised by Joy: The Shape of My Early Life* (New York: Harcourt, Brace, 1955), 208–11.

43. Newman, *Grammar of Assent*, 67.

44. Lewis, *Mere Christianity*, 138–41.

45. *Catechism of the Catholic Church*, 2nd ed. (Vatican City; Libreria Editrice Vaticana, 1997).

46. Newman, *Grammar of Assent*, 82–83.

47. Lewis, *Mere Christianity*, 153–54.

48. Ibid., 154–55.

49. Ibid., 155.

50. Avery Dulles refers to these traditions as "paracritical"; he notes the influence of Kant's philosophy on them, and lists Lutheran pietism and nineteenth-century liberal Protestantism as examples (*The Craft of Theology: From Symbol to System* [New York: Crossroad, 1995], 4).

51. Quoted in Dawkins, *God Delusion*, 285.

52. *Dei Filius* 4. Quoted in *CCC*, no. 159.

53. See Joseph P. Healy, "Faith," in *Anchor Bible Dictionary*, ed. D. N. Freedman (New York: Doubleday, 1992), 2:744–45.

54. Ratzinger, *Introduction to Christianity*, 69–79.

55. Ibid., 75.

3

Doing Theology

Faith and Reason in Theology

In this chapter, we will consider how specific Catholic theologians have viewed the relationship among faith, reason, and tradition in theology. We will begin with a thinker who is the classic model of the Catholic theologian, Saint Thomas Aquinas, and then move on to consider how two contemporary theologians, the American Avery Dulles and the Canadian Bernard Lonergan, address some of the challenges of doing theology in the modern world. We will also consider the thought of the French Protestant philosopher, Paul Ricoeur, for the illumination of these issues that he offers.

Being Itself   3.1

In the Catholic theological tradition, Thomas Aquinas holds a unique position as the primary theological teacher.[1] In this section, we will consider some of Aquinas's general principles of how faith relates to reason, and then study his specific method of doing theology in his greatest work, the *Summa Theologica (ST)*.

Let us begin by considering the foundation of Aquinas's philosophical thought, which is sometimes characterized as a "philosophy of being." First, we must attempt to grasp the importance of his concept of "being."

A child spontaneously asks very basic questions, "Why is the sky blue? Why is water wet?" But perhaps the most basic question of all can only be formulated by a childlike philosopher, "Why does anything exist at all?" In traditional philosophy, this is known as a **metaphysical** question—meaning it deals not with specific subjects, but with the ultimate questions of existence and "being" in general. Modern science (for example, physics and chemistry) attempts to explain reality as it is, and thus ignores these basic metaphysical questions—assuming that they have no practical value or sure answer.

But when we ignore metaphysical questions, we miss out on a sense of wonder at the fact of existence itself (see sec. 2.6.3). The Thomist philosopher Jacques Maritain insists that we must deliberately awaken ourselves in order to regain that primal sense of wonder. Consider any object—a tree, a person, a stone. Why is the tree there? The question is not about its immediate cause ("It grew from a seed"), but rather, "Why does it exist at all?"

Maritain's point may relate to an insight from developmental psychology. At first, an infant is unable to distinguish between his own body and the environment. Even after he has learned to make this distinction, he still has no understanding of the permanence of objects outside himself: remove a toy from his sight, and it ceases to exist for him. Only as his cognitive abilities develop is he able to comprehend that a massive, wonderful, and sometimes frightening world exists, solidly and firmly and completely separate from himself.

According to Maritain, a person's primal intuition of another object's existence is accompanied at the same moment by the person's awareness of his own limitations. Because other objects exist completely independently of me, I become aware of my limitations, my smallness, my fragility, and I have an intuition that it is possible for me not to exist. I glimpse the possibility of my own death. From that perception of solid existence of an object outside of myself, seen in light of my own limited existence, I vaguely understand that any limited existence must ultimately depend on an absolute being—a solid, unchanging reality on which all other things depend. If this absolute ground to all being did not exist, then no limited being would ever have existed at all.

It is this absolute ground of all reality that the Christian calls "God."

A key biblical story illustrates Aquinas's approach. After Moses' numinous experience of encountering God in the burning bush, Moses asks,

> "If they [the Israelites] ask me, 'What is his name?' what am I to tell them?" God replied, "I am who am." Then he added, "This is what you shall tell the Israelites: I AM sent me to you." (Exod 3:13–14)

The precise meaning of the phrase "I am who am" in Hebrew is debated. In the ancient Greek translation of the Old Testament, known as the Septuagint, the phrase was translated, "I am he that is." Early Christians understood this in a philosophical sense: God *is* — God is the Supreme Being — the ultimate source of the existence of all other things. God completely transcends all other existence, but at the same time, God is intimately connected with every existing thing — since without him nothing at all would exist.[2]

Thus Maritain shows how, in the Thomist tradition of thought, the human being is oriented toward God from the very beginning. Even before one begins to think rationally, one's very first intuition includes an intuition of God.

Aquinas on Faith and Reason   3.2

Reason Guided by Revelation   3.2.1

The human ability to reason is a true human good, but it is not adequate in itself. First, Aquinas believes that humans are directed toward the transcendent God as the ultimate goal of their lives (recall our discussion of this in secs. 1.4–7), and this transcendent goal is beyond the power of human reason to grasp. Second, although Aquinas believes that humans could know about God's existence through natural reason alone, he also thinks that such natural theological knowledge could be grasped only by a few people, and then only after a long time and with the danger of including error (*ST* 1.1.1).

Theology as Science   3.2.2

Aquinas defines a science as a search for true knowledge based on first principles that cannot be strictly proved. Proceeding from these first principles, a person uses logical reasoning to gain further knowledge.

Every science takes for granted certain first principles, such as the fundamental principle that every change must have a cause. Many sciences take for granted the principles established by other sciences: thus the study of music depends on principles established by mathematics. No scientists personally verify every scientific principle; rather they accept on authority a large body of previously established scientific knowledge (see sec. 4.3). So theology is comparable to other sciences when it accepts on authority the basic articles of faith (as stated in Scripture and Church teaching) as its starting point (*ST* 1.1.2).

From this starting point, however, the theologian then develops theological knowledge in a rational, systematic way.

Reason Answers Reasonable Objections   3.2.3

Aquinas realized that the non-Christian would not accept the Christian articles of faith as an authoritative starting point. So is any further dialogue possible with a nonbeliever on matters of Christian faith?

Yes, argues Aquinas. Theological reason cannot *prove* the truth of an article of faith to a nonbeliever, but it can answer a nonbeliever's objections that a particular article of faith is illogical or unreasonable. For example, the Christian theologian cannot prove that God is a Trinity, but he should be able to answer, by reason alone, objections that belief in the Trinity is simply illogical (for example, by showing that the three persons of God could share the same divine nature) (*ST* 1.1.8).

Aquinas's confidence that beliefs can be defended with reason is unshakeable: "Since faith rests upon infallible truth, and since the contrary of a truth can never be demonstrated, it is clear that the arguments brought against faith cannot be demonstrations, but are difficulties that can be answered" (*ST* 1.1.8).[3]

Thus Aquinas thought that Christians should never hesitate to ask a reasonable question about their faith—an answer could always be found.

Reason as Preparation for Faith   3.2.4

Theology can use philosophical reasoning due to "the defect of our intelligence, which is more easily led by what is known through natural reason (from which proceed the other sciences) to that which is above reason, such as are the teachings of this science" (*ST* 1.1.5). Aquinas holds that "faith presupposes natural knowledge, even as grace presupposes nature, and perfection presupposes something that can be perfected" (*ST* 1.2.2 ad. 1). In other words, the theologian may legitimately begin with observations about the natural world before being led to consider supernatural knowledge.

Faith and reason continually interact: our reason helps us to gain a clearer understanding of our faith, but our faith first guides our reason to help it to reason rightly. On this point, Aquinas's thought is similar to the idea of the "hermeneutical circle" that we will discuss below (see sec. 3.5.1).

Non-Christian Sources and Sciences   3.2.5

Aquinas's thought fits in well with our modern openness to diversity: he was not afraid to recognize and accept truth apart from the Christian articles of faith. In fact, Aquinas's primary guide in his philosophical thinking (for example, in his description of causes and effects) was the non-Christian philosopher Aristotle: in the *Summa*, Aquinas simply refers to Aristotle as "the Philosopher." Aquinas also interacts with the arguments of Muslim thinkers such as Avicenna and Averroes and the Jewish philosopher Maimonides.

Other sciences can help to make theological teachings clearer; Aquinas calls them the "handmaidens" of theology (*ST* 1.1.5). Theology properly makes use of these sciences, each of which is competent in its own realm of expertise: "Hence sacred doctrine makes use also of the authority of philosophers in those questions in which they were able to know the truth by natural reason" (*ST* 1.1.8). Aquinas's thinking is thus in line with contemporary Catholic leaders such as Pope John Paul II, who strongly urged dialogue between theology and modern science (see sec. 4.7).

Theological Method in the *Summa*   3.3

Aquinas's *Summa Theologica* is a summary of theology designed for beginning students of theology.[4] The work is carefully structured: it consists of four main parts, with each part divided into treatises (such as, "The One God"), and each treatise in turn divided into "points of inquiry" or "questions" (for example, "Whether sacred doctrine is a science?"). Finally, each question is divided into articles.

The article is the heart of the *Summa*'s method. It consists of five steps:

1. **Focusing the question.** A specific question is narrowed so it can be answered either "Yes" or "No." Aquinas does this to focus and sharpen the issue and avoid vague conclusions.

2. **Listing objections.** Aquinas was convinced that the only way to grasp the truth is by seriously considering all sides of an issue. He usually lists up to three objections to his own eventual conclusion, stating them in a fair and balanced way.

3. **Statement of Aquinas's conclusions, backed by authority.** Aquinas bases his answer on the authority of the Bible and of Church teachings. Here he refers to the conclusions of many previous thinkers: Augustine, Dionysius, John Damascene, and Anselm, as well as of non-Christian authorities such as Aristotle. Aquinas is careful to point out, however, that the conclusions of Christian theologians are only probable: he considers only the authority of the canonical Scriptures to be unquestionable (*ST* 1.1.8 ad. 2).

4. **Detailed explanation of Aquinas's own position.** This is the main part of the article in which Aquinas rationally justifies his answer, providing any necessary explanations and clarifications.

5. **Specific answer to the objections.** The objections to Aquinas's position (stated in step 2) are answered in detail.

The theological method of the *Summa* is thus diametrically opposed to a model of blind faith. It is true that the Christian articles of faith are the unquestioned starting point of Aquinas's thinking, but from that starting point he proceeds with the most rigorous regard for exact and precise thinking.

Proving God's Existence   3.3.1

Let us now consider in detail what is perhaps the most famous of Aquinas's articles in the *Summa*, his response to the question of God's existence. This is the third article under the question, "Whether God exists?"

1. **Focusing the question:** The first two articles of this question had focused the discussion by dealing with preliminary questions: (1) "Whether the existence of God is self-evident?" and (2) "Whether it can be demonstrated that God exists?" Once Aquinas shows that God's existence is neither (1) so obvious that everyone must accept it, nor (2) so obscure that it must be accepted on faith alone, he is then ready to ask the specific question, "Whether God exists?"

2. **Listing objections.** Here Aquinas proceeds to outline objections to arguments for the existence of God.

   - **Objection 1:** If two things are opposites, and one is infinite, then its opposite would be canceled out and cease to exist. But since God is infinitely good, then logically the opposite of good—evil—should not exist. But it does in fact exist. Therefore God does not exist.

   - **Objection 2:** Everything that occurs in the world can be explained without referring to God. Events in nature can be explained by natural causes; events caused by humans can be explained by human causes. "Therefore there is no need to suppose God's existence."

3. **Statement of Aquinas's position, backed by authority.** Aquinas refers to God's own witness to his existence in Exodus 3:14, "I am who am."

4. **Detailed explanation of Aquinas's position.** Aquinas sketches out five "ways" by which the existence of God can be proved; we will discuss these in detail below.

5. **Specific answer to the objections.**

   - **Reply to Objection 1:** God allows evil to exist, but is able to produce good out of evil.

   - **Reply to Objection 2:** Neither nature nor the human will can explain their own existence—they both point beyond themselves to a first transcendent cause.

Aquinas's Five Ways   3.3.2

We now turn to the heart of Aquinas's argument: the five "ways" to prove the existence of God. All of Aquinas's "ways" begin with empirical observations of the physical world—reality as we can see, hear, smell, taste, and touch it. By thinking rationally about physical reality, Aquinas concludes that its very existence points beyond itself to a transcendent cause. In this sense, Aquinas's ways are a philosophical expression of the experiences of transcendence that we described in sections 1.4–7. Aquinas explains in philosophical terms the common human experience that all reality in this world, because it is limited, points beyond itself to the transcendent.

The five ways may be summarized as follows:[5]

1. The fact that there is movement or change in the physical world points toward a transcendent First Mover.

2. The fact that all things and actions in the physical world are caused by something else (specifically, that they have an efficient cause) points toward a transcendent First Cause.

3. The fact that all things in the physical world exist in a contingent way (that is, it is not logically necessary that they exist) points toward a transcendent Necessary Being.

4. The fact that we can compare degrees of quality in physical things (for example, some things are better or more beautiful than others) points toward the existence of a transcendent standard (supreme degree) of those qualities.

5. The fact that everything in the physical world seems to be designed for a purpose points toward a transcendent Intelligence that gave them that purpose.

The First Cause Argument   3.3.3

In order better to understand Aquinas's approach, let's consider his second argument in more detail. Everything has a cause: nothing can cause itself to exist or to change. Thus I am able to purchase some writing paper *because* a local store stocks it. The local store has the paper *because* it was purchased by paper suppliers. The paper suppliers have the paper *because* paper factories manufactured it. The factories are able to make paper *because* there is a supply of trees. Trees exist *because* they have enough sunlight to perform photosynthesis. The sun in its turn depended upon other causes: it was caused by swirling clouds of gas pulled together by gravity.

Everything in the universe has a cause. The universe itself has a cause: currently the most widely accepted scientific theory is that the universe began with the "big bang"—an inconceivably powerful explosion and expansion of all the matter and energy in the universe. (See sec. 4.8 for a more detailed discussion of the big bang in relation to Christian thought.)

But even the big bang theory leaves one question unanswered: what caused the original energy and matter of the universe to exist before it exploded in the big bang?

Scientifically, one must presume that original energy and matter simply existed. Even if one speculates about other universes before the big bang, the same ultimate metaphysical question arises: How did these previous universes first come into existence?

Aquinas considers the possibility that the universe was eternal (Aristotle's view), concluding that one cannot know from reason alone whether the universe had a beginning in time or not. Aquinas believes that it did have a beginning in time, based on the authority of Scripture and Church teaching.[6] What we can know from reason alone, however, is that the universe must have had a cause, since we have no experience of anything simply existing without a cause.

Since the universe cannot have caused itself to come into existence, Aquinas concludes that there must have been a "First Cause," distinct from the universe itself, that caused the universe to come into being.[7]

The First Cause Argument: Avoiding Misunderstandings 3.3.4

We must think carefully about this First Cause to avoid misunderstanding.

First, a person might be tempted to object, "What caused the First Cause?" But by definition a First Cause cannot have any other cause—otherwise it would not be the first! In thinking of the First Cause, we are trying to conceive the absolute, ultimate starting point of all existence.

Second, remember that we have only two options: (1) either there is a First Cause that brought all things into existence, or (2) the universe (or any other possible universes) either exists without a cause or caused itself to come into existence. The Christian insists that option (1) is more reasonable, since we have absolutely no empirical evidence that a thing can exist without a cause or that it can cause itself to come into being.

Third, if we accept that a First Cause caused the universe, it is clear that this First Cause must be a *transcendent* cause—something that is qualitatively and absolutely different from anything else in the universe. The First Cause cannot simply be the first cause in a chain of causes, like the first billiard ball striking a series of other balls and causing them to move. It must be a cause *outside* of, *transcending* the universe, because experience and observation tell us that nothing in the universe can cause itself.

Fourth, we must understand that this First Cause is necessary, not contingent (dependent on other causes). It is necessary that this First Cause simply exists on its own, without any other cause; otherwise no other contingent things could have come into existence. God is pure Being, the source of all other being.

Fifth, Aquinas's First Cause argument is not meant to prove other aspects of the Christian view of God. It does not prove that God is kind, loving, listens to prayer, or judges sin. It simply demonstrates that some kind of transcendent power must have brought the universe into existence. In terms of this proof, we are simply calling that first transcendent power by the name of *God*.

Continuing Presence of the First Cause in the Universe   3.3.5

One final misconception should be avoided. The First Cause argument does not mean that God simply gave the universe the initial push and it has been rolling along on its own ever since. This view of God is sometimes expressed with the watchmaker analogy: God created and "wound up the watch" (the universe), but no longer interferes with its running. Such a conception is sometimes called the **Deist** view of God—a view of the divine closely associated with Enlightenment thinking.

But Aquinas's conception is completely different. For Aquinas, God is not the first in a series of causes. Since God is the First Being, God continues to be present in an intimate way to every existent thing, since God is the ultimate source of that thing's existence. "For the being of every creature depends on God, so that not for a moment could it subsist, but would fall into nothingness were it not kept in being by the operation of the Divine power" (*ST* 1.104.1). This conception of God's continuous upholding of the existence of the universe is sometimes called the *creatio continua*—the continuing creation.[8]

Of course, as we observe it now, all things in the universe are growing and changing through a myriad of natural causes: the laws of physics, natural processes of aging and decay, natural processes of birth and growth, and the natural law of evolution through natural selection. But from the perspective of the First Cause, all of these other causes can only rightfully be considered *secondary causes*. They did not cause themselves, and they only exist, and continue to exist, because they are continuously upheld by the First Cause. Brian J. Shanley notes that the "same God who transcends the created order is also intimately and immanently present within that order as upholding all causes in their causing, including the human will."[9]

The belief in God as the First Cause holding all things in existence means that God is in a real sense the cause of all things, but at the same time, does not deny the reality of these secondary causes. Shanley explains that for Aquinas, "the differing metaphysical levels of primary and secondary causation require us to say that any created effect comes totally and immediately from God as the transcendent primary cause and totally and immediately from the creature as secondary cause."[10] Thus the belief in God in no way contradicts a belief in scientifically observable laws of nature: God is in fact the ultimate foundation of those laws.

In philosophical terms, all reality in the universe—all things, all laws, all causes—are *contingent*. Their existence is not logically necessary; it is possible for them not to exist. Only the existence of the First Cause, God, is *necessary*, because without the transcendent First Cause, nothing else would exist.

Although our discussion about God as the First Cause has been rather abstract and philosophical, Thomist thinking insists that such reasoning actually puts us in touch with what is truly real. Far from being a vague, shadowy, unscientific opinion about reality, the First Cause is more real than any observable physical reality, because it is the necessary ground by which the existence of any physical or nonphysical reality is possible.

Relevance of the First Cause Argument   3.3.6

Many people today simply assume that an argument developed by a medieval theologian can carry no weight in the modern, scientific world. Such is certainly the view of biologist Richard Dawkins, who summarily rejects Aquinas's arguments as unconvincing. Let's briefly consider Dawkins's critique.

Dawkins sums up Aquinas's first three "ways," as follows: "All three of these arguments rely upon the idea of a regress and invoke God to terminate it. They make the entirely unwarranted assumption that God himself is immune to the regress."[11] In other words, asks Dawkins, why should this first cause itself not have a cause?

Dawkins fails to understand Aquinas's point—Aquinas is *not* claiming that God is simply the first in the series of causes (like the first billiard ball causing all the other billiard balls to move), and thus subject to the law of causation. Aquinas's point is that, logically, the ultimate first cause of all existence must be transcendent—a necessary ultimate being standing completely outside the chain of causation.

Dawkins again misses the point when he argues that there is no reason to ascribe to this First Cause any of the attributes normally attributed to God—such as goodness or the ability to listen to prayers: Aquinas's argument *does not claim* to prove these other attributes.

How, then, would Dawkins explain the ultimate origin of all existence? He writes that "it is more parsimonious to conjure up, say, a 'big bang singularity,' or some other physical concept as yet unknown."[12] But this is simply to say that science currently cannot explain the absolute beginning to existence.

In the Christian view this is not surprising, since the absolute beginning of the universe must logically transcend it. Since science by its nature deals with questions of cause and effect within the physical universe, there is no reason to think that science could ever come up with a scientific explanation for a First Cause that, logically, must transcend the universe.

Our discussion of Aquinas's First Cause shows us that we moderns still can learn much from a medieval theologian. At the same time, it is obvious that Aquinas's medieval Christian worldview is a limitation. In general, Aquinas's thought cannot be expected to deal adequately with many modern developments—for example, scientific theories of evolution or modern developments in ethical and political thinking that have given us a greater appreciation of democracy and tolerance of differing worldviews.

To practice theology responsibly in the world today, then, the theologian must not only be willing to listen faithfully to the tradition but also to engage critical modern developments. This double task—listening to the past and engaging the present—lies at the heart of the modern theological approaches to which we now turn.

Contemporary Examples of Theological Method   3.4

Responding to the Critics: Three Options   3.4.1

The modern world, according to the American Catholic theologian Avery Dulles, is characterized by the rise of a critical worldview, and different contemporary[13] approaches to theology can be characterized by how they react to this critical worldview.[14]

By "critical worldview" Dulles refers to the thought of philosophers such as Descartes and his theory of "methodological doubt" as well as Enlightenment thinkers such as Hume and Voltaire who directly attacked the authority of traditional Christian beliefs (see sec. 2.2.1). The rejection of religious authority continued with critics such as Karl Marx and Sigmund Freud. All of these thinkers share the critical assumption that "nothing is sacred" and all authority can be questioned, including the authority of the Bible and of the Church.

How can the modern theologian respond to these radical challenges?

One option is that of fideism: believers refuse to answer critical questions and instead retreat into their own world of faith (see sec. 2.7). Fideists tend to respond to critical questions with, "I can't explain it, but I know in my heart that it's true." Some historical traditions, such as nineteenth-century Lutheran pietism, chose this option.

Dulles contrasts the fideist approach with what he calls "countercritical theology." In this approach, the theologian tries to answer the critic with rational arguments alone. A countercritical theologian is convinced, for example, that he can prove that the Gospel stories about Jesus' life are completely accurate, or that Jesus' miracles, confirmed by many witnesses, prove that Jesus was divine. Dulles notes that Catholic neoscholastic theology of the late nineteenth and early twentieth centuries tended toward such rationalistic views.

For Dulles the fideistic option does not trust reason enough, while the "countercritical" approach trusts reason *too* much—or, rather, trusts a rationalistic understanding of reason too much (see sec.s 2.2.1 and 2.5.1).

Dulles identifies the Catholic approach as a "postcritical theology." It does not ignore the critical challenges, as fideism does, but at the same time it does not pretend that it can "prove" the truth of the Christian faith in the same way as one does a geometric proof. It accepts the broader definitions of faith and reason that we outlined in chapter 2.

Aspects of a Postcritical Theology   3.4.2

Critical Theories of Knowledge   3.4.2.1

Fideists "know" things in their hearts; rationalists "know" things through logical proof. Postcritical theologians cut through both models to ask basic philosophical questions: How do we know anything at all? When we think that we understand something, how do we know that our understanding is correct?

Philosophers have been asking such basic questions for centuries, and specific branches of philosophy have developed to focus on them. Epistemology addresses basic questions of how we know things at all, and **hermeneutics** studies the question of how we know whether our understanding or interpretations are correct.

These two fields of study are often abstract and difficult, but essential for postcritical theologians thinking about their faith tradition. These theologians must be able to show that the Christian worldview can respond to modern critical challenges in a responsible way.

We have already started to consider these necessary critical theories of knowledge and understanding in our earlier discussion. We saw that reasonable knowledge is not always based on pure logic: it is actually more often based on authority, tradition, probability, and personal experiences that cannot be expressed in precise rules (sec. 2.5.1). We saw that all thinking, especially in fields such as art, history, and philosophy, can only be done within a particular tradition (see sec.s 1.11 and 2.5.1.2). With this type of reflection, the postcritical theologian begins to show that Christian thought can still play a legitimate role in reasonable discussions about human knowledge, understanding, and truth, even in the modern, critical age.

A Hermeneutic of Trust   3.4.2.2

Dulles accepts that purely objective or "neutral" thinking about God and religious questions is impossible. Rather, all thinking must begin from fundamental presuppositions about the nature of God, life and death, and reality that are taken from a particular religious or philosophical tradition. We saw that Jane's thinking about God and the meaning of her friend's death were profoundly influenced by Christian beliefs, even though Jane herself was not an "active" Christian.

For Dulles, then, Christian theologians should begin by clearly acknowledging their commitment to the Christian faith tradition and not by pretending that they can take a completely objective position. This choice does not imply that their thinking is simply an act of blind faith, but rather a recognition that *all* thinking must begin within a tradition. "Recognizing that every affirmation rests upon some kind of faith, postcritical theology frankly relies on convictions born of the Christian faith."[15]

The theologian thus begins with a "hermeneutic of trust" in the reliability and validity of the faith tradition.[16] The traditional beliefs cannot be proven to be true beforehand, but they are accepted on the basis of trust in the authority of the tradition. This does not mean that no questions, uncertainties, doubts, or even criticisms of the tradition will arise on specific points, but simply that one's fundamental orientation is to trust the tradition.

For a Christian theologian, this basic trust includes a basic trust in specific Church authorities (see sec.s 2.5.1.1–2). "[Catholic] Theology itself demands a basic confidence in the Church and its official leadership as the transmitters of the heritage of faith."[17]

We can contrast the theologian's beginning point with a "hermeneutic of suspicion"—an intellectual starting point associated with the fundamentally antireligious attitudes of thinkers such as Marx and Freud (see sec. 1.8), whose primary orientation toward the religious traditions was one of a profound distrust. Marx and Freud were convinced that religious beliefs and actions were simply a mask for true, hidden motivations—the worker's sense of alienation due to economic oppression in Marxist philosophy, and the childlike desire for parental security in Freud's thought.

Lived Experience of the Tradition   3.4.2.3

The Christian theologian comes to a deeper understanding of the articles of faith not simply through intellectual study or purely rational understanding but also by participating in Christian worship and by attempting to live out Christian ethical principles in daily life.

This point ties in with our earlier discussion about the many ways people gain knowledge beyond strict logic (see sec.s 2.5.1.3–5). As Newman wrote, "Man is *not* a reasoning animal; he is a seeing, feeling, contemplating, acting animal" (see sec. 2.6.9). It is only through the commitment of the whole person, engaging both reason and the more emotional, imaginative, and affective aspects of the person, that more profound depths of understanding can be reached. It is only through an active participation in the Christian community, the Church, that the theologian can develop the tacit knowledge and skill (Newman's "illative sense") that is necessary for making valid theological judgments.

Consider a quick example. A Catholic theologian may understand, at the intellectual level, the belief in the Real Presence: that Christ is truly present (not just present symbolically) in the Lord's Supper. But the theologian's writing on that topic will be much fuller, more understandable, more convincing, if he or she has personally experienced the truth of that theological teaching through personal participation in the Lord's Supper over the years.

Scriptural Hermeneutics   3.5

Aquinas articulated the traditional Catholic understanding that Scripture is the foundational authority (*ST* 1.1.8 ad. 2). Accepting the tradition, then, is in large part an acceptance of Scripture.

But this raises a problem for the postcritical theologian: since the time of the Enlightenment, Scripture itself has been subjected to critical scrutiny. Who are the authors of the books? Were mistakes made as books were copied and passed down over the years? How can books that were written thousands of years ago in a very different time and culture still be relevant for Christian belief today?

A central task for the postcritical theologian, then, is to work out a valid scriptural hermeneutics—guidelines that, having fully taken into consideration the critical challenges to Scripture, could still help the reader to come to a valid and responsible understanding.

The Hermeneutical Circle   3.5.1

A fundamental concept in modern hermeneutical theory is that of the "hermeneutical circle." Let us see how this theory can help us to understand what is happening when a modern person reads a traditional text such as Scripture.

The theory begins with the insight that no reader can read a traditional text in a completely objective manner. Even before beginning to read, the reader brings certain prejudices (in the sense of "pre-judgments") or preconceived ideas to the reading.

Let's apply the theory to a reading of the first three chapters of the scriptural Book of Genesis as an example. Here we find the story of God's creation of the universe, including humans, and of humanity's first sin.

If the reader is from a predominately Christian culture, he will have many prejudgments from the Christian tradition itself. Even if reading Genesis for the first time, the reader's understandings about God, creation, sin, good, and evil will have been profoundly shaped by the scriptural tradition. A Muslim reader's understanding of the biblical story, in contrast, will be shaped by the way in which Adam is portrayed in the Qur'an. A reader from a non-Western tradition will also bring certain prejudgments about the beginnings of the universe to a reading of Genesis. These prejudgments will affect what the reader notices in the text and how it is interpreted.

Many other traditions will influence readers. A reader influenced by a rationalist worldview may find it impossible to accept the literal truth of any supernatural event described in Genesis. Because of the influence of the materialist tradition, another reader may find it difficult to accept or even fully understand biblical concepts such as creation or the belief that humans are formed in God's image. A person influenced by a tradition in which the Bible is read literally may have difficulty in understanding more symbolic or metaphorical levels of meaning.

The first step, then, for a valid interpretation of Genesis, is for readers to become intentionally aware of their own prejudgments. This does not mean that they will reject these prejudgments, only that they become aware of them and realize that they strongly influence their understanding of the text.

Engaging the Scriptural Horizon 3.5.2

In the second movement of the hermeneutical circle, readers actively engage their own horizon (view of the world, prejudgments) with the horizon of the text. The biblical text presents a definite worldview: all of creation was made directly by God and is good; humans were made in "God's image" and rule over the rest of creation; humans were tempted to disobey God and so lost their original innocence and happiness.

Gadamer's hermeneutical theory (sec. 1.11) shows us that readers can never understand a text directly. Rather, understanding takes place only in the *encounter* between two horizons, when the horizon of the reader meets the horizon of the text.

First, readers must be open to considering the scriptural worldview. It is unlikely that militant atheists would be open to considering the worldview of Genesis: if they read these chapters, they would most likely adopt a hermeneutic of suspicion, perhaps attempting to prove that the account was scientifically inaccurate or ethically questionable.

But if readers are open to considering the scriptural worldview, then a "merger of the horizons"—understanding—may take place. Readers with a rationalist worldview may perhaps become more open to a broader interpretation of symbolic meaning. Readers with a materialist worldview may be open to expanding their own understanding of reality to include spiritual realities. Muslims may merge some of their tradition's understandings of Adam with those of Genesis.

If readers encounter the traditional text more than once, the process of understanding will be ongoing. Readers first encounter Scripture with certain rationalistic, materialistic, or deterministic prejudgments. If they are open to a meeting of the horizons, they will come away from their reading with their prejudgments slightly changed. This new influence of the biblical worldview will in turn modify their own view of the world and cause them to see and experience events in their daily life in a different way. These new experiences and perspectives on daily life will in turn influence their reading when they return to the biblical text. The hermeneutical circle is an ongoing process.

Paul Ricoeur   3.5.3

The philosopher Paul Ricoeur raises a critical question with regard to the hermeneutical circle and the interpretation of Scripture: How can modern readers truly engage the biblical worldview when it is so foreign to their own way of thinking and perceiving?

Let's say that Roger has been reading accounts in the daily news of suicide bombings, school shootings, and corrupt politicians. He begins to wonder why there seems to be so much evil in the world. In an attempt to find answers, Roger turns to reading the Bible, because he knows that it is a major source for the teachings of the Christian tradition. A friend advises him to read the story of Adam and Eve in Genesis, since this provides the Christian explanation of how evil came into the world.

Roger does so, but he is disappointed. Rather than shedding light on the problem of suffering, it seems to add to his confusion. How is he supposed to believe a story in which a snake talks and a woman is formed out of a man's rib? It seems to have nothing to do with his concerns.

In Ricoeur's view, this example illustrates the fact that modern readers can no longer directly encounter a biblical text such as that found in Genesis 1–3 simply because the worldviews of the biblical text and modern people are literally "worlds apart." The biblical worldview is prescientific and symbolic; modern readers are shaped by a fundamentally scientific and literal understanding of reality. For

Ricouer, a meaningful encounter between reader and traditional text is still possible, but it can only come *indirectly*: the reader must first go through a conscious process of interpretation.

The first stage involves the use of critical reason, since modern readers do not accept certain elements of the story that are based on pre-scientific understandings of reality. For Ricoeur, this includes the story's reference to snakes crawling on their bellies due to God's curse (Gen 3:14): this should be recognized as a prescientific explanation for why snakes crawl and is considered irrelevant for modern readers.

Next, modern readers develop a critical awareness of the type of language that the story employs. It is not a historical, literal account; rather, it is the language of mythic and symbolic foundational stories through which all ancient societies expressed their encounters with the divine.

Once readers have passed through this critical phase they are in a much better position to understand the full meaning of the symbolic language. Adam and Eve are not meant to be understood as literal, historical figures; rather their lives symbolize the experiences of all humans. The exile from the Garden of Eden again is not a literal historical event: it is one of the biblical symbols used to express the human experience of sin.

Modern readers can now reflect rationally on what Genesis tells them about the divine relationship with the human and about the reality of human sin that separates people from God, the ultimate source of meaning in their lives. Far from rejecting the story because it is written in an ancient, symbolic language, modern readers will instead recognize its symbolic nature and reflect on the light it sheds on the human condition. As Ricoeur says, "the symbol gives rise to thought."

For Ricoeur, then, modern readers must engage the biblical tradition through the hermeneutical circle. Ricoeur formulates the circle thus: "We must understand in order to believe, but we must believe in order to understand."[18] "Understand in order to believe": for modern Christian believers the traditional text can only be accepted after passing through the critical questions raised by modern thought. But Christians are drawn to the text in the first place because of the traditional belief in its meaningfulness and power.

The process is not essentially different for non-Christians. They too will need to "understand in order to believe": they too will need to ask critical questions before considering the truths within the text.

Since they are not part of the Tradition, the biblical text cannot have the same meaning for non-Christians. But if they are open to bringing their own worldview into an encounter with the biblical horizon, then they too may experience a deepened understanding of the human encounter with the divine.

Lonergan's Method   3.6

Like Dulles and Ricoeur, Bernard Lonergan understands the relationship between critical reason and faith as central to the practice of theology in the modern world.

Lonergan identifies two central tasks for the Christian theologian: (1) to listen to the "word," that is, the Christian tradition, and (2) to communicate the "word," that is, to communicate the Christian tradition to others in an understandable manner. Lonergan's method is thus an attempt to help the theologian (1) to "hear," understand, and appropriate the Tradition in a way that is responsible and aware of modern critical questions, and (2) to communicate the "word" in a way that is also reasonable, responsible, and aware of the critical challenges of our times.

Theologizing in Changing Cultural Settings   3.6.1

Lonergan writes that a theology "mediates between a cultural matrix and the significance and role of religion in that matrix."[19] Theology helps to communicate religious insights to particular cultures in a clear and systematic way, or to show how religious insights may relate to scientific or other branches of nonreligious knowledge within a particular culture.

But the modern concept of culture has changed, and thus too the task of theology. In a precritical, "classicist" understanding of culture, one would think of a classic culture (for example, ancient Greece or the Middle Ages) as a stable and permanent achievement, and thus theological works could also be stable and permanent (for example, Aquinas's *Summa Theologica*). But an "empirical" view of culture appreciates its more fluid foundations and thus sees theology itself as more open to development and change as it communicates a tradition to changing cultures.[20]

We have seen how influential a particular tradition is on a person's understanding of the world. From a sociological point of view, we can relate this point to what is called the "sociology of knowledge"—the tendency of each society to reinforce certain ways of thinking that the society defines as "normal" and punish ways of thinking that deviate from that norm. Thus, in the ancient world, people were socialized to accept slavery as a natural and inevitable institution, but in modern democracies, the belief that all people are naturally equal in their basic human rights is reinforced.

In our modern, pluralistic world, we have a much livelier sense of how cultures change and develop over time. So Aquinas's *Summa*, great as it is, cannot be a permanent achievement. We no longer live in the medieval world. The language, style, vocabulary, and even thought patterns of the *Summa* must be updated and adjusted to make sense in a changed culture.

Since theology cannot rely on an unchanging cultural paradigm, Lonergan argues that theological method must be based on something that is unchanging: the way in which the human mind works. And so, in common with other postcritical theologians, Lonergan's approach is based on a critical study of how humans know and understand (see sec. 3.4.2.1).[21]

Theology as a Collaborative Effort   3.6.2

Lonergan argues that theology must be a collaboration among many different specialists working in different fields. In universities or seminaries, for example, theology was commonly divided into scriptural studies (with further specializations in Old or New Testament), historical theology (with special focus on patristic theology, medieval theology, and Reformation theology), systematic theology (the study of basic Christian beliefs from a more philosophical perspective), and moral theology.

For Lonergan, however, the more important divisions of theology are those that he calls "functional specialties": the different tasks that are necessary to do theology in a methodical way. While the tasks can be divided conceptually, they need to be closely related to one another in actual practice. Each specialty is closely related to one of the basic functions of the human mind: experience, understanding, judging, and deciding.

The first four functional specialties are related to "hearing the word"—the systematic ways in which modern theologians study the Christian tradition—and the second four to "communicating the tradition."

Functional Specialties   3.6.2.1
Hearing the Tradition

1. **Research.** Here the theologian gathers basic information by, for example, researching in a library or doing excavations at an archaeological site. Thus a historical theologian might study the life and times of Martin Luther, while a scriptural scholar might participate in an excavation in Galilee, the native province of Jesus.

2. **Interpretation.** In this specialty, the theologian gains a full awareness of the modern critical challenges to faith and learns how these challenges can be responsibly met through developing proper epistemological and hermeneutical theories (we have discussed some of these theories in sec.s 3.4–5 and more generally in chapter 2).

   Thus the theologian rejects both rationalism (the claim that we know reality directly) and idealism (the claim that we know only our own ideas, and not actual reality itself) and adopts a third position of "critical realism": we can know reality, but only through a critical analysis of our own ways of knowing, including an honest look at our own pre-judgments.

   Developing a responsible hermeneutical approach is essential for theologians as they interpret Scripture, but also as they interpret classic statements of belief such as the Nicene Creed (a fourth-century summary of Christian belief).

   We will discuss some of the issues involved in interpreting Scripture in chapter 9.

3. **History.** Within this specialty, theologians focus on particularly relevant periods in Christian history (e.g., the first centuries of Christianity, the Reformation), or on a particularly important historical figure (e.g., Augustine, Aquinas, Luther, Calvin). Again the specialist working in this area will need a critical awareness of the impossibility of writing a completely scientific and objective history, while at the same time insisting that valid historical truth is still attainable for historians who are critically aware of their own cultural biases and prejudgments.

   The theologian must understand the need to interpret historical events and historical statements within their own historical context, with a critical awareness of how particular social or cultural forces influenced the theology of a particular time. We will see in chapter

continued

continued

11 how some recent scholars have applied this historical approach to gain a better understanding of Jesus within his historical context.

4. **Dialectic.** This specialty focuses on decisive conflicts within the Christian theological tradition. So, for example, the dialectic theologian might study the issues involved in the conflict between the Roman Catholic Church and the Protestant movements of the Reformation, or the differences that led to the formal split of Eastern and Western Christianity in 1054. The aim is to gain deeper insight into the reasons underlying these conflicts. In studying the Catholic-Protestant debate on the relationship between Scripture and tradition, for example, the theologian would try to get beyond the emotional and polemical aspects of the debate, and focus on clarifying the real theological issues and alternatives.

Recent ecumenical dialogues between Catholics and non-Catholics (see sec.s 12.23, 12.25, and 12.27) are a good example of how this dialectical function can be carried out.

Communicating the Tradition

1. **Foundations.** In this specialty, the theologian attempts to describe and understand the experience of conversion: the movement from a horizon closed to the transcendent to a Christian view of the world. It does not discuss specific Christian beliefs, but presents the overall worldview within which these teachings make sense.

2. **Doctrines.** This specialty focuses on Christian teachings directly: for example, the teaching that God became human in Jesus, or that God is a Trinity. One particular consideration is to discern the extent to which Christian belief or practice developed over time. For example, the classic belief in God as a Trinity (three persons in one divine nature) is not found as such in the earliest Christian writings, including the New Testament: it is clear that this was a later theological development of the original Christian beliefs concerning the Father, Son, and Holy Spirit. The doctrinal theologian studies how the development took place and to what extent these ideas are legitimate and consistent developments of earlier beliefs (see sec. 6.14).

continued

continued

A second consideration is how the exact language of a Christian teaching might change (for example, in a different cultural setting) while retaining the same essential meaning. Thus a doctrinal theologian might consider whether the word *persons* in the phrase "God is three persons in one divine nature" still has the same sense in modern times as it did when it was first developed in early Christian debates about the precise relationship between Father, Son, and Spirit (see sec. 6.18).

3. **Systematics.** This specialty involves a critical study of Christian doctrines, considering to what extent they are consistent within themselves and consistent with one another. In showing how they relate to one another, a deeper understanding of the doctrines is gained. The role of philosophy is central in developing a systematic theology: Aquinas, for example, used Aristotelian categories to express many of the relationships in his systematic theology. Pope John Paul II raised the question of whether the natural sciences could play this same role in modern theology, providing a precise language with which to express some theological insights into the relationship between nature, humans, and God.[22]

4. **Communications.** This specialty seeks to understand the general questions of how theological beliefs can best be communicated in the modern world. A particular area within this specialty is pastoral theology, a discipline concerned with methods of communicating theological teaching to average church members who have no special theological training. **o**

Modern Theology: Faith Responding to Critical Challenges

3.7

For Dulles, Ricoeur, and Lonergan, a major task of modern theology is to demonstrate that theology is capable of making an intelligent and reasonable response to the challenges of the modern age.

These thinkers realize that theologians today cannot simply repeat past conclusions. Even if the meaning of theological truths is unchanging, the way in which these truths are studied, appropriated, expressed, and communicated must change in order to meet modern critical challenges.

Questions about the Text

1. What does it mean to say that Aquinas's theology involves a "philosophy of being"?

2. What are some examples of metaphysical questions? How are they different from questions in the natural sciences?

3. How does Aquinas understand the relationship between faith and reason?

4. Summarize Aquinas's method of discussing questions in the *Summa*.

5. What do Aquinas's "five ways" of proving God's existence have in common?

6. Logically, why must the universe have a First Cause, and why would this Cause need to transcend the universe?

7. In Aquinas's thought, what is the relationship between God as the First Cause and the laws of nature as causes?

8. In what three ways do modern theologies respond to the critical challenges of the Enlightenment, according to Dulles?

9. Explain how a Catholic approach to theology is located between a fideistic and a countercritical approach.

10. What is the difference between starting theological study with a "hermeneutic of trust" or with a "hermeneutic of suspicion"?

11. What is meant by the "hermeneutical circle" in the interpretation of Scripture?

12. What are Lonergan's "functional specialties"? Why do you think he chose these particular eight specialties?

13. What is meant by "critical realism"?

14. In what ways does Lonergan's approach to theology differ from Aquinas's?

Discussion Questions

1. Do you share Aquinas's confidence that truths of reason can never contradict truths of faith?

2. Do you think Aquinas's five-step approach to answering theological questions can still apply to theological questions today? Why or why not?

3. Think of ways in which a theologian might express the same belief differently in different cultures.

4. What are some similarities and differences between how theology was done in Aquinas's time compared with how theology is done today?

Endnotes

1. A classic statement of the central place of Aquinas's thought in Catholic theology is Pope Leo XIII's encyclical, *On the Restoration of Christian Philosophy According to the Mind of Saint Thomas Aquinas, the Angelic Doctor* (*Aeterni Patris*, 1879).

2. See the discussion of this point in Joseph Ratzinger, *Introduction to Christianity* (San Francisco: Ignatius Press, 2000; orig. pub. 1968), 116–36.

3. On these points, see Peter Kreeft, *A Summa of the* Summa: *The Essential Philosophical Passages of Saint Thomas Aquinas'* Summa Theologica (San Francisco: Ignatius Press, 1990), 45 no. 32.

4. The Prologue to the *Summa* states: "the Master of Catholic truth ought not only to teach the proficient, but also to instruct beginners."

5. See also the clear explanation of Thomas Aquinas's ways in Kreeft, *Summa of the* Summa, 60–70.

6. See William E. Carroll, "Aquinas and the Big Bang," *First Things* 97 (November 1999): 18–20.

7. When we say that the First Cause "is distinct from" or "stands outside of" the universe, this should not be understood in a physical way. We are simply using metaphorical language to try to express the logical point that the ultimate cause of the universe cannot be part of the universe itself.

8. On the *creatio continua*, see Christoph von Schönborn, *Chance or Purpose: Creation, Evolution, and a Rational Faith* (San Francisco: Ignatius Press, 2007), 75–81,

9. Quoted in William E. Carroll, "Divine Agency, Modern Physics, and the Autonomy of Nature," 14. Accessed October 8, 2008, at *www.gonzagafaithreason.org/files/pdfs/Carroll-PGA-2007.doc.*

10. Quoted in Carroll, "Divine Agency," 14–15.

11. Richard Dawkins, *The God Delusion* (Boston: Houghton Mifflin, 2006), 77.

12. Ibid., 78.

13. The reader should be aware that in many theological and philosophical discussions the term *postmodern* is used to describe a variety of contemporary intellectual trends. The term is sometimes used in rather vague ways, however, and is often associated with ethical relativism. I therefore prefer to use the term *contemporary* or simply *modern*.

14. Avery Dulles, *The Craft of Theology: From Symbol to System* (New York: Crossroad, 1995), 3–15.
15. Ibid., 13.
16. Ibid., 7.
17. Ibid., 14.
18. Paul Ricoeur, *The Symbolism of Evil* (Religious Perspectives 17; New York: Harper & Row, 1967), 351.
19. Bernard Lonergan, *Method in Theology* (Toronto: University of Toronto Press, 1990; orig. pub. 1971), xi.
20. Ibid.
21. Ibid., 14.
22. "Just as Aristotelian philosophy, through the ministry of such great scholars as St. Thomas Aquinas, ultimately came to shape some of the most profound expressions of theological doctrine, so can we not hope that the sciences of today, along with all forms of human knowing, may invigorate and inform those parts of the theological enterprise that bear on the relation of nature, humanity and God?" John Paul II, "Letter to Reverend George V. Coyne, S.J., Director of the Vatican Observatory" (June 1, 1988). Accessed October 8, 2008, at *http://www.vatican.va/holy_father/ john_paul_ii/letters/1988/documents/hf_jp-ii_let_19880601_padre-coyne_en.html.*

4

Science and Christian Faith

Christian Faith versus Modern Science? 4.1

In section 2.4 we considered some critiques of faith from a rationalist and materialist worldview. To review:

1. Religious thinking invents "spirits" and "gods" in order to explain natural phenomena. Science discovers natural laws governing the universe.

2. Religion is based on vague feelings and emotions. Science is based on hard-nosed reason and empirical facts.

3. Religion often impedes the advance of true scientific knowledge, as when the Catholic Church forced Galileo to recant his scientific conclusions. Science is dedicated to free inquiry—the scientist is free to follow where the evidence leads.

Richard Dawkins contrasts religious fundamentalist belief with scientific belief in the following way:

BACKGROUND IMAGES ROYALTY FREE FROM ISTOCK AND SHUTTERSTOCK

Fundamentalists know they are right because they have read the truth in a holy book and they know, in advance, that nothing will budge them from their belief. . . . The book is true, and if the evidence seems to contradict it, it is the evidence that must be thrown out, not the book. By contrast, what I, as a scientist, believe (for example, evolution) I believe not because of reading it in a holy book but because I have studied the evidence. . . . Books about evolution are believed not because they are holy. They are believed because they present overwhelming quantities of mutually buttressed evidence. In principle, any reader can go and check that evidence. When a science book is wrong, somebody eventually discovers the mistake and it is corrected in subsequent books. That conspicuously doesn't happen with holy books.[1]

We shall argue that the above contrasts between religion and science are overly simplistic both in their description of religion and of science. Let us begin with a consideration of scientific knowledge itself.

Intuition and Personal Insight in Science   4.2

The chemist and philosopher Michael Polanyi has shown that even in the physical sciences, scientists do not gain knowledge by strictly following the explicit rules of the scientific method. Polanyi shows scientists often work with what he calls "tacit knowledge"—an intuitive, personal way of understanding. Let us consider two examples.

How do scientists begin to do scientific research? When narrowing down a problem to be investigated or forming an initial hypothesis, scientists must draw heavily on previous personal experiences and intuition: they cannot proceed by following strict rules.

How do scientists observe data? Let us consider an astronomer recording observations of a planet's velocity. Due to a variety of factors, such observations will always vary to some degree from predicted values. The astronomer must then determine whether the pattern of variations is due to chance, or whether the variation is a clue to investigate other possible causes. No precise statistical rule of variations can help the astronomer, who must rely on personal scientific intuition to decide whether or not to follow up this clue.[2]

Newman also notes how scientists are not restricted to pure logic in their work, referring to Sir Isaac Newton's illative sense in perceiving mathematical and physical truth without strict proof.[3]

Authority and Tradition in Science   4.3

In contrast to Dawkin's idealized model of completely free scientific inquiry, both Polanyi and Thomas Kuhn have shown that science typically operates with a heavy emphasis on authority and tradition. Polanyi writes that science must be "disciplined by an orthodoxy which can permit only a limited degree of dissent, and . . . such dissent is fraught with grave risks to the dissenter."[4] Scientific orthodoxy is based on the scientific beliefs of a particular time and culture, and this orthodoxy determines (for example) whether certain research projects will be funded or papers accepted for publication based in large part on whether the proposals follow current scientific paradigms—the theoretical frameworks in which various sciences operate. Polanyi argues that such orthodoxy is necessary to weed out nonsensical theories, but it operates at the cost of occasionally ignoring or resisting legitimate scientific insights that go against the reigning paradigm.[5]

Kuhn describes scientific development as "a succession of tradition-bound periods punctuated by non-cumulative breaks."[6] A scientific community can only gain knowledge if it shares a certain paradigm of how the universe operates. Challenges to the reigning traditional paradigm are resisted: "Normal science, for example, often suppresses fundamental novelties because they are necessarily subversive of its basic commitments."[7] But eventually, when the reigning paradigm encounters problems it cannot solve, a new theory will succeed in challenging the orthodoxy, and the scientific community will then undergo what is known as a paradigm shift, a change in the theoretical framework in which that science operates.

Christian Faith and the Rise of Modern Science   4.4

We now consider another variation of the rationalist claim that faith hinders the free inquiry of science. Moderns commonly assume that the Middle Ages, because it was so dominated by the authority of the Catholic Church, was a time of ignorance and superstition hostile to scientific thought. This assumption is evident in our language: the labeling of the Middle Ages, especially their early centuries, as the "Dark Ages," and the common use of the term *medieval* to describe unenlightened and unscientific thinking.

How valid is this assumption? Granted that medieval Christian thinkers had not yet developed the modern scientific method and placed little emphasis on empirical research, the general claim that the medieval Church was hostile to science is a myth. Relying on the work of numerous historians specializing in the period, the sociologist Rodney Stark offers abundant evidence to the contrary.

The European universities, established in the middle of the twelfth century, evolved from the cathedral schools that trained monks and priests.[8] In the thirteenth and fourteenth centuries, Catholic scholastic university professors taught that the earth was round and that it turned on its axis.[9] Thomas Aquinas's teacher, Albert the Great, engaged in empirical research (he is described as "perhaps the best field botanist of the Middle Ages").[10] By the 1300s, dissection of human cadavers for anatomy lessons was common in the Italian universities.[11] Nicholaus Copernicus (1473–1543), the first to publish the heliocentric theory that the sun, not the earth, is at the center of the universe, had a doctor's degree in Church law. Copernicus's theory can be best understood not as a radical innovation but as a logical development of astronomical theories he had learned from his scholastic professors at the medieval universities he attended in Poland and Italy. He dedicated the work advancing the heliocentric theory to Pope Paul III.[12]

After the Middle Ages, we can cite many examples of how faith and scientific inquiry were considered to be entirely compatible. Galileo (1564–1642), Newton (1642–1727), and Johannes Kepler (1571–1630) were all men of deep faith.[13] To give just one example, Kepler's first major astronomical work, *The Cosmographic Mystery*, attempted to describe God's geometrical plan for the universe. The tradition of distinguished Catholic Jesuit astronomers dates back to the seventeenth century. The Austrian monk Gregor Mendel is recognized as the "father of genetics" for his discovery of the basic laws of heredity.[14]

Even in our day, religious belief and scientific achievement still correlate. In a major 1969 Carnegie survey of American university professors, 55 percent of the physical science professors identified themselves as religious; 43 percent reported regularly attending worship services.[15] To be fair, however, we should note that Dawkins does cite evidence that of the American scientists elected to the elite National Academy of Scientists, only about 7 percent believe in a personal God.[16]

Christian Worldview as Foundation for Modern Science   4.5

In direct contradiction to the myth that Christian faith held back science, scholars such as Stark have shown that Christian faith was in fact the prerequisite for the rise of modern science.

Scholars are generally agreed that the modern scientific method involving empirical observation, formation of testable hypotheses, and experimental validation arose in Europe in the sixteenth and seventeenth centuries.[17] According to the rationalist myth, this can only be explained as the result of a group of brave freethinkers such as Galileo resisting the attempts of the Catholic Church to crush free scientific inquiry.

The truth is actually the opposite. As we have just seen, the medieval Church and universities encouraged rational thought and empirical study, setting the stage for the great achievements of men such as Copernicus and Kepler.

More fundamentally, however, one can argue plausibly that a Judeo-Christian worldview was a prerequisite for the development of modern science. In Rodney Stark's words, "Christianity depicted God as a rational, responsive, dependable and omnipotent being and the universe as his personal creation, thus having a rational, lawful, stable structure, awaiting human comprehension."[18] Stark argues that far from suppressing scientific inquiry, "*Christian theology was essential for the rise of science.*"[19]

The philosopher Alfred North Whitehead also champions this claim. The early European scientists were motivated to do their painstaking research into nature because they were convinced that the universe had a rational structure. This confidence, Whitehead thinks, was based on their belief that the universe was created by a rational God. "Every detail was supervised and ordered: the search into nature could only result in the vindication of the faith in rationality."[20]

Albert Einstein, though himself not a conventional religious believer, echoes this conviction.

> What a deep conviction of the rationality of the universe and what a yearning to understand, were it but a feeble reflection of the mind

revealed in this world, Kepler and Newton must have had to enable them to spend years of solitary labor in disentangling the principles of celestial mechanics![21]

We have discussed this point already in section 2.6.2: the Judeo-Christian tradition insisted that the universe was created through God's *logos*—the power that infused the universe with a rational order. The task of the scientist was only to discover the laws through which the divine *logos* operates in the world

These scholars argue further that only the Judeo-Christian belief in a rational Creator could have provided the foundation for the modern scientific project. Whitehead argues that religious traditions that believed in inscrutable impersonal powers or in gods that acted arbitrarily could not inspire "the same confidence as in the intelligible rationality of a personal being."[22] It is for essentially these same reasons that science did not develop in otherwise highly sophisticated ancient civilizations such as China or Greece, according to Stark. Even the Islamic tradition, with its belief in a personal Creator, did not provide the foundations for modern science, since Islamic thought tends to conceive of events in the universe as shaped directly by God's will rather than through natural laws established by God.[23]

We should note also that the Christian confidence in the rationality of the Creator corresponds to the Christian confidence in the ability of the rational human to perceive that rational order in the universe. Here we must consider the Judeo-Christian belief that humans are created in God's image (Gen 1:26–27) and are thus able to share in God's *logos*.

The Galileo Affair   4.6

If it is true that the Christian worldview was a prerequisite for the development of modern science, and that the medieval Church in particular was not opposed to the use of reason and empirical research, how then do we explain the undeniable fact that the Catholic Church, in 1633, condemned Galileo and forced him to recant his scientifically based beliefs that the earth revolved around the sun?

First, we should note, with Stephen Barr, that the Catholic Church's condemnation of Galileo is in fact an anomaly: it is the only case where the Catholic Church has condemned a scientific theory.[24] The Catholic Church, it is true, has often condemned what it considers to be *theological* errors, and the precise issue on which Galileo was condemned did, in the end, involve a theological issue. Church officials judged that Galileo, by insisting categorically that the earth revolved around the sun, was rejecting the authority of Scripture. Galileo's heliocentric view was seen to conflict with certain passages of Scripture that state that the earth is immovable (e.g., Ps 93:1: "the world will surely stand in place, never to be moved") and that the sun moves across the sky (Jos 10:13: "the sun halted in the middle of the sky").

The Catholic Church's relative tolerance for scientific work even as it aggressively condemned what it considered theological heresy was true even of the infamous Spanish Inquisition (begun in 1478). Stark cites a conclusion by historian Henry Kamen:

> Scientific books written by Catholics tended to circulate freely. The 1583 Quiroga Index [a list of banned books] had a negligible impact on the accessibility of scientific works, and Galileo was never put on the list of forbidden books. The most direct attacks mounted by the Inquisition were against selected works in the areas of astrology and alchemy, sciences that were deemed to carry overtones of superstition.[25]

Even the Galileo case itself is hardly a black-and-white example of free scientific inquiry being crushed by a Church demanding blind obedience to dogma. The facts are more complex.

First, the Catholic Church had never moved to silence the Copernican theory (published in 1543, nearly a century before Galileo's trial), as long as it was presented as a hypothesis and not as fact. Galileo himself, far from being a radical freethinker, connected scientific research with an appreciation of God's creation: "the book of nature is a book written by the hand of God in the language of mathematics."[26] Galileo was personally convinced that the Copernican theory did not contradict Scripture, but only a falsely literal interpretation of Scripture.

Galileo had been an influential teacher, associated with the Medici family in Venice, who espoused the Copernican theory and taught that it did not contradict Scripture. In 1616 Galileo was warned by Church officials not to teach the Copernican theory as fact, since it appeared to contradict scriptural passages, and Galileo agreed.[27]

In 1632, however, Galileo published a book strongly supporting the Copernican hypothesis. The pope at that time, Urban VIII, at one time a friend of Galileo's, believed that Galileo had broken his earlier

Lessons of the Galileo Affair 4.7

Pope John Paul II had a particular interest in the significance of the Galileo affair and appointed a commission in 1979 to study it. In its 1992 report, the Pontifical Academy of Sciences commission concluded that at the time of the Galileo trial, "theologians . . . failed to grasp the profound non-literal meaning of the Scriptures when they described the physical structure of the universe. This led them unduly to transpose a question of factual observation into the realm of faith."[28]

In his own reflections on the report, John Paul reiterates this point. The Catholic Church officials who condemned Galileo failed to distinguish between two realms of knowledge: knowledge based on divine revelation and knowledge that can be discovered by human reason. Scripture is not competent to make judgments on the nature of the physical universe. Such judgments should be left to the experimental sciences and to philosophy, both of which are competent within their own realms.

John Paul then followed up with a crucial point: though the two realms of revelation and reason should be distinguished, they should not be separated. Precisely the opposite, in fact: advances in one field of knowledge should affect all other fields of knowledge. Thus the scientific evidence for the truth of the Copernican system should have caused theologians to question whether their own literal interpretation of scriptural passages apparently opposed to the Copernican system were accurate. John Paul insisted that the principle still applies today. "It is a duty for theologians to keep themselves regularly informed of scientific advances in order to examine . . . whether or not there are reasons for taking them into account in their reflection or for introducing changes in their teaching."[29] •

promise not to teach the theory as fact, and felt personally betrayed by the scientist. Galileo was summoned to Rome and in 1633 a tribunal condemned his theory, forced him to recant his views, and placed him under house arrest for the remainder of his life. He died in 1641.

A key point to consider is that members of the tribunal believed (along with many in Galileo's time) that the Copernican theory was factually false, or at least unproven. It seemed to contradict the common sense notion that the sun did move, and Galileo had not been able to produce convincing evidence that it did not (Galileo sought to prove the earth's motion by the movement of tides—a theory that is in fact scientifically incorrect). Cardinal Bellarmine, a leading Catholic official who had delivered the 1616 warning to Galileo, stated at the time:

> I say that if a real proof be found that the sun is fixed and does not revolve round the earth, but the earth round the sun, then it will be necessary, very carefully, to proceed to the explanation of the passages of Scripture which appear to be contrary, and we should rather say that we have misunderstood these [Scripture passages] than pronounce that to be false which is demonstrated.[30]

Bellarmine thus upheld the traditional Catholic belief that the truths of reason can never contradict the truths of faith. If the heliocentric theory had been clearly demonstrated, Bellarmine argues, this would have caused the Catholic Church to rethink its interpretation of scriptural passages that seemed to demonstrate that the sun revolved around the earth.

Long before Bellarmine's time, the great theologian Augustine (354–430) had articulated this same principle: "If it happens that the authority of Sacred Scripture is set in opposition to clear and certain reasoning, this must mean that the person who interprets Scripture does not understand it correctly."[31] This Catholic principle, then, is the exact opposite of the rigid and unreasonable fundamentalism described by Dawkins and cited at the beginning of the chapter.

The Big Bang and the Christian Doctrine of Creation 4.8

The most commonly accepted scientific theory of the origins of the universe is the "big bang" theory. According to this theory, about fifteen to twenty billion years ago all the matter in the universe was compacted into one supercondensed area. This matter exploded and began expanding outwards to form what we now see as our universe. The big bang theory has been confirmed by observations of galaxies rapidly moving apart from one another and the detection of low levels of radiation throughout the universe consistent with the hypothesis of an initial explosion.

Are the big bang theory and the Christian belief that God created the universe contradictory? The rationalist believes that they are: there is no scientific evidence of God's intervention in the big bang. A biblical literalist might argue that there is nothing in Genesis about a big bang, and so the theory cannot be correct.

It is true that the big bang theory certainly does contradict the belief that God created the universe in a literal six days, but we have seen that the Catholic tradition does not insist on a literal interpretation of that passage (see sec. 4.6). We will see later that there are good reasons for believing that Genesis should not be understood literally as a scientifically accurate description of how the universe actually began (see sec. 8.12.1).

If we understand the Genesis account of creation in a nonliteral way, we'll see that there are actually striking similarities between the biblical account of creation and the big bang theory.

The Christian View of Creation and the Big Bang 4.8.1

The big bang theory and the Christian doctrine of creation agree that the universe had a specific beginning point. Previous to the big bang theory, a common scientific assumption was that the universe simply had no beginning—one version of this idea was the "Steady State" model of the universe, which held that matter was continually being created as the universe expanded. In fact, many scientists were originally quite resistant to the implications of the big bang theory, at least in part because it opened up the possibility of a transcendent beginning to the universe that conflicted with a strictly materialist worldview.[32]

Further, the big bang theory and the Christian doctrine of creation agree that time itself had a beginning. Our common sense experience of time is that it flows at an unchanging, constant rate, by minutes, hours, days, and years. But through the work of Einstein and others, we now know that time is not a fixed constant. Rather, "time, like space, is a measure of the intervals between things and events in the physical universe."[33] Thus it makes no sense to speak about time before the universe began, since time, as a function of the physical universe, did not yet exist.

The insight that time had a beginning is not new—it was advanced centuries ago by Augustine. In the ancient world, the eternity of the universe was a common assumption (a view held by Aristotle, as we noted), and Augustine relates how some critics mocked the Christian belief that creation occurred at a specific time by asking, "What was God doing before the creation?" If God had created the universe immediately, they argued, the universe would also be eternal, but if God had waited some time before creating, why was he waiting?[34]

Augustine replies that the critics' question is based on a misunderstanding of time. Time is a constant flow of past, present, and future, while God is eternal and thus outside of—transcending—time. God is the creator of time, and thus time did not exist before the creation, in Augustine's view. Addressing God, Augustine writes, "But if there was no time before heaven and earth were created, how can anyone ask what you were doing 'then'? If there was no time, there was no 'then.'"[35]

A final intriguing convergence relates specifically to the first words that, according to Genesis, God spoke on the first day of creation: "Let there be light" (Gen 1:3). Critics have pointed out the logical problem with this verse: God does not create the sun, moon, and stars until day four (Gen 1:14–18), so how can there be light on day one? On this detail, however, the big bang theory actually coincides with Genesis: the universe, in the initial explosion, would have begun in an unimaginably huge flash of light and energy before the actual formation of stars or other heavenly bodies.[36]

The Big Bang and a Transcendent Cause of the Universe   4.8.2

Earlier we considered how the traditional "First Cause" argument (see sec. 3.3.3–6) can still be seen as a valid "way" to prove the existence of God as a transcendent cause of the universe. The big bang theory in itself in no way constitutes a proof that God exists. But it does offer striking support for the *reasonableness* of the Christian view that the universe began at a specific point in time, the result of an act of creation by a transcendent cause. As we have seen, science cannot offer a truly alternative explanation of how either matter or energy first came into existence (see secs. 3.3.3 and 3.3.6).

Arguments from Design   4.9

A common biblical belief is that the Creator can be known from observing the creation. The apostle Paul writes that even Gentiles who knew nothing about the God of Scripture could still know God: "For what can be known about God is evident to them, because God made it evident to them. Ever since the creation of the world, his invisible attributes of eternal power and divinity have been able to be understood and perceived in what he has made" (Rom 1:19–20). In making this point, Paul is drawing on previous Jewish tradition, as found for example in the Book of Wisdom, "For from the greatness and beauty of created things their original author, by analogy, is seen" (Wis 13:5). Already the psalmist maintained, "The heavens declare the glory of God; the sky proclaims its builder's craft" (Ps 19:2). These scriptural statements are often referred to collectively as the "**argument from design**": if we see evidence of a plan or design in nature, this implies the existence of an intelligent planner or designer who is ultimately responsible for that design.

Perhaps the best-known modern form of the argument from design comes from William Paley's book *Natural Theology*, published in 1802. Paley uses the example of a person finding a watch in a field. If the person carefully examines the watch, he will find many intricately designed gears and springs that function together in order to make the watch work. Although the person has never seen the designer of the watch, he knows that a designer must have made it, since it is impossible that such intricate pieces could come together spontaneously to form a functioning watch.

Paley then turns to examples of design from nature. A person observing the human eye, for example, finds many intricately designed parts (the retina, rods, cones, optic nerve) that function together for a purpose: to allow a person to see. By analogy with the watch, then, it seems reasonable to conclude that an intelligent designer must have designed the eye. Now obviously the designer of the human eye could not have been a human, and so one is led logically to the conclusion that the designer must be an intelligent power that transcends the natural world. We can call this intelligent designer "God."

In section 4.9.2 we will consider challenges to Paley's argument from the theory of evolution. First, however, we consider another variant of the argument from design.

Cosmic Argument from Design   4.9.1

Barr rightly notes that there are actually two arguments from design: a biological design argument (seeing evidence for design in animate nature) and a cosmic design argument (seeing evidence for design in inanimate nature).[37]

The cosmic design argument often focuses on the *"regularity, pattern, symmetry, and order"* in nature, for example, in the regular movement of the heavenly bodies or in the symmetrical growth of crystals.[38] In the biblical understanding of nature, this regular order is a reflection of the divine *logos* through which the universe was created (John 1:1; see sec. 2.6.2).

But just as biological order might be explained by the theory of evolution through natural selection (sec. 4.9.2), so too cosmic order may be explained as the result of natural physical laws: planets orbit the sun in regular patterns because they are obeying the laws of gravity. Once again, it seems that the need for the "God hypothesis" is removed: the cosmic order is simply the result of the working out of impersonal physical laws.

At this point, however, Barr would have us ask a basic metaphysical question: *Why* do these laws exist in the first place? (compare sec.s 2.6.3 and 3.1 on these basic metaphysical questions).

Let us consider the scientific facts. Throughout the twentieth century, physicists were able to discover ever deeper levels of reality. Moving beyond the surface order displayed in the movement of the planets or the growth of crystals, scientists penetrated to the molecular and atomic levels. Here too they discovered a precise mathematical order where, for example, each of the elements is distinguished from the others by a precise number of protons.

Earlier, James Clerk Maxwell (1831–1879) discovered that the forces of electricity and magnetism were actually united in a unified field, and he was able to express the fundamental laws of light, magnetism, and electricity in a few mathematical formulas. Though twentieth-century science was revolutionized by quantum and relativity theory, these advances only proved to be new methods of further understanding the profound unity and order in the universe. Again physicists are able to describe these relationships in exact mathematical terms; Einstein's $E = MC^2$ is only the most famous of these equations. Today, scientific research is still stimulated by the search for a "grand unified theory" that would unite all partial theories into one. With their deep faith in the rationality of the universe, researchers are confident that such a theory will eventually be articulated.

Consider also the very first moments of the universe. According to standard scientific theories, the universe began as a chaotic mixture of subatomic particles. Why did these subatomic particles spontaneously begin to combine in an orderly fashion, forming atoms and molecules, and eventually the entire ordered, predictable universe

The Rational Human Mind and the Rational Universe 4.9.1.1

The Reformed theologian and philosopher of science Thomas F. Torrance comments, "There is a fundamental harmony between the 'laws of the mind' and the 'laws of nature': that is, an inherent harmony between how we think and how nature behaves independently of our minds."[39] Our mind has an inherent drive toward making sense of things, finding (or creating) order, understanding, categorizing. Why is it that the same rationality and order, expressible in precise mathematical laws, exists outside of our minds? If nature was not rational in itself, then we could never have understood its rational laws. "We could not know anything unless the universe itself had been created by a rational mind."[40] Since the same rational order of our own minds is reflected in nature, is it really so far-fetched to assume that a rational mind outside of ourselves created nature's rational order? **o**

that we observe today? Does this imply that in the very nature of matter itself there must exist a plan, a *logos*, an inherent tendency toward order and meaning?

In the materialist or determinist worldview, this profound order in the universe is simply accepted as a given. But from a worldview open to the transcendent, the Christian allows himself to step back and ask the metaphysical question: *Why* is reality like this? Why *should* it possess such a profoundly rational order that it can be described with exact mathematical formulas? It is surely not unnatural or unreasonable for the scientist to agree with the biblical worldview: this order is evidence of the divine *logos* permeating all reality.

Biological Argument from Design 4.9.2

The Darwinian Challenge 4.9.2.1

Paley discussed the human eye as an example of intricate design that pointed toward the existence of a transcendent Designer. But modern science offers another explanation: the **Darwinian theory of evolution**. Briefly stated, the Darwinian theory holds that all forms of life on earth have evolved over billions of years from a single common ancestor. The mechanism that allows for this evolution is natural selection, the natural process by which advantageous genetic qualities are passed on and less advantageous traits gradually disappear.

All species have a certain DNA code, and as the DNA of any growing organism replicates itself, chance mutations in the code occur. Most of the time, these mutations are harmful to a species, but occasionally they are beneficial and allow the species a better chance at surviving. Members of the species with the beneficial mutation thrive and reproduce themselves, eventually replacing the nonmutated members of the species. In this way, species evolve different traits (e.g., a fish species evolves more efficient fins to help it swim faster). Over long periods of time, one species can eventually evolve into another species. Evolution of traits within a species is known as microevolution; the theory that one species can evolve into another is known as macroevolution.

The theory of Darwinian evolution is accepted by the great majority of scientists today. Since Darwin's time, the field of genetics has provided particularly striking corroborating evidence for the theory of evolution from a common ancestor. Comparison between the DNA sequences of humans with those of various animals, for example, show convincingly that humans and nonhumans share a common ancestor; at the DNA level, humans and chimpanzees are 96 percent identical.[41] The combination of the new genetic insights with traditional Darwinist theory is known as "neo-Darwinism."

For neo-Darwinian scientists such as Richard Dawkins, the implications of Darwin's theory of evolution are clear: Paley's (and any similar) argument from design for the existence of God has been demolished. Paley's analogy of God as the Divine Watchmaker has been replaced by the universe itself, evolving through random mutation and natural selection, as the "Blind Watchmaker." Since the complexity of all life can be explained through natural evolution, there is no need to believe in a "higher power" guiding the process—no need for the "God hypothesis." For Dawkins, "Darwin made it possible to be an intellectually fulfilled atheist."[42]

Reponses to Darwin: Creationism   4.9.2.2

Some Christians have responded to the Darwinian challenge by insisting on the literal truth of the creation stories in Genesis.[43] There is some variety among the creationist schools of thought, including "old earth" and "young earth" proponents. Since the "young earth" school of thought has been the most influential, we will focus on their basic beliefs.

Basic tenets of young earth creationism are (1) the earth is no more than ten thousand years old and (2) microevolution can occur within a species, but there is no true scientific evidence for macroevolution. Young earth creationists attempt to refute Darwinian evolution on scientific grounds, arguing (for example), that there is no fossil evidence for transitional forms that indicate one species evolving into another, or that carbon-14 dating methods (used to show that prehistoric animal remains are millions of years old) are flawed.

The challenges of the creationists have not been convincing— fossils of transitional forms showing evolution from one species to another, for example, have in fact been found.[44] More basically, the creationists' implicit assumption that the creation account in Genesis is a scientifically reliable account is highly misleading. As we'll discuss in more detail below, the Catholic tradition does not assume that the Genesis creation stories were intended as scientific accounts (sec. 8.12.1).

Reponses to Darwin: Intelligent Design 4.9.2.3

Another challenge to the Darwinian model comes from a school of thought known as Intelligent Design (ID).[45] Its two best-known proponents are professor of biochemistry Michael Behe and professor of science and theology William Dembski. ID thinkers accept the theory of evolution in general, but argue that it is inadequate to explain certain structures that are "irreducibly complex." A complex system such as the human eye, for example, is too complicated to have evolved through natural selection. Its existence can only be explained by the intervention of a transcendent intelligence.

As does scientific creationism, ID presents itself as a scientific alternative to the Darwinian theory. But ID is not a science in the modern sense of the term, since its claims of supernatural intervention cannot be tested or verified, and since it does not predict new findings or suggest areas for further experimentation.[46]

More generally, ID is open to criticism for its conception of the intelligent designer as a "God of the gaps." Whenever science cannot find natural causes for certain phenomena (thus leaving a "gap" in scientific knowledge), it is a natural tendency for religious believers to see this as evidence of divine intervention in nature. The problem with the "God of the gaps" approach is that science is constantly discovering natural explanations for events previously thought to have been directly caused by God or other supernatural causes. The result is that God plays an increasingly smaller role as new discoveries are made.

So, theoretically, if science one day provides satisfactory explanations for all natural phenomena, there will no longer be a need for an Intelligent Designer at all.[47]

ID has thus not proven itself as a science, and theologically it seems unnecessary to posit supernatural causation in nature on a regular basis. A better model of the relationship between supernatural and natural causes would seem to be Aquinas's view that God works through secondary natural causes (see sec. 3.3.5).

Responses to Darwin: NOMA   4.9.2.4

The biologist Stephen Jay Gould coined the acronym NOMA (nonoverlapping magisteria) for the relationship between religion and science.

> To summarize, with a tad of repetition, the net, or magisterium, of science covers the empirical realm: what is the universe made of (fact) and why does it work this way (theory). The magisterium of religion extends over questions of ultimate meaning and moral value. These two magisteria do not overlap, nor do they encompass all inquiry (consider, for example, the magisterium of art and the meaning of beauty). To cite the old clichés, science gets the ages of rocks, and religion the rock of ages; science studies how the heavens go, religion how to go to heaven.[48]

From a Catholic perspective, there is some truth in Gould's assertion. Pope John Paul II wrote, "Both religion and science must preserve their own autonomy and their distinctiveness."[49] Yet the bald statement that the two magisteria do not overlap is profoundly at odds with the Catholic tradition. All truth, both theological and scientific, is from God, and to separate them into mutually exclusive compartments is to distort the meaning of both.

Toward a Catholic Response to Darwin   4.9.3

Acceptance of Evolutionary Theory   4.9.3.1

The Catholic tradition accepts Darwinian evolution as a scientifically established theory for physical evolution. Already Pope Pius XII, in his 1950 encyclical *Humani Generis* (no. 36), taught that evolution could be investigated as a scientific hypothesis for the physical development of the human body, as long as it was not used to explain the development of the spiritual soul, which Catholic doctrine insists is "immediately created by God."

In 1985 Pope John Paul II stated,

> A belief in creation, rightly understood, and a rightly understood doctrine of evolution, do not stand in each other's way. Evolution presupposes creation; creation, seen in the light of evolution, appears as an event extended over time — a *creatio continua*, as a continuing creation — in that God becomes visible, to the eye of faith, as the "creator of heaven and earth."[50]

Catholic teaching, then, clearly accepts the validity of the theory of evolution as a reasonable explanation for the physical development of the human.

Evolution versus Evolutionism   4.9.3.2

We must be careful, however, to distinguish here between evolution as a scientific theory of physical development and a philosophical worldview espoused by certain "neo-Darwinist" thinkers that we will call *evolutionism*. The Catholic tradition accepts the validity of the former, but clearly rejects the latter.

Evolutionist thought makes several philosophical claims that its proponents believe are logical implications of the acceptance of Darwinian evolution. Among them are the following:

1. Evolution through natural selection of random genetic mutations is a satisfactory explanation for all forms and manifestations of life on earth.

2. This comprehensive explanation thus excludes any transcendent order or cause outside of the mechanism of chance evolutionary developments. It follows that God as a transcendent cause is also excluded.

3. There are no essential differences between different forms of life, since they have all evolved through chance selection from a common origin. Thus there is no essential difference between humans and so-called lower life-forms.

4. All reality can be reduced to the material basis from which it evolved. Thus "mind" is simply a function of neurons that have evolved in the brain. Concepts such as "spirit" or "soul" are meaningless fictions (see our discussion of materialism in 2.2.2).

The evolutionist worldview is thus a variation of the rationalist and materialist worldviews that we discussed in chapter 2. As such, it is liable to the same critiques that we examined in section 2.5. Let's look at a few details.

Critique of Evolutionism: Life's Origins   4.9.3.3

Let us begin by examining the first claim of the evolutionists: that evolution can fully explain all forms of life. The claim falters on at least two essential transition points: (1) the transition from non-animate substance to animate life and (2) the transition to the human from lower life-forms. Some scientists have critiqued other aspects of the theory (citing, for example, the fact that the fossil record generally shows species emerging fully formed, rather than gradually evolving), but we will limit our discussion to these two points.

At present science cannot explain life itself. One popular theory is that, at some point three to four billion years ago, life arose when chemicals combined spontaneously from a "primordial soup," perhaps catalyzed by lightning. We can analyze the chemical components of animate material, but we cannot explain how life arises from these chemical components—as is obvious from the fact that scientists cannot produce life, even when all the necessary chemical components are assembled. E. F. Schumacher rightly exposes the hubris of the evolutionist view that claims to offer a complete explanation of life when it cannot explain life itself: "To say that life is nothing but a property of certain peculiar combinations of atoms is like saying that Shakespeare's *Hamlet* is nothing but a property of a peculiar combination of letters."[51]

Obviously the very first life-form cannot have arisen from the process of natural selection, since there was nothing there to select! Furthermore, although the first life-form must have been a relatively simple single-celled organism, it must also have been complex enough to replicate its own DNA—but according to Darwinian theory such complexity can only be reached as the end result of a process of evolution. So how can a relatively complex, DNA-replicating organism have been produced spontaneously from nonorganic materials? Neo-Darwinians have proposed several speculative theories, but none has proved convincing.[52]

Since evolution cannot explain the origins of life, could an evolutionist admit the possibility that a transcendent cause—God—created the first life-form? Dawkins quickly dismisses the possibility: "But of course any God capable of intelligently designing something as complex as the DNA / protein-replicating machine must have been at least as complex and organized as that machine itself."[53] In other words, if God was complex enough to create the first single-celled life-form, how can we explain how God himself originated? Again Dawkins's strictly materialist worldview is apparent: he seems incapable of imagining the possibility of a transcendent Creator who would not be subject to the laws of evolution.

The materialist evolutionist, having made a philosophical decision (not a scientific decision) that the material world is the only reality, is stuck with the theory of evolution as the sole option — even when it is clear that it explains nothing about the origins of life itself.

Critique of Evolutionism: The Transition to Human Life

4.9.3.4

The second point at which Darwinian evolution is unconvincing is precisely the transition from the lower animals to the human. Granted that the human body evolved from lower life-forms, the theory of evolution through natural selection is simply inadequate to explain the rise of distinctly human characteristics: our high level of intelligence, our self-awareness and self-reflection, our moral conscience, our free will, and even our sense of the beautiful or the transcendent.

There can be no doubt that evolution through natural selection was *involved* in the development of all of these distinctly human characteristics. Our brain has evolved, and thus also the physical basis of our intelligence. The Christian worldview is open to recognizing the physical and even evolutionary basis (brain, neurons, nerves) for intelligence and consciousness, but it simply insists that this physical and evolutionary basis cannot be the whole explanation. The evolutionist materialist view insists that intelligence, conscience, and self-awareness are *nothing more* than their material basis.

But the human is something more. We emphasized earlier that the characteristic distinction of the human is self-transcendence: the ability of self-awareness, to think about our thinking, to stand outside of ourselves. As we noted in our discussion of determinism, the idea that a succession of chance genetic mutations would determine a person to think, "This thought is nothing but the result of a succession of chance genetic mutations," is self-contradictory (see sec. 2.5.2). Humans have the freedom to know that they are not determined completely by evolution. In Barr's words, "Spiritual powers of intellect, rationality, and freedom cannot be accounted for by mere biology."[54]

G. K. Chesterton makes a similar point in his discussion of the significance of paintings, discovered on cave walls, made by early humans. He observes that the impulse that caused the man to paint—whether he was motivated by a religious impulse or a creative one—is something that separates him by a great gulf from any other species. The picture on the cave wall is

> the testimony to something that is absolute and unique; that belongs to man and to nothing else except man; that it is a difference of kind and not a difference of degree. A monkey does not draw clumsily and a man cleverly; a monkey does not begin the art of representation and man carry it to perfection. A monkey does not do it at all; he does not begin to do it at all; he does not begin to begin to do it at all.[55]

The human attraction toward meaning, toward ethical behavior, toward beauty, are characteristics that separate us by a wide gulf from any other creature. "Man is not merely an evolution but a revolution."[56]

We should point out that some evolutionist writers grant the point that evolution cannot be a complete explanation for these characteristically human qualities. Dawkins speaks of evolution developing "rules of thumb"—general tendencies of humans (or any other species) to develop behaviors that will increase their chances for survival. He shows plausibly that even altruistic tendencies may have evolved as a survival mechanism—causing humans to be concerned for the survival of others in their kinship group, for example.[57]

Dawkins then writes, "Such rules of thumb are still with us, not in a Calvinistically deterministic way but filtered through the civilizing influences of literature and custom, law and tradition—and, of course, religion."[58] For Dawkins, too, evolution by natural selection does not offer a complete explanation of human development—humans develop also through cultural traditions.[59]

Critique of Evolutionism: An Unguided Process?   4.9.3.5

As noted above, the evolutionist believes that the comprehensive theory of Darwinism excludes any transcendent order or cause, including God, outside of the mechanism of chance evolutionary developments.

The Austrian cardinal Christoph Schönborn illustrates the evolutionist conclusion with two quotations. English author Will Provine writes, "Modern science directly implies that the world is organized strictly in accordance with deterministic principles or chance. There are no purposive principles whatsoever in nature. There are no gods and no designing forces rationally detectable." Oxford chemistry professor Peter Atkins similarly states, "Humanity should accept that science has swept away any justification for belief in the universe having a meaning or purpose." Schönborn rightly comments that these statements are not scientific, but rather philosophic expressions of worldviews closed to the transcendent.[60]

These evolutionist statements may be critiqued on two levels. First, they assume that deterministic laws sufficiently explain all reality. But we have considered several arguments (4.9.3.3–4) that suggest otherwise: the Darwinist theory in no sense is a sufficient explanation for all reality. Second, even if evolutionary or other determinist laws were sufficient to explain all observable reality, that fact would not in itself disprove the existence of transcendent reality. The evolutionist claim is based on the materialist assumption (made on faith) that the scientifically observable world is the only reality.

Schönborn (using the Aristotelian categories adopted by Aquinas) distinguishes between different types of causes: material causes (the material from which something is made), efficient causes (direct, physical causes), formal causes ("the organizing, active principles of whole living substances"), and final causes (the "plan, purpose, or design in living things"). He argues that the scientific method is rightly concerned only with observable material and efficient causes, and ignores the question of final causes. But it is an unwarranted further step to deny the existence of a final cause simply because the scientific method rightly brackets out the question.[61]

Rejecting NOMA 4.9.3.6

A possible solution to the conflict between the evolutionist and the theist is the NOMA approach (see sec. 4.9.2.4). In this scenario, God creates the world but then allows the world to unfold according to natural laws, including the laws of evolution. The scientist cannot detect God's influence, since God allows nature its own autonomy.

For Schönborn, however, this solution will not do. It is fideistic, assuming an impassable gulf between the realm of reason and the realm of faith. Its conception of God is Deistic: the Divine Watchmaker that wound up the watch, but now lets it run on its own. It ignores the traditional belief in God's providence, his loving concern for the world, and thus runs counter to the Catholic tradition.[62]

God's Hand in an Evolutionary World   4.9.3.7

Schönborn returns to traditional Catholic teaching: "The existence of God the Creator can be known with certainty through his works, by the light of human reason, even if this knowledge is often obscured and disfigured by error."[63] This of course is only a reiteration of the clear scriptural witness, found in passages such as Romans 1:19–20 and Wisdom 13:5: God can be clearly seen in creation.

Schönborn admits the reality of evolution guided by natural selection of genetic mutation. Observed scientifically, the genetic mutations are indeed random occurrences that are selected according to their ability to increase the chances of survival for the species. But if one observes the development of life on earth as a whole, Schönborn argues, a clear, purposeful pattern is evident to any unbiased observer. The mechanism of genetic variation, random from the scientific point of view, was enough "to give rise to an upward sweep of evolution resulting in human beings."[64]

E. F. Schumacher presents a clear model of this purposeful progression in nature.[65] He identifies four "Levels of Being" in nature: minerals, plants, animals, humans. Each level is *qualitatively* different from the preceding level, distinguished from that previous level by a unique "power."

Thus, plants are distinguished from minerals by the mysterious power of life—mysterious because humans can destroy life, but cannot create it. Animals are distinguished from plants by the mysterious power of consciousness—mysterious in the sense that it is again beyond human power to create or even describe accurately. It can be recognized in the fact that an animal can be knocked unconscious, while a plant cannot. Finally, humans are distinguished from animals by the even more mysterious quality that Schumacher calls "self-consciousness" (see sec. 4.9.3.4 for other ways in which humans are qualitatively distinct from animals).

For Schumacher, it is patently clear that life has progressed in a definite pattern: as one moves up from mineral to plant to animal to human, one moves from passivity to activity, from necessity to freedom. One sees progress toward ever greater intelligence, responsibility, and meaning.

Toward a Catholic Understanding of Science and Faith 4.10

In the following we will summarize some principles describing the Catholic tradition's understanding of the proper relationship between scientific thought and Christian faith.

1. Scientific and religious thought should not be kept in completely separate realms (thus rejecting fideism or NOMA). They should be in dialogue and allowed to influence one another.

2. At the same time, science and religion each have their own separate realms of expertise, and thus their own autonomy. "Each should possess its own principles, its pattern of procedures, its diversities of interpretation and its own conclusions."[66] The mistake of Galileo's judges was to make a judgment outside of their realm of competence.

3. Theological truth and scientific truth can never contradict one another. If they do seem to contradict, it is because either the scientists (e.g., through materialist presuppositions) or the theologians (e.g., through a faulty biblical hermeneutic) have strayed out of their realm of competence.

4. Theologians can learn from scientific thought. John Paul II wrote, "Science can purify religion from error and superstition."[67] Science, for example, corrected the religious belief that the sun revolved around the earth. Theologians must remain current with scientific thought and be willing to adjust their teaching in light of scientifically provable information.

5. Scientists can also learn from theologians: "Religion can purify science from idolatry and false absolutes."[68] Theologians may rightly criticize scientists who, employing rationalist, materialist, or determinist presuppositions, stray beyond their realms of competence and deny the existence of metaphysical realities.

6. Rational evidence of God's purpose and design in the universe can be discerned through a reasonable interpretation of scientific evidence (e.g., the implications of the big bang theory, the rational structure of the universe, and the clear pattern of evolution toward greater intelligence, freedom, and ethical responsibility).

7. There is a significant correspondence between the divine created order (*logos*) in the universe and the order (*logos*) in the human mind. Both are reflections of the divine *logos*.

8. Scientific and theological thought are natural allies, not opponents, as can be seen in the connection between the rise of modern science and the Christian belief in the rational order of the created universe.

Questions about the Text

1. What roles do intuition and authority play in modern scientific research?

2. How did the medieval Catholic Church support scientific research?

3. Why does Whitehead believe that modern science could only have developed among people who believed in the Judeo-Christian God?

4. Describe the basic facts in the conflict between the Church and Galileo. What lessons did John Paul II draw from this conflict?

5. What are some similarities between the big bang theory and the Christian doctrine of creation?

6. Discuss arguments for and against the cosmic argument from design. Consider especially twentieth-century discoveries of order at the molecular level.

7. What is the biological argument from design? How is the neo-Darwinist theory of evolution a challenge to this argument?

8. Discuss the strengths and weaknesses of the following responses to the Darwinist challenge: creationism, Intelligent Design, and NOMA.

9. What is the difference between an acceptance of the theory of evolution and the philosophy of "evolutionism"? What are two basic criticisms of evolutionism as a theory that tries to explain the whole of life?

10. Is there objective evidence that the evolution of life has an overall goal or direction? Why or why not?

11. What are some basic elements in a Catholic understanding of the relationship between faith and science?

Discussion Questions

1. Has reading this chapter changed your impression of the role of scientific research in the Middle Ages?

2. In your experience, do scientifically minded people tend to be less religious?

3. Is the argument from design personally convincing to you?

4. What are your thoughts on the debates on teaching evolution, creationism, or Intelligent Design in the public schools?

Endnotes

1. Richard Dawkins, *The God Delusion* (Boston: Houghton Mifflin, 2006), 282.
2. Michael Polanyi, "The Unaccountable Element in Science," in *Knowing and Being: Essays*, ed. Marjorie Grene (Chicago: University of Chicago Press, 1969), 105–20.
3. John Henry Newman, *An Essay in Aid of a Grammar of Assent*, ed. I. T. Ker (Oxford: Clarendon Press, 1985), 215.
4. Polanyi, *Knowing and Being*, 94.
5. Ibid., 79.
6. Thomas Kuhn, *The Structure of Scientific Revolutions*, 2nd enlarged ed., Foundations of the Unity of Science 1–2 (Chicago: University of Chicago Press, 1975), 208.
7. Ibid., 5.
8. Rodney Stark, *For the Glory of God: How Monotheism Led to Reformations, Science, Witch-hunts, and the End of Slavery* (Princeton, NJ: Princeton University Press, 2003), 62.
9. Ibid., 136–37.
10. Ibid., 143.
11. Ibid., 143–46.
12. Ibid., 135–36. It is true that the book was not published until Copernicus was on his deathbed.
13. Ibid., 157–72.
14. See Stephen Barr, *Modern Physics and Ancient Faith* (Notre Dame: University of Notre Dame Press, 2003), 9–10.
15. Stark, *Glory of God*, 194.
16. Dawkins, *God Delusion*, 100.
17. Stark, *Glory of God*, 146–47.
18. Ibid., 147.
19. Ibid., 123. Italics original.
20. Alfred North Whitehead, *Science and the Modern World* (New York: Macmillan, 1927), 18.
21. Albert Einstein, *Ideas and Opinions* (New York: Bonanza Books, 1954), 39.

22. Stark, *Glory of God*, 148.

23. Ibid., 150–56.

24. Barr, *Modern Physics*, 8.

25. Stark, *Glory of God*, 128. Barr also discusses cases of alleged Church persecution of scientists that are more properly understood as attacks against perceived theological errors or heresies (*Modern Physics*, 289–90 no. 12).

26. Galileo, *Confessions* 12.23–24, cited in Stark, *Glory of God*, 165.

27. For a concise account of the Galileo affair and its later mythical development as a symbol of Catholic rejection of science, see Robert P. Lockwood, "Galileo and the Catholic Church." Accessed September 18, 2008 at *http://www.catholicleague.org/research/galileo.html*. See also Stark, *Glory of God*, 163–66.

28. Cardinal Poupard, "Galileo: Report on Papal Commission Findings," *Origins* 22 (Nov. 12, 1992): 374–75. Quoted in Lockwood, "Galileo and the Catholic Church."

29. John Paul II, "Faith Can Never Conflict with Reason," *L'Osservatore Romano* 44 (Nov. 4, 1992). Accessed September 18, 2008 at *http://www.its.caltech.edu/~nmcenter/sci-cp/sci-9211.html*.

30. Quoted in "Galileo Galilei," *Catholic Encyclopedia*. Accessed September 18, 2008 at *http://www.newadvent.org/cathen/06342b.htm*.

31. Augustine, *Letter* 143.7.

32. See Barr, *Modern Physics*, 43, and Robert Jastrow, *God and the Astronomers* (New York: W. W. Norton, 1978), 112–13.

33. Barr, *Modern Physics*, 47.

34. *Confessions* 11.10

35. *Confessions* 11.13.

36. In noting this convergence, I do not suggest that Genesis 1 is a scientific account: it is simply an intriguing correspondence.

37. Barr, *Modern Physics*, 69.

38. Ibid. Italics original.

39. Thomas F. Torrance, *The Christian Frame of Mind: Reason, Order, and Openness in Theology and Natural Science* (Colorado Springs, CO: Helmer and Howard, 1989), 26.

40. Christoph Schönborn, "The Designs of Science," *First Things* (January 2006). Accessed September 18, 2008 at *http://www.firstthings.com/article.php3?id_article=71*.

41. See Francis S. Collins, *The Language of God: A Scientist Presents Evidence for Belief* (New York: Free Press, 2006), 137.

42. Richard Dawkins, *The Blind Watchmaker: Why the Evidence of Evolution Reveals a Universe without Design* (New York: Norton & Co., 1986), 10.

43. For an overview of creationist beliefs, see Ted Peters and Martinez Hewlett, *Can You Believe in God and Evolution? A Guide for the Perplexed* (Nashville: Abingdon, 2006), 35–43.

44. Ibid., 43.

45. Ibid., 47–52.

46. Ibid., 50; Collins, *Language of God*, 187.

47. See Collins, *Language of God*, 93, 194–95. Dawkins (*God Delusion*, 119–34) also rightly critiques the "God of the gaps" theory.

48. Stephen Jay Gould, *Rock of Ages: Science and Religion in the Fullness of Life* (New York: Ballantine, 1999), 6.

49. John Paul II, "Letter to Reverend George V. Coyne, S.J. , Director of the Vatican Observatory" (June 1, 1988). Accessed September 18, 2008 at *http://www.vatican.va/holy_father/john_paul_ii/letters/1988/documents/hf_jp-ii_let_19880601_padre-coyne_en.html*.

50. John Paul II, remarks at a 1985 Rome symposium "Christian Faith and the Theory of Evolution." Quoted in Christoph Schönborn, *Chance or Purpose: Creation, Evolution, and a Rational Faith* (San Francisco: Ignatius Press, 2007), 30.

51. E. F. Schumacher, *A Guide for the Perplexed* (New York: Harper & Row, 1977), 20.
52. See Dawkins, *Blind Watchmaker*, 197–237
53. Ibid., 200.
54. Stephen Barr, "Design of Evolution," *First Things* (October 1995). Accessed September 18, 2008, at *http://www.firstthings.com/article.php3?id_article=238*.
55. G. K. Chesterton, *The Everlasting Man*, in *Collected Works of G. K. Chesterton*, vol. 2, *Saint Francis of Assisi, The Everlasting Man, Saint Thomas Aquinas* (San Francisco: Ignatius Press, 1986), 177.
56. Ibid., 158.
57. Dawkins, *God Delusion*, 214–22.
58. Ibid., 222.
59. Dawkins has a theory of "memes," units of cultural inheritance that are naturally selected and passed down unconsciously through generations (*God Delusion*, 191–201). But if I understand him correctly, Dawkins would say that humans are not completely determined even by their "memes."
60. Quoted in Schönborn, *Chance or Purpose*, 28.
61. Schönborn, "Designs of Science."
62. Ibid.
63. *CCC* no. 286. Quoted in Schönborn, *Chance or Purpose*, 44.
64. Schönborn, "Designs of Science."
65. Schumacher, *Guide for the Perplexed*, 15–38.
66. John Paul II, "Letter to Reverend George V. Coyne."
67. Ibid.
68. Ibid.

5

Revelation
Can Humans Really Communicate with God?

Transcendence and Revelation 5.1

In the Christian view the very nature of God is *transcendence*: God is the *transcendent* horizon of human experience (sec.s 1.4–7); God is the First Cause that *transcends* all other causes (sec. 3.3.3). Humans and all things in the world are limited: God, by definition, is unlimited.

But since God is beyond human ability to comprehend, how can we know about God? Would not statements about God be pure speculation and not true knowledge?

According to Christian tradition, we can have no true knowledge about God *unless* the transcendent God chooses to reveal that knowledge to us. And this is exactly what Christians believe God has done.[1]

The Concept of Revelation 5.2

Christians distinguish between natural revelation (sometimes called "general revelation")—God's revelation given through the order of nature (including human nature, above all in a person's conscience), and historical revelation (sometimes called "special revelation") — God's revelation made to specific individuals or groups at specific times and places. An example of historical revelation would be God's direct communication to a person such as a prophet.[2] In Christian thought, historical revelation is closely associated with the events recorded in Scripture. Aquinas writes, "For our faith rests upon the revelation made to the apostles and to the prophets, who wrote the canonical books, and not on the revelations (if any such there are) made to the other doctors" [officially recognized teachers of the Church] (*ST* 1.1.8 ad. 2).

Although historical and natural revelation are theoretically distinct, in practice it is difficult, if not impossible, to separate them. For believers who have been influenced by the Judeo-Christian and Islamic traditions, their understanding of God's revelation in nature and conscience is already shaped by the Jewish, Christian, and Muslim theological traditions concerning God's creation and God's ethical laws.

The purpose of God's revelation, according to Catholic teaching, is to lead humans ultimately to unity with God, to receive the perfect love, peace, and harmony found only in God. In the words of *Dei Verbum (Dogmatic Constitution on Divine Revelation)*, the Vatican II declaration devoted to revelation:

> It pleased God, in his goodness and wisdom, to reveal himself and to make known the mystery of his will (cf. Eph 1:9). His will was that men should have access to the Father, through Christ, the Word made flesh, in the Holy Spirit, and thus become sharers in the divine nature. (*DV* no. 2)

Revelation in Nature   5.3

The Catholic tradition believes that the natural design of the universe reveals the intelligence of the Designer (sec. 4.9) and sees evidence in the process of evolution for a planned movement of life toward ever greater intelligence, freedom, and self-consciousness (4.9.3.7). As Paul wrote, God's "invisible attributes of eternal power and divinity have been able to be understood and perceived in what he has made" (Rom 1:20).

But nature reveals more than goodness and order, as we will now discuss.

The Problem of Evil 5.3.1

In the creation account in Genesis 1, the author repeatedly states, "God saw that it was good." This simple statement is foundational in Christian thinking: God, who is completely good, created a universe that is completely good. Humans, as part of God's creation, are also good—we are even said to be created in the "image of God" (Gen 1:26–27). The account of creation in Genesis 1 culminates with the human, created in God's image, as the crowning goodness of an all-good creation.

But aren't Christians suppressing half of the story? After all, when we observe nature, we see not only beauty and order, but also violence and disorder of all kinds. We see animals that survive by violence—killing and devouring other living creatures. We see earthquakes that level cities and tsunamis that devastate vast areas of the earth and kill thousands. And this is not even to mention the untold cruelty of humans, whose history is filled with war, mass murder, sexual violence, hatred, greed, intolerance, and prejudice. Doesn't this "other side of the story" reveal a God who is in fact cruel or, at best, indifferent to the suffering of his creation?

Before we study traditional Christian responses to the question of why evil and suffering exist in God's good creation, however, let us briefly consider one non-Christian alternative. It will help to shed some light on our options.

Christian Creation and Dualism 5.3.2

Some ancient theological traditions drew a seemingly logical conclusion: the good in the world was created by a good higher power, and the evil in the world was created by an evil higher power. The belief that reality is ultimately divided into two eternal powers of light and darkness, good and evil, is known as *dualism*. One power is purely good, the other purely evil, and they are locked in an eternal struggle for ultimate control of the universe.

The Christian view sometimes appears to be dualistic, since Christians often speak of a battle between the forces of good and evil, or a conflict between God and the devil. But if we think back to the Christian view of creation (the all-good God creating an all-good universe), we will see that the Christian view cannot be dualistic since *all things* were good in the beginning.[3]

Evil as a Corruption of Original Good 5.3.3

According to Christian thinking, there is only one possibility for the source of evil: it must have come from an original good. Pure evil cannot exist—evil can only be a corruption, or distortion, of an original good. Augustine writes, "And when I asked myself what wickedness was, I saw that it was not a substance, but perversion of the will when it turns aside from you, O God" (*Confessions* 7.16). Aquinas says similarly, "Therefore it must be said that by the name of evil is signified the absence of good" (*ST* 1.48.1).

Let us take an example of what many people understand as pure evil: the attack on the World Trade Center on September 11, 2001. If we analyze the situation, however, we see that the attackers were not motivated by pure evil. They clearly believed, in however a corrupt or distorted way, that they were doing God's will by attacking this symbol of American wealth and power. To put it another way: the 9/11 hijackers began with ideas that are good in themselves (belief in a just God, or in creating a more moral society) and distorted these ideas into a justification for killing thousands of innocent people.

What about a sadistic person, though—one who finds pleasure in being cruel? Isn't that an example of pure evil? But notice how we describe even the sadist's behavior: he gets pleasure out of being cruel. Pleasure itself is a good thing—it becomes evil only when distorted. No one does evil simply for the sake of doing evil: it's always done for the sake of some benefit or twisted pleasure. If we analyze any evil action, we will find that it is always an original good that is distorted or perverted.

We can also consider some more philosophically oriented arguments against dualism.

Dualism claims that there are two original powers, one good and one evil. But we have just seen that the idea of acting simply for the sake of evil is a contradiction. Evil is always a corruption of an original good. So it is logically impossible for a power to have been evil from the very beginning.

Further, what is the sense of calling one original power good and one evil? The terms *good* and *evil* only make sense when they are compared to a rule or standard that shows them to be bad or good. But this standard must have existed before the two powers existed— and since that standard judges the one power to be good, it must itself share that same goodness.

On this dualistic idea of pure evil, C. S. Lewis comments, "To be bad, this [evil] power must exist and have intelligence and will. But existence, intelligence and will are in themselves good."[4] Again, pure evil is a contradiction—pure evil would be simply nothing.

Christians do speak of an evil power, often identified as Satan or the devil. But Christianity is philosophically consistent in its traditional teaching that even Satan was once good. Although this tradition is not spelled out in the Bible (there are hints in passages such as Rev 12:7–9), it is discussed in some ancient nonbiblical Jewish accounts and retold in such classics of the Christian tradition as John Milton's *Paradise Lost* (see also *CCC* no. 391). A common version of the tradition is that Satan began as a good angel but eventually became jealous of God's power and rebelled against him. God and his faithful angels defeated Satan and cast him and his followers out of heaven.

Christian thought on the origin of good and evil always returns to the belief that God is the First Cause of all things, the ultimate source of all being. The First Cause *must* be a positive force, since (based on our preceding arguments) it is a logical contradiction that the original power can be evil. This is yet a further rational support for the Christian belief that God is all good, and thus that God's original creation must have been entirely good.

God is the source of all existence, and existence itself is good. Thus Aquinas says, "Goodness and being are really the same" (*ST* 1.5.1). Augustine taught that "as long as something is, it is good" (*Confessions* 7.12). These comments show us the deeply grounded Christian trust in the ultimate goodness and meaning of existence (see sec. 2.6.3–5).

Thus the Christian teaching that a good God created the whole universe has some profound implications. One is the Christian belief that evil is always a distortion of an original good. From this it follows that reality, at its deepest and most fundamental roots, is good. The Christian view of the world is thus deeply positive: good is always more powerful than evil, because good is more basic, more "real." Evil is of course also real and can be very destructive, but the Christian has the confidence that in the end, good is greater.

Why Do Bad Things Happen in Nature?   5.3.4

That evil is a distortion of an original good may perhaps explain how humans or even angels distort original good through their choices, but how can it explain the bad things in nature itself—the hurricanes, earthquakes, and tsunamis? Or how can it explain the violence, death, and destruction that seem to form a part of everyday nature: one animal feeding on another animal, the iron rule of "survival of the fittest" guiding evolution. How can it explain the fact that some children, seemingly at random, are struck with muscular dystrophy, or that some elderly people must struggle with Parkinson's disease?

The first step in responding to such questions is to admit humbly that we do not have complete answers. Schönborn cautions that we "should by no means be given too hasty an answer," and the *Catechism* also advises, "No quick answer will suffice."[5]

At the same time, neither is it helpful to conclude that pain, suffering, and destruction in nature are mysteries beyond our understanding. When we are afflicted with tragedies or diseases, we spontaneously search for theological answers. And so, with all due caution and humility, we will try to suggest some directions toward answers.

The Christian tradition itself recognizes that nature is not as it should be, that it contains violence and decay. "We know that all creation is groaning in labor pains even until now," says Paul (Rom 8:22).

So could God not have created a better world, one not so full of destruction and death? We must think carefully about this question. What exactly are we expecting when we wonder whether God could have made a better world?

In the first place, simply by the fact that the world is a creation, it can never fully reflect the perfection of the Creator. Creation will always be limited in some ways, by its very nature of being distinct from the ultimate source of being and goodness. So creation, at least as we know it now, will always be in the process of becoming, changing, and therefore limited and imperfect.[6]

Second, we should recognize that the laws of nature that sometimes cause great destruction are the same laws that generally provide order and design. In most cases, natural laws are a benefit to humans and other forms of life: they help us to live in an orderly and predictable way—we could not survive (plant crops, build homes, and so on) if the laws of nature were not predictable. So for the most part, natural laws do help humans and are in that sense good. But natural laws at times do cause destruction: a hurricane is formed by the same natural laws as a gentle summer breeze.

Schönborn points out that the 2004 tsunami was the result of a shift in continental plates. But scientists have shown that if these plates were not mobile, life would never have evolved on earth, since these mobile plates are one of the preconditions for the earth's ability to maintain a stable average temperature necessary for life.[7] The natural systems of the earth are so interrelated that if God intervened to save humans or other life in one area of the system, it might well have devastating effects in another area. If we try concretely to imagine how we would make a more perfect world than God has made, we quickly run into difficulties.

Third, we should remember that much good often arises from suffering. People can grow and mature through their suffering, or they can grow beyond their own selfishness in helping those who suffer. This fact does not imply that suffering in itself is good, or that the good that comes from it legitimates the suffering. It is simply a fact that must be taken into consideration, especially in light of the Christian belief that salvation comes through uniting one's own suffering with the suffering of Christ.

Fourth, a purely intellectual answer to the problem of pain and suffering will always be inadequate. If there is an answer, it must be a comprehensive answer of the whole human person. As Schönborn comments, "Mother Teresa, for example, was just such a living answer to the challenge of pain and evil in the world."[8]

Fifth, the Christian tradition promises that the limitations and imperfections of the universe will one day come to an end. Again, Paul writes that "creation itself would be set free from slavery to corruption and share in the glorious freedom of the children of God" (Rom 8:21). In the **eschatological** age, nature will be transformed in a way that is now beyond our understanding. Christians have the hope that at that time all suffering and pain will be healed.

Revelation in Human Nature   5.4

In our discussion of Rahner, we saw that human experience points beyond itself to a transcendent horizon (1.4). When Jeff denied that any absolute truth exists, his very denial was a claim that an absolute truth, independent of him, does in fact exist. When Clara was able to reflect on limitations of her own upbringing, she discovered within herself a freedom that allowed her to transcend them. Such experiences can be viewed as part of God's natural revelation to all humans.

We have also seen that God reveals himself in the shared human search for meaning beyond the horizons of this life, in the experience of a Moral Law, and in other signs of the transcendent (sec.s 1.4–7, 2.6.5). We turn now to a consideration of one particular aspect of God's revelation in human nature: our conscience.

Revelation in Conscience: The Natural Law

The Catholic tradition teaches that God's ethical law of right and wrong is revealed in each person's conscience. When the apostle Paul is reflecting on Gentiles who have never read or even heard of the ethical law in Scripture (such as the Ten Commandments), he insists that they still know God's ethical law naturally:

> For when the Gentiles who do not have the law [recorded in Scripture] by nature observe the prescriptions of the law, they are a law for themselves even though they do not have the [scriptural] law. They show that the demands of the law are written in their hearts, while their conscience also bears witness. (Rom 2:14–15)

In line with Paul's thinking, Catholic tradition calls this ethical law in the human heart the "**natural law**":

> The natural law is written and engraved in the soul of each and every man, because it is human reason ordaining him to do good and forbidding him to sin. (*CCC* no. 1954)

The Voice of God in Conscience

John Henry Newman points out the significance of the fact that people tend to experience their conscience as a *voice* urging them to do good, or making them feel guilty if they do wrong. When people do wrong, Newman argues, they have a natural sense not only that they have offended another person, or failed to live up to their own standards, but also that they have offended a divine person, a divine judge of right and wrong. Newman finds in the feelings of our conscience a "real apprehension of God" – that is, beyond theoretical belief, people experience a real sense of God as a person when they feel shame for doing wrong, or when they feel a sense of peace by following their conscience.[9]

In this sense, God is revealed as a personal God, not as an impersonal First Cause only: a voice urging people to do good and warning them to avoid evil. ❂

As we have seen, Lewis calls this the "Moral Law" that is recognized by all people (1.6)

Objection to the Natural Law: Moral Relativism 5.5.2

Many objections have been raised to the belief in a natural law. For example, isn't it obvious that different societies have different concepts of right and wrong? Isn't it egotistical and judgmental if one group assumes that their standards of right and wrong apply to all people in different cultures?

Furthermore, even individuals within a given culture have different standards of right and wrong. I might personally be opposed to abortion, for example, but do I have the right to impose my standards on someone who believes differently?

Isn't it also obvious that standards of right and wrong are not fixed, but rather change according to circumstances? Lying is generally wrong, but in some cases a "white lie" might do some good. Killing is generally wrong, but sometimes we might need to kill in self-defense.

So it seems there can be no "natural law" that applies in all places and at all times. Standards of right and wrong are relative: they change from person to person, society to society, and circumstance to circumstance.

Responses to Moral Relativism 5.5.3

How does the Christian tradition respond to these legitimate points? A first response to moral relativism is to ask a factual question: Do standards of right and wrong really differ fundamentally from society to society? As Lewis says, "If anyone will take the trouble to compare the moral teachings of, say, the ancient Egyptians, Babylonians, Hindus, Chinese, Greeks and Romans, what will really strike him will be how very like they are to each other and to our own."[10] To take one quick example, consider the following multicultural witnesses to the value of respecting one's elders:

- "Honor your father and your mother." (Exod 20:12)

- "Your father is an image of the Lord of Creation, your mother an image of the Earth. Your first duty is to honor them." (Hindu saying)

- "Care for your parents." (Epictetus, ancient Greek philosopher)

- "Respect the wisdom of your elders." (traditional Native American value)

- "Do good to parents." (Qur'an 6.152)[11]

Lewis admits that there are some differences: some societies allow polygamy, for example, while others insist it is immoral to marry more than one spouse. But Lewis points out that even in this example, all societies still agree on the fundamental ethical value: it is wrong for a person to sleep with any person he or she likes.

> I need only ask the reader to think what a totally different morality would mean. Think of a country where people were admired for running away in battle, or where a man felt proud of double-crossing all the people who had been kindest to him. You might just as well try to imagine a country where two and two make five.[12]

A second response to moral relativism is to ask a practical question: When societies or individuals do in fact differ in their ethical standards, are we really willing to say that each society is entitled to its own standards, and that no one else has the right to judge them as right or wrong? When societies were committing genocide or ethnic cleansing in Cambodia, Rwanda, or Bosnia, should the international community simply have allowed those societies to pursue their own standards of right and wrong? When the Taliban in Afghanistan denied the rights of women to an education, should this have been accepted as their right? Should Nazi morality, including the murder of the disabled and other "undesirables," have been accepted, since Nazi society saw these practices as ethically good?

If we are willing to judge such societies as wrong, then we obviously must do so on the basis of standards of right and wrong that apply to all humans, regardless of cultural differences. These universal standards of right and wrong are, in the Catholic view, simply another name for the natural law.[13]

Natural Law and Human Rights   5.5.4

The examples from the last section raise an issue much discussed in the world community today: human rights. The United Nations, for example, published in 1948 a *Universal Declaration on Human Rights*. But the concept of "rights" is meaningless unless it is based on commonly agreed upon standards of right and wrong. So when the *Declaration* asserts that all people have certain rights such as "life, liberty and security" (art. 3), the right to own property (art. 17), the right to freedom of thought, conscience, and religion (art. 18), the *Declaration* assumes that these universal values apply to all people.

In his reflections on the *Declaration*, Pope Benedict XVI insists that these universal rights could not be based ultimately on human laws, since human laws change. Nor could they be based on practical or utilitarian reasoning. Rather, argues Benedict,

> They are based on the natural law inscribed on human hearts and present in different cultures and civilizations. Removing human rights from this context would mean restricting their range and yielding to a relativistic conception, according to which the meaning and interpretation of rights could vary and their universality would be denied in the name of different cultural, political, social and even religious outlooks.[14]

Martin Luther King clearly understood that human rights could not be based on the legal statutes of individual societies. When he challenged the segregation laws of the American South, King had to explain how he could call these laws "unjust," since they were "just" according to the ethical standards of those Southern societies:

> How does one determine when a law is just or unjust? A just law is a man-made code that squares with the moral law or the law of God. An unjust law is a code that is out of harmony with the moral law. To put it in the terms of St. Thomas Aquinas, an unjust law is a human law that is not rooted in eternal and natural law.[15]

The natural law "expresses the dignity of the person and determines the basis for his fundamental rights and duties" (*CCC* no. 1956). If we deny that such things as natural moral law or universal standards exist, then we leave human beings, especially those who are weak and powerless, at the mercy of governments that will define right and wrong according to their own interests.

The Role of Reason in Recognizing the Natural Law   5.5.5

The Catholic tradition finds a close connection between human reason and understanding and natural law. Aquinas defines the relationship in this way, "The natural law is nothing other than the light of

Example of a Natural Law: "Do Not Lie"   5.5.6

To better understand how a specific rule of natural law works, let's consider an example: "Do not lie."

The law against lying is related to the more general law that humans naturally need to have healthy relationships with other people. If I make a habit of lying to people (even if they are seemingly harmless "white lies"), the natural consequence is that people will no longer trust me. If people no longer trust me, then I will have few friends, or the ones that I do have will not be very close. My natural human need for friendship will be unmet, and I will naturally be unhappy.

Of course the opposite is also true. Stated positively, a person should tell the truth. If I tell the truth, then people will trust me, thus making it easier for me to fulfill my natural human need to have friends.

So "do not lie" is a natural law in two senses.

- It helps us to fulfill a true need of human nature.

- It has natural consequences. Lying will naturally lead to lack of trust and unhappiness, while telling the truth will naturally lead to trust and happiness. ○

understanding placed in us by God; through it we know what we must do and what we must avoid. God has given this light or law at the creation."[16]

The pre-Christian Roman philosopher Cicero (106–43 BCE) also recognizes this link, stating, "For there is a true law: right reason. It is in conformity with nature, is diffused among all men, and is immutable and eternal."[17]

Natural Law and Human Nature   5.5.7

Humans, regardless of culture or society, share what we call "human nature." Physically, we share the need for nutritious food and adequate rest. Psychologically, we all need healthy relationships with other people, as well as a sense of meaning and purpose in our lives. Spiritually, we share a natural drive toward the transcendent, toward an ultimate truth, an ultimate freedom, an ultimate happiness. If we do things against our nature, we will become physically, psychologically, or spiritually sick.

Natural ethical laws are simply guidelines that correspond with our human nature; our reason allows us to recognize these rules. Following these natural laws tends toward happiness and health. Breaking these natural laws tends toward unhappiness and sickness.

These rules of the natural law are part of God's revelation to all humans.

Historical (Special) Revelation   5.6

In addition to natural revelation, Christians also speak of historical revelation — the belief that God has revealed himself, at certain times and places in history, in a direct way. For Christians, this direct revelation took place especially in events in Israel's history and in the words of Israel's inspired prophets. Direct revelation culminated in the person of Jesus Christ. "In time past, God spoke in partial and various ways to our ancestors through the prophets; in these last days, he spoke to us through a son" (Heb 1:1–2).

Scripture is a uniquely authoritative witness to this historical revelation. Because of the centrality of Scripture in Christian revelation, we devote separate chapters (8 and 9) to that topic.

For now, however, let us consider two fundamental questions that arise when Christians claim that God communicates to humans in special revelation: (1) Does it really make sense to say that the transcendent God "communicates" or "talks" with humans? (2) Even if the transcendent God could communicate with humans, how could those humans then communicate that personal revelation to other people in limited human language?

Can God Really Communicate? Einstein's Rejection of a Personal God   5.7

Many reasonable people reject the idea that God communicates with humans. Albert Einstein, as a result of his great insights into the order of nature, believed that the universe "reveals an intelligence of such superiority that, compared with it, all the systematic thinking and acting of human beings is an utterly insignificant reflection."[18] Einstein also spoke of the "mind revealed in this world."[19] Despite this language about "intelligence" and "mind," however, Einstein's conception of God was completely impersonal. The "intelligence" or "mind," it seems, were simply a way of speaking about the rational order in the universe, the mathematically precise laws that govern events.

Einstein firmly rejected the belief that this "mind" was in any sense personal—one could no more have a relationship with this universal mind than one could have a relationship with the law of gravity.

To think of God in personal terms, Einstein believed, was "**anthropomorphic**," a way of thinking that the world should have outgrown. Einstein called on religious leaders to have the courage to plainly "give up the doctrine of a personal God."[20]

God's Mind and the Human Mind   5.7.1

But is the idea of a personal God really outdated? Let's consider Einstein's view in a little more detail.

First, we find that behind Einstein's rejection of a personal God is a deterministic and materialistic view of the universe. With his belief that fixed laws of nature determine all events, Einstein not only left no room for a personal God, he left no room for human free will. Einstein was quite explicit on this point: "Man's actions are determined by necessity, external and internal."[21]

We have already considered the inconsistencies in a strictly deterministic view of the universe (sec. 2.5.2). We can also question Einstein's conclusions about the "mind" of the universe. Perhaps Einstein was speaking only metaphorically, comparing the rational structure of the universe to a mind. But if so, we have good reason to ask whether such a concept is more than a mere metaphor. First, if we find a common rational structure in our own mind and in the structure of the universe, is it unreasonable to suggest that the rational structure of both may have a common source in the mind of a Creator? Second, we must ask the metaphysical question: Why does the universe have a rational structure in the first place? (see sec. 4.9.1).

For Joseph Ratzinger, an intellectual structure in the universe is impossible without thought. And thought is impossible without a subject to do the thinking.[22]

We thus have reason to think that the rational structure of the universe is evidence that it was created by an intelligent power. But if this rational power is analogous to our human mind (which it seems to be), then it is more analogous to a human than to a set of impersonal mathematical laws.

To say that the universal mind is analogous to the human mind, however, is not anthropomorphic. We are not giving human characteristics to inanimate forces such as wind or lightning. We are simply recognizing a profound similarity between the workings of our own mind and the workings of the universe.

Personal Nature of God: Openness to Relationship 5.7.2

At this point in our reflections, when we speak of a "personal God," we mean only that the universal mind seems to be more analogous to a human mind than to an abstract, impersonal law.

But is a rational mind the only evidence of the personal nature of God? When we considered the "signs of transcendence" in chapter 1, we found evidence that the transcendent reality is associated with absolute truth and freedom (see sec. 1.4), the Moral Law (sec. 1.6), and the human drive to find meaning to the universe (sec. 1.5). The transcendent reality, therefore, is not simply impersonal rationality, but seems to be oriented toward a relationship with humans.

We can then think of a transcendent mind that is related to humans and the transcendent horizon of human desire for absolute truth, love, and meaning. We can thus legitimately call this transcendent mind a personal God—with "personal" understood as a being that is capable of entering into a relationship with other rational beings.

Ratzinger notes that many strictly scientific thinkers find it absurd to think that the absolute mind of the universe should be concerned with the fate of humans—an insignificant species on an insignificant planet in an obscure solar system within an ordinary galaxy, lost in the immensity of the cosmos.

But Ratzinger asks: Why do we assume that it is somehow "greater" if the consciousness of the transcendent being is unconcerned with life on the tiny speck of the universe called Earth? Would it not in fact be "greater," more "divine," if in fact there was a place of concern within that universal mind for insignificant humanity?[23]

Ratzinger points out further how the scientific mind of an Einstein assumes that "the absolute spirit cannot be emotion and feeling but only pure cosmic mathematics." But this thinking again has a hidden assumption:

> We unthinkingly assume that pure thought is greater than love, while the message of the Gospel, and the Christian picture of God contained in it, corrects philosophy and lets us know that love is higher than mere thought.[24]

Ratzinger summed up the contrast between the "God of the philosophers" that Einstein accepted and the God of biblical faith as follows:

1. The abstract God of the philosophers is "*essentially self-centered*," thought simply contemplating itself. In contrast, the God of faith is "basically defined by the category of relationship."[25] We shall explore in greater depth the category of relationship (the essence of the concept of *person*) in our next chapter on God as a Trinity.

2. The philosophical God is "*pure thought*: he is based on the notion that thought and thought alone is divine." In contrast: "The God of faith, as thought, is also love. His image is based on the conviction that to love is divine."[26]

Revelation and Language's Limitations   5.8

While the Christian tradition thinks of God as a personal God, this does not imply that Christians should think of God as a human person. In fact, the tradition agrees with Einstein that humans must resist the temptation to anthropomorphize God—to create God in the image of the human. In speaking of God, we must always keep in mind the possibilities and limitations of our human language and ideas. Let us now consider in some detail the relationship between limited language and the unlimited, eternal source of all being.

The Necessity of Language   5.8.1

The first point to clarify is that even if human language is limited, it is our only option. Even if we believe that God reveals things to us through nature and our conscience, the meaning of that revelation must be expressed in human words. If I see a rainbow, for example, and think of it as a sign from God, I will inevitably start to use language to think about its possible meaning, even if I don't express my thoughts out loud.

Let us accept, for the sake of the argument, that God did reveal himself to Moses at the burning bush (Exod 3). If Moses wished to communicate that revelation to others, his only option was to use language. All revelation must pass through the medium of human language.

Using Our Experience of God's Creation to Speak about God   5.8.2

According to the *Catechism of the Catholic Church*, "Since our knowledge about God is limited, our language about him is equally so. We can name God only by taking creatures as our starting point, and in accordance with our limited human ways of knowing and thinking" (*CCC* no. 40). God's creation reveals the Creator: "All creatures bear a certain resemblance to God, most especially man, created in the image and likeness of God. The manifold perfections of creatures—their truth, their goodness, their beauty"—all reflect the infinite perfection of God" (*CCC* no. 41).

Consider that last statement: if God's creation is a reflection of God, then couldn't we just as well say that the lies, evil, and ugliness of creation reflect God too? But we have already seen that evil can only be a corruption or distortion of an original good (see sec. 5.3.3). If we understand God as the First Cause, the transcendent source of all being, then God can only be the cause of the original, perfect goodness of all things. In this sense God can only be seen in the perfections of nature: "For from the greatness and the beauty of created things their original author, by analogy, is seen" (Wis 13:5).

True Knowledge about God through Analogies   5.8.3

Aquinas says, "Concerning God, we cannot grasp what he is, but only what he is not, and how other beings stand in relation to him" (*SCG* 1.30). In other words, humans cannot know the "essence of God"—God's nature in itself (*ST* 1.12.4). So while we can know God *indirectly* through God's creation, we must remember that "between Creator and creature no similitude can be expressed without implying an even greater dissimilitude" (*CCC* no. 43). Aquinas also notes that the **analogy** between God and his creature moves in only one direction: "A creature can be spoken of as in some sort like God; but not that God is like a creature" (*ST* 1.4.3 ad. 4).

The Orthodox Christian tradition agrees that we cannot know the essence of God, but only God's "energies"—God's acts of power in the world.[27]

An essential aspect of our language about God can be described as the **apophatic approach** — the way of negation. Orthodox Bishop Kallistos Ware explains,

> To point at this *mysterium tremendum*, we need to use negative as well as affirmative statements, saying what God is *not* rather than what he is. . . . If we say that he is good or just, we must at once add that his goodness or justice are not to be measured by our human standards. If we say that he exists we must qualify this immediately by adding that he is not one existent object among many, that in his case the word "exist" bears a unique significance. . . . Having made an assertion about God, we must pass beyond it: the statement is not untrue, yet neither it nor any other form of words can contain the fullness of the transcendent God.[28]

Our limited language "nevertheless . . . really does attain to God himself" (*CCC* no. 43). This is a crucial point. If our language did not reach God himself, then we would be forced to conclude that theological knowledge is not true knowledge, but only blind faith or unfounded opinion.

In the Catholic view we can have true knowledge about God because our being is analogous to God's being. We *have* being, but God *is* being.[29] Because humans are created in the image of God, there is a real connection between God and humans.

So, for example, we have a real knowledge of human creativity and intelligence. Because God, as the First Cause of all being, is the perfection of these characteristics, we are able to have an accurate glimpse into perfect divine creativity and intelligence. Similarly, we have experiences of human love and kindness. Because God is the perfection of love and kindness, we have a true, if limited, knowledge of God's love and kindness.

Aquinas writes, "So when we say, *God is good*, the meaning is not, *God is the cause of goodness*, or, *God is not evil*, but the meaning is, *Whatever good we attribute to creatures, pre-exists in God*, and in a more excellent and higher way" (*ST* 1.13.3).

For Aquinas, it can be true to say "that man is wise," and "God is wise." The meaning of the word "wise" in these two phrases is not identical (since there is a qualitative difference between Creator and created human), but neither is it completely different. Rather, "it must be said that these names are said of God and creatures in an analogous sense, that is, according to proportion" (*ST* 1.13.5).

Dangers of Anthropomorphism 5.8.4

Scripture often portrays God in anthropomorphic ways. Consider this passage from Psalm 7:12–14.

> God is a just judge,
> who rebukes in anger every day.
> If sinners do not repent,
> God sharpens his sword,
> strings and readies the bow,
> Prepares his deadly shafts,
> makes arrows blazing thunderbolts.

Already in ancient times, Christian commentators on Scripture were aware that these anthropomorphisms should not be taken literally. Commenting on the Psalms passage, John Chrysostom (ca. 347–407) admits that he cannot believe that there are truly bows, arrows, and instruments for sharpening swords in heaven. One must take from these words "ideas appropriate to God." But if the reader must do this with physical things, then he must also do the same with concepts such as God's "anger and wrath."[30]

Augustine, too, taught that any passages describing God with physical attributes must be taken figuratively, but so too must any passages that attribute changeable human emotions to God: "Whoever thinks that God forgets things one moment and remembers them the next, or anything like that, is certainly quite wrong." So too are those who think scriptural statements such as "I . . . am a jealous God" (Exod 20:5), or "I am sorry I made [man]" (Gen 6:7) should be taken literally (*On the Trinity* 1.1.1; see also *ST* 1.3.2 ad.2).

God's Gender 5.8.5

Traditional Christian language about God is male-centered: the Bible consistently refers to God using the male pronoun "he," and the Trinity is traditionally described as "Father, Son, and Holy Spirit." Christian believers might conclude that God actually is male. The *Catechism* addresses the issue thus:

> In no way is God in man's image. He is neither man nor woman. God is pure spirit in which there is no place for the difference between the sexes. But the respective "perfections" of man and woman reflect something of the infinite perfection of God: those of a mother and those of a father and husband. (*CCC* no. 370)

Muslim Concept of Revelation

The Second Vatican Council teaches explicitly that Muslims worship the same God as Christians do: "The plan of salvation also includes those who acknowledge the Creator, in the first place amongst whom are the Muslims: these profess to hold the faith of Abraham, and together with us they adore the one, merciful God, mankind's judge on the last day" (*LG* no. 16). Further, "They worship God, who is one, living and subsistent, merciful and almighty, the Creator of heaven and earth, who has also spoken to men" (*NA* no. 3).

Muslims agree with Jews and Christians that God has revealed himself to humans through the prophets. Islam uses the term *prophet* in a broad sense: Adam, Noah, Abraham, Jesus, and Mohammed are all called prophets. Islam recognizes that God gave revelations to the Jewish people and to the Christian people, and that these revelations are recorded in the Scriptures of the Old and New Testaments. It is for this reason that the Qur'an calls both Jews and Christians "people of the book" (see, e.g., Qur'an 2:146).

Islam, however, teaches that these earlier revelations were partial and not recorded with complete accuracy in the Old or New Testaments. According to Islam, the final and definitive revelation was God's revelation of the Muslim scriptures, the Qur'an, to the prophet Muhammad, who lived about six hundred years after the time of Jesus. Muhammad's central role as the prophet who received this definitive revelation is expressed in the fundamental belief of Islam: "There is no god but God, and Muhammad is his prophet."

According to Muslim tradition, the angel Gabriel gave a series of revealed messages to Muhammad over a period of more than twenty years. Muhammad memorized these revelations and taught them to his followers. In the generation after Muhammad's death, the revelations were written down in what is now known as the Qur'an. In the Qur'an, God (*Allah* in Arabic) is portrayed as all-powerful and all-knowing, in control of every event. He is often referred to as "the most gracious, the most merciful." In addition to frequent allusions to events in Muhammad's time, the Qur'an includes many references to characters and events familiar from the Bible: the creation; Adam and Eve; God's call of Abraham and Abraham's near sacrifice of his son (Ishmael in the Qur'an, not Isaac as in Gen 22); stories about Jesus, including Jesus' birth from the virgin Mary. In Islam,

continued

continued

Jesus is considered a great prophet, but his divine nature as the Son of God is denied (for example, Qur'an 5:72: "They do blaspheme who say, 'God is Christ the son of Mary'").

The Qur'an has a strongly **apocalyptic** feel: unbelievers and the unrighteous are frequently threatened with the fires of hell; paradise is promised for the righteous and believers. In later revelations (given at Medina, where the first Muslim community was established), the Qur'an gives a series of laws governing all aspects of society, including marriage, inheritance, and punishment for crimes.

The traditional Muslim understanding is that the Qur'an is the direct revealed word of God. As such, the words themselves have existed with God from all eternity — they were only revealed to Muhammad at a certain point in history. There is thus no possibility of human error in the Qur'an. Since God's words were revealed in Arabic, any translation of the Qur'an is not considered the Qur'an, but rather a paraphrase of the Qur'an's meaning. ◗

It follows, then, that Christians believe that one may use female analogies to describe God as well. The Bible itself occasionally uses this language. In speeches found in the Book of Isaiah, God is compared to a mother: "But now, I cry out as a woman in labor" (42:14); "Can a woman forget her infant? . . . I will never forget you" (49:15); "As a mother comforts her son, so will I comfort you" (66:13).

So too have Christian authors used female images. Clement of Alexandria wrote, "For to those babes who seek the Word, the Father's breasts of love supply milk" (*The Instructor* 1.6). The Syriac author Aphrahat spoke of the believer's love for "God his Father and the Holy Spirit his Mother," and the English visionary Julian of Norwich wrote, "God rejoices that he is our Father, and God rejoices that he is our Mother."[31]

All of these words are only analogies, of course; God's own nature is beyond male and female. Yet we must use analogies and symbols, and if God is to be pictured as a person, the analogies must necessarily be male or female.

Some feminist thinkers have called for abandoning the traditional language of Father, Son, and Spirit in Christian worship in favor of a gender-neutral formula such as Creator, Redeemer, and Sanctifier. There are, however, good reasons to think that such language would distort our understanding of God's Trinitarian nature (see sec. 6.18). Ware's thoughts on retaining the traditional male symbols are also worth noting:

> We cannot prove arguments why this should be so, yet it remains a fact of our Christian experience that God has set his seal upon certain symbols and not upon others. . . . Like the symbols in myth, literature, and art, our religious symbols reach deep into the hidden roots of our being, and cannot be altered without momentous consequences. If, for example, we were to start saying, "Our Mother who art in heaven," instead of "Our Father," we should not merely be adjusting an incidental piece of imagery, but replacing Christianity with a new kind of religion. A Mother Goddess is not the Lord of the Christian Church.[32]

Revelation in Supernatural Events (Miracles)   5.10

Vatican II's *Dei Verbum* taught that "revelation is realized by deeds and words," and spoke of "the works performed by God in the history of salvation" (*DV* no. 2). Prominent among these "works" are supernatural events: Moses splits the Red Sea and the Israelites walk across the dry ground; God rains down manna from heaven to feed the Israelites; Jesus walks on water, miraculously feeds thousands of people with only a few loaves of bread and fish, heals the sick, casts out demons from possessed people, and raises the dead. The key supernatural event in Christianity is Jesus' Resurrection from the dead.

Notice that *Dei Verbum* speaks of both deeds and words, however. In the Christian tradition, a supernatural event does not explain itself, but is interpreted through words, primarily the words of Scripture: "The words, for their part, proclaim the works, and bring to light the mystery they contain" (*DV* no. 2). The Christian tradition often speaks of supernatural events as "signs," events that carry a deeper meaning with them.

In considering supernatural events in the Bible, we will focus on two basic questions.[33] First, since the theme of our book is the relationship between faith and reason, we will need to ask whether a belief in miraculous events is compatible with a modern, scientifically grounded view of the world. Second, we will consider the deeper meaning of miraculous events from a scriptural perspective, the "words" that interpret the "works." We will have to ask, too, how well these scriptural interpretations stand up to some reasonable inquiries.

Are Supernatural Events Possible? 5.10

The Bible contains many accounts of supernatural events such as Jesus raising a person from the dead; for convenience, we'll term such events *miracles*. Modern readers can understand such events in various ways:

1. The ancient authors meant these events to be taken as metaphors or symbols.

2. The ancient authors were expressing natural facts in a naïve, pre-scientific way.

3. The ancient authors were deliberately fabricating stories (for example, in order to impress their audience with Jesus' power).

4. The ancient authors were describing actual supernatural events that took place within history.

Before making a reasonable choice from among these options, however, we must first ask a more basic question: Are miracles possible? If not, then option 4 is ruled out.

Defining a Miracle 5.11

We will not define a miracle as an event that cannot be explained by our current understanding of natural laws. Under this definition, a person from medieval times would interpret an airplane as a miracle. Rather, we define a miracle as an event, such as raising a person from the dead, that could never be explained by a natural cause, no matter how far our scientific understanding of nature develops. Its cause, by definition, is beyond nature (the literal meaning of the word *supernatural*).

C. S. Lewis defines a miracle as "an interference with Nature by supernatural power."[34] John Henry Newman defines it as "an event inconsistent with the constitution of nature."[35] Aquinas wrote, "A miracle properly so called is when something is done outside the order of nature" (*ST* 1.110.4). The Christian tradition, then, understands a miracle as an event, directly caused by God, outside of the normal laws of nature.

Miracles and Worldviews   5.12

Are events not caused by natural laws possible? Lewis rightly points out that our answer cannot be based on evidence from the senses or from historical evidence, because people's worldviews will determine how they interpret this sense data or historical evidence.[36]

Let us say that Ruth had a "near-death" experience. As she was on the operating table, her heart stopped. During that time she remembers seeing a tunnel of light and having a great sense of peace come over her. She interprets her experience as a supernatural event — an experience of a world beyond nature. Her interpretation is consistent with Ruth's worldview, since she is a Christian.

Ruth's friend Roger believes that the physical world — nature — is the only reality. Since his worldview is closed to the transcendent, he must find a natural explanation for Ruth's experience. He has read that people who are near death often see images of light because neurons in the brain fire at a great rate during the dying process. Looking at it psychologically, he knows that Ruth is a strong Christian believer who has been taught all her life about heaven as a place of peace and light, and so he is not surprised that she would picture "heaven" that way in her experience.

In the same way, a person's worldview will determine how she interprets a miracle in Scripture. A rationalist or materialist will rule out the possibility that Jesus could have healed a blind person by laying his hands on his eyes (Mark 8:25); a reader with a worldview open to the transcendent must leave open the possibility.

Bultmann's "Demythologizing"   5.13

One of the most influential New Testament scholars of the twentieth century was the German Rudolf Bultmann. For Bultmann, belief in miracles was only possible for people with a naïve, precritical worldview. This belief had no place in modern civilization:

> It is impossible to use electric light and the wireless [radio] and to avail ourselves of modern medical and surgical discoveries, and at the same time to believe in the New Testament world of spirits and miracles.[37]

Consequently the historian and scholar must rule out the possibility of supernatural events in studying Scripture:

> The historical method includes the presupposition that history is a unity in the sense of a closed continuum of effects. . . . This closedness means that the continuum of historical happenings cannot be rent by the interference of supernatural, transcendent powers and that therefore there is no "miracle" in this sense of the word.[38]

Bultmann believed that the essential truth of the New Testament could be separated from the mythological framework in which it was set. But a modern Christian would first need to *demythologize* the New Testament—to reinterpret its supernatural forces as *natural* forces. Thus, for example, demonic powers could be reinterpreted as a person's enslavement to material comfort and success, and the Holy Spirit could be reinterpreted not as a supernatural power, but as the possibility of a new life based on faith in God and not in material goods.[39]

But is Bultmann right? Does the modern scientific worldview rule out a belief in the supernatural?

The Language of Myth and the Supernatural   5.14

C. S. Lewis would have agreed with Bultmann that much of the New Testament is written in a mythic language that is hard for a modern person with an essentially scientific view of the world to accept. The reader

> finds that God is supposed to have had a "Son," just as if God were a mythological deity like Jupiter or Odin. He finds that this "Son" is supposed to have "come down from Heaven," just as if God had a palace in the sky from which He had sent down His "Son" like a parachutist. He finds that this "Son" then "descended into Hell"—into some land of the dead under the surface of a (presumably) flat earth—and thence "ascended" again, as if by a balloon, into his Father's sky-palace, where he finally sat down in a decorated chair placed a little to His Father's right.[40]

Lewis agrees, then, that some of the biblical language is mythical or symbolic. The reader of the New Testament does not need to accept such language as literally true.

Where Bultmann and Lewis part company, however, is in their interpretation of the mythic language. Bultmann insists that the modern reader can only reinterpret it to refer to *natural* events, while Lewis insists that the modern reader, while not taking the language literally, can still reasonably understand it as a poetic way of claiming that a *supernatural power* has entered into nature. Lewis's point is that the essential meaning of a statement can be accepted as true, even if we do not accept the images that go along with the message.[41]

This point is crucial, since it directs us again to the limitations of human language. Let us assume that we want to avoid mythical language about Jesus floating up to a palace in the sky, so we substitute a more sophisticated phrase, "Jesus entered into the transcendent realm."

But notice that we are still using metaphorical language. By saying Jesus "entered the transcendent realm," we are still drawing an analogy between physically entering a particular physical space, on the one hand, and spiritually passing into a transcendent realm of being, on the other. If we wish to speak of transcendent realities at all, we must accept the fact that we must use symbols, metaphors, and analogies (see 5.8.1–3). The fact that we must use such analogies, however, in no way proves that the transcendent reality does not exist.

A Power Beyond Nature? 5.15

Lewis's point about language helps us to focus on the main issue. As modern readers encounter the scriptural accounts about the miraculous, they need not accept the symbolic details as literally true. But they do need to face the essential question: Is there a power beyond nature that could, at certain times, intervene in the normal workings of nature in a miraculous way?

In the first chapters, we considered multiple reasons for thinking that a transcendent power beyond nature does exist (sec.s 1.4–7; 3.3.3). The universe does not explain itself, and thus it is reasonable to believe that a transcendent power created it. We find a rational structure in the very matter of the universe itself, implying the existence of a mind—outside of the universe—that established that order. Every single society that has ever existed has believed in a transcendent power; can that unanimous belief simply be written off as massively coincidental wishful thinking?

We are faced with solid evidence that a reality transcending nature does exist, and that this reality must be personal (5.7.1–2). If such a transcendent personal power exists, it is unreasonable to assume that this transcendent personal power would never directly cause an event that transcends the ordinary laws of nature.

Taking the Miraculous Seriously

In their analysis of scholarly studies of the Gospels, Paul Eddy and Gregory Boyd present some further reasons why the reasonable person should not reject the possibility of miracles out of hand.

1. Throughout the world, particularly in non-Western societies, the reality of miracles is largely taken for granted. Could it be, then, that an *a priori* rejection of the possibility of miracles is a bias of a narrowly scientific Western worldview? Indeed some ethnographers have argued that Western studies of non-Western societies that accept the existence of supernatural forces are skewed because of this rationalistic bias.[42]

2. Even in Western societies, a majority of people still accept the reality of supernatural interventions in nature. A 1989 Gallup poll found that 82 percent of Americans believe that "even today, miracles are performed by the power of God."[43] While this fact, of course, does not prove the existence of the supernatural, it does raise the possibility that rejection of the possibility of the miraculous is a bias of certain Western academics.

3. A person's understanding is shaped by personal experience (see sec. 2.5.1.5). Thus a New Testament scholar who has had no personal experience of the supernatural is not likely to take it seriously. Conversely, as New Testament scholar Walter Wink writes, "As a result of my own experience, I have no trouble believing in the plausibility of some events that to some of my fellow scholars simply seem impossible. . . . Because of . . . [my] experiences with spiritual healing, I have no difficulty believing that Jesus actually healed people, and not just of psychosomatic diseases."[44]

Based on these and other considerations, Eddy and Boyd rightly call for an ***open* historical-critical method** in studying the New Testament — one that does not reject from the start any possibility of a supernatural event. Such an approach would not accept all supernatural accounts uncritically. Rather, it would remain critical in the sense that, all other things being equal, it would prefer a plausible naturalistic explanation over a supernatural one for any given event. But this approach would be open to considering a supernatural explanation if no plausible naturalistic ones are available.[45] ●

The Harmony of the Natural
and the Supernatural in God's Plan   5.17

From the Christian perspective, the orderly laws of nature form part of natural revelation (sec. 5.3). Since God is the creator of nature and its natural order, in the normal course of events, God works through the causes of nature (in Aquinas's terminology, God is the First Cause, and these natural causes are secondary causes; see sec. 3.3.5). But since God is the Creator of natural laws and thus stands outside of them, God of course is in no way bound by them.

A key Christian concept is the belief in God's providence, "the foreseeing care and guidance of God . . . over the creatures of the earth."[46] Normally, God's providence works through natural causes: the regular, predictable order of nature allows humans, for example, to plant and reap crops, plan activities, and make scientific advances.

As we saw above (sec. 5.3.4), however, Christians view nature, in spite of its reflection of God's divine *logos*, as imperfect and still "groaning in labor pains" (Rom 8:22). Only at the end of history will nature's imperfections—including human diseases and suffering—be healed.

Let us apply these theological beliefs to Jesus' supernatural healings, taking as an example the story of Jesus' healing of a blind man (Mark 8:22–26). While the healing itself is supernatural, its purpose is to restore imperfect nature. It is the nature of eyes to see; Jesus restored them to their original purpose. Jesus' healing, then, is a "sign" that God intends to restore all things to their original purpose in the end.

While normally God's providential care is expressed through natural laws, in the exceptional cases of miracles, God's providence is shown directly. Yet even in these exceptional cases, natural laws and supernatural miracles are in harmony—they both are expressions of God's loving care and concern for creation.

The New Testament Greek word often translated as "miracle" is *semeion*—literally "sign." Miracles, then, are signs—special revelations from God. Based on what we have just discussed, a particular sign would have at least two meanings: (1) a reminder to humans that God the Creator is not bound by nature's law and limitations, and (2) a reminder that in the fullness of time, all of nature will be restored to perfect health and well-being.

Questions about the Text

1. Why is God's revelation necessary, in the Christian view? What is the difference between natural revelation and historical revelation? What is the ultimate purpose of revelation?

2. What is dualism? How does the dualist view differ from the Christian view regarding the origin of evil?

3. What are some possible theological explanations for evil or suffering in nature?

4. What is the Christian concept of an ethical natural law? What are some examples of specific ethical guidelines included in this natural law?

5. How would you define "moral relativism"? What are some Christian responses to this ethical philosophy?

6. How are human rights threatened by moral relativism?

7. Why did Einstein reject the belief in a personal God?

8. Discuss Christian arguments for why God must be personal, not an impersonal mind.

9. Why does the Catholic tradition teach that knowledge of God can only be expressed through analogies?

10. For Aquinas, what is the relationship between these two statements: "God is wise" and "That person is wise"?

11. What are the dangers of an overly anthropomorphic view of God?

12. Discuss different perspectives on the issue of the use of male and female analogies for God.

13. What is the Christian definition of a *miracle*?

14. Why did Bultmann call for a "demythologized" reading of the New Testament?

15. What distinction did Lewis make between the essential message of a biblical passage and the images in which it is expressed?

16. What are some reasons for accepting the possibility of miracles?

17. What does it mean to say that there is harmony between the natural and the supernatural in God's providential plan?

18. In what ways can a miracle be considered a "sign"?

Discussion Questions

1. Why do you think suffering and tragedies occur in nature?

2. Do you agree with the natural law view that there are standards of right and wrong that apply to all cultures? Why or why not?

3. Do you have one main image or analogy that helps you picture God?

4. In your own experience, are most people open to the possibility of a miracle?

Endnotes

1. See Avery Dulles, "Faith and Revelation," in *Systematic Theology: Roman Catholic Perspectives*, vol. 1 eds. F. S. Fiorenza and J. P. Galvin (Minneapolis: Fortress Press, 1991), 92.
2. Dulles, "Faith and Revelation," 94–95.
3. For a comparison between dualism and Christianity, some points of which I summarize in this chapter, see C. S. Lewis, *Mere Christianity* (London: HarperCollins, 2001; orig. pub. 1952), 42–45.
4. Ibid., 45.
5. Christoph Schönborn, *Chance or Purpose: Creation, Evolution, and a Rational Faith* (San Francisco: Ignatius Press, 2007), 93; *CCC* no. 309.
6. Schönborn, *Chance or Purpose*, 98–100.
7. Ibid., 100.
8. Ibid., 95.
9. John Henry Newman, *An Essay in Aid of a Grammar of Assent*, ed. I. T. Ker (Oxford: Clarendon Press, 1985), 73–80.
10. Lewis, *Mere Christianity*, 6.
11. Compare Lewis's list in *The Abolition of Man* (New York: Macmillan, 1947), 104–5.
12. Lewis, *Mere Christianity*, 6.
13. For this basic argument, see ibid., 13–14.
14. Benedict XVI's Address to United Nations, April 18, 2008. Accessed October 3, 2008, at: *http://www.zenit.org/article-22334?l=english.*
15. Martin Luther King, "Letter from Birmingham Jail." Accessed October 3, 2008, at *http://www.thekingcenter.org/prog/non/Letter.pdf.*
16. Quoted in *CCC* no. 1955.
17. *Republic* 3.22.33; quoted in *CCC* no. 1956.
18. Albert Einstein, *Ideas and Opinions* (New York: Bonanza Books, 1954), 40.
19. Ibid., 39.
20. Ibid., 48; see also 36–47.
21. Ibid., 39.
22. Joseph Ratzinger, *Introduction to Christianity* (San Francisco: Ignatius Press, 2000; orig. pub. 1968), 155.
23. Ibid., 145–46.
24. Ibid., 147.
25. Ibid. Emphasis original.
26. Ibid., 147–48. Emphasis original.

27. See Kallistos Ware, *The Orthodox Way* (Crestwood, NY: St. Vladimir's Seminary Press, 1995), 21–23.

28. Ibid., 14. Emphasis original.

29. Peter Kreeft, *A Summa of the* Summa*: The Essential Philosophical Passages of Saint Thomas Aquinas'* Summa Theologica (San Francisco: Ignatius Press, 1990), 90 no. 38. This theological concept of the "analogy of being" is translated in a well-known Latin phrase as the *analogia entis.*

30. Quoted in Ronald E. Heine, *Reading the Old Testament with the Ancient Church: Exploring the Formation of Early Christian Thought,* Evangelical Ressourcement (Grand Rapids, MI: Baker Academic, 2007), 148.

31. Quoted in Ware, *Orthodox Way,* 34.

32. Ibid.

33. In the Christian view, scriptural miracles are not the only types of miracles. The Catholic tradition, for example, officially recognizes miraculous healings from various times in history. We focus on scriptural miracles here since they are of primary significance in Christian theology.

34. C. S. Lewis, *Miracles* (New York: Macmillan, 1960), 5.

35. John Henry Newman, *Two Essays on Biblical and on Ecclesiastical Miracles* (Westminster, MD: Christian Classics, 1969), 4.

36. Lewis, *Miracles,* 3–4.

37. Rudolf Bultmann, et al., *Kerygma and Myth: A Theological Debate,* ed. H. W. Bartsch (New York: Harper & Row, 1961), 5.

38. Quoted in Paul R. Eddy and Gregory A. Boyd, *The Jesus Legend: A Case for the Historical Reliability of the Synoptic Jesus Tradition* (Grand Rapids, MI: Baker Academic, 2007), 44.

39. Bultmann, *Kerygma and Myth,* 18–22.

40. Lewis, *Miracles,* 68–69.

41. Ibid., 68–80.

42. Eddy and Boyd, *Jesus Legend,* 67–73.

43. Cited in ibid., 74.

44. Cited in ibid., 77.

45. Ibid., 82–90.

46. Definition adapted from *http://dictionary.reference.com.* Accessed December 8, 2008.

6

The Trinity

The Trinity:
A Reasonable Belief?

The traditional Christian belief that God is a Trinity can be summarized briefly: God is three persons in one divine nature; these three persons have traditionally been named Father, Son, and Holy Spirit. But what exactly does this mean? Does it make sense? And even if it is in fact reasonable, does it make any practical difference to anyone?

Through the ages, many critics have denied that the doctrine of the Trinity makes sense. Thomas Jefferson wrote in 1813, "It is too late in the day for men of sincerity to pretend they believe in the Platonic mysticisms that three are one, and one is three; and yet the one is not three, and the three are not one."[1]

The belief that God is a Trinity is the great dividing line between the Christian and the Jewish and Muslim conceptions of God. All three share the belief that there is only one

God, and this God is one, but only Christians believe that there exists a distinction of persons within the divine unity. Why should Christians continue to allow the doctrine of the Trinity to divide them from other monotheists?

Mystery and Reason   6.2

While the Catholic tradition insists that God can be known through natural reason alone (*CCC* no. 36), the tradition also teaches that the specific belief that God is a Trinity of three persons cannot be known by natural reason — it can only be known through special revelation (*ST* 1.32.1). In theological terms the doctrine of the Trinity is a "mystery of faith," meaning that it is an insight into God's nature not discernible by reason alone, knowable only if specially revealed by God (*CCC* no. 237). The Catholic tradition teaches that even in heaven humans will not fully understand the mystery of the Trinity.

While the Trinity is a mystery, that does not mean it cannot be understood at all. Reason can work with faith to attain a deeper understanding.

Although it is probably fair to say the average modern Christian does not spend much time thinking about the Trinity, the belief has been an essential teaching of the Church for centuries and has remained at the heart of the Church's prayer and worship. Baptism is administered "in the name of the Father, Son, and Holy Spirit," for example, and prayers generally end with that phrase. In fact the *Catechism* teaches that the Trinity is the most important truth of the faith: "It is *the* most fundamental and essential teaching in the "hierarchy of the truths of faith" (*CCC* no. 253).

What Is the Trinity?   6.3

Before trying to understand why the doctrine of the Trinity is so important, let us first consider its three essential points.

1. **The Trinity is one.** There is only one God, and God is a unity. This unity or "oneness" of God is expressed in various terms: it is said that God has one single divine "nature," "substance," or "essence" (*CCC* no. 252). Each of the persons of the Trinity, Father, Son, and Spirit, are "God whole and entire." The Fourth

Lateran Council said, "Each of the persons is that supreme reality, viz., the divine substance, essence or nature" (*CCC* no. 253).

2. **The divine persons are truly distinct from one another.** The names *Father*, *Son*, and *Spirit* are not simply identical and inter-changeable—they represent true distinctions within God's nature. Further, the persons are not simply "aspects" of God—each has its own distinct existence within the divine unity. To clarify the distinctiveness of each, the technical terms *person* (Latin: *persona*) and *hypostasis* (Greek) have been used (*CCC* no. 252).

3. **The divine persons are relative to one another.** The divine persons do not exist independently of one another, but are distinct in their different relationships with one another. Specifically, they are distinct in their origin: "It is the Father who generates, the Son who is begotten, and the Holy Spirit who proceeds" (*CCC* no. 254). We will explore the meaning of that last sentence as we continue.

We should recognize that the above definition of the Trinity does not occur in the Bible. The specialized language describing the Trinity was developed especially in the fourth century and expressed in various creeds and Church councils of that time. These creeds were themselves the end-product of much thinking, discussion, and debate among Christian theologians from New Testament times until the fourth-century Councils. The essential statement in the development of Trinitarian doctrine was the Nicene Creed (325), which taught that the Son is of the same nature (Greek: *homoousios*) with the Father. The precise language describing three persons and one nature was worked out by later theologians and expressed in further creeds. Key landmarks in this post-Nicene development include the thought of the Cappadocian theologians Gregory of Nyssa (c. 330–c. 395), Basil of Caesarea (c. 330–379), and Gregory of Nazianzus (c. 330–c. 390), and the teaching in the Creed of Constantinople [381].[2]

Unity, Plurality, and Ultimate Reality   6.4

At this point, let us step back and remember our main goal in discussing theology. Theology tackles the "big questions" of life: Does the universe have ultimate meaning? Why does the universe exist at all? Did the universe have a beginning and will it have an end? How do I know what is truly right and wrong? What happens when I die?

The question of God is a question about ultimate reality. We have already considered several approaches to this question: What is the first cause of all things (sec. 3.3.3)? Does reality have an ultimate meaning (sec. 1.5)? Is there an absolute truth that grounds and upholds the partial truths we see in this world (sec 1.4)?

As humans, we experience this world not as a unity, but as a *plurality*, an endless variety. People are divided on the basis of gender, ethnicity, beliefs, and other issues. Within the nonhuman world, we also see a wondrous variety: oceans, deserts, glaciers, starfish, stars, molecules, galaxies. Yet as humans we seem to have a need to seek an underlying unity that holds together all of this variety, this plurality. It seems to be one expression of our deep desire to make sense of the universe, our need to find meaning.

Consider a teaching from an ancient Hindu text:

> In the beginning there was Existence alone — One only, without a second. He, the One, thought to himself: Let me be many, let me grow forth. Thus out of himself he projected the universe, and having projected out of himself the universe, he entered into every being.[3]

The Greek philosopher Plotinus (c. 205–270) taught, "The One is all things and not a single one of them."[4]

The *Tao-te ching*, the ancient Chinese Taoist scripture, teaches,

> There is a thing confusedly formed, born before heaven and earth. Silent and void, It stands alone and does not change, goes round and does not weary. It is capable of being the mother of the world.[5]

Ancient Greek philosophers sought the unity of all things by identifying the one single element that formed the basis for all reality. Thales claimed that it was water, Anaximenes argued for air.[6] Though science is much more sophisticated today, we are still searching for a single Grand Unified Theory that will explain all of reality. Einstein identified "cosmic religious feeling" as the desire "to experience the universe as a single significant whole."[7]

In philosophy, part of the speculation about ultimate reality involves this question of "the one and the many": trying to understand the relationship between unity and plurality. If reality began as a unity, why does it now appear as a plurality? As Plotinus asked, "How then do all things come from the One, which is simple and has in it no diverse variety, or any sort of doubleness?"[8] What is more real: the plurality that we see and touch now, or the unity that we believe must have been there originally?

The question of the one and the many is not simply philosophical. As Einstein rightly saw, it is also a religious question: a desire of people to get beyond the limitations and divisions of this world and to experience ultimate reality. In Hindu thought, for example, the ultimate goal of life may be understood as "liberation from the limitations of space, time, and matter through realization of the immortal Absolute."[9]

So we can see that Christian Trinitarian discussions about unity and plurality within God are not unique. They are simply a way of trying to make sense of common human questions about the divine, about ultimate reality.

Trinity: A Unique Way of Understanding Ultimate Unity   6.5

The Trinitarian view of God offers a unique way of understanding the relationship between the ultimate unity and plurality. Ultimate reality—God—is not just pure unity. Rather, God is a unity already containing a kind of plurality: a relationship of three persons forms the one God. The doctrine of Trinity answers the question of the "one and the many" by going beyond both. Ultimate reality is a One formed through a unity of "many."

According to the New Testament, "God is love" (1 John 4:16). Far from being just a sentimental slogan on a greeting card, this biblical phrase is, according to Christian thought, a philosophically precise description of ultimate reality. Within the oneness of ultimate reality is a plurality: the three persons of the Trinity are united in a relationship of love.

Peter Kreeft explains how the doctrine of the Trinity does not diminish the oneness of God:

> Far from God's Trinity lessening His unity, it increases it; for the oneness of love, which is the glue that holds that Trinity together, is a closer and more perfect union than the one of mere quantitative, arithmetical oneness.[10]

Joseph Ratzinger agrees:

> To him who believes in God as tri-une, the highest unity is not the unity of inflexible monotony. The model of unity or oneness toward

which one should strive is consequently not the indivisibility of the atom, the smallest unity, which cannot be divided up any further; the authentic acme of unity is the unity created by love. The multiunity that grows in love is a more radical, truer unity than the unity of the "atom."[11]

We can extend Ratzinger's analogy. In ancient Greek philosophy, the "atom" (the word literally means "that which cannot be cut") was conceived as the smallest bit of matter that could not be divided further, and so was absolutely "one." Modern physics, however, has shown us that this basic unit is in fact composed of relationships among electrons, protons, and neutrons: a model of unity formed from a plurality.

The Christian view of **salvation**, of heaven, then, is not one in which humans overcome division and plurality by losing their individuality in the Absolute, as a drop of water is immersed in the ocean. Rather, it is "the entry of God's creatures into the perfect unity of the Blessed Trinity" (*CCC* no. 260). Salvation involves people joining in the relationship of love among the Father, Son, and Holy Spirit.

We catch a glimpse of this Trinitarian vision of salvation in Jesus' prayer before his death, as recorded in the Gospel of John. Here Jesus speaks of his followers participating in the unity that he and the Father already shared before the creation of the universe:

> I pray not only for them, but also for those who will believe in me through their word, so that they may all be one, as you, Father, are in me and I in you, that they also may be in us, that the world may believe that you sent me. And I have given them the glory you gave me, so that they may be one, as we are one, I in them and you in me, that they may be brought to perfection as one, that the world may know that you sent me, and that you loved them even as you loved me. Father, they are your gift to me. I wish that where I am they also may be with me, that they may see my glory that you gave me, because you loved me before the foundation of the world. (John 17:20–24)

Trinity: God as Person   6.6

But let's not move too quickly here. When we speak of God as a Trinity of three persons who love one another, aren't we being too anthropomorphic? Aren't we reducing the mystery of God to our level? To prevent misunderstanding, we need to consider the meaning of this language more carefully.

We have already considered reasons for concluding that absolute being, the First Cause of all reality, is more like a person than like an abstract, impersonal power, since humans experience absolute being as intelligent and concerned with human meaning, freedom, and standards of right and wrong (secs. 5.7.1–2). To the extent that absolute being reveals these characteristics, it makes sense to use terms such as *person* (rather than simply abstract terms such as *power*) to describe it.

Consider the term *person* more deeply. Strictly at the human level, what is the difference between an "individual" and a "person"? We can see a clue in the related term *personality*. We say that Susie has a lively, bubbly personality, while Lorraine's personality is more reserved and private. What we mean by "personality," then, is a person as she is revealed in her relationships with other people. Thomas Torrance writes, "You cannot be a person all by yourself, as a separated individual. You can be a person only along with other persons—you need interpersonal relations to be a person."[12]

We develop our personalities, our characters, largely through our interactions with other people. Our parents and family who raise us influence us in profound ways, ways of which we are often not explicitly aware. The attitudes, opinions, likes and dislikes of our friends and acquaintances again profoundly shape our own attitudes and opinions (think of how powerful peer pressure is, for example). It is impossible to develop our personality or character in isolation—we cannot separate who we are from the people with whom we interact.

The "interpersonal" character of the term *person* makes it appropriate in speaking of the Trinity. Father, Son, and Holy Spirit in the Trinity are not defined as independent entities, but rather on the basis of their relation to the other Trinitarian persons (see sec. 6.3).

Ratzinger applies this insight to God's nature: "The unrelated, unrelatable, absolutely One could not be a person." As with all theological terms, of course, the word *person* is analogous: the persons within God's nature are not the same as human persons. But they are analogous in the sense that both human and divine persons are oriented outside of themselves.[13]

Both Torrance and Ratzinger argue that the concept of person as an individual oriented toward relationships with others was not known in the ancient world—it arose only as the early Christians reflected on the relationships of Father, Son, and Spirit within the one divine nature.[14]

The classic Christian theologians also see the essence of "person-hood" as relationships with others. Aquinas expresses the idea this way: "a divine person signifies a relation as subsisting" [*to subsist* means to exist in a stable way] (*ST* 1.29.4). Augustine shows how the traditional names for the first two persons of the Trinity—Father and Son—relate to the concept of person. "He is not called Father with reference to himself but only in relation to the Son; seen by himself he is simply God."[15] The very word *Father* points beyond itself toward relationship with another—either a son or a daughter. The name "Father" thus refers not to God conceived as absolute oneness, but rather defines God in relation to another.

The belief in God as a Trinity, then, is the claim that ultimate reality is not simply based on the independent existence of absolute unity: rather ultimate reality contains within itself interpersonal relationships.

Trinity and Modern Science   6.7

The Trinitarian view of ultimate reality is thus not of a static, unchanging One, but rather of a dynamic relationship.

Christian theology teaches us that we know God, ultimate Reality, only through analogy to God's creation (see sec. 5.8.3). Torrance argues that for James Clerk Maxwell, the great scientist (and devout Christian) who first described the relationship between electricity and magnetism, the situation was, in a sense, reversed. Looking at the world through the static paradigm of Newtonian physics (which understood reality as composed of fixed, independent objects connected through forces such as gravity), scientists had been unable to develop an adequate theory to explain electricity and magnetism. Only when Clerk Maxwell, who had been trained by his Christian faith to understand ultimate reality as relational and dynamic, applied this Trinitarian paradigm to his scientific observations was he able to develop the dynamic theory of interrelated electromagnetic fields.[16]

Clerk Maxwell's insight was a crucial stepping-stone on the path toward Einstein's dynamic theory of relativity, where time and space are conceived not as absolute, independent substances, but rather as a flexible fabric of space-time, "which could bend and quiver in response to the matter and energy that moved around on it."[17]

Trinitarian Persons and John's Gospel   6.8

Ratzinger ties in his reflections on the relational definition of *person* with a study of Jesus' relationship with his Father in the Gospel of John.

The Gospel begins by describing the dynamic unity between the two distinct persons of Father and Word, "In the beginning was the Word, and the Word was with God, and the Word was God" (John 1:1). Later the Gospel explicitly identifies the Word with Jesus, God's Son, "And the Word became flesh, and made his dwelling among us" (John 1:14). Even in his earthly status, however, the Son speaks of his unity with the Father, "Whoever has seen me has seen the Father," (14:9), and "the Father and I are one" (10:30).

Yet many of the statements in the Gospel also seem to give Jesus, the Son, an inferior status to God the Father. Jesus says, "I cannot do anything on my own; I judge as I hear, and my judgment is just, because I do not seek my own will but the will of the one who sent me" (5:30), and, "My teaching is not my own but is from the one who sent me" (7:16).

For Ratzinger, the paradox is explained by the idea of relation. The words *Father* and *Son* reveal the relationship between the two persons: the Father is the source, and the Son comes forth from this source. In theological terms, "It is the Father who generates, the Son who is begotten" (*CCC* no. 254). But these are analogical terms. In human terms, a father must precede his son in time. Within the divine nature—a nature that completely transcends created concepts of time and space (see sec. 3.3.4)—there can be no time (see sec. 4.8.1). So the relationship between Son and Father within the divine unity can only be understood as eternal: the Son, as the Word, has always been coming forth from the source of the Father.

In Trinitarian theology, the Father gives everything he has, his very being, as a free gift to the Son. In this sense, the Son receives everything he has from the Father. This would seem to put the Son in an inferior, subordinate position, but Ratzinger argues that it is not so. By not insisting on his own independence or his rights as an individual, but accepting his entire existence from the Father, the Son is able to accept everything from the Father. Since the Son has (or is) everything that the Father has (or is), then they are in fact equal.

This same paradoxical sense is reflected in many of Jesus' sayings elsewhere, "For whoever wishes to save his life will lose it, but whoever loses his life for my sake and that of the gospel will save it" (Mark 8:35). "Whoever exalts himself will be humbled; but whoever humbles himself will be exalted" (Matt 23:12).

Trinitarian Doctrine and the Bible: Old Testament   6.9

Jefferson criticized the doctrine of the Trinity as unreasonable; others, including some Christian churches, have criticized Trinitarian doctrine for two further reasons: (1) it is not found directly in the Bible, and (2) the doctrine uses philosophical terms (such as *homoousios*) that are also unbiblical.

The Catholic tradition, however, argues that (1) the essential seeds for Trinitarian belief are in the Bible, and the later Trinitarian definitions are a faithful development of those seeds, and (2) the use of clearly defined philosophical terms was necessary in order to protect the biblical ideas from misinterpretation.

By way of analyzing this controversy, let us start with the evidence of the Old Testament. We will find that while the Old Testament certainly does not portray God as a Trinity, it does raise, in a variety of ways, the question of some type of plurality within the divine unity of God.

Unity of the Transcendent God   6.9.1

In the ancient world in which the Hebrews and later the Jews lived, societies worshipped many different gods. By teaching that there was one God alone, Jews of the **Second Temple period** (from the Babylonian Exile in 587 BCE until the destruction of the Jerusalem Temple by the Romans in 70 CE) were considered quite odd. Historically speaking, there is no doubt that monotheistic belief was a gradual development: at first, although the Hebrews worshipped the God of Israel alone (at least in theory), they recognized that other nations also had their own gods. By the time of the prophecies recorded in the second portion of the Book of Isaiah (most likely written during the Babylonian Exile (sixth century BCE), the claim is made that the God of Israel is the only God: "I am the LORD and there is no other, there is no God besides me" (Isa 45:5).

"LORD" in this quotation from Isaiah is the English translation of the divine name in Hebrew: YHWH (sometimes written out fully as Yahweh). YHWH (Lord) is the personal name of the God of Israel, applicable only to this one God alone and not to any other god.

Yet even when the existence of other gods was considered possible, biblical writers insisted on the unity of this one God. A classic statement of the faith of Israel, still recited by Jews today, is the *Shema*, "Hear, O Israel! The LORD is our God, the LORD alone!" [sometimes translated as "the LORD is one"] (Deut 6:4).

Divine Manifestations on Earth   6.9.2

Several Old Testament passages reveal a distinction between God imagined in his own eternal, invisible nature, and God's visible presence on earth. The patriarch Jacob, after wrestling all night with "a man" who refuses to tell Jacob his name, says at the end of this encounter, "I have seen God face to face" (Gen 32:23–31). After speaking with the angel (or "messenger") of the Lord; Sarah's servant Hagar exclaims, "Have I really seen God and remained alive?" (Gen 16:7–13). In Moses' famous encounter at the burning bush, the narrative first reports, "*An angel of the Lord* appeared to him in fire flaming out of a bush," but then as Moses approaches, relates, "When the LORD saw him coming over to look at it more closely, God called out to him from the bush" (Exod 3:2–4, emphasis added).

In a similar fashion, concepts such as the "glory of the Lord" are used to indicate God's presence on earth, yet in a way that is distinct from God in his eternal invisible nature.

> Then Moses said, "Do let me see your glory!" He answered, "I will make all my beauty pass before you, and in your presence I will pronounce my name, 'LORD'; I who show favors to whom I will, I who grant mercy to whom I will. But my face you cannot see, for no man sees me and still lives. Here," continued the LORD, "is a place near me where you shall station yourself on the rock. When my glory passes I will set you in the hollow of the rock and will cover you with my hand until I have passed by." (Exod 33:18–22)

> [After the priests deposited the Ark of the Covenant within the Holy of Holies,] the cloud filled the temple of the LORD so that the priests could no longer minister because of the cloud, since the LORD's glory had filled the temple of the LORD. (1 Kgs 8:9–10)

The ancient Hebrews and Jews believed that God was one (Deut 6:4). But we see in the above passages that the biblical authors were trying to find language to describe God as absolutely separate and beyond human senses and comprehension, and God as he appeared in a form comprehensible to the senses. The texts struggle to express the idea that the visible form is truly God, but at the same time is not God in his own invisible nature, but rather God's presence manifested as an angel, a man, or glory.

We thus see that questions about the divine unity and some kind of distinction within that unity had already arisen in Old Testament times.

Plurality within the Divine Unity?   6.9.3

Similar questions arose in other contexts. When John says that God created the world through the Word (*logos*), he was drawing on an extensive Jewish theological and philosophical background (John 1:1–3; sec. 2.6.2). Proverbs describes God's Wisdom as working alongside him to establish the heavens and fix the foundations of the earth (Prov 8:22–31). The Book of Wisdom describes God's Wisdom in similar terms: "For she is an aura of the might of God . . . the spotless mirror of the power of God. . . . She reaches from end to end mightily and governs all things well" (Wis 7:25–8:1). The first-century Jewish philosopher Philo wrote of how God created the universe by using his divine *logos* as the model and pattern; he could even refer to the *logos* as "a second god" (*Questions and Answers on Genesis* 2.62).

Again we can see the ancient Jewish reflection on a kind of plurality within the divine nature, especially in regard to God's act of creation.

Two Powers in Heaven   6.9.4

Related to this speculation about a power through which God created the world is further ancient Jewish speculation about "two powers" in heaven. Alan Segal has shown that Jewish rabbis were concerned with what they saw as heretical claims about a second divine power in heaven alongside the one God.[18] A text such as Daniel 7 could easily be understood this way, with its reference to "thrones" in heaven, and the great power and authority granted to the "one like a son of man." Another text that aroused this speculation, at least in early Christianity, was Psalm 110:1: "The LORD says to you, my lord: 'Take your throne at my right hand, while I make your enemies your footstool.'"

In its original context, this Psalm spoke of God ("the LORD") giving authority to the Hebrew king ("my lord" as a title of respect, similar to the English title, "sir"). But in Second Temple Jewish and early Christian thought, this reference to a "second Lord" could easily be understood (and was understood by some) as a reference to a second divine power, a "second Lord" who existed beside God.

Divine Intermediaries   6.9.5

Second Temple Judaism also had a lively interest in what we can term "divine intermediary figures." Philo's conception of the *logos* is a good example of such a figure: the *logos* is clearly subordinate to God, but at the same time is in some sense divine ("a second god") and thus "above" the rest of creation: a divine intermediary between heaven and earth. Angels too could fulfill this role.

Second Temple texts also reflect on human beings raised up to a divine status and given some of God's functions. The Book of Daniel (likely written in the decade of the 160s BCE) records Daniel's vision of

> One like a son of man coming, on the clouds of heaven;
> When he reached the Ancient One and was presented
>   before him,
> He received dominion, glory, and kingship;
>   nations and peoples of every language serve him.
> His dominion is an everlasting dominion that shall not be
>   taken away,
>   his kingship shall not be destroyed. (Dan 7:13–14)

"One like a son of man" is a roundabout phrase for a figure who appears to be human. This human has been taken up into God's (the "Ancient One's") presence in heaven and has been given an authority that would seem only applicable to God: "everlasting dominion," a kingship that "shall not be destroyed." Significantly, Daniel's vision began with him seeing "thrones set up and the Ancient one took his throne" (7:9) — the "one like a son of man" is clearly intended to sit enthroned in heaven beside God.

The "one like a son of man" is not identical with God, yet he has been raised up to a divine level of authority in heaven and shares some of God's functions of ruling the universe.

Summary of the Old Testament View   6.9.6

Let us summarize the results of our quick survey of the Old Testament and of Second Temple Jewish beliefs. First, the ancient Jews believe in one God. At the same time, however, many writers refer to some kind of plurality or distinction within the unity of God—a plurality or distinction that does not deny the unity. These distinctions are seen in two ways: (1) a presence of God, visible on earth, that is distinct but not separate from God's eternal, invisible nature, and (2) a distinction within God's own nature, labeled as *Word* or *Wisdom*, through which God creates the universe. In addition, there was speculation about other powers who could be considered divine but who were ultimately subordinate to God, including "one like a son of man" (i.e., one like a human) who had been raised to divine status.

So while Second Temple Judaism clearly does not speak in a Trinitarian fashion of three distinct persons subsisting within the divine unity, it allowed the possibility for the development of such a belief.

Trinitarian Doctrine
and the New Testament   6.10

Second Temple Judaism had developed ways of thinking in which it was possible to accept two sets of related ideas. First, within the divine unity itself there was the possibility of some type of distinction; second, the belief in one God did not rule out a belief in divine intermediary figures who would share some of the divine functions of God.

Christian Worship of Jesus   6.10.1

The first Christians were Jews and thus worshipped the one God alone, the one Creator of the universe. This is the God whom Jesus called "Father" and taught his disciples to call "Father" as well (see, e.g., Matt 6:9). Shortly after Jesus' death, however, his followers, Jewish and non-Jewish, were applying the divine name "Lord" to Jesus and were baptizing and healing people "in his [Jesus'] name." They claimed that Jesus was enthroned at the "right hand of God" in heaven. They expected him to return to judge the living and the dead. They addressed prayers to him, "Come, Lord Jesus" (*Marana tha* in Aramaic, see 1 Cor 16:22; Rev 22:20), or to God through Jesus' name (for example, Rom 1:8). Some writers identified him with God's Word and Wisdom that had existed eternally within the divine unity (John 1:1–14). How did this happen?

What Did Jesus Claim?   6.10.2

Some well-known Christian thinkers have simply assumed that Jesus himself must have claimed to be God, and his followers were persuaded by his claim. C. S. Lewis writes:

> Among these [strictly monotheistic] Jews there suddenly turns up a man who goes about talking as if He was God. He claims to forgive sins. He says He has always existed. He says he is coming to judge the world at the end of time.[19]

Lewis goes on to say that this claim to forgive sins would have raised some questions. If a Jewish man was claiming to forgive sins, not just sins committed against him personally, but sins of all people in general, then he was claiming to be God. But if Jesus was claiming to be God, then we can no longer conclude that Jesus was simply a religious or moral teacher:

> A man who was merely a man and said the sort of things Jesus said would not be a great moral teacher. He would either be a lunatic — on a level with the man who says he is a poached egg — or else he would be the Devil of Hell. You must make your choice. Either this man was, and is, the Son of God: or else a madman or something worse. You can shut Him up for a fool, you can spit at Him and kill Him as a demon; or you can fall at his feet and call Him Lord and God. But let us not come up with any patronizing nonsense about His being a great human teacher. He has not left that open to us. He did not intend to.[20]

Lewis's argument is dramatic and moving, but it is also too simplistic. Lewis simply begs the question of whether Jesus actually did claim to be God, and, if so, in what sense.

Did the historical person Jesus actually make the claims that are recorded in the Gospels, or were these claims perhaps embellished or even invented by the Gospel writers themselves? And what does it mean to say that Jesus claimed to be God? Was he claiming to be identical with God the Father? Or was he claiming to be an intermediary divine figure, such as the "Son of Man" mentioned in Daniel?

We shall address these questions in chapters 10 and 11. For now, however, let us simply say that we cannot assume the answers that Lewis does without further study.

The Earliest Christian View of Jesus   6.10.3

The "Lord" Jesus   6.10.3.1

Ancient Jews believed that God's holy name, YHWH, was so sacred that it should not be pronounced. So in reading the Scriptures aloud, they would not pronounce the name YHWH but instead say "my Lord" (*Adonai* in Hebrew; equivalent to "sir") as a title of respect. The name "Lord" could thus range in meaning from a simple title of respect to a substitute for the divine name.

When the Hebrew Scriptures were translated into Greek by Greek-speaking Jews (a translation known as the Septuagint), they used the Greek word *kyrios* as their translation of YHWH. The word in Greek has a similarly broad range of meaning.

So when Jesus is called *Lord* in the Gospels, it is not always apparent which meaning is intended. When a Gentile woman calls Jesus *Lord* (Mark 7:28), this is most likely simply a title of respect. But when the apostle Paul calls Jesus *Lord*, it's clear that he means far more:

> Indeed, even though there are so-called gods in heaven and on earth (there are, to be sure, many "gods" and many "lords"), yet for us there is one God, the Father, from whom all things are and for whom we exist, and one Lord, Jesus Christ, through whom all things are and through whom we exist. (1 Cor 8:5–6)

When the early Christians confessed that "Jesus is Lord," they did so because they believed that God had given this divine name to Jesus:

> Because of this, God greatly exalted him
> and bestowed on him the name
> that is above every name,
> that at the name of Jesus
> every knee should bend,
> of those in heaven and on earth and under the earth,
> and every tongue confess that
> Jesus Christ is Lord,
> to the glory of God the Father. (Phil 2:9–11)

Seated at the Right Hand of the Father   6.10.3.2

In trying to understand the identity of Jesus, the earliest Christians turned to the Old Testament. Their attention was drawn especially to what we have called the "two powers in heaven" passages (sec. 6.9.5). They focused on Psalm 110:1, "The LORD says to you, my lord: 'Take your throne at my right hand, while I make your enemies your footstool.'"

In early Christian understanding, the passage meant that God the Father had placed the Lord Jesus in a position of equality at his right hand, making him Lord over all other powers in the universe. We see this imagery in many different New Testament writings:

> Then comes the end, when he [Jesus] hands over the kingdom to his God and Father, when he has destroyed every sovereignty and every authority and power. For he must reign until he has put all his enemies under his feet. The last enemy to be destroyed is death. (1 Cor 15:24–26)

> Jesus Christ, who has gone into heaven and is at the right hand of God, with angels, authorities, and powers subject to him. (1 Pet 3:21–22)

> You crowned him with glory and honor, subjecting all things under his feet. (Heb 2:7–8)

> Raising him from the dead and seating him at his right hand in the heavens, far above every principality, authority, power, and dominion, and every name that is named. (Eph 1:20–21)

Related to Jesus' identity as Lord is his role as judge of humans (Matt 25:31–46).

We can draw several conclusions from these passages (and others like them):

1. Jesus is not thought of simply as one of the divine intermediary powers between heaven and earth. Paul clearly says that although there are many "lords," Jesus is the one unique Lord. The other passages show that Jesus is above *every* other power in the universe, whether it be an earthly power or spiritual power.

2. Jesus is given the divine name "Lord."

3. Jesus as Lord is clearly distinct from God the Father.

Clearly the early Christians must have had some concept of possible distinction within the divine unity of God the Father. They claimed that Jesus shared the divine name and authority with God the Father, while still remaining distinct from the Father.

Jesus as God's Word and Wisdom   6.10.3.3

The Gospel of John's statement that "In the beginning was the Word, and the Word was with God, and the Word was God" is perhaps the clearest New Testament expression of the belief in a distinction within the divine unity. The belief that God created through this distinct power was widespread in Second Temple Judaism (6.9.3); Christians were unique only in identifying this distinct power with Jesus.

But the Gospel of John was not alone in identifying Jesus with this distinct creative power of God:

> He is the image of the invisible God, the firstborn of all creation.
> For in him were created all things in heaven and on earth,
> > the visible and the invisible,
> > > whether thrones or dominions or principalities or powers;
> > all things were created through him and for him.
> He is before all things, and in him all things hold together.
> (Col 1:15–17)

> In these last days, he [God] spoke to us through a son, whom he made heir of all things and through whom he created the universe, who is the refulgence of his glory, the very imprint of his being. (Heb 1:2)

All these passages show that the Son is distinct from the Father and far above all the rest of creation. In the Colossians passages, where Jesus is called "firstborn," it is possible that the author believed that God created the Son first and then through him created the rest of creation, although some scholars argue this reference to "firstborn" should be taken as a metaphorical phrase intended to distinguish the Son from the rest of creation.[21] John clearly places the Word within the divine unity; Hebrews seems to do something similar in designating the Son "the very imprint of his [the Father's] being."

The Bible and the Holy Spirit   6.11

When we turn to the biblical evidence concerning God's Spirit, we find a similar dynamic: the Spirit is described in a way distinct, but not separate, from God himself.

In the Old Testament, God's spirit is associated with the gift of prophecy—the gift of receiving and communicating God's messages. We read that "the spirit of God rushed upon" Saul, and he joined a band of prophets (1 Sam 10:10); the Lord took some of his spirit from Moses and gave it to the elders, and they were able to prophesy also (Num 11:25).

The word *spirit* in Hebrew (as in Greek) can also be translated as "wind" or "breath." We read in the creation story that "a mighty wind"—a phrase that can also be translated as "a wind of God" or "the spirit of God"—swept over the waters (Gen 1:2). It is the breath or spirit of God that gives life to humans: "The Lord God formed man out of the clay of the ground and blew into his nostrils the breath of life, and so man became a living being" (Gen 2:7).

In the New Testament, the Spirit is also connected with the "new creation" of God's Son in human form: Mary conceived Jesus not through ordinary human means, but "through the Holy Spirit" (Matt 1:20). The distinction of the Spirit within the unity of God is shown elsewhere in the New Testament as well. Paul writes, "For the Spirit scrutinizes everything, even the depths of God. . . . No one knows what pertains to God except the Spirit of God" (1 Cor 2:10–11).

Just as the spirit was associated with the gift of prophecy in the Old Testament, so the New Testament speaks of the Spirit giving spiritual gifts to the followers of Jesus, including the gifts of prophecy and "speaking in tongues" (1 Cor 12). At the feast of Pentecost, the Holy Spirit comes upon the apostles, the followers of Jesus, giving them the power and confidence to go out into the world and preach their message about Jesus Christ (Acts 2:1–4). The Spirit assists in prayer, "for we do not know how to pray as we ought, but the Spirit itself intercedes with inexpressible groanings" (Rom 8:26). The Spirit is also connected with the written word of God in the Scriptures. The authors of Scripture were inspired by the Holy Spirit: "All scripture is inspired" (2 Tim 3:16). The Greek word for *inspired* translates as the wonderfully expressive "God-breathed" (see sec. 8.2 on scriptural inspiration).

The Spirit is also intimately connected with Christ. In the Gospel of John, the Father will send the Spirit (also called the Comforter, or Advocate) to Jesus' followers after Jesus has returned to the Father. Jesus tells his disciples, "The Advocate, the holy Spirit that the Father will send in my name—he will you teach you everything and remind you of all that I told you" (John 14:26). Just as Jesus comes in the Father's name, so the Spirit comes in Jesus' name.

Paul teaches that the Spirit enables a believer to accept Christ: "No one can say 'Jesus is Lord' except by the Holy Spirit" (1 Cor 12:3).

The Trinity in the New Testament   6.12

Although the New Testament does not use the word *Trinity*, several passages show an intimate relationship between Father, Son, and Spirit that surely foreshadows later Trinitarian doctrine

Notice the intimate connection between Father, Son, and Spirit in Jesus' words to his disciples:

> But when he comes, the Spirit of truth, he will guide you to all truth. He will not speak on his own, but he will speak what he hears, and will declare to you the things that are coming. He will glorify me, because he will take from what is mine and declare it to you. Everything that the Father has is mine; for this reason I told you that he will take from what is mine and declare it to you. (John 16:13–15)

The intimate connection between the workings of Father, Son, and Spirit in Paul's thought is also clear:

> As proof that you are children, God sent the Spirit of his Son into our hearts, crying out, "Abba, Father!" (Gal 4:6)

> You received a spirit of adoption, through which we cry, "Abba, Father!" The Spirit itself bears witness with our spirit that we are children of God, and if children, then heirs, heirs of God and joint-heirs with Christ. (Rom 8:15–17)

> There are different kinds of spiritual gifts but the same Spirit; there are different forms of service but the same Lord; there are different workings but the same God who produces all of them in everyone. (1 Cor 12:4–6)

> The grace of the Lord Jesus Christ and the love of God and the fellowship of the holy Spirit be with all of you. (2 Cor 13:13)

The classic foreshadowing of Trinitarian thought comes at the end of the Gospel of Matthew, when the risen Jesus instructs his disciples to baptize "in the name of the Father, and of the Son, and of the holy Spirit" (Matt 28:19). From the beginning of the Christian movement, baptism was an essential ritual for joining the Christian community; it is significant that the wording accompanying this essential ritual refers to Father, Son, and Spirit.

Orthodox Bishop Kallistos Ware identifies further Trinitarian passages in Scripture.

Irenaeus (c. 130–200) spoke of the Son and the Spirit as the "two hands of God the Father in creation." Irenaeus finds evidence for this image in John 1 (God creating through the Word), the reference to the Spirit (translated as "mighty wind" in some Bibles) in Gen 1:2 (hovering over the waters at creation), and passages such as Psalm 33:6: "By the Lord's word the heavens were made; by the breath [spirit] of his mouth all their host."

The Incarnation—God becoming human—also has a Trinitarian shape: God sends the Holy Spirit upon Mary, and, after her acceptance, she conceives the Son of God in her womb (Luke 1:35).

Finally, the Orthodox tradition sees Jesus' baptism as a revelation of the Trinity. After Jesus was baptized in the Jordan River by John, "the heavens were opened," the Spirit of God descended upon him "like a dove," and the Father declared from heaven, "This is my beloved Son, with whom I am well pleased" (Matt 3:16–17).[22]

Summary of the Biblical Data   6.13

The above survey shows that we have good reason to see a profound unity between the later, more technical and philosophical creedal statements about the Trinity and the biblical evidence. Both the Old Testament and New Testament are familiar with the idea of distinction within the divine unity of God, and a great variety of New Testament passages show a deep sense of the unity of Father, Son, and Spirit, even though this unity is never expressed in precise, technical language.

Development of Doctrine   6.14

The Catholic tradition teaches, then, that the doctrine of the Trinity developed from its scriptural roots into the more precise language of the fourth-century creeds. This concept of "**development of doctrine**" is essential to Christian thought. John Henry Newman provides an influential discussion of the concept in his classic work, *An Essay on the Development of Christian Doctrine* (1845).

Newman argues that it is natural for a complex "idea" to develop over time. Consider an example from the political realm. Most Americans take it for granted that the United States was founded on the "idea" of democracy—the belief that the people have both the natural right and the ability to govern themselves. Yet when the United States was first founded, few people had the right to vote and participate in the democracy. White men who did not own property, African American slaves, Native Americans, and all women were excluded. As the years passed, however, the "idea" of democracy developed to the point where the rights of these excluded groups to participate in the democratic process became clear. The essential idea of democracy remained the same, but it was *developed* to include greater portions of the American population.

A Rocky Road 6.14.1

In tracing the development of the doctrine of the Trinity from New Testament times, Newman does not argue that the belief developed in a smooth and unbroken line. Quite the opposite: Newman, with characteristic boldness and intellectual honesty, points out that many of the great theologians who lived before the Council of Nicaea (325) would have rejected the teaching that God is three divine persons in one nature. Judged by the later, developed Trinitarian doctrine, Ignatius of Antioch (c. 35–c. 107) did not adequately distinguish between the three persons, and Justin (c. 100–c. 165) and Eusebius (c. 260–c. 340) failed to recognize the Son's full equality with the Father.[23]

Newman argues further that sometimes historical circumstances force a vague or embryonic idea to be developed more clearly. This was precisely the case with the doctrine of the Trinity: the Arian controversy (in which Arius's followers denied that the Son was equal to the Father) forced the Church to clarify its understanding of the Trinity.

The Arian Controversy 6.14.2

Arius (d. 336) was an Alexandrian priest whose teaching sparked a complex theological movement known generally as *Arianism*. There were actually distinctive schools of thought among the so-called Arians, but a basic, shared teaching of the movement was that the Son, who was accepted as the Savior and whose death atoned for sins, was nevertheless considered clearly subordinate to God the Father, not just in his human nature, but in his divine nature as well. In Arian thought, God the Father created the Son as his first act of creation and then created the rest of the universe through the Son.

The Arians were able to point to many scriptural texts to support their position. They were especially fond of passages concerning the human Jesus found in the Synoptic Gospels: "But of that day or hour [i.e., the time of the coming of the Son of Man in glory], no one knows, neither the angels in heaven, nor the Son, but only the Father" (Mark 13:32), or Jesus' answer to the rich man, "Why do you call me good? No one is good but God alone" (Mark 10:18). From John they favored John 14:28, "The Father is greater than I."

But the Arians also argued that the Son was subordinate to the Father not only when he was incarnate as a human, but also before his Incarnation ("The LORD begot me, the first-born of his ways," Prov 8:22) and after his Incarnation ("When everything is subjected to him, then the Son himself will also be subjected to the one who subjected everything to him, so that God may be all in all," 1 Cor 15:28).

Orthodox opponents of the Arians responded with their own proof-texts. The great Arian opponent Athanasius (c. 296–373) cited passages showing that the Son and the Father shared the same "being," including Hebrews 1:3: the Son "is the refulgence of his [God's] glory, the very imprint of his being." Athanasius was especially fond of Jesus' words in the Gospel of John, "The Father and I are one" (10:30), and, "Whoever has seen me has seen the Father" (14:9).

Note that Scripture alone could not resolve the issue—both sides had scriptural support.

The Significance of the Arian Controversy   6.14.2.1

For the early Christians, the debate over the Son's equality with the Father was not an abstract philosophical question. On the contrary, it involved basic issues of how God was understood and how humans could attain salvation. Arius had taught that although the Son was less than the Father, he was still the Savior who saves humanity from their sins. Athanasius replied that since only God could save people from their sins, if the Son was not truly God, then Christians are not truly saved. "For if the Lord had not become man, we have not been redeemed from sins" (*Discourses against the Arians* 1.43).

Answering the Arians: Linguistic Precision 6.14.2.2

Scripture alone, then, could not settle the Arian controversy: both sides could "prove" their position from Scripture.

Part of the problem was that the scriptural terms used in the debate (such as *Father* and *Son*) were too ambiguous. The Arians exploited this ambiguity, insisting that it is only logical that a Father must exist prior to his Son. The orthodox countered that the Arians were taking the analogy too literally.

Thus when Christian bishops drew up the Creed at the Council of Nicaea in 325 in an attempt to settle the Arian controversy, wishing to avoid ambiguity, they felt compelled to go beyond scripturally based language.

The first step was to define the Son's relationship with the Father with a philosophically precise term. They settled on *homoousious*, which is usually translated in English as "one in being." (The prefix *homo* means "the same," while the root word *ousia* means "being.")

Answering the Arians: Trinitarian Analogies 6.14.2.3

In addition to using precise philosophical language, the Nicene Creed also employed analogy to clarify the relationship between Father and Son.

In the phrase "light from light," God the Father, the ultimate source of all things, is compared to the sun. The Son is compared to the rays of light streaming forth from the sun. The rays of sunlight are distinct from the sun itself, but at the same time, they are the very essence of the sun: they are sunlight. The analogy shows how something can be both unified with, yet distinct from, something else.

The analogy also addresses well the issue of time. As soon as the sun came into existence, rays of sunlight began to stream forth from it. There was no interval of time, not even a fraction of a second, between the beginning of the sun and the first rays of sunlight. In the same way, there is absolutely no interval of time in between the existence of the Father and the existence of the Son. Both are eternal; from all eternity, the Son has been streaming forth from the source of the Father. ○

Ousia, a term common in Greek philosophy, means the essence of a certain thing: that which makes a thing what it is and not something else. We have already seen how this process of philosophical clarification continued in later years, until the point where the Christian tradition defined the Trinity as three persons in one divine nature.

Aquinas acknowledged that some words used in the Church's official declarations are not biblical, but insisted that "the urgency of confuting heretics made it necessary to find new words to express the ancient faith about God" (*ST* 1.29.3 ad. 1).

Modern Issues in Trinitarian Thought   6.15

The Immanent and the Economic Trinity   6.15.1

In the Old Testament (see sec. 6.9.2), we recognized a distinction between describing God's presence in the world ("God's glory" or "God's angel") and God's transcendent presence. In the Orthodox tradition, a similar distinction is made between God's essence (God in his own nature, unknowable to humans) and God's energies (God's activities in the world; see sec. 5.8.3).

The Catholic tradition also distinguishes between what it calls the *economic Trinity* and the *immanent Trinity*.[24] The word *economic* in this case has nothing to do with buying or selling; it is rather a theological word that refers to how God deals with the world, in particular God's plan for salvation. God's plan for helping humans become liberated from limitations and evil and become united to God. The economic Trinity, then, is the persons of the Trinity in their relation to humans, especially as we see this relationship recorded in Scripture.

To consider the immanent Trinity, in contrast, is to consider how the three persons of God relate to one another within the divine nature itself, without reference to humans.

At this point we may reasonably ask how we could ever know anything about the immanent Trinity. Isn't it all pure speculation, beyond us as humans? If we accept that God can reveal himself, shouldn't we just accept what we know of God from the economic revelation and not speculate about what God is in his own hidden nature? Doesn't the Christian tradition itself tell us that we cannot know God in his essential nature (see sec. 5.8.3)?

Karl Rahner makes a bold proposal regarding this point; he insists that "the 'economic' Trinity is the 'immanent' Trinity and the 'immanent' Trinity is the 'economic' Trinity."[25] For Rahner, it is fundamental that what is revealed in the relationship of the Father, the Son, and the Holy Spirit to humans also reveals the truth about how the Father, the Son, and the Holy Spirit relate to one another within the mystery of God.

Rahner, of course, knows the general Christian teaching that we can know God only by analogy with his creation. His point here, though, is that we can have not merely knowledge about God in general, but can gain specific insights into God's Trinitarian mystery within the divine reality by observing how the divine persons function in the world.

Economic Trinity: The Father Sending Son and Spirit 6.15.2

Revelation shows us an economic Trinity of God the Father sending his Son (the Word) and Spirit into the world. Consider the following passages.

God the Father sent forth his Son:

> And the Word became flesh, and made his dwelling among us. (John 1:14)

> God did not send his Son into the world to condemn the world. (John 3:17)

> But when the fullness of time had come, God sent his Son, born of a woman, born under the law. (Gal 4:4)

In the same way, God the Father sent the Spirit:

> When you send forth your breath [spirit], they are created, and you renew the face of the earth. (Ps 104:30)

> Then afterward I will pour out my spirit upon all mankind. (Joel 3:1; see also Acts 2:17)

> The Advocate, the holy Spirit that the Father will send in my name. . . . (John 14:26)

> God sent the spirit of his Son into our hearts, crying out, "Abba, Father!" (Gal 4:6)

Jesus' words to his disciples in the Gospel of John also speak of the Son sending the Spirit (from the Father):

> When the Advocate comes whom I will send you from the Father, the Spirit of truth that proceeds from the Father, . . . (John 15:26)

For if I do not go, the Advocate will not come to you. But if I go, I will send him to you. (John 16:7)

And when he had said this, he breathed on them and said to them, "Receive the holy Spirit." (John 20:22)

Immanent Trinity: The Father Sending Son and Spirit   6.15.3

The Father's "sending" activity, revealed in the economic Trinity, must reflect an analogous activity within the immanent Trinity, according to Rahner's principle. The traditional language of the creeds does in fact reflect these two "sendings": "It is the Father who generates, the Son who is begotten, and the Holy Spirit who proceeds" (*CCC* no. 254). The Father is understood as the origin, the source, the beginning point of all reality. The Son is "eternally begotten from the Father" (as the Nicene Creed expresses it); the Spirit then flows forth "from the Father and the Son." The Trinitarian image of God is dynamic, full of movement.

Before going further, we should note a controversial point regarding the "sending" of the Spirit within the Trinity. The Nicene Creed as read in Western churches today states that the Spirit "proceeds from the Father and the Son." This is not the original wording of the Creed. "And the Son" (*filioque* in Latin) was added later by Western churches; the addition was not accepted by Eastern Orthodox churches.[26] The *filioque* controversy was one contributing factor leading to the split between the Eastern and Western churches in 1054. Though still controversial, the issue is not so divisive today, as a result of **ecumenical dialogues**.[27]

The two "sendings" within the divine nature reveal that God's nature is not inwardly directed, divinity contemplating itself. On the contrary, it is directed outward, in a movement of love, reaching out to another outside itself.

A key conclusion from Rahner's thesis of the identity of the economic Trinity and the immanent Trinity is that in meeting the Son and the Spirit in the world, humans truly meet God. God has not sent out a messenger, or an intermediary, but rather *communicates himself,* gives himself, to humanity. "God relates to us in a threefold manner, and this threefold, free, and gratuitous relation to us is not merely a copy or an analogy of the inner Trinity, but this Trinity itself, albeit as freely and gratuitously communicated."[28] Although our language about God is always limited and analogous, according to this teaching we actually do encounter the true God in Jesus and in the Spirit.

Trinity and Creation 6.16

This outward movement of the Trinity is closely tied with the doctrine of creation. In Christian teaching, it is precisely this outward movement of the Son and the Spirit that results in the creation and sustaining of the universe. As we noted above, ancient Christian writers such as Irenaeus picture the Son and the Spirit as God's "two hands" in his act of creation (sec. 6.12).

The creation of the universe is another act of love. Sometimes people suggest that God created the universe and life within it because he was lonely. But this is not the Christian view. Within the Trinity itself, the relationships of love are perfect and complete—God had no need to make anything else. But God chose freely to (in a sense) overflow himself, creating other beings out of nothing for the sheer joy of sharing his love. Aquinas writes, "Creatures came into existence when the key of love opened his hand."[29]

In Lewis's view,

> We begin at the real beginning, with love as the Divine energy. This primal love is Gift-love. In God there is no hunger that needs to be filled, only plenteousness that desires to give. . . . God, who needs nothing, loves into existence wholly superfluous creatures in order that He may love and perfect them.[30]

So Christians say that the deepest, most profound roots of reality are a relationship of love; the ultimate nature of reality is love.

This Trinitarian worldview thus contradicts the materialist or atheist view that sees the universe as based simply on chance events of cause and effect. The Christian alternative is to imagine the universe as arising from a meaningful, intelligent relationship of love.

Moreover, the Christian view contradicts what many would see as a more "realistic" view of the world. Our world, in fact, is full of things that are opposed to love: corruption, greed, violence, sexual exploitation. In thinking about all these negative and destructive motivations and events, it is easy for a person to become depressed. But in the end, no matter how violent, oppressive, or dark the world becomes, Christianity teaches that love will win out, because love is the force that created all things in the first place.

This profound insight into ultimate reality is expressed at the end of Dante's *Divine Comedy* (canto 33) when the poet speaks of the "love which turns the sun and the other stars."

Limitations of Language   6.17

In the end, language about God, even the more philosophically sophisticated language of the fourth-century creeds, can only be limited and analogical. Thus Ratzinger writes that unity and "threeness" are the essential points of the Trinity. The use of the terms *substance* and *person* are not necessarily the only terms adequate to describe these concepts.[31]

In fact, Rahner has questioned the continued usefulness of the term *person* in describing the Trinity today. The problem is the vast majority of Christians do not understand *person* as a precise theological term describing the relationships within the divine unity. On the contrary, a common modern understanding is that *person* means an independent, self-sufficient center of consciousness. If one applied this common understanding to the Trinity, the result would be a belief in three Gods.[32] Instead of *person*, then, Rahner tentatively suggests the phrase "distinct manner of subsisting."[33] Catherine LaCugna, however, rightly points out that such phrases would make no sense to nonspecialists and would be unsuitable for preaching. The traditional term *person*, if accepted properly as an analogy, still has the advantage of implying that Father, Son, and Holy Spirit are more appropriately compared to human persons capable of relationships with others than with impersonal powers or functions.[34]

LaCugna also discusses the critiques by feminist theologians such as Mary Daly and Rosemary Radford Ruether, who assert that the traditional wording, "Father, Son, and Spirit," is too patriarchal. She notes that in some worship services, one hears "Creator, Redeemer, Sustainer" as a more inclusive description of the Trinity. For LaCugna, however, the problem in describing the Trinity in this way is that it focuses exclusively on the *function* of each person within the world. It thus risks breaking the connection between the economic Trinity (how the Trinity functions in the world) and the immanent Trinity. If this is done, as Rahner notes, then we can lose our assurance that we are meeting the true God in Jesus and in the Spirit. We might also add that the focus on function tends to make the Trinity less personal.

LaCugna notes further that the traditional image of Trinity as a community of persons is in fact an image more compatible with feminist values of community and shared responsibilities than the Unitarian model of God that some feminists have called for.

LaCugna ends her reflections by calling for a use of both masculine and feminine images for the Trinity, together with a constant awareness of the limitations of each. She notes that the Christian tradition already has feminine Trinitarian images; she refers to the Eleventh Council of Toledo (675), which used the phrase "from the womb of the Father" as a synonym for "the substance of the Father."[35] We may also recall Aphrahat's reference to the Holy Spirit as mother (see sec. 5.8.5).

Summary   6.18

The traditional doctrine of the Trinity is criticized from many directions today. Thinkers in the rationalist tradition of Jefferson argue that it is irrational; some Christian churches criticize it as unbiblical and a corruption of the simple gospel. Many Jews and Muslims see it as compromising or confusing the essential teaching that God is one. Even for the many Christians who accept the teaching, the belief seems to make little practical difference.

And yet the concept of Trinity remains central to the Christian tradition. Christians baptize in the name of the Father, Son, and Holy Spirit. Traditional Christians begin each prayer with the sign of the cross, in the name of Father, Son, and Holy Spirit. The Orthodox worship service is profoundly Trinitarian, as are many of the prayers in the Roman Catholic Mass.[36]

Trinitarian belief is not a set of contradictory statements about how three really equals one. The doctrine answers a religious and philosophical puzzle with which every culture and religion has struggled: our profound sense that reality depends ultimately on a single, unified source seems to be contradicted by the fact that we experience reality as pluralistic and fragmented. The Trinitarian insight is that the ultimate source of reality is a dynamic unity that includes within itself a kind of plurality.

The central Trinitarian insight—that ultimate reality is not a single, static unity, but is a dynamic unity of relationships—has been confirmed in surprising ways by the insights of modern quantum physics and relativity theory. Far from being an outdated medieval relic, the Trinitarian doctrine that God is a *relationship* of persons anticipated the insights of Einstein that reality can only be described in terms of *relationships* between space, time, and forces.

The doctrine of the Trinity explains to us that ultimate reality is based on relationships of love. For this reason, the universe, and human life as its highest creation, has a meaning: it was called out of nothingness in order to share in the divine relationship of love.

Questions about the Text

1. What are the three essential points in the Christian doctrine of the Trinity?

2. What are some common objections to the doctrine of the Trinity?

3. What is the philosophical and theological problem of the relationship between the unity and plurality of the universe? How is the doctrine of the Trinity an answer to this "problem"?

4. At the human level, how is a "person" distinct from a single individual? Why does the Christian tradition apply this word to the relationships in the Trinity?

5. How does a Trinitarian view of reality resemble the view of reality in modern physics?

6. What are some Old Testament passages that distinguish between the transcendent God and God's manifestations on earth?

7. What are some Old Testament examples of possible distinctions within the divine unity?

8. What is meant by the phrase "divine intermediary figure"?

9. What evidence from the New Testament indicates that early Christians considered Jesus to be divine?

10. How would you summarize the evidence for the role of the Spirit in the Bible?

11. How does Newman understand "development of doctrine"?

12. What were the basic issues in the Arian controversy? How did the controversy lead to a development of Trinitarian doctrine?

13. What is the difference between the "economic" and the "immanent" Trinity? Why does Rahner insist that they are the same?

14. What is the relationship between the Father "sending" the Son and the Spirit in the immanent and in the economic Trinity?

15. What is the relationship between the Father's "sending" of the Son and Spirit and the doctrine of creation? Consider especially the Christian understanding of the role of love within the Trinity and in the act of creation.

16. What are the basic issues regarding whether the term *person* is appropriate for describing the relationships within the Trinity?

17. What are the basic issues regarding whether the male-centered description of the Trinity as Father, Son, and Spirit should be replaced with gender-neutral terms, such as Creator, Redeemer, and Sanctifier?

Discussion Questions

1. Can you think of references to the Trinity in art, literature, or Christian worship? Elaborate.

2. Do you agree that human beings have a basic desire to understand or experience the unity of all reality? Why or why not?

3. Which of the objections to the doctrine of the Trinity seems most important or persuasive to you? Why?

4. Can you think of examples of the "development of doctrine" or development of basic ideas in your own field of study or in another field in which you are interested?

5. Are you persuaded that there are significant connections between the Trinitarian worldview and the worldview of modern physics? Why or why not?

Endnotes

1. Quoted in Stephen Prothero, *American Jesus: How the Son of God Became a National Icon* (New York: Farrar, Straus, and Giroux, 2003), 22.
2. The "Nicene Creed" that is still recited in many Christian churches today is actually a combination of the creeds written at the Council of Nicaea (325) and the Council of Constantinople (381). So technically, it should be called the *Niceno-Constantinopolitan Creed*, although most churches understandably use the short form.
3. *Chandogya Upanishad*, quoted in Mary Pat Fisher and John Kelsay, *Living Religions*, 6th ed. (Upper Saddle River, NJ: Prentice-Hall, 2005), 75.
4. Plotinus, *Enneads* 5.2.1, in *Plotinus*, trans. A. H. Armstrong (Cambridge, MA: Harvard University Press; London: Heinemann, 1984), 5:59.
5. Quoted in Fisher, *Living Religions*, 181.
6. Frederick Copleston, *A History of Philosophy*, vol. 1, *Greece and Rome* (Garden City, NY: Image Books, 1962), 38–44.
7. Albert Einstein, *Ideas and Opinions* (New York: Bonanza Books, 1954), 38.
8. *Ennead* 5.2.1
9. Fischer, *Living Religions*, 75.
10. Peter Kreeft, *A Summa of the Summa: The Essential Philosophical Passages of Saint Thomas Aquinas'* Summa Theologica (San Francisco: Ignatius Press, 1990), 112 no. 75.

11. Joseph Ratzinger, *Introduction to Christianity* (San Francisco: Ignatius Press, 2000; orig. pub. 1968), 179.

12. Thomas Torrance, *The Christian Frame of Mind: Reason, Order, and Openness in Theology and Natural Science* (Colorado Springs: Helmers & Howard, 1989), 150.

13. Ratzinger, *Introduction to Christianity*, 180.

14. Torrance, *Christian Frame of Mind*, 150; Ratzinger, *Introduction to Christianity*, 160, 182.

15. Quoted in Ratzinger, *Introduction to Christianity*, 183.

16. Torrance, *Christian Frame of Mind*, xxvi–xxxi, 150–53.

17. Stephen Barr, *Modern Physics and Ancient Faith* (Notre Dame: University of Notre Dame Press, 2003), 39.

18. Alan Segal, *Two Powers in Heaven: Early Rabbinic Reports about Christianity and Gnosticism* (SJLA 25; Leiden: Brill, 1977).

19. C. S. Lewis, *Mere Christianity* (New York: HarperCollins, 2001; orig. pub. 1952), 51.

20. Ibid., 52.

21. See Eduard Lohse, *Colossians and Philemon* (Hermeneia; Philadelphia: Fortress, 1971), 48–49.

22. Kallistos Ware, *The Orthodox Way*, rev. ed. (Crestwood, NY: St. Vladimir's Seminary Press, 1999), 35–36.

23. John Henry Newman, *An Essay on the Development of Christian Doctrine* (Westminster, MD: Christian Classics, 1968), 15–17.

24. See Catherine Mowry LaCugna, "The Trinitarian Mystery of God," in *Systematic Theology: Roman Catholic Perspectives*, eds. F. S. Fiorenza and J. P. Galvin (Minneapolis: Fortress, 1991), 174–76.

25. Karl Rahner, *The Trinity* (New York: Seabury, 1974), 22. Emphasis original.

26. For a brief sketch of the controversy, see Lacugna, "Trinitarian Mystery," 184–86.

27. A 2003 statement issued by the North American Orthodox–Catholic Theological Consultation includes the following recommendations: (1) that theologians become more aware of their limitations in making definitive statements about the inner life of the Trinity; (2) that the churches not label as heretical understandings of the procession of the Spirit that differ from their own; (3) that the Catholic Church because of the undisputed authority of the 381 creed of Constantinople should "use the original Greek text alone [a version not containing the "and the Son" addition] in making translations of that Creed for catechetical and liturgical use." See "The *Filioque*: A Church Dividing Issue? An Agreed Statement of the North American Orthodox and Catholic Theological Consultation" (October 25, 2003). Accessed September 23, 2008, at *http://www.usccb.org/seia/filioque.shtml*.

28. Rahner, *Trinity*, 35.

29. Quoted in *CCC* no. 293.

30. C. S. Lewis, *The Four Loves* (New York: Harcourt, Brace, 1960), 175–76.

31. Ratzinger, *Introduction to Christianity*, 180–81.

32. Rahner, *Trinity*, 42–45, 56–57, 103–13.

33. Ibid., 109–15.

34. LaCugna, "Trinitarian Mystery," 179.

35. Ibid., 180–84.

36. See Ware, *Orthodox Way*, 36–38; LaCugna, "Trinitarian Mystery," 187.

7

Human Nature and Human Destiny

Christian Anthropology

Anthropology is generally defined as the science of human beings that deals with their origin, behavior, beliefs, and their physical, social, and cultural development. A branch called philosophical anthropology studies human beings at another level: their nature and essence, purpose and meaning, and their status in the universe. This chapter focuses on philosophical anthropology; specifically, we examine the traditional Christian view of human nature, in other words, Christian anthropology.

In modern Western culture, we commonly refer to the human person as composed of "mind, body, and spirit." A heath-care professional who favors a holistic view of health, for example, might speak of integrating these three elements in a complete health plan.

But there is no universal agreement on just what these three terms mean. A materialist might ask, "What do you mean by *mind*? Isn't that just neurons firing in the brain?"

BACKGROUND IMAGES ROYALTY FREE FROM ISTOCK AND SHUTTERSTOCK

A rationalist might challenge, "What do you mean by *spirit*? Can you measure spirit? Is there any proof that spirit actually exists?" A worldview closed to the transcendent might conclude that the only reality is "body," the physical component of the human.

In this chapter we will begin with a quick overview of Christian anthropology. We will then turn to a more detailed consideration of some elements of the Christian view, including a response to some critical challenges to Christian beliefs. We will find that Christian ideas about human nature are closely tied to Christian views on the ultimate destiny of human beings—specifically, what happens to people after death and at the end of history. In the Christian worldview, this earthly life and the afterlife are inseparably connected.

Brief Sketch of Christian Anthropology 7.2

Christians believe that God created humans as the summit and crown of all creation. Only humans are created in the image of God, and only humans are given authority to rule and exercise stewardship over the rest of creation (Gen 1:26–27). Furthermore, humans—alone out of all creation—are both spiritual and physical, having both a physical body and an eternal soul.

In the symbolic language of the first chapters of Genesis, human life is portrayed ideally: originally, humans lived a life of meaningful work and of harmony with nature, with each other, and with God. In the Christian understanding, this ideal life of peace, harmony, and health is God's intention for all humans—the reason that God created the universe.

Chapter three of Genesis, however, narrates what the Christian tradition interprets as humanity's "**Fall**." Humans, through a misuse of free will, turned away from God (an action Christians call "sin"). The Christian tradition speaks of a **fallen human nature**—one that, although it is still in the image of God, is also prone to selfishness, deceit, and violence. Far from the original state of harmony, humans must now struggle with harsh realities of suffering, sickness, and death.

Nevertheless, in the Christian view, God did not abandon fallen humanity. God continued to communicate with humans through natural and historical revelation, inviting humans to return to him and the original life of harmony and fulfillment. The ultimate act of God's efforts to recall fallen humanity was the **Incarnation**, when God's Word took on human form, reconciling the divine and the human in Jesus. Because of this action, all humans now have the opportunity for what Christians call "salvation": the overcoming of sin, sickness, suffering, and even death in a return to that lost, original harmony with God.

Christian anthropology understands this salvation as holistic: it begins already in this life and is completed in a transcendent unity with God; it involves the healing and renewal not only of the "spirit," but the resurrection and transformation of the body as well.

We now consider some details of the Christian view, beginning with the scriptural sources.

Scriptural Anthropology: Old Testament   7.3

Within the Christian Scriptures, we have two basic worldviews and thus two distinctive anthropologies: the Semitic (found largely in the Old Testament) and the **Hellenistic** (influencing some later Old Testament and all the New Testament books). Semitic anthropology tends to be more holistic, as the ancient Hebrews did not make a sharp distinction between the physical and spiritual, between body and soul.

Consider a quotation from Psalms: "O God, you are my God—for you I long! For you my body (Hebrew: *basar*) yearns; for you my soul (Hebrew: *nephesh*) thirsts" (Ps 63:2). In this passage, it is clear that the two words *basar* and *nephesh* both refer to the same person, but seen from two distinct points of view.

Basar is often translated as "flesh." It refers to the whole human person, but the person looked at from the perspective of essential human fragility. The prophet Isaiah says, "All mankind (*basar*) is grass, and all their glory like the flower of the field. The grass withers, the flower wilts" (Isa 40:6–7).

The basic verbal meaning of the Hebrew word *nephesh* is "to breathe." For the ancient Hebrews, breath is what distinguished a living body from a dead body, and so one basic sense of *nephesh* is the "life-force" that causes a body to live. Thus "the Lord God formed man out of the clay of the ground and blew into his nostrils the breath of life, and so man became a living being (*nephesh*)" (Gen 2:7). As does *basar*, *nephesh* refers to human life as a whole (including what moderns would call body and spirit), but focuses on the "aliveness" of the person. The *nephesh* cannot exist apart from the body; an individual who has died and is in *Sheol* (the realm of the dead) is never called a *nephesh*.

Scriptural Anthropology: New Testament 7.4

The clear distinction in Christian thought between physical and spiritual reality results from the influence of Greek anthropology. According to Plato, the soul (Greek: *psyche*) is clearly distinct from the body: it is an immortal, invisible force that governs the physical body. For Aristotle, in contrast, body and soul, although distinct, are essentially united: the soul is the "form" of the body, the principle of its life. Aquinas (and with him mainstream Catholic thought) follows Aristotle in seeing body and soul as essentially united; Aquinas also defines the soul as the form of the body.

Christianity sometimes describes humans as formed of body and spirit (Greek: *pneuma*); other times, a tripartite division is made, as in Paul's Letter to the Thessalonians: "May you entirely, spirit, soul, and body, be preserved blameless for the coming of our Lord Jesus Christ" (1 Thess 5:23). The *Catechism* does not make a sharp distinction between spirit and soul (*CCC* no. 367). The Orthodox tradition, however, does at times make a clear distinction: "soul" is essentially the life-force (Aristotle taught that even plants and animals have lower-order souls) within living things, but spirit is a unique gift that pertains to humans alone. Through the spirit (also known as the "spiritual intellect" or *nous* in Greek), humans can understand eternal truths about God and his creation in a supernatural way, through an intuitive "spiritual perception."[1]

In New Testament thought, the "spirit" of a person is distinct from God's "Holy Spirit," although there is a clear connection between the two. Paul at times refers to a person's spirit as a supernatural gift given to one who has become a follower of Christ: "But you are not in the flesh; on the contrary, you are in the spirit, if only the Spirit of God dwells in you" (Rom 8:9). Elsewhere Paul contrasts the "spiritual" (*pneumatikos*) person and the "natural" (*psychichos*) person (1 Cor 2:14–15): only the spiritual person can understand the things that pertain to God's Spirit.

The New Testament thus makes a clear distinction between the "natural" (*psychichos*) human life and the "life in Christ," a spiritual (*pneumatikos*) life that a person receives after conversion to Christ and baptism. Paul contrasts the two kinds of life in this way: "We know that our old self was crucified with him, so that our sinful body might be done away with, that we might no longer be in slavery to sin" (Rom 6:6). "So whoever is in Christ is a new creation: the old things have passed away; behold, new things have come" (2 Cor 5:17).

In "natural" human life there is indeed much beauty, goodness, creativity, and love, but there is also suffering, deceit, weakness, violence, and death. One way of understanding the Christian concept of salvation is to see it as a process in which a person moves from this natural life, with all of its limitations, to the life of the "new creation." In the Orthodox tradition, the process is called divinization or deification.[2] In the words of the New Testament, humans are destined to "share in the divine nature" (2 Pet 1:4).

At times Christian description of this process seems to imply a conflict between the "spiritual" world and the "natural" world. But it is better understood as a purification of the natural world, a lifting up of the entire human, both spirit and body, to a higher level of existence.

Does Christianity Despise the Body? 7.5

The German philosopher Friedrich Nietzsche (1844–1900) exemplifies the misunderstanding of Christianity as "anti-body." In a typical passage from his *Thus Spoke Zarathustra*, Nietzsche mocks Christians as "hair-shirted despisers of the body."[3]

It is undeniable that, historically, some strands of the Christian tradition (e.g., the Puritans) have viewed the physical body negatively, seeing it largely as a source of temptation to sin. But in fact Scripture and mainstream Christian thought celebrate and glorify the human body as good.

Genesis tells us that God found the physical creation to be good, and the human body is part of that good creation. The Old Testament Song of Songs is an unabashed love song, in which two lovers celebrate physical beauty and the pleasures of physical love: "Let him kiss me with kisses of his mouth! More delightful is your love than wine!" (Song 1:2); "Your lips are like a scarlet strand; your mouth is lovely. . . . Your breasts are like twin fawns. . . . You are all-beautiful, my beloved" (Song 4:3–7).

Paul reminds the Corinthians, "Your body is a temple of the holy Spirit . . . Therefore, glorify God in your body" (1 Cor 6:19–20). The Vatican II Council teaches explicitly that "man may not despise his bodily life. Rather he is obliged to regard his body as good and to hold it in honor since God has created it and will raise it up on the last day" (*GS* no. 14).

Other religions and philosophies of the ancient Mediterranean world in which Christianity developed did have a fundamentally negative view of the body. Platonist philosophy, for example, tended to denigrate the value of the body, regarding it as part of the fleeting, changing, material world, and therefore far less "real" and valuable than the eternal world of unchanging "ideas." The body, too, is the realm of unpredictable and irrational emotions, in contrast to the stable, rational mind. Several of Plato's dialogues use a phrase built on a Greek wordplay: the body (*soma*) is the tomb (*sema*) of the soul (*Gorgias* 493A; see also *Phaedo* 66B; *Cratylus* 400C).

Ancient **Gnostic** thought takes an even more negative attitude toward the body. Gnosticism was a widespread religious and philosophical movement that combined elements of Christian, Jewish, Greek, and other strands of thought. The Gnostic view is dualistic, distinguishing sharply between the good spiritual realm and the evil material world. In Gnostic mythology the physical world in which we live is the creation of a lesser god. Souls from the spiritual realm have fallen into the evil material world and become trapped in physical bodies. Salvation means the release of the spirit from the prison of the body so that it can return again to the heavenly realms.[4]

Gnostic and Platonist ideas about the body influenced some Christian writers. The great theologian Origen (c. 185–c. 254), for example, taught that souls pre-existed in the heavenly realms and had been sent to earth in bodies as punishment for sins (*On First Principles* 1.8). This view, however, does not represent the Christian mainstream. Let's consider some further evidence.

Christian Respect for the Body   7.6

Essential Unity of Body and Soul   7.6.1

According to Pope John Paul II, the Christian doctrine that the body will be raised from the dead influenced Aquinas to abandon more Platonist ways of thinking and adopt Aristotle's view that body and soul cannot be separated; they belong together essentially "To be united to the body belongs to the soul by reason of itself" (*ST* 76.1.1).[5]

In the words of the *Catechism*:

> The unity of the soul and body is so profound that one has to consider the soul to be the "form" of the body: i.e., it is because of its spiritual soul that the body made of matter becomes a living, human body; spirit and matter, in man, are not two natures united, but rather their union forms a single nature. (*CCC* no. 365)

Christian Respect for the Body: The Incarnation   7.6.2

Christian respect for the body is best illustrated in the doctrine of the Incarnation. According to this teaching, God himself, in the second person of the Trinity, took on a human body. This doctrine that the eternal *logos* of the universe could take on a limited human body was so contrary to common ways of thinking about the divine that it took centuries to bring out the teaching in its full clarity (see sec. 10.1.5 for discussion of the fourth-century Christian councils that drew out the implications of this belief).

How is it possible that the eternal, unlimited First Cause of the universe could be confined to a mere human body? The Christian tradition has struggled to find language to express this concept accurately. One branch of thought, known as **Docetism** (closely allied with Gnostic thought), claimed that the spiritual Christ did not take on a *truly* human body; he only "appeared" (Greek: *dokeo*) to have one. For Docetists it was impossible that the spiritual Christ could have a true connection with the fallen material world.

The orthodox Christian tradition, however, insists that Christ did take on a *true* human body with all of the limitations of that body, while at the same time remaining truly divine: Christ was true God and true man. The doctrine of the Incarnation, therefore, implies the highest possible respect for the body. The human body is both capable and worthy of being united in a real way to the absolutely perfect and transcendent source of all things: God.

Respect for Physical Reality   7.6.3

John Henry Newman taught that the Incarnation is the central "idea" of Christianity.[6] The Incarnation demonstrates the Christian conviction that the physical and the spiritual are not opposites, but rather work together to form an essential unity. The spiritual God created the physical universe and continues to reveal himself through that physical universe. From this central idea flows also the basic Catholic principle concerning the **sacraments**: God gives spiritual benefits to humans through physical means (the water of baptism, the bread and wine of the Lord's Supper, the oil of the Anointing of the Sick). Pope John Paul II's "Theology of the Body," in which the pope interprets our physical sexual nature as a sign that humans were meant to be in communion and community with one another, sharing not only words and ideas but intimately sharing our physical selves as well, is only a natural development of the long tradition of Christian respect for the body.[7]

Destiny of the Body: The Resurrection   7.7

Many people today, including many Christians, hold a rather Platonic view of life after death. They assume that the material body is left behind to decay and only our souls or spirits "move on" to the next world.

Such a view, however, is actually not Christian. The Christian tradition has always insisted that our bodies, after dying and decaying, will rise again at the end of time. As the Apostles' Creed, the ancient summary statement of Christian belief, says simply, "I believe in the resurrection of the body."

But is this a reasonable belief? It is a fact that living bodies decay and disintegrate after death, and we have no scientific proof of a dead body ever coming back to life again. It seems we have here a clear contradiction between faith and reason.

Is Resurrection Reasonable?   7.7.1

First, let us consider carefully what the Christian claim is. Christians, including Christians in New Testament times, know that in nature dead bodies stay dead. If such an event as the resurrection of a dead body has ever occurred, it could only be as the result of an intervention in nature by a power outside of nature, a supernatural power. So the more fundamental question is: Is it reasonable to think that a supernatural power could intervene in nature?

We have argued already that such a view is reasonable (sec. 5.15). We have considered multiple reasons for thinking the existence of a transcendent power outside the universe is a reasonable possibility (sec.s 1.4 – 7; 3.3.3), and we have considered evidence that this transcendent power is most reasonably understood as a personal God (see sec.s 5.7.1–2).

The Christian claim is that God intervened in nature to raise Jesus from the dead: "God raised him [Jesus] from the dead; of this we are witnesses" (Acts 3:15).

Christians do not consider God's supernatural interventions in nature to be arbitrary. Rather, Christians believe that such miraculous events are fundamentally in harmony with the natural laws, since God is the ultimate source of *both* natural laws and miracles (sec. 5.17). As Aquinas taught, "grace presupposes nature, and perfection supposes something that can be perfected" (*ST* 1.2.2 ad. 1).

In the natural world, bodies that are hurt naturally work to heal themselves, and people who are hurt physically or emotionally also have a natural tendency to seek healing. Jesus' miraculous healings in the Gospels, then, are a supernatural aid to restoring the sick to their *natural* state of health. The resurrection of the body is simply the logical final step of a process of human healing and salvation: humans who have overcome sin, sorrow, and suffering in their own lives are destined finally to overcome death itself. Jesus' Resurrection is not understood as an isolated event. It is rather a foreshadowing of the destiny of all humans: "But now Christ has been raised from the dead, the firstfruits of those who have fallen asleep" (1 Cor 15:20).

Christ's Resurrection is a revelation, a sign that God intends the complete healing and salvation of all humans.

Paul on the Resurrection of the Dead 7.8

As many modern people consider the resurrection of the body to be strange or unreasonable, so too did many in ancient times. Paul's church at Corinth must have had similar concerns, for they questioned Paul, "How are the dead raised? With what kind of body will they come back?" (1 Cor 15:35). It is probable that these residents of Corinth, a Greek city, were influenced by Plato's philosophy. They could understand the belief that a spiritual soul could survive death, but they were confused by the idea that a *material* body could be raised again (see sec. 11.7.2 for ancient beliefs about life after death).

When Paul speaks of a resurrected body, he is by definition speaking of a supernatural body—a body that exists outside of the normal workings of nature, since a strictly natural body obviously does not come back to life. So Paul answers the Corinthians in the only way that a question about a supernatural reality can be answered: by analogy (see sec. 5.8.3). The resurrected body is like a seed, "a bare kernel of wheat" that is sown in the ground (1 Cor 15:37). Like a seed, the human body is "sown corruptible; it is raised incorruptible. It is sown dishonorable; it is raised glorious. It is sown weak; it is raised powerful. It is sown a natural (*psychikos*) body; it is raised a spiritual (*pneumatikos*) body" (1 Cor 15:42–44).

Paul relates his comparison between the *psychikos* and the *pneumatikos* to a comparison between Adam (representative of the "natural" human being) and Christ (representative of human beings who have overcome sin and death and attained the *pneumatikos* life). "Just as we have borne the image of the earthly one, we shall also bear the image of the heavenly one" (1 Cor 15:49).

The resurrected body, then, will not be a resuscitated corpse, a dead body with the principle of life (the soul) put back into it. Rather, it will be a *different kind of body*: a "spiritual body," an immortal, incorruptible body (15:53–54). At the same time, it is not simply a completely new body; Paul's analogy of the seed only makes sense if the spiritual body is a transformation, not a replacement, of the physical body.

We can thus see how Paul's discussion fits our broader conception of Christian salvation: the complete healing and renewal of the "natural" human being.

The Transformed Body: The Example of Jesus' Resurrected Body   7.9

We can get some further insights into the Christian understanding of the nature of the resurrected body by considering the accounts of Jesus' Resurrection in the Gospels. As we have seen (1 Cor 15:20), Paul thought of Jesus' Resurrection as a foreshadowing of the resurrection of all people. Because Christ is the "last Adam" (1 Cor 15:45), his Resurrection represents the destiny of all people.

In the accounts of Jesus' Resurrection from the dead, the Gospel writers go out of their way to emphasize that Jesus' *body* rose, not just his spirit. First, all four Gospels report that when women came to Jesus' tomb on the first day of the week, they found the tomb empty: his body had risen. When the risen Jesus appears to his disciples, it is true that in some aspects he seems like a pure spirit: longtime followers do not recognize him at first (Luke 24:15–16; John 20:14), and he can appear and disappear suddenly (Luke 24:31; John 20:19). Yet other passages emphasize that there is still some sort of physicality to Jesus' risen body. In Luke his sudden appearance frightens the disciples into thinking that they have seen a ghost, and Jesus admonishes them, "Look at my hands and my feet, that it is I myself. Touch me and see, because a ghost does not have flesh and bones as you can see I have" (Luke 24:39). Jesus then takes a piece of fish and eats it in their presence (Luke 24:42–43). The risen Jesus also admonishes "doubting Thomas," "Put your finger here and see my hands, and bring your hand and put it into my side, and do not be unbelieving, but believe" (John 20:27).

The Gospel accounts, then, seem to be a fair illustration of Paul's teaching about the "spiritual body." Jesus' body retains characteristics that we think of as physical: the ability to eat, the ability to be touched. At the same time, his body has clearly transcended physical limitations as we know them. It has passed into a different, supernatural plane of existence.

The Resurrected Body and Salvation 7.10

The doctrine of the resurrection of the body is thus in perfect harmony with Christian teaching on salvation. Salvation is not a completely new experience, cut off from earthly reality. It is rather a perfection of earthly reality. There is an essential continuity between earthly and heavenly life.

An essential Christian principle is that the transcendent life with God ("heaven" in traditional Christian language) is the fulfillment and perfection of everything good on earth. Thus the body too, since it was created good (Gen 1:31), will find its perfection in heaven.

Following the philosophical tradition of Aristotle and Aquinas (who taught that the soul is the "form" of the body), on the one hand, and the scriptural teaching of the unity of the human (the holistic anthropology of the Old Testament and the teaching of Paul and the Gospels on the resurrection of the body) on the other, the main lines of Christian thought have insisted that the physical body is *essential* to what it means to be human. This teaching is a decisive rejection of the Gnostic view that devalues the body and the physical world. It is only to be expected, then, that this essential element in human nature would also need to be present in eternal life. If a person is saved, it is the whole person who is saved.

Resurrection of the Body
and the Renewal of Nature   7.11

Paul's Letter to the Romans reveals an intimate connection between salvation, including the "redemption of our bodies" and the renewal of all physical creation.

> For creation awaits with eager expectation the revelation of the children of God; for creation was made subject to futility, not of its own accord but because of the one who subjected it, in hope that creation itself would be set free from slavery to corruption and share in the glorious freedom of the children of God. We know that all creation is groaning in labor pains even until now; and not only that, but we ourselves, who have the firstfruits of the Spirit, we also groan within ourselves as we wait for adoption, the redemption of our bodies. (Rom 8:19–23)

Describing the Future Life   7.12

In thinking theologically about these traditional teachings concerning resurrection and the ultimate destiny of the world, we must remember the limited ability of human language and reason to express fully a supernatural reality (see sec. 5.8).

The traditional Christian teaching is that the risen body is the same as a person's earthly body (see *ST* 3.79.1 *Supp.*). But how can the body be the same if it has already decayed and scattered?

This question raises a problem that is actually more imagined than real. Even in earthly life, at the purely physical level, our bodies are in fact constantly changing. "Although people may think of their body as a fairly permanent structure, most of it is in a state of constant flux as old cells are discarded and new ones generated in their place."[8] Science shows us that even our present physical identity does not depend on retaining the exact same cells and molecules.

Theologically, then, the key principle is that there is a *continuity* between the person's self (composed of both body and spirit) in this world and the same person (composed of a spiritual body) in the future state. ●

Christian doctrine teaches us that all creation, all nature will be renewed. Nature, as we can see in its patterns of death and decay (futility and corruption), is not as God intended it to be. In the end times, in the renewal of all things, however, a renewed nature will arise, along with the renewed body: "a new heaven and a new earth" (Rev 21:1). Aquinas teaches, "Wherefore at the one same time, the world will be renewed, and man will be glorified" (*ST* 3.91.1 *Supp.*).

Again we see how these doctrines are in harmony with the principle that God created all things good, and heaven is the perfection and completion of all natural goodness.

Soul as the Life Force of the Body   7.13

Now that we have considered the Christian view of the body, we turn to a more detailed consideration of Christian beliefs about the soul. Once again we will find Christian ideas to be distinctive, differing markedly from ancient philosophies and religions, just as they differ from modern materialistic beliefs.

In contrast to the Platonic and Gnostic models of a soul descending into a body, "the Church teaches that every spiritual soul is created immediately by God" at the moment of conception (*CCC* no. 366). Souls do not pre-exist in heaven before entering the human body. This teaching brings out again the profound unity between soul and body in Christian thought: at the exact moment of the physical uniting of the sperm and the egg, the spiritual soul is also created.

The soul, however, is not a *result* of the physical union of sperm and egg. Rather, the soul is the principle of life that cannot be defined in a material way. It is the mysterious power that brings matter to life, the power that the Bible describes as the breath of God: "The LORD God formed man out of the clay of the ground and blew into his nostrils the breath of life, and so man became a living being" (Gen 2:7).

To call the soul the "mysterious power of life" is not unscientific. As we have seen (sec. 4.9.3.3), even when scientists are able to identify all the chemical components of life they are unable to produce life itself. Life remains a mysterious "extra" beyond the mere combination of chemicals.

We saw too that the theory of evolution by natural selection is no help in explaining how life evolved from nonliving materials: how can something nonliving naturally select a characteristic that will help it to survive?

Spirit, Reason, and the Transcendent Horizon of the Human 7.14

Stephen Barr writes, "When religious believers say that we have a 'spiritual soul,' therefore, they are not referring to something occult or magical; they are referring to the faculties of intellect and free will that are familiar to and constantly employed by all human beings."[9]

Barr is certainly correct that the Christian tradition refers to abilities such as our intellect and free will as spiritual. He is perhaps not correct, however, to say that the "spiritual soul" is the intellect and free will. The *Catechism* expresses the thought more indirectly:

> With his openness to truth and beauty, his sense of moral goodness, his freedom and the voice of his conscience, with his longings for the infinite and for happiness, man questions himself about God's existence. In all this he discerns signs of his spiritual soul. The soul, the "seed of eternity we bear in ourselves, irreducible to the merely material," can have its origin only in God. (*CCC* no. 33; the quotation is from *GS* no. 18)

The soul and spirit are especially connected with the human ability to reason. Irenaeus writes, "But man, being endowed with reason, and in this respect like to God, having been made free in his will and with power over himself, is himself the cause to himself" (*Against Heresies* 4.4.3). Bishop Kallistos Ware explains that in the Orthodox tradition, spirit "is sometimes termed *nous* or spiritual intellect"—the power that allows humans to understand the eternal truth about God and the "inner essences" of created things.[10] Reason or intellect is also necessary for other "signs" of human transcendence: only through our reason can we be presented with choices and thus have true free will; only through our reason can we have a sense of what is morally right and wrong: "Conscience is a judgment of reason" (*CCC* no. 1778); "The Natural Law is nothing other than the light of understanding placed in us by God" (*CCC* no. 1955).

Another possible definition of spirit is to say that it is that within us that orients us to the transcendent. Such a definition is consistent with Rahner's approach, which speaks of the "transcendent horizon" of the human. The spirit, then, includes the "higher" faculties of free will, the search for meaning, conscience, and reason. But it would

Spirit and the New Life in Christ
7.15

We saw that Paul closely connects the "spirit" of a person with the new life in Christ: "But you are not in the flesh; on the contrary, you are in the spirit, if only the Spirit of God dwells in you" (Rom 8:9). Paul contrasts the "spiritual" (*pneumatikos*) person and the "natural" (*psychichos*) person (1 Cor 2:14–15). The old way of life is crucified (Rom 6:6); Paul says, "Yet I live, no longer I, but Christ lives in me" Gal 2:20).

For Paul, then, "spirit" means above all the spirit of Christ. A follower of Christ, a member of the body of Christ no longer lives the old, "natural" way of life (a life animated by a "natural" soul), but a life animated by Jesus' spirit. "Now those who belong to Christ [Jesus] have crucified their flesh with its passions and desires" (Gal 5:24). This new life animated by the spirit will be characterized by "love, joy, peace, patience, kindness, generosity, faithfulness, gentleness, self-control" (Gal 5:22–23). •

---

also include what we can call our more affective aspects, our desire for beauty, our restlessness with the limitations of this world, and our desire for perfection.

The notion of "spirit" is closely connected in Christian thought with scriptural teaching that humans, and no other creatures, are created in the image of God (Gen 1:26–27). Bishop Ware sums up, "Fundamentally, the image of God in man denotes everything that distinguishes man from the animals, that makes him in the full and true sense a *person*—a moral agent capable of right and wrong, a spiritual subject endowed with inward freedom."[11]

Human Role in Nature
7.16

Humans and Animals
7.16.1

Christian teaching boldly and without apology places humans in the center of the universe.

> Then God said, "Let us make man in our own image, after our likeness. Let them have dominion over the fish of the sea, the birds of the air, and the cattle." (Gen 1:26)

The Christian tradition is united in claiming that all creation was created for humans. Humans are "the only creature on earth that God has wanted for its own sake" (*GS* no. 24). The second-century *Letter to Diognetus* reads, "For God loved mankind for whose sake he made the world" (10.2). Aquinas says, "Now plants and animals were made for the upkeep of human life" (*ST* 3.91.5 *Supp*.). The *Catechism of the Catholic Church* teaches, "Animals, like plants and inanimate beings, are by nature destined for the common good of past, present, and future humanity" (*CCC* no. 2415).

This Christian view runs counter to much of modern thinking. English evolutionary biologist Olivia Judson may be cited as a representative example of modern thought:

> Many people would like to think that we men are the product of a special creation, separate from the other forms of life. I do not think this, I am happy that it is not so. I am proud to know that I am part of the tumult of nature, to know that the same forces which produced me also produced the bees, the giant fern and the microbes.[12]

In reality, the Christian tradition agrees with much of Judson's observations. Humans do in fact share the mystery of life with bees and ferns and microbes: Christianity is in no way embarrassed by this fact. Medieval scholastic theologians such as Aquinas were not ashamed of the human link with animals: they followed Aristotle in defining humans as "rational animals." They simply insisted that, while sharing much in common with other animals, we also transcend them in many other ways.

Humans and Animals: Key Differences   7.16.2

In the Christian tradition, only humans are made in God's image, and this distinguishes them decisively from any other animal.

This is not to deny that other species, such as the primates, have some sort of limited intelligence. But it is absurd to pretend that human intelligence and animal intelligence are in the same category. Human intelligence has built incredibly complex technological systems capable of producing spacecraft that can travel to other planets. Animal "technology" can, at the most, produce simple tools and shelters.

We need not deny, either, that animals may have some rudimentary sense of right and wrong. But animals are still essentially bound by laws of instinct and conditioning. Only humans are free enough to wonder whether a certain planned action is morally right or wrong.

It is also true that sometimes human actions are morally *worse* than those of animals. No animal can match the sadistic, calculated cruelty of a serial killer or rapist. But, ironically, such sadistic behavior is only possible because humans have the transcendent gift of free will. As Giovanni Pico della Mirandola (1463–1494) wrote, "You are just as free to distort yourself into subhuman forms as you are free, by your own choice, to be reborn into higher and divine forms."[13] Humans have the freedom to shape their character to the level of the divine or distort and corrupt it to a level below that of the animals.

Ironically, only a human can claim to be essentially no different from the rest of nature. A chimpanzee cannot make that claim, for a chimpanzee cannot conceive of the abstract idea of "nature," nor is a chimpanzee free enough from the bonds of instinct and conditioning to ask such a self-reflective question.

In the Christian view, God appoints humans to use their freedom and intelligence to care for nature, not to exploit or destroy it. If we deny that humans are essentially different from the animals, then we deny our responsibility to care for creation properly. Can we seriously think that we should let monkeys or great apes take over our role as the stewards of nature? While it is true that humans, through often irresponsible and unthinking actions, have threatened and damaged nature, it is also true that only humans are in a position to save nature from those human-produced threats.

The Challenge of Human Freedom   7.17

Genesis 3: A Story of Freedom   7.17.1

The story in Genesis 3 about humans disobeying God's commandment and eating from the tree of knowledge of good and bad can plausibly be understood as a story about human freedom.

In interpreting this account, sometimes people wonder, Why did God have to "set up" Adam and Eve for failure by giving them a commandment that he knew they would be tempted to break? Couldn't God simply have left humans in this paradise of peace and harmony?

But such a question may come from reading the story too literally (see 5.8.4 on Chrysostom and Augustine's warning against literalism). If we understand Genesis as a symbolic story, with Adam and Eve representing all humans, we can make better sense of it. Seen in this light, it is reasonable to interpret God's commandment as God's desire to provide humans with free choices. To be truly free, a human must have the ability to choose. In relation to God, the source of all goodness and true happiness, a free choice can only be framed in terms of obeying God (choosing the true good and true happiness) or disobeying God (choosing only an apparent or temporary good or happiness). So in giving them the commandment, God creates the space of their freedom; he provides options that allow them to exercise their freedom to choose.

There is no doubt that an all-powerful God could have created humans in such a way that we would never have disobeyed him and never turned from doing good to a corruption of good. But in that case, God would have created mere robots—creations that could only react in ways that had been preprogrammed.

In giving humans true freedom, God "ran the risk" (to put it anthropomorphically) that humans would abuse that freedom and disobey him—the source of true good. And so in fact humans have done. But God must have considered the gift of freedom to be so great that it was worth the risk.

Only the ambiguous gift of freedom makes us human—otherwise we would merely react instinctively like animals, or in a preprogrammed way like machines. On a daily basis, our free choices form our character: we become more trustworthy or untrustworthy, more courageous or less courageous, based on our choices. That same freedom gives us the ability to love. We cannot force someone to love us; love is truly love only if it is given freely. And so God, having created us in a free act of love (sec. 6.16), showed an even deeper love in allowing us the freedom to love or not to love him in return. "Where there is no freedom, there can be no love."[14] As Lewis writes, "Free will, though it makes evil possible, is also the only thing that makes possible any love or goodness or joy worth having."[15]

Reformation Debate on Free Will   7.17.2

The Christian tradition has not always agreed on how to reconcile several theological beliefs that can at times seem contradictory: that humans have free will, that humans have a fallen nature, and that God is all-powerful and all-knowing. Several of the Reformers, for example, in their emphasis on the essentially sinful nature of humans over against the almighty power and plans of God, drew the conclusion that free will was an illusion.

In his work, *On the Bondage of the Will* (1525), Luther wrote,

> For if we believe it to be true, that God fore-knows and fore-ordains all things; that He can be neither deceived nor hindered in His Prescience and Predestination; and that nothing can take place but according to His Will, (which reason herself is compelled to confess); then, even according to the testimony of reason herself, there can be no "Free-will"—in man,—in angel,—or in any creature! (no. 167)

The Fall had so corrupted human nature that it was impossible for humans to turn toward God of their own free will—the fallen human will could only choose evil. It is only through the influence of God's grace that humans can turn toward God, but humans are powerless to do anything to earn that grace, or even to accept it or cooperate with it on their own power.

The Reformer John Calvin (1509–1564) wrote similarly, "When the will is enchained as the slave of sin, it cannot make a movement towards goodness. . . . Such is the depravity of his nature, that he cannot move and act except in the direction of evil" (*Inst.* 2.3.5).

Catholic Defense of Free Will   7.17.3

Responding to the Reformers and seeking to clarify authentic Catholic teaching, the Council of Trent's (1545–1563) *Decree on Justification* sought to balance the reality of human free will with Christian doctrines on the fallen nature of humans and the necessity of God's grace for salvation.

The Council agreed that the first movement in the process must be God's grace: no one can turn toward God without the help of the Holy Spirit. But once this initial help is offered, the person is free either to turn toward God "assenting to and cooperating with" God's grace, or to reject that grace. Free will, although weakened by the human fall into sin, "was by no means extinguished."[16]

Modern Lutheran-Catholic Agreement   7.17.4

Four centuries after the **Reformation** debates, however, Lutherans and Catholics are in a position to reevaluate their stances. In October 1999, the Lutheran World Federation and the Catholic Church issued a *Joint Declaration on the Doctrine of Justification*. This same document was later also officially adopted by the World Methodist Conference.

The document concludes that "a consensus in basic truths of the doctrine of justification exists between Lutherans and Catholics," although the consensus still allows for differences in language and emphasis (no. 40). Both parties agree that, "By grace alone, in faith in Christ's saving work and not because of any merit on our part, we are accepted by God and receive the Holy Spirit, who renews our hearts while equipping and calling us to good works" (no. 15).

The *Declaration* also addresses the issue of free will: "When Catholics say that persons 'cooperate' in preparing for and accepting justification by consenting to God's justifying action, they see such personal consent as itself an effect of grace" (no. 20). As for Lutherans, "When they emphasize that a person can only receive (mere passive) justification, they mean thereby to exclude any possibility of contributing to one's own justification, but do not deny that believers are fully involved personally in their faith" (no. 21). The differences, then, seem to be different ways of describing the relationship between human will and divine grace, rather than mutually exclusive understandings.

Sin   7.18

The Christian tradition teaches that humans fell away from God through sin, that fallen human nature is sinful, and that salvation involves overcoming this sinful nature. In order to grasp rightly Christian anthropology, then, we must have a clear sense of what Christians mean by *sin*.

One online dictionary defines *sin* as "1. transgression of divine law; 2. any act regarded as such a transgression, especially a willful or deliberate violation of some religious or moral principle."[17] This concept of sin, however, seems to be gradually disappearing in modern thought. Let us consider some factors.

From a materialist or determinist point of view, this definition makes no sense—our actions are determined by forces that we cannot control, and so there can be no "*willful or deliberate* violation." Determinist-influenced language is quite common: "It was the alcohol talking, not me." "I can't help losing my temper, that's just the way I am." "Boys will be boys." All of these expressions put the responsibility for negative actions outside of the person acting, thereby eliminating the traditional concept of sin.

Ethical relativism (see sec. 5.5.2), also rejects the reality of sin. If right and wrong are determined solely by individual circumstances, then there can be no universal "religious or moral principles." And a person can't violate what doesn't exist.

As societies (especially Western societies) become more religiously pluralistic, it is increasingly difficult to agree on the specifics of a "divine law." As (especially Western) societies become more secular, the whole concept of "divine law" gradually loses meaning.

Despite these modern challenges, Christian anthropology maintains that the concept of sin is essential for true human dignity. God has revealed universal ethical standards, not only through differing religious traditions, but in the natural law that is accessible to all (sec. 5.5). The human person has been given real knowledge of good and evil, and the true freedom to choose between them. Sin is simply the failure to choose rightly.

Sin as Turning from God to Self   7.19

The *Catechism* defines *sin* as "an offense against reason, truth, and right conscience; it is a failure in genuine love for God and neighbor caused by a perverse attachment to certain goods" (*CCC* no. 1849).

The essence of virtually any moral wrong can be traced back to a focus on the self (and thus a failure of love) — we steal, lie, cheat, and even murder because we selfishly think we (or our group) will get some kind of benefit from it.

"Sin is an offense against God" (*CCC* no.1850) because God is the source of all goodness and of the natural law of right and wrong. As we have seen, all humans, whether they belong to a specific religion or not, have a sense of the transcendent and a sense of the moral law. As Paul says, "For what can be known about God is evident to them. . . . As a result, they have no excuse" (Rom 1:19–20). In the Christian view, even atheists or agnostics can be considered sinful if they act against what God has revealed to their conscience as right and wrong.

In refusing to submit to God and God's laws, humans rebel against God and, in essence, set themselves up as their own measure of right and wrong: we become our own god.

Original Sin: Sinful Babies?   7.20

According to the *Catechism*, the Catholic Church baptizes infants in order to cleanse them from the **original sin** that they inherited from Adam and Eve (see *CCC* nos. 417; 1250). For many today this teaching is inexplicable. How can an innocent baby be sinful? How can a baby commit "an offense against reason, truth, and right conscience" (*CCC* no. 1849) even before reaching the age of reason? How can the idea that a baby "inherits" sin be compatible with the principle that persons are responsible for their own sins (see Ezek 18)?

Original Sin and Fallen Human Nature   7.20.1

The Catholic tradition agrees that it would be absurd to hold a baby personally accountable for sin. To sin means, at some level, to make a choice (the *Catechism* defines *sin* as an offense against *reason*) for something that our reason tells us is wrong. Obviously babies do not have the mental or emotional development to make true choices.

But think about what happens when babies begin to reach the age of reason. As they grow into toddlers, at some point they begin to make conscious choices, at the same time developing an understanding of right and wrong. So consider, will a given child at some point freely choose to do certain things that he or she knows are wrong? For example, will she choose to disobey her mother, because she enjoys seeing Mom get frustrated? Will he choose to keep some toys to himself, when he knows he should share them with his younger brother?

As the child continues to develop, will she ever choose to do anything selfish? Will he ever gossip about another person who is not around to defend herself? Will she ever be jealous of another girl who is more athletic or more popular?

To these questions we must answer "yes." And we could easily add to the list of examples. In fact, each of us would probably have to admit that every day we do something that we know is wrong (judging other persons without knowing their full story, telling a "white lie," not keeping a commitment because we are too tired, etc.). Furthermore, truth be told, we actually enjoy doing certain things we know are wrong. We somehow enjoy gossiping, overeating, drinking too much, watching pornography, being lazy—otherwise why would we do these things so often?

Since *all* people *inevitably* sin when they are old enough to choose between right and wrong, it is only logical to conclude that sinning is part of human nature. To be more precise, we can say that the attraction toward sin, the tendency toward sin, or even the enjoyment we get out of sin—must also be part of human nature. That tendency is somehow innate in us.

The Christian tradition tells us that these negative tendencies and attractions are part of our fallen, not our original, nature. Our own experience can confirm this teaching in a more subtle way. Though doing wrong is common, we typically do not experience it as "normal." Unless our consciences have become hardened, we usually find our wrong actions to be shameful, we are frustrated with ourselves when we do wrong, or perhaps we try to rationalize our negative behaviors. Why would we react in this way if we really found doing wrong natural or normal? Deep within ourselves it seems that we know that human nature was not meant to be like this.

This "fallen," negative condition of humanity is what the Catholic Church calls original sin. Original sin is simply "human nature deprived of original holiness and justice"; it is "a state and not an act" (*CCC* no. 404).

The *Catechism* continues, "As a result of original sin, human nature is weakened in its powers; subject to ignorance, suffering, and the domination of death; and inclined to sin. (This inclination is known as 'concupiscence.')" (*CCC* no. 418)

So when the Catholic tradition says that a baby is born with original sin, it simply means that the baby is born with a human nature that is "wounded," is weak when it comes to doing what is right, and will be all too inclined to give in to selfishness and sin when that person reaches the age of reason.

We have discussed how our own experience tends to support the truth of this doctrine. But human history in general, with its long, unhappy record of wars, violence, racism, slavery, drug and alcohol addictions, and sexual exploitations, also supports its truth. From this perspective, G. K. Chesterton was right to conclude that far from being an unintelligible teaching, the doctrine of original sin "is the only part of Christian theology which can really be proved."[18]

To say, then, that babies "inherit" original sin does not mean that original sin is passed down like some kind of genetic disorder. Rather, it means that Adam and Eve, in their symbolic role as representatives of all humans, simply passed on *human nature* to succeeding generations—unfortunately, it was a fallen human nature. Original sin involves "the transmission of a human nature deprived of original holiness and justice" (*CCC* no. 404).

For Catholicism, the doctrine of original sin is not pessimistic, it is realistic. When we analyze our own selves, and when we analyze human history, it is only wishful thinking that would allow us to avoid the conclusion that there is something deeply flawed in our human nature.

Hell: Missing Out on Salvation 7.21

Difficulties with the Doctrine of Hell 7.21.1

Throughout this chapter, we have considered the close connection, in the Christian view, between life in this world and life in the transcendent realm after death. We saw that salvation—the overcoming of sin and suffering—is a process that begins in this world and is simply perfected in the transcendent realm. Heaven is simply the fulfillment and completion of all that is good on earth.

If the idea of heaven as the eternal perfection of earthly goodness is perhaps the most attractive and popular of Christian teachings, the opposite seems to be the case concerning Christian teachings about hell. Catholic theologian Peter Kreeft writes, "Hell is certainly the most unpopular of all Christian doctrines. It scandalizes almost all non-Christians."[19] We might add that the doctrine of hell—the belief that God condemns unrepentant sinners to eternal punishment—scandalizes many or even most Christians too.

The reasons for the scandalized reaction are not far to seek, because the doctrine of hell seems to contradict not only basic modern values such as tolerance but basic Christian teachings as well. Christians are taught, for example, that God is forgiving, but then taught that there is no forgiveness in hell—the punishment is eternal.

Or again, Jesus taught his followers to love their enemies and pray for those who persecute them (Matt 5:44). But the traditional Christian imagination of hell is filled with seemingly vindictive, even sadistic portraits of the suffering of sinners. In the classic Christian literary description of hell, the *Inferno*, Dante (1265–1321) describes some sinners tortured in a river of boiling blood, others chased eternally by ferocious dogs, others forced to lie on burning sand while fiery flakes rain down upon them. The images of Scripture, while less graphic, are no less horrible. Jesus himself speaks of a "fiery furnace, where there will be wailing and grinding of teeth" (Matt 13:42), "the eternal fire prepared for the devil and his angels" (Matt 25:41), and "eternal punishment" (Matt 25:46). The Book of Revelation describes a "pool of fire" (20:14–15).

Christians claim that God is love, but God seems to have no love for those he punishes (or allows to be punished) in hell. Since Christians believe that God is just, it is understandable that those who have committed great crimes would be punished or corrected in some way, but why is the punishment eternal, with no chance for repentance?

With these objections in mind, we turn to a deeper consideration of the Christian doctrine regarding hell.[20]

Describing Hell   7.21.2

We begin with a reminder of the limitations of our language. Since hell, according to Christian doctrine, is a supernatural reality, it can only be described in analogies (sec. 5.8.3). A teaching of the German Catholic Bishops' Conference made the point this way:

> Holy Scripture teaches us the *essence of hell* in images. When it speaks of the fire of hell, it is not to be understood in a grossly realistic sense. Much less should we think of sadistic tortures. But neither does a purely spiritual understanding do justice to the declaration in Scripture. The image expresses a reality of a much deeper nature. God in his holiness is a consuming fire for evil, deceit, hate, and violence (Isaiah 10:17). Just as heaven is God himself, won forever, so hell is God himself as eternally lost.[21]

The images of Scripture, or other images such as those in Dante, or popular images of devils and pitchforks, need not be taken too literally. They are meant to describe a state of existence after death and not a physical "place." Images of fire and pain are ways of expressing the essential Christian understanding of hell—that it is separation from God.

Hell as Eternal Separation from God   7.21.3

In the Christian understanding, we may define heaven as simply "being-with-God." God is the ultimate source of goodness, truth, beauty, love—everything meaningful in life. Persons united in heaven with God experience and enjoy the fullness of beauty, truth, love, and every conceivable goodness.

Hell, in contrast, is simply "being-without-God." It is thus an existence without goodness and without meaning. Such an existence is hard to imagine, but we can perhaps just begin to conceive of it. Just as we have many glimpses of heaven in our experiences of goodness and love in daily life, so too do we have many glimpses of hell. Whenever we experience any sort of distortion or twisting of an original good, we have some insight into what hell is like.

To experience the pain and emptiness of hell, we do not have to call up images of flames and devils with pitchforks. We have only to imagine a life that is cut off from all goodness. Instead of true friendship, only relationships of fear and mistrust. Instead of true love, only selfishness and self-centeredness. Instead of true joy, only the twisted pleasure of cruelty. Instead of true communication and sharing, only isolation. Instead of hope, only a cynical despair. Instead of trust and honesty, lies and deception. This sort of existence, most truly and without exaggeration, would be hell.

When we say that hell does not necessarily have devils with pitchforks, this does not mean that demons or devils do not really exist, or that they are merely metaphors. The Christian tradition is quite clear that demons do exist, and no doubt they in some way have a place in the pains of hell. They do not necessarily have horns, tails, and pitchforks, however. C. S. Lewis, in *The Screwtape Letters*, imagines the demons of hell organized in an office bureaucracy; each demon is polite and smiling on the surface, but inwardly always scheming and conniving, ready to stab his partner in the back if it suits his purpose. Again, the essence of hell is the distortion of all good—selfishness, deceit, cringing fear, and twisted pleasures reign supreme.

Hell Is Freely Chosen   7.21.4

How, then, would a person come to be in this state-without-God? We have already outlined the answer in our earlier discussions. All humans have a fallen human nature, and thus we all have a tendency toward sin and selfishness. We are born with these tendencies, yet we are free, in each individual instance, to cooperate or not to cooperate with these tendencies. According to Christian anthropology, however, we can never overcome this sinful aspect of our nature by our own power—we will always fall short, and fall back into selfish, deceitful tendencies. Thus we need to accept God's help to overcome sin, we need to accept God's grace in order to achieve that original happiness that God intended for us.

But it is precisely that "accepting help" that is the problem. The human situation is analogous to the observation counselors often make: the hardest step in overcoming any addiction is for persons to admit that they have a problem that they cannot handle on their own.

It is just so with human pride. Before persons can cooperate with the offer of God's freely given grace, they must first admit that they are too weak to overcome their sins on their own. And this is precisely what is so difficult for humans—the giving up of our own sense of control over our own lives and the acceptance of divine help. Humans have a natural tendency to hold on to the old way of life with all of its distortions, deceits, and corruptions—under the illusion that we are still in control.

The New Testament plainly describes what is involved in this process. Jesus tells his disciples, "For whoever wishes to save his life will lose it, but whoever loses his life for my sake and that of the gospel will save it" (Mark 8:35). Paul says, "We know that our old self was crucified with him, so that our sinful body might be done away with, that we might no longer be in slavery to sin" (Rom 6:6). Accepting Christ involves a dying to one's old way of life, a crucifying of oneself, and people are naturally not eager to make such a hard decision.

In Catholic anthropology, humans are truly free to cooperate with or to reject God's offer of help (sec. 7.17). By the innumerable free decisions persons make in their lives, they orient their lives toward God or away from God. Persons can either make a fundamental decision to humble themselves (as Christ did) and accept God's will for their lives, or they can decide to hang onto the illusion that they are really in control of their lives. The one choice ultimately leads to the life-with-God (heaven); the other choice leads to the life-without-God (hell).

In this sense, God does not "send" people to hell; the Day of Judgment simply reveals the fundamental choice that a person has already made. In the end, as C. S. Lewis says, there are only two kinds of people: those who say to God, "Thy will be done," and those to whom God says, "Thy will be done."[22]

In the Catholic understanding, God does not torture people in hell, nor does he allow the demons to torture those in hell. God continues to love (it is impossible for God to stop loving, since his nature is to love), but the inhabitants in hell do not experience his love as love. In their self-centered anger, hatred, and fear, Kreeft imagines, they experience God's love as a burning pain. [23]

Eternal Hell? 7.21.5

But why is hell eternal? Why not punish sinners for a certain amount of time, or until they repent? We can suggest two considerations.

First, the "eternity" of heaven and hell is *not* an endless amount of time; recall the basic theological principle that we cannot describe supernatural realities directly with human concepts (see sec. 5.8). In the supernatural realm, human conceptions of time no longer apply.[24]

Second, it seems to be an essential element of true human freedom that a human must, at some point, make a final, definitive decision. If we are really truly free, at some point we must make a final, irrevocable decision for or against God. If we choose to go against God and what we know in our hearts is right, but in the back of our mind we are thinking, "I can always change my mind later"—then we are not really choosing, we are still avoiding that final decision. But God insists (so to speak) that we exercise our freedom to choose—one way or another.

Who Is in Hell?   7.21.6

The Catholic tradition's answer to the question, "Who is in hell?" is simply, "Anyone who has made the final, definitive choice against God." As the *Catechism* says, "This state of definitive self-exclusion from communion with God and the blessed is called 'hell'" (*CCC* no. 1033).

But do we know for sure whether any particular person is in hell? Many people would answer "Yes," listing such people as Judas, Hitler, or Stalin. Based on the idea that people cannot save themselves from sin, some Christians would say simply, "Anyone who has not accepted Jesus as Savior." We will discuss this last point in more detail in section 12.28.

There is, however, a strand of Catholic thought that is much more cautious in its assertions. Thus the German Bishops' Conference declares that "neither Holy Scripture nor the Church's Tradition of faith asserts with certainty of any man that he is actually in hell."[25]

As the Swiss Catholic theologian Hans Urs von Balthasar shows, there are hints both in Scripture and in Tradition that *all* people *might* be saved.[26] Thus Paul says, "For God delivered all to disobedience, that *he might have mercy upon all*" (Rom 11:32, emphasis added). Paul's letter to Timothy asserts that God "wills everyone to be saved and to come to knowledge of the truth" (1 Tim 2:4). If God wills that all people be saved, can God's will truly be opposed? Mystics such as Mechtilde of Hackeborn (d. 1299) and Julian of Norwich (c. 1342–c. 1416) received private revelations from Christ that support the hope of universal salvation.[27]

Von Balthasar's thinking is also influenced by the absolute, qualitative difference between good and evil. If evil really is a corruption of good, if pure evil is nothing—than can hell truly be eternal? Gregory of Nyssa, for one, taught that evil could not be absolute, and so there must be a limit to the pains of hell.[28] Similarly, von Balthasar also notes the possible implications of Paul's train of thought in Romans 5:12–21: "Just as through one transgression [of Adam] condemnation came upon all, so through one righteous act [of Christ] acquittal and life came to all" (Rom 5:18).[29]

Theologians such as de Lubac, Rahner, Ratzinger, the great Reformed theologian Karl Barth, as well as C. S. Lewis, all took seriously the possibility of universal salvation. These thinkers do not claim that all people *will* be saved—such a belief (attributed to Origen) has been officially condemned in Church teaching.[30] "Hell is always held before our eyes as *real possibility*."[31] Von Balthasar concludes that Christians are entitled to *hope* that each individual person might be saved, but they should in no way assume that universal salvation is inevitable.[32]

Purgatory: Final Cleansing in Heaven   7.22

To finish our reflections on human nature and final destiny of humans, we consider Catholic teaching on purgatory. Once again, the doctrine is controversial: the Reformers Luther and Calvin, for example, flatly rejected the Catholic teaching on purgatory (see, for example, Calvin's *Institutes* 3.5.6–10).

Misconceptions about Purgatory   7.22.1

Many Christians misunderstand the Catholic doctrine of purgatory to mean a third option between heaven and hell. This is not the case: the Catholic tradition agrees with the entire Christian tradition that there are only two options after death: life-with-God (heaven) or life-without-God (hell).

We have already discussed the reasons why the Christian tradition believes that salvation cannot be attained by a person's own power, but only through God's grace in Christ. In Catholic anthropology, however, even the person who is saved through Christ is not completely passive: the person must cooperate with God's grace offered through Christ. One aspect of this cooperation is known as repentance—a genuine regret of having done wrong, and a serious commitment to try (with God's help) to live a better life.

To attain salvation, union with God, a person must be cleansed of all sins. Since God is pure goodness and holiness, no one can be in God's presence unless all sins have been completely cleansed.

What happens, though, if a person dies without having repented of certain sins? Let us consider a hypothetical example. Let's say Mrs. Matthews, a good moral person who believes in Christ, dies at age eighty. Although everyone in her community recognizes that she was a good person, still there will be certain wrongs in her life that she has not fully cleansed. All people, according to Christian anthropology, have weaknesses or faults in their lives, large or small, that they have either ignored or not completely faced. In Christian terms, Mrs. Matthews is indeed saved through Christ, but these faults remain.

In the Catholic view (a view shared by the Orthodox tradition), even after her death Mrs. Matthews must go through a process of cleansing those remaining wrongs and faults. Purgatory is simply this final process of cleansing before a person enters fully into God's presence.

The *Catechism* expresses the teaching thus,

> All who die in God's grace and friendship, but still imperfectly purified, are indeed assured of their eternal salvation; but after death they undergo purification, so as to achieve the holiness necessary to enter the joy of heaven. (*CCC* no. 1030)

Thus the Catholic tradition sees purgatory not as a "third place" between heaven and hell, but rather as sort of an "entryway" into heaven. A soul in purgatory will eventually be fully in God's presence.

Notice again, however, the limitations of our language. We speak of "going" to heaven, hell, or purgatory as if they were physical places, but of course they are not — they are transcendent realities, states of supernatural being rather than "places."

Let us consider another hypothetical example of this process of purgatory. Imagine someone who was a criminal and a murderer but who, some time before his death, repented and turned toward God. At his death, the man is saved, but has he truly cleansed the guilt and stain of all his crimes? Perhaps in the process of purgatory, the man would have to "relive" his crimes, but this time from the point of view of his victims. He would have to know in the depths of his own soul the pain and suffering that he inflicted on others, and this would help him in the process of cleansing his own soul.

The doctrine of purgatory implies that even in heaven those who are saved will still go through progress, change, and development. They will continually grow deeper in purity and holiness, growing ever deeper in their knowledge and experience of God.

Purgatory and Scripture   7.22.2

The Reformers objected to the teaching on purgatory in part because it is not found in Scripture. Admitting that it is not explicit in Scripture, the Catholic tradition nevertheless understands the teaching as a legitimate development of doctrine — a growth in our understanding of the scriptural teachings about salvation.

A passage from one of Paul's letters, while not a direct support of purgatory, nevertheless shows that the concept of a final cleansing is not too far from the apostle's mind:

> For no one can lay a foundation other than the one that is there, namely, Jesus Christ. If anyone builds on this foundation with gold, silver, precious stones, wood, hay, or straw, the work of each will come to light, for the Day [of Judgment] will disclose it. It will be *revealed with fire*, and the fire [itself] will test the quality of each one's work. If the work stands that someone built upon the foundation, that person will receive a wage. But if someone's work is burned up, that one will suffer loss; the *person will be saved, but only as through fire*. (1 Cor 3:11–15, emphasis added)

The Catholic tradition has sometimes spoken of the number of "years" that a soul spends in purgatory, but such language is metaphorical. As Pope Benedict teaches, "It is clear that we cannot calculate the 'duration' of this transforming burning in terms of the chronological measurements of this world."[33]

The pope suggests further that the doctrine of purgatory may be one way of imagining the encounter with Christ on the Day of Judgment:

> Some recent theologians are of the opinion that the fire which both burns and saves is Christ himself, the Judge and Saviour. The encounter with him is the decisive act of judgment. Before his gaze all falsehood melts away. This encounter with him, as it burns us, transforms and frees us, allowing us to become truly ourselves.[34]

The pope's understanding of purgatory opens much common ground between Protestant and Catholic ways of thinking about salvation.[35]

Prayers for the Dead   7.22.3

In line with their critique of purgatory, the Reformers also rejected the Catholic tradition's practice of praying for the dead.[36]

For many people, the concept of praying for the dead makes no sense. In traditional Christian thought, the moment of death is definitive—a person is judged, and "goes" to heaven or hell. What difference would the prayers of another person make at that point?

First, we must recall the principle that God is not confined to the human concept of chronological, sequential time. For God, all time is the present moment. Thus a prayer said on behalf of a person after his death is not heard by God *after* the person's death. It is heard by God from all eternity, and thus may benefit that person in the time (from a human perspective) *before* his death. Pope Benedict writes, "It is never too late to touch the heart of another, nor is it ever in vain."[37]

Second, the Catholic teaching is that prayers of the living can help a person through the process of Purgatory, the final cleansing of sins. In this understanding, we can say metaphorically that prayers can "lessen" a person's "time" in Purgatory.

The Catholic tradition also finds justification for this practice in the Second Book of Maccabees, when Judas Maccabeus "made **atonement** for the dead that they might be freed from this sin" (2 Macc 12:46).[38]

Human Nature and Human Destiny 7.23

In this chapter, we have tried to get an overview of the Christian understanding of what it means to be human. We have also considered several objections and challenges to Christian anthropology, together with some Christian responses to those challenges.

The Christian view of human nature and destiny cannot be summed up neatly as "optimistic" or "pessimistic." On the one hand, it is extremely optimistic: it claims that humans are the high point of the entire created universe and that the final destiny of humans is nothing less than absolute, unimaginable joy, contentment, peace, and love. On the other hand, it is also (in the eyes of many) deeply pessimistic: it claims that innocent babies are born with "original sin" and that humans are so weak and enmeshed in sin that they cannot free themselves; they must rely completely on God's help.

For Christians, however, these seemingly contradictory extremes can be reconciled. The supposed pessimism is simply an honest look at the limitations, weakness, and tendency to selfishness and corruption that lie deeply in every human. The seeming optimism is attained when persons, having "died" to the "natural" self-centered way of life with all of its attractions, open themselves up to God and begin to live a new way of life, a life of joy and fulfillment far surpassing the wildest dreams of their earlier life.

Questions about the Text

1. What are the basic meanings of the Hebrew terms *basar* and *nephesh*?

2. What is the basic difference between Plato and Aristotle in their views of the relationship between the soul and the body?

3. How does the Christian view of the body compare with that of Gnosticism or Platonism? What are the implications of the doctrine of the Incarnation and the resurrection of the body for Christian anthropology?

4. In what ways can Christian anthropology be called holistic?

5. How does Christian belief in the resurrection fit into the Christian view on miracles?

6. What are the similarities between Paul's discussion of the resurrection of the body and the Gospel reports of Jesus' resurrected body?

7. What is the relationship between the Christian view of salvation and the Resurrection of Jesus?

8. How does the Christian tradition define *soul* and *spirit*?

9. In what ways are humans essentially different from other animals, in the Christian view?

10. How are free will and the possibility of sin connected in the Christian view?

11. Why did Luther and Calvin deny the reality of free will? What was the Catholic response to their views? How do modern Lutherans and Catholics view the issue of the relationship between God's grace and human free will?

12. How is *sin* defined in the Christian tradition, and what are some modern challenges to the concept of sin?

13. What is the Catholic understanding of original sin?

14. What are some challenges to the Christian doctrine of hell?

15. Why do modern theologians caution against taking images of hell too literally?

16. What does it mean to say that "hell is freely chosen"?

17. What is the evidence for the possibility of universal salvation in Scripture and Tradition? What is von Balthasar's view on the question of universal salvation?

18. What is the Catholic view concerning purgatory? Why did the Reformers reject the belief? How does Pope Benedict XVI's view on purgatory serve to connect traditional Protestant and Catholic views?

Discussion Questions

1. How would you define the terms *soul* and *spirit*? How do your definitions compare with traditional Christian definitions?

2. What is your view of what happens to the body and soul after death? How does your view compare with the traditional Christian view?

3. Are you familiar with some accounts of "near death experiences"? How do the descriptions of the afterlife in these experiences compare with traditional Christian teaching?

4. Do you agree that the concept of sin is losing meaning in modern society? If so, what factors do you think are contributing to this decline?

Endnotes

1. Kallistos Ware, *The Orthodox Way*, rev. ed. (Crestwood, NY: St. Vladimir's Seminary Press, 1999), 48.
2. Ibid., 74.
3. Friedrich Nietzsche, *Thus Spoke Zarathustra* part 3.10.2. See Walter Kaufmann, ed., *The Portable Nietzsche* (New York: Viking, 1968), 300.
4. See D. S. Noss and B. R. Grangaard, *A History of the World's Religions*, 12th ed. (Upper Saddle River, NJ: Pearson Prentice Hall, 2008), 483–84.
5. John Paul II, "The Resurrection and Theological Anthropology," *L'Osservatore Romano*, English ed., December 7, 1981, p. 3.
6. John Henry Newman, *An Essay on the Development of Christian Doctrine* (Westminster, MD: Christian Classics, 1968), 36.
7. On the "Theology of the Body," see John Paul II, *The Theology of the Body: Human Love in the Divine Plan* (Boston: Pauline Books & Media, 1997). A more popular and accessible summary of the pope's ideas are found in Christopher West, *Theology of the Body for Beginners* (West Chester, PA: Ascension Press, 2004).
8. Nicholas Wade, "Your Body Is Younger than You Think," *New York Times*, August 2, 2005, page D1.

9. Stephan Barr, *Modern Physics and Ancient Faith* (Notre Dame: University of Notre Dame Press, 2003), 168.

10. Ware, *Orthodox Way*, 48.

11. Ibid., 51.

12. Olivia Judson, "Our Place in Nature's Riotous Order," *International Herald Tribune*, January 3, 2006; cited in Christoph Schönborn, *Chance or Purpose: Creation, Evolution, and a Rational Faith* (San Francisco: Ignatius Press, 2007), 108.

13. Giovanni Pico della Mirandola, *Oration on the Dignity of Man*, quoted in Schönborn, *Chance or Purpose*, 111.

14. Ware, *Orthodox Way*, 76.

15. C. S. Lewis, *Mere Christianity* (London: HarperCollins, 2001; orig. pub. 1952), 48.

16. Council of Trent Session VI, "Decree on Justification," accessed October 3, 2008, at *http://www.ewtn.com/library/COUNCILS/TRENT6.htm*.

17. *http://dictionary.reference.com*, accessed October 3, 2008.

18. G. K. Chesterton, *Orthodoxy* (Peabody, MA: Hendrickson, 2006; orig. pub. 1908), 10.

19. Peter Kreeft, *Everything You Ever Wanted to Know about Heaven—but Never Dreamed of Asking* (San Francisco: Ignatius Press, 1990), 213.

20. For further objections to the Christian doctrine of hell, see ibid., 219–25.

21. *The Church's Confession of Faith: A Catholic Catechism for Adults* (San Francisco: Ignatius Press, 1987), 346–47. Emphasis original.

22. C. S. Lewis, *The Great Divorce* (New York: Macmillan, 1946), 72.

23. Kreeft, *About Heaven*, 219.

24. For a discussion of the time of the material world (*chronos*), spiritual time (*kairos*), and eternity, see Kreeft, *About Heaven*, 151–71.

25. *Catholic Catechism for Adults*, 346.

26. Hans Urs von Balthasar, *Dare We Hope "that All Men Be Saved"?* (San Francisco: Ignatius, 1988).

27. Ibid., 98–102.

28. Discussed in ibid., 244.

29. Ibid., 39–40.

30. The doctrine attributed to Origen is known as the *apokatastasis*: the belief that all of creation, including the demons, would be restored.

31. *Catholic Catechism for Adults*, 346.

32. Von Balthasar, *Dare We Hope*, 211–21.

33. Pope Benedict XVI, *Saved in Hope: Encyclical Letter (Spe Salvi)* (San Francisco: Ignatius Press, 2007), no. 14.

34. Ibid.

35. On the possibility of reconciling traditional Protestant and Catholic views on Purgatory, see Kreeft, *About Heaven*, 61–62.

36. For example, Calvin, *Inst.* 3.5.10.

37. Benedict XVI, *Spe Salvi*, no. 48.

38. The canonical status of 1 and 2 Maccabees is not accepted by churches in the Protestant tradition.

8

The Christian View of Scripture
Inspiration and Inerrancy

What Is Scripture?   8.1

The word *scripture* simply means "writing" (from the Latin *scripto*, "to write"). In religious traditions, however, the word means "holy writings" or "authoritative writings."

Virtually all religious traditions that have a written language have scriptures, which are writings those traditions consider holy and authoritative. Thus Judaism has the Tanak: the Torah, Prophets, and Writings, which Christians call the Hebrew Scriptures or Old Testament. Islam has the Qur'an. The Hindu tradition has the Vedas. The Raveda Buddhists have the Pali Canon, while the Mahayana Buddhist tradition has other scriptures such as the Lotus Sutra. Nonliterate traditions also have something analogous to scripture in their sacred stories of the gods and spirits.

It seems, then, that all literate religious traditions have some kind of inner dynamic that results in a written scripture. Perhaps it involves the need to fix traditional teachings in an unchangeable form—virtually all the written scriptural traditions began as oral traditions that were eventually written down.

While Christian Scripture today includes both the Old Testament and New Testament, the earliest Christians had only the Jewish Scriptures. Thus all references to "Scripture" in the New Testament refer to these Jewish sacred writings. Later we will consider the historical process (known as **canonization**) by which early Christian writings came to be considered Scripture and the concept of a New Testament developed.

First, however, we will focus on the Christian belief that the Holy Spirit inspired the scriptural authors.

Inspiration of Scripture   8.2

Christians commonly call the Bible the "Word of God." By this Christians do not imply that God wrote the Bible directly, but rather that God "inspired" the biblical authors to write. The theological task is to ask some reasonable questions about **inspiration** in order to understand the belief at a deeper level. We begin with the following questions:

1. What does it mean to say that God inspired the biblical authors? Did God dictate a message word-for-word? Or was this inspiration indirect, like the inspiration of a poet or painter?

2. How does inspiration affect the author? When God inspired the author, did the author know everything that God knows? Did the author make errors? Or did the author receive no supernatural help at all, but did God work through the author's natural abilities toward a divine purpose?

We will explore these questions primarily from within the Catholic tradition, giving special attention to the Vatican II teaching on revelation, *Dei Verbum*. But in order to present a fuller picture of the issues raised in the theological discussion on inspiration, we will also consider some non-Catholic ideas, particularly the 1978 *Chicago Statement on Biblical Inerrancy*, a document signed by more than two hundred evangelical leaders and adopted by the Evangelical Theological Society. It is worth noting that virtually every principle in the *Chicago Statement* has been taught by a Catholic theologian at some point in history.

The Word Church 8.3

As we discuss inspiration and Scripture, we will make frequent use of the term *Church*, since the Church plays a key role in recognizing and interpreting Scripture. The meaning of the word, however, is ambiguous. As used in this book, *Church* with a capital *C* generally refers to the one, holy, catholic, and apostolic Church as expressed in the Nicene Creed, the community of Christians (including Orthodox, Protestant, Roman Catholic, and evangelical churches) who share essential beliefs and practices, especially as they are found in the New Testament and the Apostles' and Nicene creeds. However, *Church* in some instances will refer specifically to the Roman Catholic Church, especially when it is referenced in Vatican II documents. Chapter 12 addresses the theological understanding of *Church* more precisely; for now, we simply call attention to the occasional ambiguity in order to avoid confusion. **o**

What Is Inspiration? 8.4

The Bible says, "All Scripture is inspired by God and is useful for teaching, for refutation, for correction, and for training in righteousness, so that one who belongs to God may be competent, equipped for every good work" (2 Tim 3:16). The Greek word translated as "inspired" is *theopneustos*, literally "God-breathed." Similarly, our English word *inspiration* is derived from the Latin verb *inspiro*, "to breathe into."[1]

The word for "breath" in both Greek (*pneuma*) and Latin (*spiritus*) can also mean "spirit." The Christian tradition thus presents a metaphorical picture of the Holy Spirit inspiring the biblical authors—breathing into them. The Christian tradition consistently identifies the Spirit as the inspirer of the scriptural authors. *Dei Verbum* affirms that the Church

> accepts as sacred and canonical the books of the Old and the New Testaments, whole and entire, with all their parts, on the grounds that, written under inspiration of the Holy Spirit (cf. John 20:31; 1 Tim 3:16; 2 Pet 1:19–21; 3:15-16), they have God as their author. (*DV* no. 11)

Inspiration and Prophecy 8.5

Early Christians closely identified the inspiration of Scripture with the gift of prophecy. Already a New Testament writer says,

> We possess the prophetic message that is altogether reliable. . . . There is no prophecy of scripture that is a matter of personal interpretation, for no prophecy ever came through human will; but rather human beings moved by the holy Spirit spoke under the influence of God. (2 Pet 1:19–21)

Early Christian apologists tended to think of God's inspiration of a biblical author as virtually the same as God's inspiration of a prophet—the Holy Spirit essentially speaking through the human.[2] Thus Justin Martyr (c. 100–c. 165) wrote, "You must not suppose that they [scriptural passages] are spoken by the inspired [writers] themselves, but by the Divine Word who moves them" (*1 Apology* 36). Athenagoras (c. 133–190) believed that the biblical authors, "lifted in ecstasy above the natural operations of their minds by the impulses of the Divine Spirit, uttered the things with which they were inspired, the Spirit making use of them as a flute-player breathes into a flute"(*A Plea for the Christians*, no. 9).

Aquinas also saw biblical inspiration as a type of prophecy.[3] Scholastic theologians such as Aquinas used the different types of cause in Aristotelian logic to describe the relationship between God and the inspired author: God is the primary efficient cause, and the human author is the instrumental cause of Scripture. Scholastic authors, however, had different interpretations of "instrumental cause." Some thought this meant the Spirit essentially used an author as a writer uses a pen—there is no true human influence in the process of writing. Other scholastics sought to give more credit to an author's free cooperation with the inspiring Spirit.[4]

Human and Divine in Scripture 8.6

This scholastic discussion raises a key question in the theology of biblical inspiration: what is the exact relationship between the human and the divine? Does the Holy Spirit dictate the very words of Scripture and the author simply copy them down? At the other extreme, is the writing a completely human process in which God is the ultimate cause of the writing, since God created the author and his intellect, but otherwise does not interfere with the human author?

Dei Verbum affirms that because they were "written under the inspiration of the Holy Spirit," all biblical books have "God as their author [Latin: *auctor*]" (*DV* no. 11). But this phrase need not imply that God himself actually wrote the words. *Auctor* can mean "literary author," but can also mean "source" or "originator."[5]

Dei Verbum at several points affirms true human involvement in the process of writing. God "made full use of their [the sacred writers'] powers and faculties" so that they were "true authors" (*DV* no. 11). In Scripture, "God speaks to men in human fashion," and thus a central task of the biblical interpreter is to "carefully search out the meaning which the sacred writers really had in mind" (*DV* no. 12).

In the end, however, according to *Dei Verbum*, one cannot separate the human author and the Holy Spirit: the author wrote "whatever he [the Spirit] wanted written, and no more" (no. 11); the meaning that the author intended is "the meaning which God had thought well to manifest through the medium of their words" (no. 12). "All that the inspired authors, or sacred writers, affirm, should be regarded as affirmed by the Holy Spirit" (no. 11).

The *Chicago Statement* also credits humans with a role in the process: God "utilized the distinctive personalities and literary styles of the writers whom He had chosen and prepared" (art. 8); "in determining what the God-taught writer is asserting in each passage, we must pay the most careful attention to its claims and character as a human production" (art. 18).

Concrete Examples   8.7

In discussing scriptural inspiration, Catholic biblical scholar Raymond Brown rightly insists that we should avoid starting with theoretical assumptions about what we think biblical inspiration must mean, and rather start from the facts and work back toward theories of what the biblical authors actually were doing and saying.[6] So how did biblical authors in fact go about their writing?

Luke's Introduction   8.7.1

A good place to start is with the Gospel of Luke, because Luke specifically tells us something about how he wrote his account about the life, death, and Resurrection of Jesus. In the following table, we set down Luke's opening account along with some explanatory comments.

Luke 1	Explanatory Comments
1:1 Since many have undertaken to compile a narrative of the events that have been fulfilled among us,	Luke acknowledges that many people have either written or passed down by word of mouth accounts about Jesus and his first followers. Most scholars believe that Luke was writing approximately fifty years after the death of Jesus.
1:2 just as those who were eyewitnesses from the beginning and ministers of the word have handed them down to us,	Since Luke lived after the time of Jesus, he must rely on the accounts of eyewitnesses who heard and saw Jesus, and also on the "ministers of the word" who passed down these accounts either in oral or written form. The "ministers of the word" apparently were Christians who made sure that the accounts about Jesus were passed down and taught accurately.
1:3–4: I too have decided, after investigating everything accurately anew, to write it down in an orderly sequence for you, most excellent Theophilus, so that you may realize the certainty of the teachings you have received.	Luke personally checked the accuracy of these accounts, put them in order, and used them as sources in writing his own story of Jesus. He is now sending his completed Gospel to a man named Theophilus, most likely a recently baptized Christian and Luke's patron—the person who supported Luke financially while he worked on his Gospel. Ancient authors often dedicated their works to their patrons. Luke hopes that his account will help Theophilus become more confident about the accuracy of the oral teaching about Jesus that Theophilus had already received.

Luke's introduction shows us that he worked in much the same way as any historian in ancient or modern times: he gathered accounts from eyewitnesses, checked the accounts for accuracy, and then arranged them in a logical or chronological sequence.

The Christian tradition tells us that, as a biblical author, Luke was inspired by the Holy Spirit. Examining Luke's own statements, a theologian can thus draw the reasonable conclusion that inspiration by the Holy Spirit does not necessarily imply divine word-for-word dictation. Rather, God's inspiration may involve ordinary human practices of writing. In fact, the inspired author need not know or think of himself as "inspired" at all—Luke's account certainly gives no indication of this awareness.

Use of Sources by Biblical Writers   8.7.2

Many biblical authors used a variety of sources. In the Old Testament, Ezra quotes from a copy of a letter from the Persian king Artaxerxes (Ezra 7:12–26). The author(s) of the books of Kings and Chronicles refers to other historical sources: "The rest of the acts of Hezekiah, all his valor, and his construction of the pool and conduit by which water was brought into the city, are written in the book of the chronicles of the kings of Judah" (2 Kings 20:20). The Book of Proverbs includes collections of wise sayings from various sources, including sayings from "Lemuel, king of Massa" (Prov 31:1). These biblical authors made use of conventional human sources just as other historians or collectors of wise sayings do.

Paul's Letters   8.7.3

Paul, author of many New Testament books, similarly shows little or no awareness of being directly inspired by the Holy Spirit in his writing. Rather, Paul appears to be focused on the human business of corresponding with other people: "I am writing you this not to shame you, but to admonish you" (1 Cor 4:14); "I, Paul, write this in my own hand" (Philemon 19); "Greet Prisca and Aquila, my co-workers in Christ Jesus" (Rom 16:3); "Have a little wine for the sake of your stomach" (1 Tim 5:23); "When you come, bring the cloak I left with Carpus in Troas" (2 Tim 4:13). Accepting on faith that Paul is inspired, the evidence suggests that Paul's inspiration took a routinely human form.

In certain passages, however, Paul shows an awareness of the Spirit's guidance in his teaching: "I think that I too have the Spirit of God" (1 Cor 7:40; see also 1 Cor 14:37). But Paul's letters give no indication that he thought the Spirit was directly guiding his writing.

The Prophets   8.7.4

We now consider one type of biblical writing that does seem to credit direct inspiration from God: the words of the prophets. Jeremiah asserts that God spoke to him directly: "The word of the LORD came to me thus, 'Before I formed you in the womb I knew you, before you were born I dedicated you'" (Jer 1:4–5). Jeremiah then says explicitly, "Then the LORD extended his hand and touched my mouth, saying, 'See, I place my words in your mouth!'" (Jer 1:9).

But granted that Jeremiah claims a verbal revelation from God (received, apparently, in a dream or vision), this tells us nothing about how this initial revelation came to be *written down* in Scripture. Prophecy in ancient Israel, as a general rule, was an oral phenomenon. It followed a general pattern: a prophet, claiming that he was inspired by God, would deliver his message orally to the people. "Stand at the gate of the house of the LORD, and there proclaim this message: Hear the word of the LORD, all you of Judah who enter these gates to worship the LORD" (Jer 7:2). At times, the divine message was not even delivered orally, but rather in symbolic actions (see Jer 13:1–6).

The prophet Jeremiah himself did not write these oral proclamations down. Only after having received revelations is Jeremiah instructed by God to record them: "Take a scroll and write on it all the words I have spoken to you against Israel, Judah, and all the nations, from the day I first spoke to you, in the days of Josiah, until today. . . . So Jeremiah called Baruch, son of Neriah, who wrote down on a scroll, as Jeremiah dictated, all the words which the LORD had spoken to him" (Jer 36:2–4). It is difficult to imagine, at the strictly human level, how Jeremiah could have remembered the exact wording of revelations from a thirty-year time span. We might also wonder how accurately Baruch recorded the words or how Baruch's copy was then preserved.

While claiming that God revealed a message to them, Jeremiah and the other prophets spare us the details of their revelatory experience. It is interesting that even though the prophets record a verbal message, the "word of the LORD," their books often describe their revelatory experience as a *vision* (see Isa 1:1; Micah 1:1; Habakkuk 1:1). If the prophet was inspired as a human—and all Christians teach that God did not simply overpower the humanity of the inspired author—then it is reasonable to conclude that *he would have heard God's words as a human.* In other words, the prophet would have understood God's words through his own experiences and insight. But if this is so, then there is no way of separating God's pure message from how the human author received, understood, and communicated it.

The Ten Commandments   8.7.5

Sometimes, inconsistencies in the Scriptures themselves lead us to ask some historical and critical questions. By "critical" we simply mean reasonable questions that ask for evidence. Two versions of the Ten Commandments narrative provide a case in point.

According to Scripture, the Ten Commandments were "inscribed by God's own finger" on tablets of stone (Exod 31:18; Deut 9:10). When we examine the biblical record, however, some critical questions arise, since we have two scriptural versions of the Ten Commandments (Exod 20: 1–17; Deut 5:6–21). While several of the commandments are the same in both versions, others differ. A striking example is the commandment to keep the Sabbath. Note the italicized passages:

Exodus 20:8 - 11	Deuteronomy 5:12 - 15
Remember to keep holy the sabbath day. Six days you may labor and do all your work, but the seventh day is the sabbath of the LORD your God. No work may be done then *either* by you or your son or daughter, or your male or female slave, *or your beast,* or *by* the alien who lives with you. *In six days the Lord made the heavens and the earth, the sea and all that is in them, but on the seventh day he rested.* That is why the Lord *has* blessed the Sabbath day *and made it holy.*	*Take care* to keep holy the sabbath day *as the Lord your God commanded you.* Six days you may labor and do all your work; but the seventh day is the sabbath of the LORD your God. No work may be done, then, *whether* by you, or your son or daughter, or your male or female slave, *or your ox or ass or any of your beasts,* or the alien who lives with you. *Your male and female slave should rest as you do. For remember that you too were once slaves in Egypt, and the Lord, your God, brought you out from there with his strong hand and outstretched arm. That is why the* LORD, *your God, has commanded you to observe the sabbath day.*

The basic commandment to keep the Sabbath is obviously the same in both versions, but the rationale for keeping the Sabbath is completely different. If we assume that Scripture recorded God's words exactly, we are forced to ask: Which version was the original written by God?

Beyond the critical problem of the two versions, we also have to ask further historical and critical questions about how God's words were recorded and eventually written down in the books of Exodus and Deuteronomy.

So even in the case of the Ten Commandments, we cannot escape the theological conclusion that writing Scripture was a thoroughly human process—we simply do not have the exact words of God apart from any human influence on those words.

"Plenary Verbal Inspiration"   8.8

Dei Verbum affirms that all scriptural books and every part of those books were written "under the inspiration of the Holy Spirit" (*DV* no. 11). This rules out any opposing theory that only certain parts of the Bible are inspired (for example, books of the prophets), whereas other parts are not necessarily inspired (for example, historical books).

The authors of the *Chicago Statement* teach similarly, with an important addition: "We affirm that the whole of Scripture and all its parts, *down to the very words of the original*, were given by divine inspiration" (art. 6, emphasis added). This doctrine is sometimes referred to as "plenary verbal inspiration"—*plenary* meaning "full" or "complete."

We will use the term *verbally inspired* to refer to the theological belief that *every word* is inspired by God. The belief that God verbally inspired biblical authors raises a number of critical issues.

Textual Criticism   8.8.1

One critical problem with the belief that original writings of the scriptural books are verbally inspired is that we simply do not have the original text of any of the books of the Bible. Modern scholars possess only copies of these original writings, handwritten by ancient scribes—but no two of these copies are exactly the same. Through a process known as textual criticism, scholars study these copies in an attempt to find out what the original writing was. Let us briefly consider that process.

In the case of the New Testament, scholars have collected approximately five thousand handwritten, ancient Greek manuscripts. The earliest New Testament manuscript is a fragment of the Gospel of John that dates to around 100 CE—probably less than twenty years after the Gospel was first written. In the case of the Old Testament, Hebrew manuscripts of the various books date back to 150 years before Christ. The earliest Old Testament copies were found among the Dead Sea Scrolls—manuscripts found at Qumran, a community not far from Jerusalem in the Judean desert.

Trying to establish the original wording of the author, scholars compare the manuscript evidence for each biblical book. In most cases, especially among the New Testament manuscripts, the copies are quite close in wording, but there are some discrepancies. Some copies of the Gospel of Mark, for example, have "The beginning of the gospel of Jesus Christ, the Son of God" (Mark 1:1), while others read only, "The beginning of the gospel of Jesus Christ" and do not have "the Son of God." From the viewpoint of verbal inerrancy, then, we would have to ask, "Which version is inspired by God?" Some manuscripts of Hebrews 13:21 read, "May he carry out in *you* what is pleasing," while other manuscripts read, "May he carry out in *us* what is pleasing." Hundreds of other examples could be given. Depending on the evidence, in many cases we can be quite sure of the original wording, but in other cases, we can only make an educated guess.

The writers of the *Chicago Statement* are aware of these textual problems. They thus state that "inspiration, strictly speaking, applies only to the autographic text [the text written by the original author] of Scripture." Since textual criticism allows us to know the original text "with great accuracy," the writers of the *Statement* believe that the doctrine of verbal inspiration is still valid (art. 10).

But if we can never know the exact words—as is the case at a number of points in the manuscript tradition—does the doctrine of exact verbal inspiration make any practical sense?

Recent studies of the Dead Sea Scrolls raise even deeper challenges not only to the theory of verbal inspiration but also to our conception of inspiration itself. The ancient Jewish community at Qumran possessed several manuscripts of almost all of the biblical books, and of course there are some minor variations in the wording. But for certain books, the differences are so major that we must speak of two different *editions*. Such is the case with Exodus, Numbers, and Jeremiah—whole chapters are quite different.[7] And yet apparently the community accepted both versions as inspired.

Inspiration and Human Authorship   8.8.2

In the end, then, can we reconcile the belief that the Spirit inspired every word of Scripture with all this evidence for human composition? And can a human have true free will and still have his very word choice determined by the Spirit? The *Chicago Statement* indeed says, "We deny that God, in causing these writers to use the very words that He chose, overrode their personalities" (art. 8). But if every word is chosen by a power outside of him, how can an author be truly free to express his own personality? (It also seems odd to claim that such mundane comments as Paul's request to Timothy to bring his cloak are verbally inspired by the Spirit [2 Tim 4:13].)

The *Chicago Statement* does not claim that the Spirit dictated the Scripture word-for-word, affirming instead that the "mode of divine inspiration remains largely a mystery to us" (art. 7). Yet as we have noted, we cannot separate the pure "word of God" from the influence of the humans who received and recorded that word. Any theory of inspiration must do justice to this fact.

Inspiration and Communal Authorship   8.9

In traditional discussions about inspiration, theologians assume that a single author wrote a particular biblical book. This assumption works well in some cases: historical and literary studies support that Paul was indeed the single author of such letters as Romans and Galatians. We note, however, that Paul did dictate on at least some occasions (see the reference to his secretary Tertius in Rom 16:22).

But a critical evaluation of biblical books reveals that many of them had more than one author. This is obvious, for example, at the ending of the Gospel of John, "It is this disciple who testifies to these things and has written them, and we know that his testimony is true" (John 21:24). Who is the "we"? If we grant that "this disciple," called the "disciple whom Jesus loved" (John 21:20), is the main author of the Gospel, it seems there must be at least one other author or editor who was involved in writing the Gospel, and who in 21:24 comments on the trustworthiness of the disciple's testimony.[8]

We have evidence of a complex literary process in other biblical books as well. Consider some differences when we compare the first two chapters of Genesis in their accounts of creation.

Genesis 1:1 – 2:3	Genesis 2:4 – 25
• God is called "God" (in Hebrew, *Elohim*)	• God is called "LORD God" (in Hebrew, *Yahweh Elohim*)
• Creation occurs in six days	• No time frame for creation is given
• Fish, birds, and land animals (1:20 – 25) are created first, humans last (1:26 – 27)	• Man is formed first (2:7), before the plants (2:5) and before the animals (2:19 – 20)
• God creates humans in the divine image, male and female (1:27)	• LORD God forms Adam (2:7) and then later Eve from his rib (2:21 – 22)
• God creates things by speaking ("Let there be")	• LORD God forms things by working with his hands (2:7, 19, 22)

One can see from this comparison why many scholars believe that there were originally two stories of creation that were combined by a later editor. Scholars have labeled these hypothetical sources the Priestly (P) source (Gen 1) and the Yahwist (J) source (Gen 2).[9]

Finally, consider what modern scholarship tells us about a composition such as the Book of Judges. Stories in Judges began as oral traditions passed down by various tribes. After circulating for centuries, they were gathered into two written collections, a northern (Israel) and a southern (Judah) collection. The two collections were eventually united by an editor (or editors). After the **Babylonian Exile** (after 587 BCE), the same editors who put together the Book of Deuteronomy also further edited the Book of Judges. Finally, another editor added still more material, including an introduction and appendices. The entire process took some eight hundred years.[10]

The extended process involved in writing the Book of Judges is not an isolated exception. Scholarship has shown that the Book of Isaiah, for example, is composed of different sections that were written over a period of centuries.[11]

We should recall here also the evidence from the Dead Sea Scrolls, which shows that certain biblical books were rewritten in different editions (see sec. 8.8.1).

Our historical-critical evidence (see sec. 9.1) seems to call for a more social concept of biblical inspiration: a group of authors or editors, or perhaps a "school," composing some inspired books of Scripture over a period of centuries.[12]

James Barr thus suggests,

> If there is inspiration at all, then it must extend over the entire process of production that has led to the final text. Inspiration therefore must attach not to a small number of exceptional persons . . . it must extend over a larger number of anonymous persons . . . it must be considered to belong more to the community as a whole.[13]

We will return later to Barr's suggestion that inspiration belongs to the community as a whole.

Inerrancy and Inspiration   8.10

Christians have traditionally tended to identify inspiration with **inerrancy**. The word *inerrant* means "incapable of making a mistake." As applied to Scripture, inerrancy refers to the belief that God protected the biblical authors from making errors.

Many writers, both Catholic and non-Catholic, have assumed that inspiration and inerrancy logically cannot be separated. If God, who is perfect, inspired an author to write, then it follows that the author's writing must also be perfect—inerrant or without mistakes.

Theological theories of inerrancy are also closely tied with issues of the authority or trustworthiness of Scripture. If there are mistakes in Scripture, how can it be trusted? The issue of the trustworthiness of Scripture is critical for all scriptural religions, since Scripture is generally regarded as the highest religious authority.

The *Chicago Statement* affirms, "Scripture, having been given by divine inspiration, is infallible, so that, far from misleading us, it is true and reliable in all the matters it addresses" (art. 11). The scope of this inerrancy was clearly expressed in the introduction to the statement: "Scripture is without error or fault in all its teaching, no less in what it states about God's acts in creation, about the events of world history, and about its own literary origins under God, than in its witness to God's saving grace in individual lives." Scripture thus has no errors regarding any topic, including how the world was created and historical events. We will refer to this view that the Bible has no mistake of any kind as *strict inerrancy*.

Dei Verbum expresses itself with more caution. Because the authors were inspired by the Holy Spirit, "we must acknowledge that the books of Scripture, firmly, faithfully and without error, teach that truth which God, for the sake of our salvation, wished to see confided to the sacred Scriptures" (*DV* no. 11). The truth of Scripture, then, is that truth that God wished to see written "for the sake of our salvation."

What is this truth that God wished to see written? The statement in *Dei Verbum* is open to interpretation. Some Catholic interpreters have concluded that it means (in line with the *Chicago Statement*) that there is no error of any kind, since Scripture must contain a fully trustworthy truth that leads to salvation. The vast majority of Catholic biblical scholars and Church leaders, however, understand the wording of *Dei Verbum* to place a limitation on the truth that Scripture teaches "without error." It is only the truth that is recorded "for the sake of our salvation" that the faithful should regard as "without error." This interpretation leaves open the possibility that other biblical information that is not necessary for salvation (for example, historical accounts or descriptions of nature) could contain errors.[14] We shall refer to this view as *limited inerrancy*: the belief that only the truths necessary for salvation are to be considered inerrant.

The evidence we have considered so far in our chapter makes the second interpretation more reasonable. Yet even if we accept the theological theory that only biblical truth that is necessary for salvation is without error, we are still faced with questions. Exactly what truth is it that is necessary for salvation? Most Christians would agree that a teaching such as "Christ died for our sins" (1 Cor 15:3) is central, or the teaching that Christ rose from the dead. But would a believer, for example, have to believe that the teaching that Christ rose *bodily* from the dead is "without error"? Or could a believer accept, for example, that the accounts of Christ's Resurrection are generally correct, but might have some errors in detail? It seems difficult to make clear distinctions between biblical claims necessary for salvation and those not necessary for salvation.

All Christians believe that the Bible is the essential record of God's special revelation; Catholic theologians such as Aquinas taught that Scripture is the fundamental source of God's revelation (*ST* 1.1.9). So the question of whether the Bible is accurate and trustworthy is essential. But the issue whether the inspired Bible is inerrant or in what precise way it is inerrant is probably not the most helpful way to phrase the question. More helpful is to ask *in what ways* the Bible is *trustworthy and true*. We shall try to answer that question in the following sections.

The Differing Truths of Differing Genres 8.11

Regarding the understanding of truth, *Dei Verbum* teaches that "truth is differently presented and expressed in the various types of historical writing, in prophetical and poetical texts, and in other forms of literary expression" (*DV* no. 12).

The *Chicago Statement* grants the same point.

> In inspiration, God utilized the culture and conventions of his penman's milieu. . . . So history must be treated as history, poetry as poetry, hyperbole and metaphor as hyperbole and metaphor, generalization and approximation as what they are, and so forth. (*Exposition*, III C)

Most Christians would agree, I think, that Jesus' parables are not meant as literal historical facts: Jesus told stories to illustrate points. Thus in his story of the son who wastes his father's inheritance, but eventually repents and is forgiven (Luke 15:11–32), few would insist that the details of the story must be literally true.

Jonah: A Didactic Story 8.11.1

What about the story related in the Book of Jonah? The book itself presents Jonah as a prophet every bit as historical as Jeremiah: "This is the word of the LORD that came to Jonah son of Amittai" (Jon 1:1).

But if we read the story critically, we find several unbelievable details. A "large fish" swallows Jonah, and he remains in its belly for three days (Jon 2:1). In the main action of the story, Jonah preaches to the people of Nineveh for one day, and they repent and believe God's message (3:5). But how is this possible, historically speaking? The Assyrian people of Nineveh believed in their own gods, and no doubt the vast majority had never even heard of the God of Israel. How could they have been converted by one sermon? On an even more basic level, how would the Assyrian-speaking people even have understood the Hebrew-speaking Jonah?

Some would answer these historical-critical questions by relying on faith. If we accept that God can perform miracles, why can't we say that God sent a miraculous fish and that God miraculously caused the

Ninevites to understand Jonah and to believe miraculously in the God of Israel instead of their own gods?

Yet this hypothetical string of miracles seems to contradict Scripture's usual way of portraying supernatural events. In our earlier discussions of miracles, we saw that typically biblical miracles work *in harmony* with natural events (sec. 5.17).

If we compare the story of Jonah to an account of Jesus healing a blind man in the Gospels (see Mark 8:22-26), for example, we'll notice some essential differences:

1. When Jesus restores the blind man's sight, he works miraculously to restore nature's original purpose (eyes that see). In contrast, the insides of large fish were never naturally meant to serve as human transportation.

2. The setting of the Gospel story is historically plausible: Jesus is a first-century Jew healing a fellow Jew in a Galilean village. The entire setting of Jonah is implausible: polytheist, non-Hebrew-speaking Assyrians converted by the monotheistic Hebrew Jonah.

The author of Jonah, furthermore, never tries to convince his reader that the events are miracles. He does not say that God miraculously intervened and translated Jonah's speech into the language of the Assyrians; he simply glosses over that point and narrates events in a straightforward, historical way, as would the author of any realistic fictional story.

The literary genre of Jonah, therefore, is not history, but a parable, or a didactic story (a story meant to teach a point).[15] The basic genre of telling a fictional story in order to convey a moral lesson is found in every culture: think of *Aesop's Fables* or the fairy tales or legends of innumerable cultures. Their truth is found in the lesson, not in the history.

Jonah is a didactic story. Its truth is not a literal historical truth, but rather the truth that the God of Israel is also concerned with the salvation of Gentile peoples.

Job as Didactic Story   8.11.2

The Book of Job raises critical questions—not so much historical or scientific questions as theological and ethical ones. In the story, God essentially makes a bet with Satan to see whether Job will remain faithful to him. God allows Satan to test Job—a test that includes killing all of his children (Job 1). Are we really to believe that a loving God would make such cruel deals with Satan?

On these ethical grounds alone we have good reason to question whether Job is literally true. Already Augustine (354–430) developed this principle of biblical interpretation: "Anything in the divine writings that cannot be referred either to good, honest morals or to the truth of the faith, you must know is said figuratively."[16]

Another clue that the story is not meant to be historical is its almost complete lack of specific references to historical time and place. The only locater is the very general beginning sentence: "In the land of Uz there was a blameless and upright man named Job" (Job 1:1).

We can reasonably conclude that Job is meant as a didactic story. The clear point of the long speeches and dialogues in the book is to deal with the question of why good people suffer. In order to dramatize the issue, the author(s) develops a story of a good man (Job) who suffers terrible tragedies.

The truth of Job is thus not a historical, literal truth. Its truth emerges in its wrestling with answers to the age-old question of why bad things happen to good people, and in its conclusion that a person should continue to trust God even when answers to such questions are beyond human understanding (Job 38).

Cultural Limitations on Scriptural Truth 8.12

Dei Verbum teaches, "Rightly to understand what the sacred author wanted to affirm in his work, due attention must be paid both to the customary and characteristic patterns of perception, speech and narrative which prevailed at the age of the sacred writer" (*DV* no. 12).

Our examples above (8.7) show that inspired authors worked very much as human authors, and to be human is to be part of a particular human culture. The biblical authors lived in ancient Hebrew, Jewish, and Hellenistic cultures. When we consider the biblical evidence, we find no reason to think that God's inspiration took them beyond the moral and intellectual limitations of those cultures.

Again, let's consider some specific examples, and then draw some conclusions.

Cultural Limitations on Scientific Knowledge 8.12.1

The biblical authors lived and wrote in a time before modern science. It is hardly surprising, then, that they thought that the sun literally moved across the sky:

> Joshua prayed to the LORD, and said in the presence of Israel: Stand still, O sun, at Gibeon, O moon, in the valley of Aijalon! And the sun stood still, and the moon stayed, while the nation took vengeance on its foes. Is this not recorded in the Book of Jashar? The sun halted in the middle of the sky; not for a whole day did it resume its swift course. (Jos 10:12–13)

Nor is it surprising that there are discrepancies between the accounts of creation in Genesis and the views of modern science:

Genesis	Modern Scientific View
The sun, moon, stars, earth and all its life forms were created in six days (Genesis 1).	The universe itself is approximately 12–14 billion years old; our sun and the earth are approximately 4.5 billion years old.
There were three evenings and mornings (Gen 1:1–13) before the sun was created (Gen 1:16).	How can there be evening and morning if there is no sun?
Plants were created on day three (Gen 1:11), one day before the creation of the sun (Gen 1:14–18).	The sun formed billions of years before the first plant life. Since plants need sunlight for survival, it is impossible to have plant life without the sun.
If we add up the ages of the generations recorded in the Bible (by using records such as the one found in Gen 5) from Adam and Eve until modern recorded history, the earth would be about six thousand years old.	The earth is about 4.5 billion years old.

The author(s) of Genesis did not have access to modern scientific information and thus simply communicated the story of God's creation of the earth in a way that would be understandable to their own culture. Notice how they describe God "working" for six days and "resting" on the Sabbath — this is exactly the cultural pattern of work and rest observed by the ancient Hebrews. To take the story literally would be theologically unreasonable, since it suggests that almighty God literally needed a twenty-four-hour break from his activity. No, the story clearly describes God's working in a manner analogous to human working, and thus puts the doctrine of God's creation of the world into culturally comprehensible terms.

This observation supports our earlier conclusions: even granted (from a faith perspective) that the authors were inspired, they still wrote as human beings who were limited by the knowledge of their own ancient cultures.

Cultural Limitations on Ethical Values　　8.12.2

Although certainly ethical evil exists still today, many would argue that the human race as a whole has made some ethical progress over the centuries. The modern world, for the most part, has gained a better understanding of the dignity and equality of all people, for example. This increased understanding has led us to such ethical advances as the abolition of slavery and increased opportunities for women.

Since the biblical authors wrote as human members of ancient cultures, it again should not surprise us that they shared many of the ethical limitations of their cultures as well.

The biblical authors shared in the ancient world's general acceptance of the institution of slavery as natural and normal. The great patriarchs of Hebrew history, such as Abraham (Gen 12:16), Isaac (Gen 24:35), and Jacob (Gen 32:6), all owned slaves. One of the Ten Commandments that we studied above (8.7.5) presupposes ownership of slaves. Even in the New Testament, slavery is seen as normal: Paul's Letter to the Ephesians advises, "Slaves, be obedient to your human masters" (Eph 6:5), and Paul himself sent a runaway slave back to his master (Philemon).

It is true that the Bible argues that slaves should be treated well: the Ten Commandments say that the slave should also rest on the Sabbath, and Paul insists that there is no essential difference between slave and master, "for the slave called in the Lord is a freed person in the Lord, just as the free person who has been called is a slave of Christ" (1 Cor 7:22). In one famous passage, Paul describes the Christian community in this way: "There is neither Jew nor Greek, there is neither slave nor free person, there is not male or female; for you are all one in Christ Jesus" (Gal 3:28). These differences are not essential — people are equal as members of the Body of Christ.

Despite recognizing the equality of all in Christ, neither Paul nor any other New Testament writer took what to a modern reader would seem to be the next logical step by calling for the end of slavery. No doubt slavery simply seemed natural to the cultures at that time, as philosophers such as Plato and Aristotle had taught.

The Christian tradition did indeed come to realize that slavery is intrinsically evil, no matter how well masters treat their slaves. When Pope Gregory XVI forbade Catholics from engaging in slavery or the slave trade (in the encyclical *Supremo Apostolatus* in 1839), one could argue that this position developed from scriptural seeds such as Paul's teaching that there is no slave or free person in Christ, or the teaching that all people are created in the image of God (Gen 1:26–27). But the scriptural authors did not take this step, and to that extent were limited by their cultural beliefs.

Development of Truth in the Bible　8.13

Even within Scripture there is a dynamic process of reinterpretation.[17] The process could occur even within a single book. Historical-critical studies have shown that books such as Isaiah grew and developed over centuries as new material was added to reinterpret and update the old in the light of new experiences of the people of Israel. Thus at the time of the Babylonian Exile, the prophecies of "Deutero-Isaiah" were added to the centuries-old oracles of the original prophet Isaiah.

The process of development also took place as a sort of "dialogue" that occurred when differing viewpoints of different books were read as part of the same Scripture. Let's take a look at some examples.

Group-Oriented Personality and Individual Responsibility　8.13.1

Sometimes the partial insights of an earlier time were challenged or complemented in later writings. Consider one of the Ten Commandments:

> For I, the LORD, your God, am a jealous God, inflicting punishment for their father's wickedness on the children of those who hate me, down to the third and fourth generations. (Exod 20:5)

The Book of Ezekiel states,

> Only the one who sins shall die. The son shall not be charged with the guilt of his father, nor shall the father be charged with the guilt of his son. The virtuous man's virtue shall be his own, as the wicked man's wickedness shall be his. (Ezek 18:20)

At the verbal level, the two statements flatly contradict each other: Exodus says that God punishes the children for their fathers' sins, and Ezekiel says God does not. But such a comparison involves a static concept of truth. Applying the idea of development within the biblical tradition, we can see that both passages express *partial* truths that must be held in tension to attain a fuller sense of the truth.

Looked at from a historical-critical view, we can say that the cultural values evident in the Exodus passage emphasize the value of the social group over the individual; a person in such a culture would have a "group-oriented personality."[18] This perspective, common in ancient Mediterranean cultures, saw children not so much as independent persons in their own right, but as family members who received their identity from the family as a whole. From this perspective it would be natural to speak of the child being punished for the sins of the father.

The Ezekiel passage, written at the time of the Babylonian Exile, centuries after the Exodus account, marks a development from this group-oriented perspective. By Ezekiel's time, the Jewish culture was able to view the individual more as an independent person responsible for his or her own actions.

So we see a development in ideas, but the partial truth of the earlier insight is still valuable. If we were to consider the truth of both passages, we might say that together they give us a more holistic view of the person. Each person is ultimately responsible for his or her own actions, as Ezekiel saw. But no person is an island — each individual is influenced profoundly, often in unconscious ways, by others around him, especially close friends and family — a truth to which the Exodus passage still witnesses today.

Sacrifice   8.13.2

The Bible commands various types of sacrifices to be offered (for example, in Leviticus 1–7). But what kind of "truth" can these passages have, now that neither Christians nor Jews literally offer sacrifices?

Traditionally, Christians have understood the laws of sacrifice (and the Torah in general) in two ways: (1) as scriptural commandments foreshadowing later Christian beliefs or practices (for example, the sacrifices foreshadow Christ's ultimate sacrifice of offering his life on the cross); (2) as part of a temporary covenant between the Jewish people and God before the coming of the Messiah. A passage from the Letter to the Hebrews may reflect elements of both perspectives:

> He [Jesus] has no need, as did the high priests, to offer sacrifice day after day, first for his own sins and then for those of the people; he did that once for all when he offered himself. (Heb 7:27)

From a Christian perspective, many of the practices and beliefs found in Old Testament times developed into specifically Christian practices and beliefs.

Yet even within a specifically Jewish perspective we can see development in understanding, from a literal understanding of sacrifice to a more spiritual one. The psalmist can say, "For you do not desire sacrifice; a burnt offering you would not accept. My sacrifice, God, is a broken spirit" (Ps 51:18–19). Such developments allowed the Jewish people to worship God in the synagogue instead of simply through sacrifice offered at the Temple.

Other Examples of Development and Dynamic Tension   8.13.3

Consider a few other developments within Scripture. Many of these developments are a result of a "dialogue" taking place on particular issues between authors who are separated by both time and cultural perspective. Yet when the community (either of Israel or of the Church) places these divergent writings into the same collection of Scripture, fresh, dynamic insights often arise from the encounter.

1. **A debate on God's reaction to good and evil.** Some passages present a black-and-white view that righteous people are always rewarded and the wicked are always punished (Ps 1 and 112). Others (especially Job) passionately dispute this view as too simplistic. As Job complains, "Why do the wicked survive, grow old, become mighty in power?" (21:7).

   Both views contain truth, and the biblical reader is challenged to see how they relate. Wickedness always has some negative consequences (even if it only harms the wicked person's own conscience and soul), and good behavior always has its own intrinsic reward, yet Job is right to insist that the realities of life are too complex to be conveyed by simply asserting that God rewards the good and punishes the wicked.

2. **Development in the view of the afterlife.** The early Hebrews believed that all the dead, good and bad, exist in a shadowy sort of way in Sheol (see Gen 37:35; Ps 9:18); in later passages we see the belief in the resurrection of the dead and reward and punishment in heaven and hell (for example, Dan 12:2; Matt 25:31–46).

3. **Differing views on faith, action, and salvation.** Paul says, "For we consider that a person is justified by faith apart from works of the law" (Rom 3:28). But James asserts, "See how a person is justified by works and not by faith alone" (Jas 2:24).

    As the biblical reader struggles to reconcile these two perspectives, other insights may emerge. Thus, for example, the reader may understand more deeply that a person's actions or "works" are such an intimate part of who they are that they cannot be neatly separated from that person's fundamental faith.

Biblical scholar James Sanders argues that these and other tensions within the Bible constitute a strength and not a weakness.

> There can be no program that can be constructed on the basis of the Bible which can escape the challenge of other portions of it: this is an essential part of its pluralism. No one person, no denomination, no ideology, can exhaust the Bible or claim its *unity*. It bears with it its own redeeming contradictions, and this is a major reason it has lasted so long and has spoken so effectively to so many different historical contexts and communities. . . . The whole Bible, of whichever canon, can never be stuffed into one theological box.[19]

Truth and Error in the Bible 8.14

In understanding truth and the trustworthiness of the Bible, then, we must pay special attention to the literary form in which a truth is expressed and also to the cultural limitations of the authors. But in addition to these considerations, it is clear that the Bible also contains what can only be called errors.

Consider the following examples.

1. David killed the Philistine "Goliath of Gath" whose javelin shaft "was like a weaver's heddle-bar" (1 Sam 17:4 – 50, esp. 17:7).

2. A later account, however, claims that a man named Elhanan killed Goliath: "There was another battle with the Philistines in Gob, in which Elhanan, son of Jair from Bethlehem, killed Goliath of Gath, who had a spear with a shaft like a weaver's heddle-bar" (2 Sam 21:19).

3. The author of 1 Chronicles, who used the books of Samuel as a source, saw the discrepancy and tried to smooth it out: "Once again there was war with the Philistines, and Elhanan, the son of Jair, slew Lahmi, the brother of Goliath of Gath, whose spear shaft was like a weaver's heddle-bar" (1 Chron 20:5).

It is clear that all three accounts cannot be historically accurate. Concerning the first two accounts, either David killed Goliath, or Elhanan did. One could possibly argue that there were two men named "Goliath of Gath," both of whom owned a spear "like a weaver's heddle-bar," but this would be a stretch. It seems clear we have two different versions of the same event. The author of Chronicles saw the historical problem and tried to solve it by saying that Elhanan killed the brother of Goliath, not Goliath himself. We do not know if the author of Chronicles had additional information, or simply changed the account so that it would no longer be a contradiction.

Any theory of inspiration, therefore, must account for the fact that the biblical authors were not only limited in their understanding of truth, but plainly made errors.

Toward a Communal Model 8.15

Traditional Christian views of biblical inspiration seem to hold the following process as a paradigm: the Holy Spirit inspires a single prophet to write a book and thus ensures that God's word will be recorded without any serious errors (or with no errors at all, if one follows strict inerrancy).

In light of historical and critical understandings of the Bible, however, such a model is no longer adequate. Using some suggestions from within the Catholic tradition, we now consider how the traditional model of inspiration might be adapted to reflect the reality of biblical authorship.

Communal View of Inspiration: Israel and the Church 8.15.1

While Paul's Letter to the Galatians, for example, is the product of one author at one point in time, the authorship of many other biblical books is better understood as a process. This process may have included an oral stage before writing, and rewriting over a period of centuries. It also seems appropriate to speak of the inspiration of the *community* in which oral and written traditions were passed down: Israel and the Old Testament, the Church and the New Testament. This suggestion does not imply some vague notion that every member of the community was inspired in some way, but rather the reasonable theological insight that the God who plays a role in gathering people together as a community of faith also guides that community in its vital task of finding written expression of its fundamental beliefs and tasks in Scripture.

The Canonization Process 8.15.2

The books of the Bible are known as a **canon**. The Greek word *kanon* originally meant a measuring tool or, metaphorically, a standard or rule by which things are evaluated. As applied to the Bible, *canon* refers to the authoritative list of books that, according to the faith community (Israel or the Church), meet the standard of faith. All books of the canon are considered by Christians to be inspired by the Holy Spirit.

Let's briefly consider the process of canonization as it applies to New Testament writings. Jesus himself did not write, and his earliest followers preached his message orally (see the speeches in the Acts of the Apostles, for example). For the earliest communities of Jesus' followers, the standard measure of a true teaching about Jesus was the oral tradition that had been passed down from Jesus' closest disciples (also known as apostles). So Paul reminds the Corinthian church, "For I handed on to you [orally] as of first importance what I also received [orally]: that Christ died for our sins in accordance with the Scriptures [the Old Testament]; that he was buried; that he was raised on the third day in accordance with the Scriptures" (1 Cor 15:3-4). When writings such as Paul's letters or the Gospels appeared, their truth was measured against the standard of this oral tradition. The tradition is also known as the "apostolic tradition," since it was associated with Jesus' earliest followers (see chapter 9 on apostolic tradition).

Over time, then, a body of writings came to be accepted as "canonical"—writings that were considered to witness faithfully to the apostolic tradition. Such writings were read aloud in Christian worship (see Col 4:16; Rev 1:3). The authors of these writings, thought to be apostles or followers of the apostles, were considered to be inspired by the Holy Spirit.

At first, individual churches began a generally informal process of judging whether a particular writing was "canonical" and should be accepted as trustworthy. At a later stage, we see bishops and theologians concerned with establishing a canon of sacred writings for the whole Church. Certain writings were widely accepted as canonical (and thus inspired) by the second century, but the exact list of twenty-seven books that are now part of the New Testament canon does not appear until the later fourth century (367, Athanasius's *Festal Letter*). Catholic theologians have made it clear that the Church does not have the authority to *grant* inspiration to a particular writing after the fact—it only has the authority to *recognize officially* at a later date that a particular writing was inspired by the Holy Spirit.[20]

An analogous process took place in which the community of Israel also recognized and accepted certain writings that formed its scriptural canon.

Canonization and Inspiration   8.15.3

In the catholic Christian view, the communities of faith, Israel and the Church, had the authority to recognize and accept which books would be considered inspired and canonical. Yet even before authority had evolved to that point, the process by which a book was written took place within the authority and oversight of the community of faith.

Thus biblical scholar Bruce Vawter concludes, "Inspiration should be thought of primarily as one of the qualities bestowed upon the community of faith by the Spirit of God that has called it into being."[21] Individuals (such as Jeremiah or Luke) are of course inspired, but they are inspired as members of a faith community.

Rahner speaks of the inspired writing of Scripture as a "constitutive element" of the Church. In other words, the Christian Church was in a certain sense not fully established until the inspired Scripture was written and recognized.[22] In the process of writing and later canonizing Scripture, the Church expresses its own self-understanding in a more objective way and produces a concrete, visible standard or canon that the later generations of Christians can follow. In Scripture, "the apostolic Church interprets itself for later ages."[23]

A Dynamic View of Truth 8.16

A traditional theory of biblical inspiration tended to regard biblical truth as static: God directly revealed a truth to a biblical author, and the author recorded it.

More recent literary, critical, and historical studies of Scripture have shown us that the writing of Scripture was very much a *human* process. While accepting that God inspired the author, these studies show that inspiration worked through human channels.

We thus have a more lively sense that different truths may be expressed in different literary genres. We have a greater appreciation for how human culture influenced, shaped, and at times limited the way in which divine truths were expressed. We understand better that the full truth often is not expressed best in a single passage, but rather in the dynamic tension between more than one passage in a variety of biblical books. And finally, we can perhaps grasp the idea that the expression of divine truth does not rule out simple human error.

To accept a more dynamic view of truth is by no means to accept the idea that truth is subjective, or that truth is always relative, not absolute. On the contrary, the dynamic view has the highest regard for truth, but simply insists that truth cannot be relegated to one unchanging, static form.

As Raymond Brown reminds us (sec. 8.7), it is better to avoid reading Scripture with preconceived ideas of what biblical inspiration must mean (e.g., that it must mean that every word is inerrant). If a reader, while accepting on faith that Scripture is inspired, wrestles honestly and critically with what Scripture actually says, he or she may find that the inspiration of the Holy Spirit works in some unusual and unexpected ways.

Questions about the Text

1. What purpose or purposes do scriptures serve in any religious tradition?

2. What is the basic meaning of the theological belief that Scripture is inspired by the Holy Spirit?

3. In what ways did early Christians identify a biblical author's inspiration with the gift of prophecy?

4. Compare how the Gospel of Luke was written with how the Book of Jeremiah was written.

5. What does the fact that there are two versions of the Ten Commandments imply for a theory of biblical inspiration?

6. What does "plenary verbal inspiration of Scripture" mean? What are some historical and critical challenges to this belief?

7. What is the evidence that some biblical books were written by more than one author?

8. What is the theory of biblical inerrancy, and why is it important for theology? What is the difference between strict and limited inerrancy? What are some criticisms of both views?

9. What does it mean to say that different literary genres have different truths? Give examples of the difference between an ethical or didactic truth, and a historical or literal truth.

10. What are some examples of how the scientific understanding of the biblical authors was limited? How would this insight have applied to the Galileo affair?

11. How is the institution of slavery regarded in the Bible? What does the biblical view of slavery imply for theories of biblical inspiration?

12. Discuss some examples of the development of ideas within Scripture (e.g., of sacrifice or views of the afterlife). What are the implications of such development for theories of biblical inspiration and inerrancy?

13. Differing views on the roles of faith and good works for salvation offer one example of "dynamic tension" within Scripture; what are some others? What implications does such dynamic tension have for theories of biblical inspiration, inerrancy, and the concept of truth in Scripture?

14. Discuss evidence of factual errors in Scripture. What are the implications for theories of biblical inspiration and inerrancy?

15. Why is there a trend toward a more "communal" understanding of biblical inspiration? How is communal understanding related to the process of canonization of Scripture?

16. In what ways have literary, historical, and critical studies of Scripture led to a more dynamic view of scriptural truth?

Discussion Questions

1. Are you familiar with the scriptures of other religious traditions? What are some similarities and differences that you have noted?

2. In what ways would the inspiration of a poet or a painter be different from the inspiration of an author of Scripture?

3. Do you think that if an author is inspired by God, his writing should be inerrant in some sense? Explain your reasoning.

4. Besides the examples given in the text, what are some other examples of different kinds of truth?

5. Does an individual or a communal sense of inspiration make more sense to you? Explain.

Endnotes

1. It should be noted that the passage in 2 Tim 3:16, seen in its historical context, refers only to the Scripture of what Christians today call the "Old Testament"; the New Testament had not yet been recognized books of the Scripture.
2. See Bruce Vawter, *Biblical Inspiration*, Theological Resources (Philadelphia: Westminster, 1972), 20–42.
3. Aquinas discusses biblical inspiration under the general heading of "Prophecy" (*ST* 2 /2. 171–74).
4. See Vawter, *Biblical Inspiration*, 43–75.
5. See Raymond F. Collins, "Inspiration," in *NJBC*, 1027–28.
6. R. E. Brown, *The Critical Meaning of the Bible* (New York: Paulist Press, 1981) 18–19.
7. See Eugene Ulrich, "The Bible in the Making: The Scriptures Found at Qumran," in *The Bible at Qumran: Text, Shape, and Interpretation*, ed. P. W. Flint (Grand Rapids, MI: Eerdmans, 2001), 59–64.
8. For the scholarly theory of a "Johannine school" that composed the Gospel, see Pheme Perkins, "The Gospel According to John," in *NJBC*, 946–47.
9. For a scholarly view on the four major sources of the Pentateuch (the first five books of the Bible), including *P* and *J*, see R. E. Murphy, "Introduction to the Pentateuch," in *NJBC*, 4–5.
10. See Vawter, *Biblical Inspiration*, 104–5.
11. See C. Stuhlmueller, "Deutero-Isaiah and Trito-Isaiah," in *NJBC*, 329–30.
12. For "social theories" of inspiration, see Collins, "Inspiration," in *NJBC*, 1032.
13. Quoted in ibid.
14. For a discussion of these points, see ibid., 1030.
15. See A. R. Ceresko, "Jonah," in *NJBC*, 580.
16. Augustine, *On Christian Doctrine*, 3.14.
17. See the Pontifical Biblical Commission's "The Interpretation of the Bible in the Church," in *The Scripture Documents: An Anthology of Official Catholic Teachings*, ed. D. P. Béchard (Collegeville, MN: Liturgical, 2002), 284–89.

18. See Bruce J. Malina, *The New Testament World: Insights from Cultural Anthropology*, rev. ed. (Louisville, KY: Westminster / John Knox, 1993), 65–73.

19. James Sanders, *Canon and Community: A Guide to Canonical Criticism* (Philadelphia: Fortress Press, 1984), 37.

20. Collins, "Inspiration," in *NJBC*, 1029.

21. Vawter, *Biblical Inspiration*, 158.

22. Karl Rahner, *Inspiration in the Bible*, Quaestiones Disputatae (New York: Herder and Herder, 1961), 47–50.

23. Karl Rahner, "Scripture and Tradition," in *Theological Investigations* (London: Darton, Longman & Todd; New York: Seabury Press, 1974), 6:102.

9

Understanding the Bible

God's Word in Human Words

A basic Christian belief is that the Holy Spirit inspired the authors of Scripture. But as we discussed in the last chapter, accepting this belief by no means leads to the conclusion that the Holy Spirit took away all human limitations from the authors. On the contrary, the scriptural evidence leads to the theological conclusion that an inspired author still has human limitations of knowledge and cultural perspective.

To gain a deeper understanding of Scripture, then, a reader must consider the historical and cultural context of a biblical author, since these conditions had a profound influence on how an author thought and wrote. To get a good sense of this context, the biblical scholar may legitimately use any of the historical and critical tools that are used to study any culture.

Yet at the same time, the Christian faith perspective insists that the books of the Bible are not the same as any other writing—they are authoritative writings composed under the inspiration of the Holy Spirit.

Vatican II's *Dei Verbum* acknowledges that both the human and the divine factors should be considered when interpreting Scripture. "[I]n sacred Scripture, God speaks through men in human fashion. . . . The interpreter of sacred Scriptures . . . should carefully search out the meaning which the sacred writers really had in mind." At the same time, "sacred Scripture must be read and interpreted with its divine authorship in mind" (*DV* no. 12).

In this chapter, we will consider these two aspects of interpretation.

The Historical-Critical Method   9.1

In Scripture studies, the umbrella term for the approaches focusing on understanding the human author in his cultural and historical contexts is the **historical-critical method.**[1]

Scholarly and religious communities today continue to debate the value and limitations of the historical-critical method. The term itself is somewhat misleading, since it suggests there is *one* clearly defined historical-critical method. This is not the case. While most scholars could agree that certain approaches are essential to the method (for example, textual and source criticism), other approaches (such as literary or genre criticism or various sociological approaches) may or may not be labeled "historical-critical" by different scholars.

We will define as *historical* those methods used to understand any historical writing (religious or otherwise), especially those methods whose goal is to clarify the historical context in which a work was written. We will define *critical* not as a hostile or suspicious approach to the text but simply one that asks reasonable questions about all aspects of a text's human authorship, including such tough questions as whether an author shows bias or makes mistakes. Again, if we take seriously the true humanity of the scriptural author (see chapter 8), we cannot rule out error or bias simply because we believe an author is inspired.

We turn now to a consideration of some specific historical-critical approaches.

Textual Criticism 9.2

Before we can interpret an author's work, we first need to establish as nearly as possible precisely what he wrote. This can only be done by comparing differences between manuscripts and making critical decisions about which readings are most likely to be original (see sec. 8.8.1). Even Christians with conservative views of verbal inspiration and strict inerrancy agree that textual criticism is the first step in interpreting a biblical text.

As we have seen, however, textual criticism and other historical-critical disciplines have implications for theories of inspiration. Textual criticism shows us, for example, that manuscripts of the Gospel of Mark have several different endings. The earliest manuscripts end after 16:8, while others include the so-called longer ending (16:9–20), and still others also add a "shorter ending" (found after v. 20 in some modern translations). Textual critics have shown that the original manuscript of Mark most likely ended after verse 8. So does this mean that the other verses should not be accepted as part of the inspired text, since, traditionally, Christians have considered Mark the inspired author, and not the copyist or scribe who first added the additional endings? The same question must be raised about John 8:1–11, the well-known text about Jesus and the woman caught in adultery, since it too is missing from the earliest manuscripts.

These examples show again that it makes more theological sense to consider inspiration (the guidance of the Holy Spirit) as a gift given to the Church as a whole rather than to an individual author. Only from this perspective is it reasonable to accept these later scribal additions as inspired and canonical.

Nor are these additions to Mark and John exceptional. The Dead Sea Scrolls include various editions of books, and the Book of Isaiah shows evidence of a centuries-long composition process (although admittedly there is no textual evidence of an "original" first Isaiah). Thus we err when we focus narrowly on the "inspired" text of the original author. Rather, we must consider the whole process of composition as inspired if we regard the current text as inspired.

Questions of Authorship 9.3

For interpreting any writing, some knowledge about the author can be helpful. When you are writing a research paper for a class, for example, it is essential to cite your sources, since this information will help the reader judge whether your information is trustworthy.

Thus, in interpreting a biblical text, we can ask: Who was the author (or authors)? When was the text written? To what extent can we determine the author's (authors') original purpose for writing?

In interpreting the Gospel of Matthew, for example, it would help to know whether the author is the apostle Matthew who was a companion of Jesus (Matt 10:3), a later writer, or even more than one writer or editor.[2] The Gospel itself does not identify the author (the attribution to Matthew is a later addition).

The Author's Use of Sources   9.3.1

Many biblical authors used sources in their work, both oral and written (see sec.s 8.7.1–2). To answer critical questions about the reliability and trustworthiness of the biblical authors, we need to have a good sense of the sources they used. Thus when writing a historical account, did the author(s) have access to eyewitness accounts, or is he (are they) relying on secondhand information? We will discuss some of these questions as we consider the Gospel accounts about Jesus in our next chapter. The effort to identify an author's sources is known, naturally enough, as *source criticism*.

A particular approach for analyzing an author's sources is known as *form-criticism*. This approach attempts to determine a source's original oral structure, the original social context in which it developed, and how it was subsequently passed down in oral tradition. Thus, for example, scholars have recognized the form of the *pronouncement story*—a relatively fixed form of narrating a story that culminates in a saying of Jesus (see, for example, the stories in Mark 2). The method is associated especially with Old Testament scholar Hermann Gunkel (early twentieth century) and New Testament scholar Rudolf Bultmann (1884–1976; see sec. 10.9.1 for criticism of the assumptions of this method).

We refer to the study of how an author adjusted or adapted his sources as *redaction criticism* (*redactor* being another word for *editor*). Identifying how an author adapts or adjusts sources can give us insights into that author's particular interests. Thus, assuming that Matthew used the Gospel of Mark as one of his sources (a theory accepted by many critical scholars), we can often see how Matthew's rewriting of an account emphasizes Jesus' Jewish identity (compare Mark 6: 7–13 and Matt 10:5–15).

Historical and Cultural Context 9.4

A correct understanding of historical and cultural context is crucial for understanding the Bible. For example, to interpret Paul's teaching that women should wear head coverings in the church at Corinth (1 Cor 11:3–16), we need to know the cultural expectations regarding women's dress at that time, as well as the cultural significance and symbolism of head coverings. When the Letter of James instructs a sick person to call the elders of the church to pray and anoint him with olive oil (Jas 5:14), we need to understand the meaning of anointing and the significance of olive oil in the ancient world. When we read that Jesus cast out a "mute and deaf spirit" (Mark 9:25), it helps to be familiar with ancient beliefs about spirits and causes of illness. To understand why a pig is "unclean" and thus not fit for food (Lev 11:6–7), we need a sense of what "unclean" meant in ancient Hebrew culture and why a pig was considered unclean.

An uncritical reading of Scripture can in fact cause great harm, as when Scripture was used to justify slavery (see sec. 8.12.2). A clear understanding of how culture inevitably shapes and conditions the biblical message is essential for a reasoned interpretation of Scripture.

Literary (Genre) Criticism 9.5

Literary criticism is a broad term, and many thinkers would distinguish it sharply from historical criticism. We use it here to mean a critical evaluation regarding the type (*genre*) of literature to which a work belongs. As we have seen, it makes a good deal of difference whether we think the story of Job is a historical account or a didactic story. Determining the literary genre is also essential in determining the writer's original intent. Both *Dei Verbum* (no. 12) and the *Chicago Statement* (art. 18) emphasize the importance of understanding genre.

For these and related reasons the Pontifical Biblical Commission (PBC) document *Interpretation of the Bible in the Church* (1993) calls the historical-critical method "indispensable":

> The historical-critical method is the indispensable method for the scientific study of the meaning of ancient texts. Holy Scripture, inasmuch as it is the "Word of God in human language," has been composed by human authors in all its various parts and in all the sources that lie behind them. Because of this, its proper understanding not only admits the use of this method but actually requires it. (I A)[3]

Critiquing Historical-Critical Method 9.6

Yet the use of the historical-critical method in scriptural studies has been criticized for various reasons in recent decades.[4] Some of the criticisms are listed here.

- Historical-critical studies focus on detecting sources and historical background at the expense of the text's literary power and beauty as well as its general and religious meaning.

- The historical-critical method's Enlightenment roots bias it against Church authority.

- The method ignores the fact that all interpretation is influenced by subjective factors and biases.

- Its "scientific" orientation intimidates the average reader of the Bible.

- Once a text is written, the historical context in which it was created is no longer relevant as the text either creates a narrative world of its own or its meaning is a product of the reader's beliefs, biases, and understandings.

Defending the Historical-Critical Method 9.7

Before attempting to show that the proper use of the historical-critical method is essential to Catholic and Christian theology, we should point out that the modern Roman Catholic Church accepted the legitimacy of the historical-critical method only slowly and grudgingly. As late as the first half of the twentieth century, the Roman Catholic hierarchy remained suspicious of the approach and Catholic scholars were restricted in its use. The Pontifical Biblical Commission, set up in 1902, issued a series of ultraconservative teachings (for example, that Moses was the author of the first five books of the Bible, that Genesis 1–3 was to be understood literally, and that the Book of Isaiah was composed by a single author). It was only after Pius XII's encyclical *Divino afflante Spiritu* (*On the Promotion of Biblical Studies*; 1943) that the use of the historical-critical method began to be employed freely by Catholic scholars.[5]

By 1993, the Pontifical Biblical Commission was able to describe the historical-critical method as necessary. Among the many distinguished Catholic biblical scholars in the second half of the twentieth century, Raymond Brown and Joseph Fitzmyer have been leading practitioners and defenders of the method.

Using some of the insights of Brown, Fitzmyer, and the Commission, as well as other sources, we can suggest some elements of a Catholic response to criticisms of the historical-critical method.

1. **Criticism:** The historical-critical method is an inappropriate tool to use in the study of divinely inspired Scripture. **Response:** Use of the method is consistent with the belief that humans are *true authors* of Scripture (*DV* no. 11). If they truly acted as humans, then insights into their historical and cultural context, their use of sources, and their methods of redaction are essential in reaching a correct interpretation.

2. **Criticism:** The historical-critical method is at best agnostic and rationalistic, and at worst intentionally anti-Christian (or at least anti-Church hierarchy). **Response:** The historical-critical method itself is essentially neutral.[6] It is true that rationalists and Church critics pioneered application of this method to Scripture. These critics brought rationalist presuppositions (above all, their denial of the supernatural) to their work, together with biased presuppositions, such as their assumption that earliest Christian worship was free and spontaneous, and any evidence of concern for structure, rules, or sacramental interpretation of rituals was a later development.[7] Yet there is no reason why these misleading presuppositions cannot be separated from the method itself. In fact, correct application of the method will call into question such mistaken presuppositions.

3. **Criticism:** The historical-critical approach cannot determine the influence of the Holy Spirit on an author. **Response:** The influence of the Holy Spirit is not open to precise rational examination. Christianity teaches that the Holy Spirit works through the humanity of the author (see chapter 8), and no method can neatly separate these human and divine elements.

4. **Criticism:** The historical-critical method implicitly claims that it is the only legitimate method for studying Scripture; other methods are considered "precritical" or naïve. **Response:** The historical-critical method should not be used in isolation. It is essential

in answering specific questions about the human process of authoring a text, but its insights can and should be supplemented by the use of other methods (for example, approaches that focus more on the literary art of Scripture).

From a Catholic perspective, a true understanding of the inspired text cannot stop with the insights gleaned from historical-critical research or from strictly literary approaches, but must be supplemented by considering its meaning within the whole of Scripture and in light of the general teachings of the Church (see below for further discussion of these points).

5. **Criticism:** Proponents claim that the historical-critical method is "scientific" and "objective," and thus mask their own biases and presuppositions. **Response:** No interpreter can come to a text without presuppositions (see sec. 3.5.1). But in using the method (for example, in trying to determine the original intention of the author), interpreters can and should be open about their presuppositions while striving for fairness and objectivity.

   In addition, feminist, liberationist, and similar approaches can help the scholar who takes a predominately historical-critical approach to appreciate and understand aspects of the text that have been overlooked in the past. At the same time, exclusive use of these newer approaches will result in a one-sided perspective that can distort the original meaning of a text.[8]

6. **Criticism:** The historical-critical method ignores narrative and reader-response insights that show how meaning does not lie "objectively" in the text alone, but rather is created through an interplay between text and reader. **Response:** The Catholic tradition seeks a balanced, critical-realist approach to interpretation. Such an approach accepts that the reader's presuppositions do indeed influence the meaning of a text, but denies that they determine it. Rather, meaning occurs through a "fusion of horizons" (as Gadamer teaches) when readers allow their presuppositions to encounter the meaning of a text — they do not simply impose their own meaning on it (see secs. 3.5.1–2). The encounter with the text's meaning can come only through a critical reading of the text (as Ricouer insists), and it is precisely the tools of the historical-critical approach that allow this critical reading to occur (see sec. 3.5.3; see also Lonergan's thoughts on critical realism as an approach to interpretation: sec. 3.6.2.1).

The Historical-Critical Method and the Literal Sense 9.8

Official Catholic approval of the historical-critical method finally came in 1943. The delay resulted from specific historical circumstances such as the early association of the method with Enlightenment and anti-Catholic thought, and not from any inherent incompatibility between the method and the Catholic theological tradition. In fact, the historical-critical method is completely consistent with the traditional Catholic synthesis of faith and reason. Specifically, the method is consistent with the Catholic emphasis on the literal and historical meaning of the text as the foundation of Scripture's meaning. In the following we take a closer look at that relationship.

The Catholic Church has long taught that Scripture has different "senses." [9] In medieval times, for example, a common understanding was that Scripture had four senses:

1. Historical or literal sense

2. Allegorical sense: the symbolic meaning that points beyond itself

3. Moral sense: the ethical meaning or lesson taught in Scripture

4. Anagogical sense: the meaning as found in the eschatological fulfillment of God's plan

Let us now consider how Aquinas understood the senses of Scripture and then relate his view to the historical-critical approach (*ST* 1.1.10).

In the first question of the *Summa*, Aquinas discusses the "nature and extent of sacred doctrine." For Aquinas, the study of Scripture was essentially identical with the study of theology (sacred doctrine): "For our faith rests upon the revelations made to the apostles and prophets, who wrote the canonical books" (*ST* 1.1.9). Henri de Lubac writes that this view of the centrality of Scripture was a Catholic consensus, especially before the Reformation. In a sense, "all of revelation is contained in Scripture" and thus, in the interpretation of Scripture, "all of theological science is encompassed." [10]

Aquinas (*ST* 1.1.10) divides the four traditional senses of Scripture into two basic categories: (1) the historical or literal sense, and (2) the spiritual sense (allegorical, moral, anagogical).

Peter Kreeft gives examples for each of Aquinas's three spiritual senses:

1. **Allegorical sense:** "Moses (symbolic of Christ) leading the Hebrews (symbolic of the Church, Christ's Body) through the exodus (symbolic of salvation) from slavery (symbolic of sin) to Pharaoh (symbolic of Satan), ruler of Egypt (symbolic of this fallen world), across the Red Sea (symbolic of death), through the wilderness (symbolic of Purgatory) to the Promised Land (symbolic of Heaven)." The primary meaning of the allegorical is to find in the Old Testament a prefiguring of Christian realities.

2. **Moral sense:** Jesus' washing his disciples' feet (John 13) symbolizes the requirement of followers of Jesus to serve one another.

3. **Anagogical sense:** Jesus' miracles of healing a blind man symbolize the clear vision that those who are saved will have of God in heaven.[11]

Aquinas is clear that the historical or literal sense is foundational, and the spiritual sense "is based on the literal, and presupposes it." Aquinas states further,

> All the senses are founded on one—the literal—from which alone can any argument be drawn, and not from those intended in allegory, as Augustine says (*Epistle* 48). Nevertheless, nothing of Holy Scripture perishes on account of this, since nothing necessary to faith is contained under the spiritual sense which is not elsewhere put forward by the Scripture in the literal sense.

Aquinas identifies the literal sense with "that which the author intends." Understanding the literal sense includes an awareness of when an author is using a metaphor: thus, the "literal sense" of the scriptural phrase "God's arm" is the metaphorical meaning of God's power to act. Aquinas also includes explanations of historical events under the literal sense.

The *Catechism*, referencing Aquinas, teaches that "the *literal sense* is the meaning conveyed by the words of Scripture and discovered by exegesis, following the rules of sound interpretation: 'All other senses of Sacred Scripture are based on the literal'" (*CCC* no. 116). In his 1943 encyclical *Divino afflante Spiritu (On the Promotion of Biblical Studies)*, Pope Pius XII, although he did not refer specifically to the historical-critical method, explicitly stated that historical and critical techniques are necessary for recovering the literal sense:

> What is the "literal" sense of a passage is not always as obvious in the speeches and writings of the ancient authors of the East as it is in the works of our own time. For what they wished to express is not to be determined by the rules of grammar and philology alone nor solely by the context; the interpreter must, as it were, go back wholly in spirit to those remote centuries of the East and with the aid of history, archaeology, ethnology, and other sciences accurately determine what modes of writing, so to speak, the authors of that ancient period would be likely to use, and in fact did use.[12]

The Catholic insistence on the permanent value of the historical-critical approach to interpreting Scripture is part of the Catholic tradition's commitment to reason and its rejection of fideism (see sec. 2.7).

Interpreting the Bible: God as Author 9.9

The historical-critical approach is essential for establishing the literal and historical meaning of Scripture and thus for understanding its human authorship. But if one is to understand Scripture as divinely inspired and discern how it addresses the spiritual needs of people today, other approaches to interpretation are necessary as well. *Dei Verbum* addresses this issue:

> But since sacred Scripture must be read and interpreted with its divine authorship in mind, no less attention must be devoted to the content and unity of the whole of Scripture, taking into account the Tradition of the entire Church and the analogy of faith, if we are to derive their true meaning from the sacred texts. (*DV* no. 12)

The *Catechism* summarizes *Dei Verbum*'s teaching in three points:

1. Be especially attentive "to the content and unity of the whole of Scripture."

2. Read the Scripture within "the living Tradition of the whole Church."

3. Be attentive to the "analogy of faith" (defined by the *Catechism* as "the coherence of the truths of faith among themselves within the whole plan of Revelation," *CCC* nos. 112–14).

We may also add a fourth principle, recognized by the *Catechism*:

4. All other senses are based on the literal (*CCC* no. 116).

These four principles, in the Catholic view, help the interpreter to recover, in a responsible way, the "spiritual" senses of Scripture, and thus help the interpreter to apply the spiritual or moral lesson of Scripture to his own situation in the modern world, a process known as *actualization*.[13]

Interpretation within the Tradition of the Church and Individual Interpretation 9.10

Dei Verbum's first three principles are actually contained within the second, that is, that Scripture should be read within "the living Tradition of the whole Church." But before we explore what this means, let's take a brief look at two challenges to this Catholic principle.

The Protestant Reformation 9.10.1

The Protestant Reformation was a direct challenge to the belief that the Bible must be read and interpreted in the context of Church Tradition. In the early 1500s, the Reformation began under the leadership of Martin Luther and other Reformers. The movement eventually led to the formation of new Christian denominations, including the Lutheran and various Reformed churches. One of the major issues that led to these groups splitting away from the Catholic Church was precisely the Reformers' belief that Church authority was distorting the true meaning of the Scriptures.

One of the most famous slogans of the Reformation is summed up in the Latin phrase, ***sola scriptura***: "Scripture alone!" For Luther and other Reformers, this phrase expressed their principle that the Scriptures should be the sole authority on which Christian teachings are based. In their view, the Catholic Church had overstepped its authority by developing teaching and practices that were not based directly on the Bible (for example, teaching that there are specifically seven sacraments, or that only priests have the authority to forgive sins).

One of Luther's driving motivations was to get the Bible into the hands of ordinary people so that they could read it for themselves and thus protect themselves from Church distortions—to facilitate this he produced his great translation of the Bible into German.

Today, centuries after the Reformation, the issues dividing the Catholic and Protestant churches do not seem as overwhelming. Constructive dialogues have been held between Roman Catholics and various faith communities since the Second Vatican Council, including a Lutheran-Catholic dialogue, and the sides have discovered more common ground in their respective beliefs about the Bible and Church authority (see secs. 12.25–27).

Nevertheless, important differences remain, not least regarding differing understandings of the relationship between Scripture and Church. In the following discussion, we will explore why Catholic thought does not accept the principle of *sola scriptura* as held by the Reformers. We will see that many of the Catholic principles, however, are today also recognized as legitimate by other Christian churches as well.

Modern Individualism　9.11

A second challenge to the principle that the Bible should be read and interpreted within the Tradition of the Church is rooted in the values of modern Western culture, a culture that stresses individuality, democracy, and intellectual freedom. Many Western Christians simply assume that individuals have the right to interpret the Bible for themselves. It makes no sense, according to this view, that an educated, modern reader would have to depend on the "living Tradition of the whole Church" to understand Scripture properly or fully.

We will explore, then, how the Catholic and catholic traditions have responded to these challenges.

Scripture as a Product of the Church　9.12

At the beginning of this book (sec. 1.1), we defined the term *tradition* as "a way of life or customs that are passed down through the generations." If you think about it, only an organized community that shares the same religious beliefs can pass down a religious tradition, "a way of life." In the Christian tradition, this community is the Church.

The very concept of "scripture" presupposes an organized community of faith. *Scripture* usually means "holy writing"—but "holy" for whom? The Qur'an is scripture for the Muslim community, the Tanak is scripture for the Jewish community, the Vedas are scripture for the Hindu community, and the Bible is scripture for the Christian community.

Scripture is formed by a community. As we saw earlier (8.15), it was the community of faith, either Israel or the Church, that officially recognized a particular writing as inspired by God and thus as Scripture. The Bible as the combination of Old and New Testaments would have remained unknown unless first recognized by the Church. "By means of the same Tradition the full canon of the sacred books is known to the Church" (*DV* no. 8).

Historical-critical investigations have shown that we can go farther in this understanding: the very books themselves are the products of a faith community. The Book of Isaiah, for example, was put together over a period of centuries under the guidance of the faith community.

Distinguishing Scripture and Tradition 9.13

The word *tradition*, as we have seen, can have a broad meaning: the phrases "the Jewish tradition" or "the Christian tradition" can be synonymous with Judaism as a whole or with Christianity as a whole. The essential beliefs and practices of Christianity may also be called the *gospel* or the *deposit of faith* (*CCC* no. 84).

In Catholic theology, however, **Tradition** (note the capital *T*) also has a narrower definition, referring to Christian beliefs and customs that are *not* directly in Scripture. "This living transmission, accomplished in the Holy Spirit, is called Tradition, since it is distinct from Sacred Scripture, though closely connected to it" (*CCC* no. 78).[14] The entire deposit of faith, then, has been passed down in "two distinct modes of transmission": in the Tradition of the Church and in the Scriptures (*CCC* no. 81).

We will now consider why the Catholic Church makes this distinction between Scripture and Tradition, and at the same time get a better sense of the meaning of Tradition itself.

Tradition Apart from Scripture 9.14

Apostolic Tradition Before the New Testament 9.14.1

The earliest Church passed down the deposit of faith long before the New Testament books were written (see sec. 8.15.2). The apostles and their close associates passed down the essential Christian teachings through oral preaching and instruction—only later did the idea of creating a written deposit of faith (a scripture) emerge.

The New Testament is filled with witnesses to this oral tradition. Paul refers to the essential teachings that he had passed on to the Corinthians, "For I handed on to you as of first importance what I also received: that Christ died for our sins in accordance with the Scriptures; that he was buried; that he was raised on the third day in accordance with the Scriptures" (1 Cor 15:3–4).

In numerous other passages, Paul and other New Testament authors refer to these oral teachings.

> I praise you because you remember me in everything and hold fast to the traditions, just as I handed them on to you. (1 Cor 11:2)

> For you know what instructions we gave you through the Lord Jesus. (1 Thess 4:2)

> Stand firm and hold fast to the traditions that you were taught, either by an oral statement or by a letter of ours. (2 Thess 2:15)

This apostolic tradition was not composed of oral teachings alone, but also of firmly established Church practices. Paul's letters (the earliest of the New Testament documents) show that baptism (Rom 6:3; 1 Cor 1:14) and the Lord's Supper (1 Cor 11:23–34) were firmly established practices in the churches already in Paul's time.

Yves Congar points out that nowhere in the New Testament is there a systematic teaching about the practice and significance of the Lord's Supper in the early Christian churches. Various questions are thus left unanswered. Should children receive? Who should preside? What prayers should be said during the ceremony? We have some stray remarks by the apostle Paul about the Supper, but this is only because the Corinthians had raised specific issues for Paul to address (1 Cor 10:16–22; 11:17–34).

Congar's point is that the New Testament writings, especially Paul's letters, were never meant to give a systematic overview of Christian belief and practice. Rather, they were written to address specific issues that arose in specific churches. Paul's writings (and other New Testament texts) presuppose that a more systematic instruction had already been given orally in prebaptismal teaching. Thus we cannot expect to find the full apostolic tradition in the Scriptures.[15]

Furthermore, Scripture itself does not claim to be the only basis of Christian teaching. Thus in one passage referenced above (2 Thess 2:15), Paul admonishes his community to hold fast to his teachings, expressed both in his letters and in oral traditions; Scripture itself shows that it is not self-sufficient for Christian faith.[16] *Dei Verbum* teaches, "The Church does not draw her certainty about all revealed truths from the holy Scriptures alone" (no. 9). The apostolic tradition before the New Testament shows that, in theory, it is possible to live and transmit the Christian life even without Scripture.[17] It is in this sense that *Dei Verbum* teaches that "Tradition transmits in its entirety the Word of God which has been entrusted to the apostles by Christ the Lord and the Holy Spirit" (*DV* no. 9).

Further Examples of Tradition Apart from Scripture   9.14.2

Today we no longer have direct access to the apostolic oral traditions not recorded in Scripture. We do have indirect access, however, in the living Tradition of the churches as it has been passed down since apostolic times. Beliefs and practices passed down through nonscriptural Tradition include:

1. **Canonization of Scripture.** The process of recognizing which writings should be accepted as scriptural obviously stands outside of Scripture itself. Only a nonscriptural authority can determine the canon of Scripture.

2. **Sunday worship.** The first Christians, as Jews, celebrated the Sabbath on Saturday. The tradition of Christians meeting on Sunday (in honor of Jesus' Resurrection) rather than Saturday is neither commanded nor justified in Scripture (though there may be an allusion to this practice in 1 Cor 16:2; see also Rev 1:10). In fact, the tradition of weekly worship itself is not described, explained, or commanded in the New Testament.

3. **Infant baptism** (see further discussion in sec. 9.18.1). The New Testament itself explicitly mentions only the baptism of adults. Yet the tradition of infant baptism is accepted by the Roman Catholic Church, the Orthodox churches, the Anglican Church, and the main churches of the Reformation (Lutheran and Reformed). Infant baptism is rejected by traditions that have their roots in the Anabaptist movement (a radical branch of the Reformation).[18]

4. **Authority of the creeds.** The process of writing brief, systematic summaries of the main Christian beliefs lies outside of Scripture. The Christian tradition recognizes especially the authority of the Apostles' Creed and the Nicene-Constantinopolitan Creed.

5. **Living experience of the Church.** Tradition includes the living experience of the Church through the centuries: the teachings of the great theologians (Augustine, Aquinas, Gregory of Nyssa, Luther, and Calvin); various liturgies and prayers; the sacraments; sacred music (Gregorian chant, Bach's Masses, contemporary Christian music); great religious art (icons of the Orthodox tradition, Michelangelo's paintings on the Sistine Chapel, the great medieval cathedrals); and Church symbols (the crucifix, the act of making the sign of the cross). All of these and many more are powerful, essential mediums by which the faith has been passed down outside of Scripture.[19]

Congar compares this living sense of Tradition to the process of education. A child receives an ethical education (learning right from wrong) not so much from direct instruction as through a living process of daily experience, learning especially from the examples of parents or other loved ones.[20] We can compare this sense of Tradition with our earlier critiques of the rationalist view of knowledge (sec. 2.5). In that discussion we saw that humans learn not simply by a strictly logical study of a written text, but rather through more indirect methods: by accepting authority and tradition, making decisions based on probabilities, and letting themselves be guided by intuitions that cannot be reduced to strict rules.

What is passed down in the Christian Tradition is Christianity itself, in all of its lived experience—an experience so rich and mysterious that it can never be summed up in a few written formulas.

Tradition Interprets Scripture: The Magisterium 9.15

One crucial role of Tradition as distinct from Scripture is to provide Christians with an accurate interpretation of Scripture. Every Christian tradition recognizes some type of authority that guides it in its approach to Scripture. Many churches accept the creeds as a guideline to what is most important in Scripture. In the Lutheran tradition, Luther's principle that a person is justified by faith alone has served as an interpretive guideline, leading that tradition to emphasize the letters of Paul over the Letter of James, for example.

In the Roman Catholic tradition, the official teaching authority is known as the **Magisterium**, the teaching authority composed of bishops and the pope. A central task of the Magisterium is the interpretation of Scripture: "the task of giving an authentic interpretation of the Word of God, whether in its written form or in the form of Tradition, has been entrusted to the living teaching office of the Church alone" (*DV* no. 10).

The Magisterium is closely associated with Christ's apostles. In the Catholic view, the apostles, in a process known as **apostolic succession**, handed down this teaching authority to the bishops, so that the deposit of faith would be passed down fully and accurately (*DV* no. 2.7; *CCC* nos. 77–78). Irenaeus, writing around the year 180, insists that Christians of his generation can "contemplate clearly the tradition of the apostles manifested throughout the whole world; and we are in a position to reckon up those who were by the apostles instituted bishops in the churches, and [to demonstrate] the succession of these men to our own times" (*Against Heresies* 3.3.1). As the bishop of Rome, the pope has a unique teaching authority among the bishops. "The task of interpretation has been entrusted to the bishops in communion with the successor of Peter, the Bishop of Rome" (*CCC* no. 85; for further discussion of the "apostolic tradition," see sec.s 12.13–16).

In the Catholic view, it is essential to have a final, definitive authority in order to resolve the inevitable theological disputes that arise in the life of the Church. In the Arian controversy (6.14.2), both orthodox theologians (who believed that the Son was equal to the Father) and Arian theologians (who believed that the Son was less than the Father) found support in Scripture. It was only when the Church's Magisterium spoke through its councils and creeds, using nonscriptural, philosophical language to add precision to its teaching, that the conflicts were resolved.

Dei Verbum is careful to qualify this authority when it adds, "Yet this Magisterium is not superior to the Word of God, but its servant" (no. 10). The Magisterium cannot reveal divine truths, the Church teaches, rather its task is to clarify and explain the divine truths that have already been revealed.

Tradition Interprets Scripture: Further Examples 9.15.1

During the first centuries, the Church made authoritative judgments on which particular writings would be considered Scripture (the process of canonization). When writings such as Paul's letters or the Gospels were first circulated, their truth was measured by the Church against the standard of apostolic tradition, and these various writings were eventually placed together as a single canon of Scripture.

By the very act of placing different books together in a single canon, a religious community already has begun the process of interpretation. Israel's community of faith decided the Exodus statement on sons being punished for their fathers' sins must be interpreted together with Ezekiel's insistence on individual responsibility (see sec. 8.13.1). In addition to inheriting Israel's canonical interpretations, the community of the Church determined that Paul's insight that "a person is justified by faith apart from works of the law" (Rom 3:28) must be balanced with the assertion of James that "a person is justified by works and not by faith alone" (Jas 2:24; see sec. 8.13.3).[21]

The Church's statement of faith in the Nicene Creed became the key by which the Catholic Tradition interpreted Scripture: "By means of the same Tradition . . . the holy Scriptures themselves are more thoroughly understood and constantly actualized in the Church" (*DV* no. 8). Many early Christian writers witness to this principle. Irenaeus writes that presbyters of the Church "expound the Scriptures to us without danger" (*Against Heresies* 4.36.5). Origen insists, "The key to the Scriptures must be received from the tradition of the Church, as from the Lord himself."[22] "I would not believe in the Gospel," writes Augustine, "had not the authority of the Catholic Church already moved me" (*Against the Epistle of Manichaeus* 5.6). The liturgy of the Church also interprets Scripture by selecting certain texts to be read together in a single worship service. For example, the modern Roman Catholic liturgy of the Mass combines an Old Testament account of the Hebrews eating manna ("the bread from heaven"; compare John 6:32–33) in the desert (Exod 16) with a New Testament text in which Jesus proclaims, "I am the bread of life" (John 6:35).

The whole process of a tradition providing authoritative interpretations to its scriptural texts is common throughout history. It is a process central to the way in which civilizations develop. In living the life of Judaism, orthodox Jews consult not only the Tanak but the traditional rabbinic teachings preserved in the Mishnah and Talmud. Traditional Muslims base beliefs and practice not on the Qur'an alone but also on the Hadith (traditions of Mohammed) and the guidance of the Ulama (community of religious scholars). In Mahayana Buddhism one consults not only the original teachings of the Buddha preserved in the Pali Canon but also later interpretive scriptures such as the Lotus Sutra.

In the Christian tradition, the way in which a reader understands a text such as the Bible has already been profoundly shaped by a certain tradition of interpretation (sec.s 1.11 and 3.5.1). Thus a reader instructed in the doctrine of the Trinity and the teachings of the Nicene Creed will read the New Testament in a way that is quite different from a person not familiar with those traditional teachings.

A purely individual interpretation of Scripture apart from the Tradition of the Church is impossible. The presuppositions of the reader about God and Jesus (for example) have already been shaped by years of interpretation through creeds, councils, and various other informal methods of passing down the faith. If the New Testament is to be read at all, it must be through the lens of a tradition; the Catholic claim is that the Catholic Tradition is the most trustworthy lens.

Recent Developments on Scripture and Tradition 9.16

As a result of the sharp divisions of the Reformation, the tendency of the Protestant churches has been to emphasize the principle of *sola scriptura*, while the Catholic reaction has been to defend the authority of Scripture and Tradition. In recent decades, however, this sharp dichotomy has softened, as many Protestant and evangelical churches are recovering a sense of the importance of Tradition and Catholic theologians are recovering a sense of the centrality of Scripture within the Catholic synthesis of Scripture and Tradition. Part of this ongoing convergence has been a clarification of the theological meaning of Tradition.

Tradition and Traditions 9.16.1

The nonscriptural traditions of the Catholic Church are not all of equal value. Some traditions have been relevant only to certain times and cultures. Thus the Roman Catholic Church, as a result of the renewal associated with the Second Vatican Council, changed centuries-old traditions such as fasting from meat on Fridays and saying the Mass in Latin. The phrase "sacred Tradition," however, as it is used in *Dei Verbum*, refers to essential teachings and practices that are not subject to change, for example, the clarification given to the doctrine of the Trinity by the councils of Nicaea and Constantinople. Congar thus distinguishes between unchanging Tradition (capital *T*) and traditions that are subject to change (lowercase *t*).[23]

This same distinction was made in a 1963 statement on Scripture, Tradition, and traditions of the Faith and Order Commission of the World Council of Churches, an alliance of a broad range of more than three hundred Christian churches, including Orthodox and Protestant churches. "We can speak of the Christian Tradition (with a capital *T*), whose content is God's revelation and self-giving in Christ, present in the life of the Church" (no. 46).[24] The statement uses the word *traditions* (lowercase *t*), to refer to the "diversity of forms of expression" in the Christian Tradition, and "also what we call confessional traditions, for instance, the Lutheran tradition or the Reformed tradition" (no. 39).

The Faith and Order statement speaks of a living Christian Tradition in a sense very similar to that of Congar:

> We exist as Christians by the Tradition of the Gospel (the *paradosis* of the *kerygma*) testified in Scripture, transmitted in and by the Church through the power of the Holy Spirit. Tradition taken in this sense is actualized in the preaching of the Word, in the administration of the sacraments and worship, in Christian teaching and theology, and in mission and witness to Christ by the lives of the members of the Church. What is transmitted in the process of tradition is the Christian faith, not only as a sum of tenets, but as a living reality transmitted through the operation of the Holy Spirit. (no. 46–47)

In this broad sense, then, Tradition includes Scripture.

Evangelical and Protestant Recovery of Tradition   9.16.2

The 1963 Faith and Order report does not hold a strict *sola scriptura* position: "The very fact that Tradition precedes the Scriptures points to the significance of tradition" (no. 42). The report also concurs with *Dei Verbum*'s teaching that the Scripture must be interpreted within the context of Church Tradition:

> The Tradition in its written form, as Holy Scripture (comprising both the Old and the New Testament), has to be interpreted by the Church in ever new situations. Such interpretation of the Tradition is to be found in the crystallization of tradition in the creeds, the liturgical forms of the sacraments and other forms of worship, and

also in the preaching of the Word and in theological expositions of the Church's doctrine. (no. 50)

Many Protestant and evangelical writers are becoming aware of the value of interpreting Scripture not solely as individuals, but as self-conscious members of a two-thousand-year-old tradition.[25] The Faith and Order report asks, "Should we not study more the Fathers of all periods of the Church and their interpretations of Scripture in the light of our ecumenical task?" (no. 55). Representative of this renewed interest are a number of ongoing series published by traditionally evangelical presses. Baker's Press, for example, is publishing the Evangelical Resourcement series, meant "to address the ways in which Christians may draw upon the thought and life of the early church to respond to the challenges facing today's church."[26]

Two series, the *Ancient Christian Commentary on Scripture* (Inter-Varsity) and The Church's Bible (Eerdmans), have adopted the ancient Christian *catena* method for reading Scripture. Using this method, passages from biblical books are quoted, followed by exegetical comments on the passages drawn from the influential early Christian theologians known collectively as the "Fathers of the Church" (writers such as Irenaeus, Tertullian, and Augustine).

The principle of interpreting Scripture within the Church community is also evident in the interpretive approach known as *canonical criticism* associated with the Protestant biblical scholar James Sanders. Sanders champions the vision of a scholar who, while accepting modern critical approaches to Scripture, is also "openly willing to be a servant of the believing communities."[27] Canonical criticism thus studies the canonical process: how the communities of Israel and the Church interacted with their Scripture, constantly renewing and updating them to apply to new situations. This same process, Sanders argues, must continue in the believing communities today.

A Renewed Catholic Sense of the Centrality of Scripture 9.16.3

Roman Catholic theology after the Reformation, in large part as a reaction against the *sola scriptura* principle of the Reformers, tended to describe Scripture and Tradition as two separate forms of God's revelation. Yet many theologians within pre-Reformation tradition recognized the centrality of Scripture.

The Centrality of Scripture
in Earliest Christianity   9.16.3.1

Even before the canonization process that resulted in the New Testament began, the earliest Church already had a Scripture: the Scripture of Israel. In fact, it is not an exaggeration to say that the essence of Christian theology was—and is—an interpretation of the Scriptures of Israel in light of Jesus Christ. Recall how Paul reminds the Corinthian church of his basic teachings to them:

> For I handed on to you as of first importance what I also received: that Christ died for our sins *in accordance with the scriptures*; that he was buried; that he was raised on the third day *in accordance with the scriptures*. (1 Cor 15:3–4; emphasis added)

All of the essential New Testament titles of Jesus are interpretations of the Old Testament (see sec. 6.10).

- **Christ.** Meaning "the anointed one," this title had as its primary reference Israel's king and thus drew on the multiple scriptural references to this figure, often portrayed in ideal terms (for example, Ps 2:8, "Only ask it of me, and I will make your inheritance the nations").

- **Son of Man.** This title's primary referent is the mysterious figure in Daniel 7:13, "one like a son of man" coming on the clouds to be presented before God's throne.

- **Lord.** This title (at least in some instances) applies the scriptural title given to the God of Israel to Jesus.

- **Word.** Though the title *Logos* itself is borrowed most directly from Greek philosophy, it is also a philosophical interpretation of scriptural passages such as Proverbs 8:22–31 that portray God creating the universe through his Wisdom.

Furthermore, all of Paul's essential teachings are based on Scripture interpreted through Jesus Christ, both the traditions Paul received ("according to the scriptures" in 1 Cor 15:3–4), and his more distinctive teachings (such as his teaching that Gentile followers of Jesus did not have to follow Torah).

The Primary Authority for Christian Faith 9.16.3.2

The later Catholic and catholic tradition also recognizes the centrality of Scripture. As noted above (sec. 9.8), de Lubac writes of a pre-Reformation consensus that, in a sense, "all of revelation is contained in Scripture" and thus, in the interpretation of Scripture, "all of theological science is encompassed."[28] Aquinas teaches that Scripture is the foundation of the Christian faith: "For our faith rests upon the revelation made to the apostles and prophets who wrote the canonical books" (*ST* 1.1.8 ad. 2). Aquinas recognizes other theological authorities, especially the teachings of the popes and the Church Councils, but believes that the authority of Scripture is primary. If Tradition or Church teaching claimed to teach something that contradicted Scripture, it would be false, Aquinas argues, and the faithful ought to reject it.[29] According to one strand of Catholic theology, then, we can say that "Scripture contained, in one way or another, all the truths necessary for salvation."[30]

Congar writes that, for a Catholic, "the holy Scriptures have an absolute authority which Tradition has not. . . . They are the supreme guide to which any others there may be are subjected."[31] Rahner even speaks of a "Catholic *sola scriptura*" principle. Rahner argues that the saving truths of the Catholic faith are all based on Scripture alone — but on Scripture as it has been recognized and interpreted by the Church and its Magisterium. Such interpretation, for Rahner, includes the principle of the "development of doctrine" — that in some cases Scripture contains the seeds of truths that were later developed within Church Tradition.[32]

The Inseparability of Tradition and Scripture 9.17

Dei Verbum was careful to say that Tradition and Scripture are not two separate sources of God's revelation. "Sacred Tradition and sacred Scripture make up a single sacred deposit of the Word of God, which is entrusted to the Church" (no. 10). The two "are bound closely together and communicate one with the other"; "both of them, flowing out from the same divine well-spring, come together in some fashion to make one thing and move towards the same goal. . . . Hence, both Scripture and Tradition must be accepted and honored with equal feelings of devotion and reverence" (*DV* no. 9).

Congar writes that "no article of the Church's belief is held on the authority of Scripture independently of Tradition, and none on the authority of Tradition independently of Scripture."[33] Scripture is the primary witness to the Christian faith. But Scripture cannot be separated from Tradition and from the teachings of the Magisterium that interpret it. *Dei Verbum* sees all three as intimately cooperating in order to achieve the ultimate purpose of the salvation of humanity:

> It is clear, therefore, that in the supremely wise arrangement of God, sacred Tradition, sacred Scripture and the Magisterium of the Church are so connected and associated that one of them cannot stand without the others. Working together, each in its own way under the action of the one Holy Spirit, they all contribute effectively to the salvation of souls. (no. 10)

Development of Doctrine   9.18

Essential to the Catholic understanding of the relationship between Scripture and Tradition, as Rahner noted, is the principle of "development of doctrine." We have already considered a classic example of this Catholic principle: the gradual development of Trinitarian doctrine from its scriptural roots by means of more precise, philosophically sophisticated terminology (sec. 6.14.2).

We have also considered the evidence of development of ideas within Scripture itself: ideas concerning the afterlife, sacrifice, God's punishment of the wicked and reward of the good (sec. 8.13). As John Henry Newman insists, "The whole Bible, not its prophetical portions only, is written on the principle of development."[34]

Newman argues further that it would be unreasonable to expect development of doctrine to end with the writing of the last book of Scripture. An obvious example of this ongoing development is the fact that the Church took two centuries after the writing of the last book of the New Testament to discern the precise canon of the New Testament.[35]

A basic principle of the faith communities of Israel and the Church is that Scripture should be updated and applied to new circumstances. In particular, a crisis in the life of the community (such as the Babylonian Exile) can spark the need to reinterpret Scripture to fit a new situation. Sanders argues that the process of reinterpretation of Scripture and the application of Scripture to new situations is and should be ongoing in the Church.[36] In their application to new situations, however, scriptural ideas develop and deepen.

Jesus himself, in the Gospel of John, supports this theory of development in understanding. He says to his disciples, "I have much more to tell you, but you cannot bear it now. But when he comes, the Spirit of truth, he will guide you to all truth" (John 16:12–13).

We now consider some specific illustrations of the "development of doctrine" principle.

Sacraments   9.18.1

Today the Catholic Church teaches that there are seven sacraments (*CCC* no. 1113), but the teaching that there are precisely seven did not arise until centuries after New Testament times. As part of his efforts to return to a more scriptural basis, therefore, Luther taught that there are only two sacraments: baptism and the Lord's Supper.

Baptism

How did the sacrament of baptism develop? The New Testament clearly teaches that baptism cleanses a person from sin (Acts 2:38). The New Testament, however, is silent on whether an infant should be baptized. All the specific scriptural examples show adults being baptized, but was this meant as a general rule? What about passages which refer to the baptism of a woman "and her household" (Acts 16:15) and a man "and all his family" (Acts 16:33) — is it not possible, even likely, that "household" and "family" would have included children? But Scripture is silent, and so a development of doctrine was necessary to answer the question.

A second question emerged: granted that baptism cleansed a person from sin, how would sins committed after baptism be cleansed? Since the answer was unclear, some early Christian believers avoided baptism until they were on their deathbed to ensure that they would commit no other sins that might not be forgiven before they died. Newman argues that over the years the practice of verbal confession to a priest developed as an answer to this problem.[37] The sacrament of penance (not explicitly described in Scripture), then, developed from the practice of baptism (recognized explicitly in Scripture).[38] ○

But as Raymond Brown points out, the New Testament does not use the term *sacrament* at all, and in fact has no general term to discuss rituals such as baptism and the Lord's Supper.[39] Thus while Scripture certainly has many references to baptism and the Lord's Supper, as well as to other rituals that are closely connected with Catholic sacraments (for example, James 5:14 is seen by the Catholic Church as the basis for the sacrament of the anointing of the sick), it has no overall doctrine of sacraments.

The *Catechism* explicitly refers to a process of development with regard to sacraments: "Thus the Church has *discerned over the centuries* that among liturgical celebrations there are seven that are, in the strict sense of the term, sacraments instituted by the Lord" (*CCC* no. 1117; emphasis added). Nor is this principle of development only a recent idea. Congar writes, " 'Apostolic traditions' do not necessarily imply, in the eyes of the Fathers, that the rite or practice in question was instituted materially or historically by the apostles in its *present* form."[40]

Other Examples of Development of Doctrine   9.18.2

Brown judges that the doctrines of the Trinity and of the sacraments have an "abundant but incipient basis in Scripture."[41] Brown also provides other examples of Catholic doctrine that do not have direct support in the New Testament. Under the category of "doctrines that have a slender basis in Scripture," Brown discusses Jesus' virginal conception, his bodily Resurrection, and the office of the papacy.[42] Under the category of "doctrines about which the Scriptures are virtually silent," Brown discusses three Catholic doctrines regarding Mary, mother of Jesus: her perpetual virginity, her Immaculate Conception (the doctrine that Mary was born without original sin), and her Assumption (the doctrine that Mary was taken body and soul into heaven).[43]

Development or Corruption of Scriptural Teaching?   9.18.3

Granted that certain Catholic (and other Christian) doctrines and practices go beyond the Scriptures (see sec. 9.14.2 and Brown's examples above), how are we to know whether they are faithful developments of Scripture or corruptions and betrayals of scriptural teaching? After all, this was the criticism of the Reformers, who believed that the Catholic Church had corrupted the faith by adding beliefs and practices that either went beyond or flatly contradicted Scripture.

Newman discusses seven "notes" or characteristics of developments that show them to be true developments and not corruptions.[44] To illustrate his thinking, we will discuss one such note—logical development.

Newman himself thought that "the Incarnation is the central aspect of Christianity" and that the sacramental system was a logical development of this central aspect.[45] The Incarnation shows that God can take on physical form; the sacramental teaching that God's grace can be communicated through the physical agents of water (in baptism) and bread and wine (in the Lord's Supper) flows logically from this central idea.

Conclusions   9.19

In the Roman Catholic tradition, a valid interpretation of Scripture requires paying attention to its two inseparable aspects: the human and the divine. Proper understanding of the human author of a scriptural book involves interpreting that author within his historical and cultural context, and thus requires the application of a variety of historical-critical and literary tools to the text. Paying attention to the divine aspect of the text involves not so much developing a completely separate "spiritual" approach as a conscious reading of Scripture in the context of the Tradition of the Church.

There are many aspects to reading Scripture within Church Tradition. One essential principle is that Church Tradition, especially its teaching authority (Magisterium), serves as a guide to interpretation. Just as Tradition was the guide that first discerned the specific books of the scriptural canon, the Tradition also guides the faithful in a legitimate development of scriptural teaching.

In the Catholic vision, Scripture and Tradition are inseparable. In its widest sense, Tradition is simply the passing down of the Christian faith from generation to generation in all of its fullness: the official teachings, the sacraments, the art and literature, the daily religious experience of the faithful. Scripture is a unique, privileged, and essential expression of that Tradition.

It is a hopeful sign of future Christian unity that understanding of the relationship between Scripture and Tradition among Catholic and other Christian communities is converging, as churches with roots in the Reformation recover a sense of the importance of Tradition and Catholics recover a sense of the centrality of Scripture within the Tradition.

Questions about the Text

1. What did *Dei Verbum* mean by saying that Scripture should be interpreted with both its human and divine aspects in mind?

2. What is the historical-critical method? Define textual, source, and redaction criticism.

3. What are some reasons why a modern reader should be aware of the cultural background of Scripture?

4. What are some objections to the historical-critical method of interpreting Scripture? Why do both "conservative" interpreters of Scripture (e.g., those who read Scripture more literally) and "liberal" interpreters of Scripture (e.g., liberationist or feminist) raise objections?

5. How does the historical-critical approach fit into the general Catholic view of the relationship between faith and reason? What are some Catholic answers to specific critiques of the historical-critical method?

6. What is the relationship between Aquinas's view of the "literal sense" of Scripture and the results of historical-critical study of Scripture?

7. What are the specific Catholic principles for reading Scripture "with its divine authorship in mind"?

8. How do the beliefs of the Protestant Reformation and of modern individualism challenge the Catholic principle of interpreting Scripture within Church Tradition?

9. What are the two basic senses of "Tradition" (capital *T*) in Catholic theology? What are the various meanings of "tradition" or "traditions" in Catholic and Christian theology?

10. How does the apostolic tradition show that Tradition was passed down apart from Scripture?

11. What are some specific beliefs held generally by Christian churches that are not in Scripture?

12. In Catholic thought, what is the Magisterium and what is its function? Why does the Catholic tradition regard the Arian controversy as an example of the Church's need for the Magisterium?

13. What are some other historical examples of how Church Tradition has interpreted Scripture?

14. In what ways have modern Protestant and evangelical churches recovered a sense of the importance of Tradition?

15. What are some examples of how the Catholic and catholic traditions before the Reformation accepted Scripture as the central authority? What does Rahner mean by a "Catholic *sola scriptura*"?

16. How does *Dei Verbum* sum up the relationship between Scripture, Tradition, and Magisterium?

17. In what ways does Scripture demonstrate a development of doctrine within itself?

18. How are the practices of infant baptism and the Catholic sacrament of penance examples of development of doctrine beyond Scripture?

19. How did Newman see the sacramental system as a logical development of the Incarnation?

Discussion Questions

1. Discuss some nontheological examples of how a text requires interpretation by a reliable tradition. (Think of the U.S. Constitution or other codes of law, or interpretations of classic literary texts such as those by Shakespeare.)

2. Think of how liberationist or feminist interpretations have challenged traditional interpretations of American history (e.g., the role of Columbus). How do these challenges compare to similar challenges to historical-critical interpretations of the Bible?

3. What are your own experiences or knowledge of the relationship between Scripture and Tradition in Christianity?

Endnotes

1. For a fuller description of the historical-critical method, especially as it is used in scriptural studies, see Joseph A. Fitzmyer, *The Interpretation of Scripture: In Defense of the Historical-Critical Method* (New York: Paulist Press, 2008), 63–66.

2. For a convincing case that the Old Testament quotations in Matthew were produced by a group of early Christian scribes, see Krister Stendahl, *The School of St. Matthew and Its Use of the Old Testament* (Ramsey, NJ: Sigler Press, 1991).

3. Quotations from the PBC's *Interpretation of the Bible in the Church* are from *The Scripture Documents: An Anthology of Official Catholic Teachings*, ed. D. P. Béchard (Collegeville, MN: Liturgical, 2001), 244–315.

4. For other discussions of criticism of the historical-critical method, see "Introduction" in PBC's *Interpretation of Scripture*, (Béchard, *Scripture Documents*, 246–48); see also Luke Timothy Johnson and William S. Kurz, *The Future of Catholic Biblical Scholarship: A Constructive Conversation* (Grand Rapids, MI: Eerdmans, 2002), 14–17, 127–30, 161–62.

5. On this history, see Béchard, *Scripture Documents*, 318–29 (examples of the ultraconservative teachings are on pp. 187–211); Fitzmyer, *Interpretation of Scripture*, 3–6.

6. See Fitzmyer, *Interpretation of Scripture*, 66–69. For an opposing view, see Johnson and Kurz, *Catholic Biblical Scholarship*, 15–17.

7. See Johnson and Kurz, *Catholic Biblical Scholarship*, 20.

8. On the value and limitations of these approaches, see the PBC's *Interpretation of the Bible* (Béchard, *Scripture Documents*, 269–73); R. E. Brown, *Biblical Exegesis and Church Doctrine* (New York: Paulist Press, 1985), 23–24.

9. See Henri de Lubac, *Medieval Exegesis*, vol.1, *The Four Senses of Scripture* (Grand Rapids, MI: Eerdmans/Edinburgh: T & T Clark, 1998). See also *CCC* nos. 115–19. Different schools of thought arranged or divided these senses in different ways (some, for example, spoke only of three senses).

10. De Lubac, *Medieval Exegesis*, 24.

11. Peter Kreeft, *A Summa of the* Summa: *The Essential Philosophical Passages of Saint Thomas Aquinas'* Summa Theologica (San Francisco: Ignatius Press, 1990), 49–50 no. 37.

12. Pope Pius XII, Encyclical Letter *On the Promotion of Biblical Studies (Divino afflante Spiritu)* no. 20 in Béchard, *Scripture Documents*, 128.

13. See Johnson and Kurz, *Catholic Biblical Scholarship*, 159–60.

14. See also Yves Congar, The Twentieth Century Encyclopedia of Catholicism, *The Meaning of Tradition* (New York: Hawthorne Books, 1964) 10.

15. Ibid., 37, 96–98.

16. Ibid., 36–37.

17. Ibid., 22–23, 95.

18. Ibid., 36–47, 96–105.

19. Ibid., 14–18.

20. Ibid., 26–27.

21. There is much scholarly debate about the precise limits of the Jewish canon in the time of Jesus. Certainly, however, the Torah of Moses (the first five books) and the writings of prophets such as Ezekiel were accepted as scriptural.

22. Quoted in Congar, *Meaning of Tradition*, 83.

23. See ibid., 46–47.

24. "Scripture, Tradition and Traditions," in *The Fourth World Conference on Faith and Order, Montreal, 1963*, eds. P. C. Rodger and L. Vischer (London: SCM Press, 1964), 50–61.

25. See references in Congar, *Meaning of Tradition*, 89–90.

26. See Ronald E. Heine, *Reading the Old Testament with the Ancient Church: Exploring the Formation of Early Christian Thought* (Grand Rapids, MI: Baker Academic, 2007).

27. James Sanders, *Canon and Community: A Guide to Canonical Criticism* (Philadelphia: Fortress, 1984), xvi.

28. De Lubac, *Medieval Exegesis*, 24.

29. See the discussion in Congar, *Meaning of Tradition*, 95. See Aquinas, *On Truth*, 14.10, ad. 11: "We believe the successors of the apostles and prophets only in so far as they tell us those things which the apostles and prophets have left in their writings."

30. Congar, *Meaning of Tradition*, 44. Other Catholic theologians believed that an "objective or material imperfection" in the Scriptures needed to be supplemented by nonscriptural traditions (ibid.).

31. Congar, *Meaning of Tradition*, 94–95.

32. Rahner, "Scripture and Tradition," in *Theological Investigations* (London: Darton, Longman & Todd; New York: Seabury Press), 6:107–8.

33. Congar, *Meaning of Tradition*, 45.

34. John Henry Newman, *An Essay on the Development of Christian Doctrine* (Westminster, MD: Christian Classics, 1968), 65.

35. Ibid., 68.

36. Sanders, *Canon and Community*, 35.

37. Newman, *Development of Doctrine*, 60–63; 384–88.

38. Scriptural passages such as John 20:22–23 and Matt 16:19 and 18:18 also support the general theology behind the sacrament of penance.

39. Brown, *Biblical Exegesis*, 33–34.

40. Congar, *Meaning of Tradition*, 40.

41. Brown, *Biblical Exegesis*, 31.

42. The virgin birth and bodily Resurrection of Jesus technically do not involve development of doctrine beyond Scripture, since certain Scriptures plainly teach them. Brown includes them, however, because only a limited number of New Testament writings witness to them.

43. Brown, *Biblical Exegesis*, 26–53.

44. For an overview of the seven notes, see Newman, *Development of Doctrine*, 169–206.

45. Ibid., 36, 325.

10

Christology

The Christian View of Jesus

In this chapter, we consider a specific field of study within Christian theology known as Christology. This area of study focuses on the theological understanding of Jesus Christ within Christian faith. As Jesus Christ is central to the faith, so too is Christology to Christian theology.

The Incarnation   10.1

Shock and Offense I:
The Particularity of Jesus   10.1.1

Make no mistake: the Christian understanding of Jesus is a shock and an offense to millions of people. For millions more it is simply incomprehensible.

The traditional Christian belief is that one human being, Jesus, who lived two thousand years ago in a remote village in the Roman province of Galilee, is the key to understanding

God's ultimate plan for the universe. Christians claim nothing less than that the salvation and ultimate happiness of every person who has ever lived depends on Jesus.

Many people are understandably shocked and puzzled by this claim. How can it be that out of all the billions of people who have lived, *one person* would have this central role? Given the thousands and even millions of religious teachers and leaders over the centuries, isn't it unbelievably arrogant to assume that only one of them would be the key to bring all people back to a saving relationship with God? Anyone who is not shocked and even offended by this Christian teaching probably has not understood it.

Let us try to understand, then, why Christians make a claim that seems so unbelievable or unacceptable to so many.

The Logic of Jesus' Particularity   10.1.2

We begin by recalling some basic points from earlier chapters. Humans, all humans, desire the transcendent, even if this desire may be expressed only implicitly: frustration with human limitations, striving for meaning in life, hoping for existence beyond death, and so on. Likewise, all cultures have developed religions that seek to connect humans with the transcendent, often understood as God.

But humans are frustrated in their striving for God. To use Christian vocabulary, humans are caught in sin and cannot save themselves from it. This sin separates them from God, the source of truth, love, and meaning, and humans cannot overcome this separation on their own efforts.

The logic of the Incarnation is this: when the Second Person of the Trinity humbled himself to become human, humans were given the opportunity for reconciliation with the divine. Jesus is unique, different from every other human, in that he was both divine and human, and thus God and humanity truly met in him. In Jesus, the great gap was overcome.

But why, in the Christian view, is the separation between the human and the divine overcome only in this one individual? Theoretically, we might speculate, the great chasm between the human and the divine might have been bridged in another way.

According to Christianity, for reconciliation and salvation to occur it is essential that the human and the divine come into a real contact. Thus it was necessary that Jesus be both truly God and truly human. But to be a true human means to suffer, to doubt, to worry, to laugh, to love—and one can only do these things *as an individual*, in one particular time period, in one particular culture, in one particular sex. There is no such thing as a *generic* human being. So if God were to come concretely into contact with humanity, it would need to be through an individual person, in one culture, one time in history.

This is the logic, then, behind the Christian teaching that God has (to speak analogically) humbled himself in order to meet humans at their own level of experience and understanding. In Jesus, God has entered into human history—not abstractly or theoretically, but in the flesh.

Shock and Offense II: The Humility of God   10.1.3

Besides the scandal of its particularity (that the Savior of humanity lived at only one certain place and time), the view of God implicit in the Incarnation also scandalizes many. Christianity claims that the ultimate power of the universe, the perfect source of all goodness, became a limited human—not merely that God *appeared* as a human, or that God *revealed* himself through the human Jesus, but that God *became* human.

For many this makes no sense. The concept is a scandal for Islam, which holds a strict view of God's absolute difference from all created things. It can thus only be a source of great confusion, if not blasphemy, to say that God could become human. "Far is it removed from his transcendent majesty that he should have a son" (Qur'an 4:171). If it is inconceivable that God should have a divine Son, far less could it be held that God could become human.

This belief that the divine would (or could) thus humble itself, then, is central to the uniqueness of Christianity. The divine Son, the Second Person of the Trinity, "emptied himself, taking the form of a slave, coming in human likeness" (Phil 2:7). In this regard Paul says, "For the foolishness of God is wiser than human wisdom, and the weakness of God is stronger than human strength" (1 Cor 1:25).

Development of Doctrine: True God and True Man   10.1.4

The central idea that God became human in Jesus, though present in Christianity from the beginning, went through a long period of development during which its various implications were worked out and expressed more clearly. This is not surprising: as we've just discussed, the idea that the unlimited divine became human in the man Jesus of Nazareth runs counter to human expectations on many levels.

Already in the earliest documents of the New Testament, Paul's letters, Paul thinks of Jesus as divine in the fullest sense of the word (Jesus is Lord of the universe and shares the divine name; see sec. 6.10.3.1), while at the same time regarding him as fully human: Jesus was "born of a woman, born under the law" (Gal 4:4), died and was buried (1 Cor 15:3–4). Yet the precise understanding of the divine and human natures, as well as their relationship within the one person of Jesus, would continue to develop in the early centuries of the Church.

> The unique and altogether singular event of the Incarnation of the Son of God does not mean that Jesus Christ is part God and part man, nor does it imply that he is the result of a confused mixture of the divine and the human. He became truly man while remaining truly God. Jesus Christ is true God and true man. During the first centuries, the Church had to defend and clarify this truth of faith against the heresies that falsified it. (*CCC* no. 464)

We have already discussed the great Arian controversy; the assertions of Arius and his followers (who claimed that Jesus did not fully share the divine nature) prompted the orthodox to clarify that Jesus was fully God (see sec. 6.14.2).

The Relationship Between the Human and the Divine in Jesus   10.1.5

How were the two natures related to one another? In the course of the fourth and fifth centuries, many different models of understanding this relationship emerged and were debated. The Nestorian belief, for example, accepted that Jesus did have both a human and divine nature, but could not accept the idea that the two could truly be interrelated. The Nestorians believed that divinity and humanity are so essentially different that the two must in practice always remain separate.

For the Nestorians, then, Mary could be called the mother of the human Jesus but could by no means be called "Mother of God"—it would be an obvious absurdity to think that a human woman could be the mother of the uncreated source of the universe.

In answering the Nestorians, Cyril of Alexandria and the Council of Ephesus (431 CE) insisted that Jesus must be thought of as *one* person: he was not an unnatural combination of a human nature and a divine nature living in the same body. The Son of God "assumed" human nature and "made it his own," "the Word" united "to himself in his person the flesh animated by a rational soul" (*CCC* no. 466). Since the two natures are intimately and integrally bound in Jesus, it is entirely appropriate to call Mary "Mother of God," since she bore a human son whose nature was united in the closest possible way with the nature of God.

In reflecting on the Nestorian controversy, we see that effects of the Christological developments are not limited to Christian understanding of Jesus, but also have deep implications for the Christian understanding of the human. The belief that human nature can be so intimately related with the divine that the two can form one person underscores both the immense potential of the human for good and the reality of the human destiny of divinization—the participation of the human in the Trinitarian life. Mary, in receiving the title "Mother of God," reveals the enormous dignity and potential for good of the human in God's plan. "Human nature, by the very fact that it was assumed, not absorbed, in him, has been raised in us also to a dignity beyond compare" (*GS* no. 22).

Around the same time as the Nestorian controversy, the so-called Monophysite teaching was insisting that if the all-powerful divine nature of the Word had assumed human nature, then the weak human nature must have essentially been overwhelmed. This teaching again tends in a Docetic or Gnostic direction, convinced that although the divine Jesus may have appeared to be human, he could not truly have been a weak, limited human being.

Reacting against the Monophysite view, and again emphasizing the dignity of human nature, the fourth **ecumenical council** at Chalcedon (451) published a classic definition of the relationship between the human and divine natures of Jesus. In Jesus are "two natures without confusion, change, division, or separation" (*CCC* no. 467). Beyond all expectation, the Council insisted, the limited human and the all-powerful divine had truly reconciled in Jesus Christ.

The New Adam   10.2

Just as Adam (or Adam and Eve) represents all human nature, so too Jesus, in becoming human, took on human nature as a whole. By uniting himself to the human nature of the particular man Jesus, the divine Word also took on human nature.[1]

In becoming human, the Word of God provided humans a new model of humanity. Paul brings out this point by contrasting Adam—the representative of human nature enslaved to selfishness and sin—with Christ—the representative of human nature freed from sin. "For if, by the transgression of one person, death came to reign through that one, how much more will those who receive the abundance of grace and of the gift of justification come to reign in life through the one person Jesus Christ" (Rom 5:17).

Christ is thus the goal of humanity. Paul writes that Adam was "the type of the one who was to come" (Rom 5:14). Adam thus symbolizes humanity in its incompleteness, and Christ represents humanity in its fullness and completeness. Paul writes, "Just as we have borne the image of the earthly one, we shall also bear the image of the heavenly one" (1 Cor 15:49). Since Christ is the perfect image of the Father (Col 1:15; Heb 1:3), Christ is the model for restoring humanity's own image of God, distorted by sin, to its original destiny of perfect harmony with nature and God.

Christ as the Goal of Creation   10.3

But what can it mean, specifically, that Christ is the goal of humanity? Let us consider the teaching from a scientific point of view.

E. F. Schumacher suggests that life has evolved in a definite pattern: moving up from mineral to plant to animal to human, one moves from passivity to activity, from necessity to freedom. One sees progress toward ever-greater intelligence, responsibility, and meaning (see sec. 4.9.3.7). We also see a greater potential (not always fulfilled) to leave aside self-centeredness and develop the capacity to think about, feel empathy for, and truly love others.

Expanding our view, we can say that the entire universe has been evolving toward this goal. Through the billions of years since the big bang, conditions in the universe have slowly evolved to the point where it was possible to produce intelligent beings. Hydrogen and helium were the only elements existing after the big bang. It was only after stars had formed from the dust of the original explosion that processes involving nuclear fusion began to produce the other elements—including carbon, the basic element of life. After its birth billions of years ago, the earth slowly cooled and conditions slowly developed to the point where earth could support life. The entire cosmos has been evolving toward the goal of producing intelligent life—a life that can reflect on and understand itself within the universe.

Some modern trends in Catholic thought have combined this evolutionary view of the universe with the biblical understanding of Christ as the "last Adam"—the goal of humanity. The man Jesus Christ, who lived two thousand years ago, is obviously not the last human being in terms of time. But he can be understood as the goal to which humanity is striving: the goal of a human life that is ever more free, ever more responsible, ever more "meaning-full." Joseph Ratzinger has written that in his total willingness to live for God and for others, Jesus Christ achieved the goal of humanity: the overcoming of selfishness and self-centeredness.[2]

Pierre Teilhard de Chardin (1881–1955), the French priest and paleontologist, also attempted to relate the theory of evolution to Christology. In his scientific studies, Teilhard sees evidence of the universe moving "to ever greater complexity and inwardness, from matter to life to mind."[3] The universe is moving toward what Teilhard called the Omega point. Yet this Omega point can also be conceived of as the Alpha point—the ultimate creative power that first made the universe.[4] Teilhard identifies this Omega point as Christ—the Word through which all things in the universe were made.

Earlier we studied the scientific evidence that the physical world is governed by rational laws (4.9.1), right down to the molecular and atomic levels. In Christian terms, this is seen as evidence that God created the universe through the Word. Teilhard argues that this intelligibility of the universe is not static, but shows rather that the universe is evolving back toward its beginning source (Christ) in its movement toward ever higher levels of life, freedom, and self-consciousness.

This Omega point, the ultimate source of intelligibility and meaning, must be personal. As Ratzinger points out, an intelligible structure is impossible without thought, and thought is impossible without a personal subject to do the thinking.[5]

Teilhard thus brings a modern scientific perspective to Christ's words, "I am the Alpha and the Omega, the first and the last, the beginning and the end" (Rev 22:13). Or as Paul writes, "For in him [the Son, the Alpha point] were created all things in heaven and on earth . . . all things were created through him and for him" [Omega point] (Col 1:16). Understanding the Incarnation as an event that God had planned from the creation of the universe—and thus an event that affects all time, both before and after the historical time of the

Incarnation—Teilhard interprets this central event as God "immersing himself in matter" and "descending into nature to superanimate it and unite it with himself" (see sec. 10.6.1.3 on the timeless nature of the Incarnation).[6]

Teilhard's work has been criticized both scientifically, for his too simplistic view of evolution as a continuous process of the universe becoming more complex, and theologically, for understanding Christ too much within natural, rather than supernatural, categories.[7] Ratzinger, however, while recognizing limitations in Teilhard's work, judges that he grasped New Testament ideas of Christ gathering all things to himself and made them accessible in modern language.[8]

The *Logos* in Incarnation and Creation 10.4

Karl Rahner believes that the immanent Trinity (God within his own nature) is the same as the economic Trinity (God working in the world; see sec. 6.15). Thus we should expect a profound unity between the activities of the *Logos* within God's nature (immanent to God) and the activities of the *Logos* "outside of God" (so to speak) in the world, both in the creation and in the Incarnation. In the immanent Trinity, the Father eternally "sends forth" the Son: the Father eternally commands the Son, and the Son eternally accepts in complete love the command of the Father. This eternal sending is mirrored in the Father's "economic" activity of sending the Son out into the world, not only in the Incarnation, but also in the creation.

We will first consider the Father's "sending" the Son in the act of creation. According to Christian belief, God did not create the universe out of necessity. God is love, and thus the persons of the Trinity already shared a relationship of perfect love before the creation. In creating the world, the Trinitarian God acted freely, out of a completely free desire to share his goodness and his love.

But truly to share his goodness and love, God would need to create a creature who would be capable of receiving, understanding, and responding to that love, a creature made in God's image. That creature of course was the human being, the only creature willed to exist for its own sake (*GS* no. 24).

When the *Logos* became human in the Incarnation he "emptied himself," taking on the human condition (Phil 2:7). This self-emptying of the Son in the Incarnation corresponds to a self-emptying in the initial creation. The *Logos* also emptied himself at that time, creating the universe (and humans as the crown of the universe) in order to have another intelligent subject with whom to share his love. In Rahner's words, "the goal of the world [the reason for its creation] is God's self-communication to it."[9]

For Rahner, the "self-expression of God is his self-emptying." The human being can be defined as "that which comes to be when God's self-expression, his Word, is uttered into the emptiness of the Godless void in love." "When God wants to be what is not God, man comes to be."[10] The human is the result of God's desire to share love beyond the love within the Trinity.

If human nature itself is God's self-emptying, we can understand why humans, by nature, are oriented toward the transcendent, toward that point from which we originated. We can see that the whole process centers on communication: it is the Word (reason, rational expression) that empties himself in loving desire to communicate; it is the rational human that desires to respond in love, to reach beyond him or herself in love.

The Incarnation and Salvation   10.5

If we think of human nature as oriented toward God, toward truth, toward meaning, then salvation simply means the fulfillment of human nature. But human nature, in its desire for complete meaning and love, can only be fulfilled in the encounter with the transcendent God.

It is in this sense that Christians believe that Jesus is the Savior of all people. The *Logos* took on human nature in the one man Jesus Christ. Since he is the *Logos* of God, however, Jesus as an individual human being can also represent humanity as a whole. What Jesus does as an individual human, then, Jesus does for all of humanity. De Lubac sums up early Christian thought on the matter: "Whole and entire he will bear it [human nature] then to Calvary, whole and entire he will raise it from the dead, whole and entire he will save it."[11] In the famous phrase of Athanasius (c. 296–373), "he indeed assumed humanity, that we might become God" (*On the Incarnation*, no. 54). As von Balthasar says, Christ "must somehow have adopted human nature as a whole. If this is so, it also becomes credible that his work of atonement has affected the whole of human nature."[12]

Salvation means the fulfillment of the whole person: body, mind, and soul. Against the teachings of Apollinarius (c. 310–c. 390) that Jesus (since he was the divine *Logos*) did not truly have a human mind, Gregory of Nazianzus (c. 329–c. 390) writes, "That which was not assumed is not healed; but that which is united to God is saved" (*Epistle* 101, 32). Because the Word took on all of human nature—mind, body, and spirit—so too all aspects of the human person may be saved, that is, fulfilled, and so achieve the destiny of wholeness for which humans were created.

The Incarnation and the Atonement 10.6

The Christian doctrine of atonement is essentially an attempt to understand the earliest teaching of the Church that "Christ died for our sins" (1 Cor 15:3). As C. S. Lewis notes, however, different theological explanations of the atonement have been offered over the course of the centuries.[13] One popular version, known as the doctrine of satisfaction, is associated with Anselm (c. 1033–1109). Anselm thought of sin as a violation against divine justice. If I lie or cheat, the divine order of justice in the universe, in a sense, has become unbalanced. Something positive must be done in order to restore the balance. Or to alter the metaphor slightly, when I violate the divine order, I put myself in debt to God, the source of that divine order. In order to reestablish justice, I must pay that debt.

But since humans have a fallen nature, we will never be able to pay the debt completely (see sec. 7.2). Lewis explains paying the debt, repenting of one's wrongdoing, in this way:

> Now repentance is no fun at all. . . . It means unlearning all the self-conceit and self-will that we have been training ourselves into for thousands of years. It means killing a part of yourself, undergoing a kind of death. In fact, it needs a good man to repent. And here comes the catch. Only a bad person needs to repent; only a good person can repent perfectly.[14]

True repentance, true turning back to God, is nothing less than a "willing submission to humiliation and a kind of death." The essence of human sin is self-centeredness; I lie or am selfish because my attention is focused on myself (sec. 7.20.1). In my fallen human nature, I cannot overcome that basic selfish orientation on my own. Enmeshed in this fallen nature, humans could never pay the debt of sin.

The only way out of the dilemma, in the Christian understanding, is the Incarnation:

> But supposing God became a man—suppose our human nature which can suffer and die was amalgamated with God's nature in one person—then that person could help us. He could surrender His will, and suffer and die, because He was man; and He could do it perfectly because He was God.[15]

Critiques of the Doctrine of the Atonement   10.6.1

To avoid misunderstanding this central Christian doctrine, we need to consider some possible objections.

Why Can't God Just Forgive?   10.6.1.1

If God is just and merciful, why doesn't God simply forgive our sins without demanding satisfaction or payment of debt?

While the idea that God could simply "forgive and forget" sounds plausible at first, on closer examination this way of dealing with sin violates some strongly held human convictions. The sense that we must "make up" or "atone" for a wrong lies deeply within our human consciousness.

Let us say, for the sake of the argument, that someone like Adolf Hitler had a complete and genuine change of heart. Imagine that in the last days of World War II, Hitler had voluntarily given up power and asked the Jewish people for forgiveness. Despite his genuine repentance, wouldn't our sense of justice demand that Hitler not be forgiven so easily? Wouldn't we have a deep sense that Hitler needed to atone in some way for his crimes (if it were even possible), that simply forgiving and forgetting would be impossible?

Daily experience seems to confirm this idea. Let's say George and Claudia have been dating for a long time and have gotten to know each other well. One day they have an argument, and George, losing his temper, says something hurtful that offends Claudia terribly. They don't speak to each other for several days.

Once George has calmed down he feels ashamed and wishes to apologize. But instinctively he knows that saying "I'm really sorry" isn't enough. He's fairly sure that Claudia will accept his apology. And yet George feels that words alone aren't sufficient. Somehow he needs to "make up for it" to Claudia. He feels the need to do something positive, something generous and kind, that will somehow "balance out" or "make up" for the wrong that he has done. Perhaps he'll buy some flowers, or offer to take Claudia out to supper, or do some other act of kindness for her.

George is feeling, at a basic level, the need to make atonement. When we do something wrong, we often have an instinctive sense that we need to do something good to make it right again.

The history of religions reveals another aspect of the human need to make atonement. Nearly every ancient religion offered some sort of sacrifice as a way of worshipping their gods. The Hebrews offered sheep, cattle, grain, and wine, the Greeks and Romans offered bulls, the ancient Aztecs had human sacrifices. While such sacrifices were not always done to "make up" for a sin—they might be given in thanksgiving, or in an effort to appease the anger of a god—the need to offer something personal or precious as a sacrifice is a common theme across cultures.

The Old Testament Book of Leviticus connects the idea of atonement with the blood of an animal:

> Since the life of a living body is in its blood, I have made you put it on the altar, so that atonement may thereby be made for your own lives, because it is the blood, as the seat of life, that makes atonement. (Lev 17:11)

The idea seems to be that humans must offer something precious to the divine powers, especially when atoning for sin. The blood of animals is especially important because it is symbolic of life, the most precious gift a human has. It is possible that animals owned by a person in some sense were thought to represent that human. So instead of a human paying for his sin with his own life, it is possible that the ancient Hebrews (at least originally) believed that God allowed humans to "pay" or "atone" for sin with the life of one of their animals.

While the human need to offer atonement and sacrifice can be manipulated and distorted, it nevertheless seems to be a genuine human need.

Christ's Death for Others   10.6.1.2

What does it mean to say that Christ died for my sins? How could someone's death two thousand years ago affect any person of today?

To answer, we reiterate our earlier point that in his Incarnation, Christ took on human nature as a whole. Thus each individual, in a sense, can participate with Christ in paying the debt. Consider the following quotations from some early theologians.

- Athanasius wrote, "All men were condemned to death; but he, the Innocent One, surrendered his body to death for all; thus all men, being dead through him . . . should be freed from sin and the curse and be raised from the dead." (*Contra Arianos* 1.69)

- Gregory Nazianzus teaches that Christ "bears me, in my entirety, with all my misery, within himself. So he eliminates the evil, as fire melts and consumes wax." (*Oration* 30:6)

Atonement, Violence, and Abuse

10.6.1.3

Theologians such as Rita Nakashima Brock have raised some fundamental criticisms of the atonement, arguing that basic concepts behind it have legitimated violence and oppression. The divine Father sending his innocent Son to redeem the world "looks uncomfortably to some like a charter for child abuse, with an innocent son sent to bear the wrath of a 'heavenly father' to make things right for the entire extended family."[16]

These theologians correctly point out the potential to distort the Christian message in certain interpretations of the atonement. But other theologians such as Hans Urs von Balthasar have shown that the danger for distortion lies not so much in the doctrine itself as in certain interpretations of it:

One thing we must never forget: the atonement wrought by Christ must not be interpreted as a penance imposed on the Son by the divine Father; rather, as we have often repeated, it goes back to that salvific decision made by the Trinity. Jesus Christ sees himself as coming forth from that decision in perfect freedom.[17]

Von Balthasar here refers to the doctrine (6.15.1) that the immanent and economic Trinity mirror one another. Within the immanent relationship of love in the Trinity, the three persons together make the decision to send forth the Son from the Father. It would then be just as true to say that the Son "volunteered" to offer his own

continued

continued

life as it is to say that the Father sent him. Again it is important to bear in mind the limitations of our analogical language.

This connection of the immanent and economic Trinity prompts yet another question and reflection. Part of the "scandal of particularity" of the doctrine of the Incarnation is that it occurred at a specific time in history, approximately two thousand years ago. If the Second Person of the Trinity was going to unite himself to human nature in order to save it, why didn't he do so earlier, from the beginning of the human race? Do those who lived before Jesus have no chance at salvation?

The answer is relatively simple. Because the Son united himself to a concrete, individual human being, the Incarnation itself could only occur at a specific point in time. Yet since the Word taking on human nature in time is simply a reflection of the "self-emptying" of the *Logos* within the immanent Trinity, the effect of the Incarnation cannot be limited to time. As von Balthasar says, "The assumption of 'flesh' — which, seen from eternity, is timeless — is already an integral part of the original world plan."[18] o

In Paul's thought, the sufferings of humans who are "in Christ" can be united to the suffering of Christ in bringing about salvation. Paul says, "I rejoice in my sufferings for your sake, and in my flesh I am filling up what is lacking in the afflictions of Christ" (Col 1:24). Paul refers frequently to the followers of Christ participating in Christ's suffering:

- Or are you unaware that we who were baptized into Christ Jesus were baptized into his death? (Rom 6:3)

- [We are] always carrying about in the body the dying of Jesus. (2 Cor 4:10)

- I have been crucified with Christ. (Gal 2:19)

In Paul's view, the death of Christ could affect the follower of Christ because the follower was intimately connected with him. We'll explore further this concept that a follower can be "in Christ" in our discussion of the "Body of Christ" (see sec. 12.6).

A Historically Accurate Portrayal of Jesus?   10.7

For two thousand years, the Church, through Scripture and Tradition, has passed down a portrait of Jesus as true God and true man, the incarnate Word; the Son sent by the Father to save the world from sin and death through his own life, death, and Resurrection.

From the beginning, however, there have been challenges to this portrait. Already in the New Testament, the apostle Paul condemns others who present a different understanding of Christ: "But there are some who are disturbing you and wish to pervert the Gospel of Christ. . . . If anyone preaches to you a gospel other than the one you received, let that one be accursed" (Gal 1:7–9). The First Letter of John also speaks of some who deny basic Christian beliefs and declares, "Who is the liar? Whoever denies that Jesus is the Christ" (1 John 2:22).

Paul and John clearly do not tolerate other perspectives about the identity of Jesus. Both declare in the strongest terms that these other ideas are false and should not be followed.

Challenges to the Historical Accuracy of the Gospels   10.7.1

Beginning roughly in the Enlightenment, a scholarly tradition emerged challenging the historical accuracy of the Church's portrayal of Jesus. Basing their work on historical-critical study of the Gospels and often using rationalist presuppositions, researchers working in this tradition argued that Jesus, as a historical figure, was actually quite different from the Gospel portraits. Some of these scholars produced their own "lives of Jesus" intended to correct the misleading Gospel portraits. The beginning of this "quest for the **historical Jesus**" is typically traced to the work of Hermann Samuel Reimarus (1694–1768). Other well-known products of the quest included biographies by David Strauss (1835) and Ernest Renan (1863).[19]

Consistent with their Enlightenment worldview, the early questers rejected the historical accuracy of the Gospels since they recorded supernatural events that, according to the questers' worldview, were impossible (see sec. 2.2.1). These scholars did accept, however, that Jesus was a historical figure who had lived and died in first-century

Palestine. They claimed that they could separate the actual "Jesus of history" from the legendary "Christ of faith."

Challenges to the historical accuracy of the Gospels—and attempts to recover the "real" Jesus of history—continue to this day. Discussions about these challenges have not been relegated to academic circles: on a regular basis (usually around Christmas or Easter), popular news magazines run cover stories about the latest attempts to recover the "real Jesus," and the distinction between the actual Jesus and the Church's later (supposedly distorted) portrait of him is the theme of many popular books and films.

Was There a "Historical Jesus"?   10.7.2

There is no serious doubt that Jesus of Nazareth actually lived. In addition to the four Gospels, we have the witness of numerous other early Christian writings, both canonical and noncanonical. More importantly for historical evidence, Jesus is mentioned (briefly) by ancient non-Christian sources who were either indifferent or hostile to the Christian movement, and thus are more likely to be "objective" historical witnesses. For example, the Jewish historian Josephus (born shortly after Jesus' death) calls Jesus a "wise man," a "doer of startling deeds," and a "teacher" (*Antiquities* 18.3.3.63–64). The Roman historian Tacitus (c. 57–c. 118) mentions "Christ, who during the reign of Tiberius, had been executed by the procurator Pontius Pilate" (*Annals* 15.44). Pliny the Younger (c. 61–112), a Roman official in Asia Minor, writes of Christians in his district who sang hymns "to Christ as to a god" (*Letter* 10.96).[20]

Relevance of the Historical Jesus   10.7.3

For a non-Christian believer (whether a believer in Judaism, Islam, Hinduism, or some other belief), the search raises questions about the truth of Christianity. If it can be shown that the historical Jesus is quite different than the Gospel portraits, this may lend support, for example, to Judaism's view that Jesus was an ordinary human teacher, or Islam's view that Jesus was a great prophet but not the Savior or the divine Son of God.

For a nonbeliever, the search for the historical Jesus is relevant simply for its historical interest. Jesus, whoever he was, is at the center of the world's largest religion (Christianity) and holds a place of honor in the world's second largest religion (Islam). Even for the person hostile to the Christian faith, the search for the historical Jesus is relevant because, if it can be shown that the real Jesus was quite different from the Gospels' portrayal of him, the Church's claims about him can be dismissed.

On the other hand, some Christians have denied that the historical Jesus is relevant for faith—for example, Catholic author Luke Timothy Johnson.[21] Johnson criticizes the approach of historians who dissect New Testament documents for historical information, since these documents were not intended to provide such information. For Johnson, the "real Jesus" cannot refer to a historical reconstruction by scholars, but can only refer to contemporary Christians' claims to encounter the "real Jesus" in their religious experiences and convictions that are based on the New Testament. Because it is based on private religious experience, the Christian claim to encounter the "real Jesus" is not open to historical challenge, though it is open to religious, theological, or moral challenges.[22]

Johnson is certainly correct to point out the limitations of historical research into the Gospels and the tendency of many scholars to claim more than they can know (as responsible historians) about the history of earliest Christianity.[23] He is also correct to say that the Christian faith cannot be based on the results of a historical-critical investigation of Jesus. The object of the Church's worship, in the Catholic view, can only be Jesus as made known through Scripture and Tradition (including the sacraments, liturgy, and the interpretation of Scripture as found in the creeds). As Avery Dulles writes, "But in no case does the method [i.e., historical method] provide a religiously adequate portrait, one that can take the place of Jesus Christ as proclaimed by the Church and received in faith."[24]

Nevertheless, Johnson's criticism tends to border on fideism (sec. 2.7). As we have stressed throughout this book, the Catholic tradition insists that faith and reason cannot be separated, and so we should by no means conclude that historical research is irrelevant to Christian faith. Just as the Catholic tradition rejects a NOMA (nonoverlapping magisterial) response that would partition faith and science into separate and mutually exclusive realms (sec. 4.9.2.4), so too the tradition rejects separating history and faith into separate realms.

Dei Verbum explicitly recognizes the importance of the historical trustworthiness of the Gospels. The Catholic Church firmly maintains,

> The four Gospels just named, whose historicity she unhesitatingly affirms, faithfully hand on what Jesus, the Son of God, while he

lived among men, really did and taught for their eternal salvation, until the day when he was taken up. (*DV* no. 19)

Since the Catholic Church makes such historical claims, they are legitimately open to historical scrutiny.

As Aquinas wrote, the Christian tradition cannot *prove* the truth of an article of faith to a nonbeliever, but it can answer a non-believer's objections that a particular article of faith is illogical or unreasonable (*ST* 1.1.8; sec. 3.2.3). Thus when critics attack traditional beliefs about Jesus from a historical perspective (for example, asserting that neither Jesus nor his followers claimed that he was the Messiah until long after his death), then the Christian should be able to demonstrate that these beliefs are at least historically plausible.

In dealing with historical questions, however, the Christian should not adopt uncritically a rationalist model of doing history. As Bernard Lonergan argued, one of the "functional specialties" of theological method is engaging in historical research. While such research rightly rejects the impossible goal of complete objectivity, it insists, while striving to be aware of its own cultural biases and prejudgments, that the search for historical truth is valid (see sec. 3.6.2.1).

Noncanonical Gospels and the "Historical Jesus" 10.7.4

Scholars investigating the historical Jesus rightly insist that historians should use any source that provides historically accurate information. This could include noncanonical Christian sources, since it is possible that these sources preserve accurate information not found in the canonical Gospels.

Contemporary scholars such as Burton Mack and John Dominic Crossan, in fact, argue that use of noncanonical sources allows us to recover a more accurate picture of who Jesus really was. Relying on hypothetical early versions (dating to within twenty years of Jesus' death) of the *Gospel of Thomas* and the sayings gospel "Q" (a hypothetical collection of Jesus' sayings that many scholars believe was used by Matthew and Luke), Mack, Crossan, and others, especially a group of scholars known as the Jesus Seminar, argue that the historical Jesus was essentially a wise man who taught a radical form of social equality.[25] Beliefs that Jesus was the Messiah, the Son of God, the Savior, that he rose from the dead, and other "apocalyptic" ideas are all later developments that have little to do with the actual Jesus of history, these scholars argue.[26] Thus the earliest Christian communities who composed *Thomas* and Q thought of Jesus as a human teacher only, and did not believe in his atoning death or Resurrection.

Their work, then, is a direct challenge to traditional Christian views of Jesus. Thus, for example, the introduction to *The Five Gospels*, a publication of the Jesus Seminar, argues that it was only by the work of critical scholars, beginning in the Enlightenment, that "the discrepancy between the Jesus of history and the Christ of faith emerged from under the smothering cloud of the historic creeds."[27]

Scholars such as N. T. Wright, a bishop in the Church of England, have shown that the challenges of Mack and Crossan can be answered on a historical basis. Wright notes that the arguments of these scholars are built on a series of shaky hypotheses. First, they must hypothesize that there were earlier "layers" of both the *Gospel of Thomas* and Q (since we have no textual evidence for earlier versions) that included only the nonapocalyptic wisdom sayings of Jesus. It is especially questionable to hypothesize layers in Q, since Q itself is a hypothetical source.

Second, these scholars make the unwarranted assumption that these earlier versions of Q and *Thomas* represent the comprehensive theological view of entire Christian communities. Simply because these hypothetical communities read a hypothetical collection of Jesus' sayings that do not refer to Jesus' atoning death or Resurrection does not imply that readers of these documents had no such theological beliefs, however; they may well have had other writings (or oral traditions) that did refer to these beliefs.[28]

Thomas is not the only noncanonical gospel known from early Christianity. Others, such as the *Gospel of the Hebrews* and the *Gospel of the Ebionites* (both preserved only in fragmentary form) come from Jewish-Christian sources, followers of Jesus who still kept the Torah. We also have copies of the ancient *Gospel of Peter*, the *Gospel of Mary*, and the recently published *Gospel of Judas*. These gospels, however, shed little light on the actual Jesus of history. They all date from the second century and were written after the Synoptic Gospels and most likely after John, and appear to be dependent on traditions found in the canonical Gospels.[29] Works such as the *Judas* and *Thomas* gospels show a Gnostic influence (see sec. 7.5): Jesus is interpreted as a spirit who only pretended to have a human body. In the *Gospel of Judas*, for example, Jesus says to Judas, "For you will sacrifice the man that clothes me," interpreting his death as the liberation of his soul from the body.

It is true that some of these works almost certainly include material older than the second century. For example, the *Gospel of Thomas*, a collection of 114 sayings attributed to Jesus, seems to have versions of Jesus' sayings that can be traced back to the historical Jesus. Other sayings, however, are clearly later and reflect Gnostic influence, such as saying 113, "Woe to the flesh that depends on the soul! Woe to the soul that depends on the flesh!" *Thomas* ends with an exchange between Jesus and Simon Peter that reflects an ancient association of maleness with spirit:

> Simon Peter said to them: "Let Mary go away from us, for women are not worthy of life." Jesus said: "Lo, I shall lead her, so that I may make her a male, that she too may become a living spirit resembling you males. For every woman who makes herself a male will enter the kingdom of heaven." (Saying 114)

The noncanonical gospels, then, contribute little to our understanding of the actual historical Jesus. Although they demonstrate that Jesus was understood in diverse ways in the ancient world, especially in a Gnostic direction, we must rely essentially on the canonical Gospels to recover a sense of the "historical Jesus."[30]

Questioning the Gospels' Accuracy 10.8

Given that the four Gospels are our only solid source for knowledge of the historical Jesus, why not simply accept them as historically accurate? Several reasons prevent a critical reader from doing so:

1. The Gospel of John presents Jesus quite differently from Matthew, Mark, and Luke (known collectively as the Synoptic Gospels). John has much material not found in the other three. More significantly, John has long discourses by Jesus not found in the Synoptics (for example, John 14–17), and his Jesus makes far more explicit claims of divinity than the Jesus of the other Gospels (for example, "the Father and I are one" [John 10:30] and "before Abraham came to be, I AM" [John 8:58]).[31] The uniqueness of John's Gospel, then, raises questions about its historical accuracy.

2. According to the most widely accepted critical scholarly theory, the Gospel of Mark was the first of the Gospels, written approximately 65–70 CE. Since Jesus died around the year 30, we must

assume a gap of approximately thirty-five to forty years during which historical traditions about Jesus' life were passed down orally. The gap raises historical and critical questions. What was changed, or lost, in that period? Could Jesus have been transformed from a simple human teacher to a divine Messiah during that time?

3. Jesus spoke Aramaic; the Gospels are written in Greek. We must consider the possibility of some serious misunderstandings in the translation from one language to another.

4. The very fact that the Gospels record supernatural events raises questions. This objection actually takes two forms: (1) If one believes the supernatural is impossible, then the Gospels are by definition untrustworthy as historical documents. (2) If one accepts the possibility of supernatural events, one could argue that the supernatural cannot be investigated historically since it is (by definition) beyond the natural world.

5. Because the Gospel writers were explicitly writing to encourage faith, some scholars argue that they were *not* interested in historical accuracy. John writes, "But these [signs of Jesus] are written that you may [come to] believe that Jesus is the Messiah, the Son of God" (20:31); Luke writes his account to Theophilus "that you may realize the certainty of the teachings [basic theological beliefs about Jesus] you have received" (1:4). Thus the Gospel writers cannot be accepted as objective witnesses to historical events.

Catholic Responses to Historical Challenges 10.9

In describing a Catholic (and catholic) response to these historical challenges, we will refer especially to a 1964 publication of the Pontifical Biblical Commission (PBC), *Instruction on the Historical Truth of the Gospels*, *Dei Verbum* (which relied heavily on the *Instruction*), and to various New Testament scholars, including N. T. Wright.

In considering these critical challenges to the historicity of the Gospels, it is essential for us to develop a concrete view of how the actual traditions about Jesus were passed down. The *Instruction* acknowledges this need by referencing the three stages of the transmission of accounts of Jesus' sayings and actions (VI, 2):

1. Living witness of Jesus himself and his disciples (c. 27–c. 30)

2. Oral transmission of Jesus traditions by the apostles (c. 30–c. 70)

3. Writing of the Gospels: Mark (c. 60–c. 75), Matthew (c. 80–c. 90), Luke (c. 80–c. 90), and John (c. 80–c. 110)[32]

Stage 1: Jesus and His Disciples as Eyewitnesses 10.9.1

Even nontraditional reconstructions of the historical Jesus acknowledge that he was a teacher. This fact greatly increases our confidence in the historical reliability of the Gospels.

The *Instruction* states, "Jesus himself attached to himself certain chosen disciples (cf. Mark 3:14; Luke 6:13) who had followed him from the beginning (cf. Luke 1:2; Acts 1:2–22), who had seen his works and heard his words, and thus were qualified to become witnesses of his life and teaching" (VII).

Much New Testament scholarship, influenced by the assumptions of form-criticism (see sec. 9.3.1), works with a model in which Jesus traditions were passed down anonymously by early Christian "communities," and thus were subject to change due to the particular needs of those communities.[33]

In contrast to this assumption, the *Instruction* stresses the role of the disciples as eyewitnesses. It makes the historically well-supported point that Jesus deliberately chose twelve close companions who lived with him from the beginning of his public ministry and who were eyewitnesses of his life and teaching. They would have heard Jesus' teaching over the course of three years, both publicly and privately (see Mark 4:1–20 and 10:1–12 for examples of Jesus teaching publicly and then explaining the teaching in more detail privately with the disciples). Even during the lifetime of Jesus, the disciples were already preaching (see Mark 6:7–13): they very plausibly began collections of Jesus' sayings, either oral or written, at this point.

There were, in addition to the Twelve, numerous other eyewitnesses of the events. Richard Bauckham has argued that when the Gospels mention an incidental name in a narrative, they are referring to the eyewitness of the account (for example, the mention of Simon of Cyrene and his son in Mark 15:21).[34] Against scholars who argue that these names are a later addition to the original traditions, Bauckham argues that our historical evidence shows no definite pattern of adding names to a tradition as it is passed down, and that the names attested in the Gospels are popular, contemporary Palestinian names.[35] Finally, we should recall Luke's own statement that he received his information about Jesus from "those who were eyewitnesses from the beginning and ministers of the word" (Luke 1:2).

The Gospel records themselves show the central role of Peter, James, and John as witnesses of events. Jesus takes only these three with him on certain extraordinary occasions: raising a girl from the dead, his transfiguration, his final prayer in the Garden of Gethsemane (Mark 5:37; 9:2; 14:33). In addition, Peter (Acts 2:14–36; 3:12–26) and John (Acts 4:13) are portrayed as preaching about Jesus after his death. Paul acknowledges that Peter, John, and James (the brother of the Lord) were known as "pillars" of the Jerusalem church (Gal 2:9).

Papias (c. 60–130), a bishop of Hierapolis in Asia Minor, called the Gospel writer Mark an "interpreter" of Peter who wrote down accurately, although not in order, what he heard from Peter concerning the words and actions of Jesus.[36] Irenaeus (c. 130–c. 200) also refers to Mark as "the disciple and interpreter of Peter, [who] did also hand down to us in writing what had been preached by Peter" (*Against Heresies* 3.1). Justin refers to the Gospel of Mark as the "reminiscences" of Peter (*Dialogue* 106.3).[37]

Jesus the Teacher   10.9.2

The Swedish scholar Birger Gerhardsson has drawn out some of the implications of the fact that Jesus was a Jewish teacher (*rabbi* in Hebrew) and that his twelve disciples were his students – the primary meaning of the Greek word *mathetes*, translated as "disciple," is "learner" or "student." Jesus taught his disciples in ways that would fix his teachings in their memories. Above all, Jesus taught in parables (Hebrew *meshalim*): short, well-crafted sayings and stories that could be remembered easily and

accurately. Gerhardsson shows how these essentially fixed *meshalim* would be passed down along with a more flexible commentary. Thus Jesus' parable of the sower (Mark 4:1–9) was fairly fixed, whereas its interpretation (Mark 4:10–20) had more flexibility.[38]

Because Jesus was regarded as an authoritative teacher by his disciples, it stands to reason that, from the start, his disciples were concerned to preserve his exact words as faithfully as possible.[39] ●

Stage 2: The Oral Tradition of the Apostles   10.9.3

Paul and the Tradition   10.9.3.1

We saw above (sec. 9.14.1) how Paul refers often to the "traditions" that he has passed on to his congregations: "I praise you because you remember me in everything and hold fast to the traditions, just as I handed them on to you" (1 Cor 11:2).

From whom did Paul receive his traditions? Paul himself did not know the historical Jesus, but he did know and spend time with Jesus' disciples: "I went up to Jerusalem to confer with Kephas [the Aramaic name for Peter] and remained with him for fifteen days" (Gal 1:18).

Gerhardsson concludes that in 1 Corinthians 15:3, Paul "quotes a *logos* which he had received as an authoritative tradition, undoubtedly from Jerusalem."[40] He shows that in this passage Paul uses precise, technical language to describe how he handed on authoritative tradition that he had in turn received from Jesus' apostles in Jerusalem: "I handed on to you . . . what I also received."[41] Gerhardsson, drawing on his knowledge of similar transmission of tradition in later rabbinic circles, clarifies what the concrete process must have been:

> Either the apostle has passed the text on in a written form which the congregation then has at its disposal, or he has presented the text orally, and impressed it upon them in such a way that the congregation (or, more precisely, one of its leaders) knows it by heart. To "hand over" a text is not the same as to recite it once. It rather means that the text is presented to the hearers in such a way that they "received" it and possess it.[42]

Gerhardsson does point out that after passing on the fixed text, Paul felt free to add his own interpretive comments. For example, the phrase "most of whom are still living, though some have fallen asleep" (1 Cor 15:6) seems to be Paul's own addition to a fixed text.[43]

This evidence from Paul directly contradicts a common scholarly assumption that the oral traditions about Jesus were passed down by anonymous communities. It also fits in well with recent folkloric studies that stress the importance of an authoritative individual carrier of a tradition rather than the involvement of an entire, anonymous community in passing down oral traditions.[44]

Eyewitnesses and the Tradition 10.9.3.2

In his analysis of Papias's statement (see 10.9.1) of how he received traditions, Bauckham makes an important distinction between *oral tradition* (the passing down of traditions beyond one generation) and *oral history* (the passing down of traditions within the lifetime of eyewitnesses).[45] Papias, referring to a time around the year 90, refers to a process in which named disciples of Jesus (he refers to John the Elder and Aristion) were still handing down traditions. Bauckham does not deny that church communities would also have had communal traditions (for example, recited during worship) about Jesus, but he notes that a historian such as Papias prefers to rely on named, known eyewitnesses. The process is one of oral history, not oral tradition.

The Twelve, the Jerusalem Church, and Authoritative Handing Down of Tradition 10.9.3.3

We have seen that Jesus' twelve disciples were the central eyewitnesses to what Jesus said and did. After Jesus' death, we know that the Twelve, along with James, brother of the Lord, became leaders of the first church in Jerusalem (see Acts 6:2; Gal 2:9). Bauckham thus agrees with Gerhardsson that "we should certainly expect them [the Twelve] to have been authoritative transmitters of the traditions of Jesus and to have had something like an official status for their formulation of those traditions."[46]

The Twelve would have had assistance in preserving, formulating, and interpreting the traditions from Jesus. The Jerusalem community was bilingual, composed of both Greek- and Aramaic-speaking believers (see Acts 6:1); the community also included "a large number of priests" (Acts 6:7) as well as Pharisees (Acts 15:5).

The Jerusalem church did not produce a full written Gospel. But as Gerhardsson has shown, the church must have worked intensively with the early traditions about Jesus. This work included translation from Aramaic to Greek as well as reflection on Jesus' life and teaching in the light of Scripture. Traditions were arranged either in writing or in "oral texts" so that they could be passed down accurately to other communities. The Jerusalem community had an authoritative status as the original source of the Jesus traditions; even Paul, who emphasizes his own independence as an apostle, acknowledged the authority of the Jerusalem church to approve the legitimacy of his understanding of the Jesus' tradition (see Gal 2:2).[47]

The earliest traditions about Jesus, then, were developed in a highly educated bilingual community (including priests and scribes) led by Jesus' closest followers and eyewitnesses. They would have carefully preserved the traditions while also interpreting them in light of Scripture.

Outside the Jerusalem church, the Jesus traditions were also handed on by authoritative individuals. The New Testament often refers to "teachers" (Acts 13:1; Rom 12:7; 1 Cor 12:28–29; Eph 4:11; Heb 5:12; Jas 3:1) who would have taught the traditions, and Luke refers to the "ministers of the word" (Luke 1:2).[48] "Presbyters" (elders), appointed by the apostles, also played a role in handing on tradition and teaching (see Acts 14:23; 1 Tim 4:13–14; 5:17; Titus 1:5–9).

Our evidence, then, shows that it is a false dichotomy to suggest that the Gospel writers were interested in faith and not in history. Rather, we find that a systematic effort was made to preserve historical traditions in order to give solid support to faith: this is certainly Luke's understanding as he records it in his preface (Luke 1:1–4).

The Pontifical Biblical Commission, then, is correct to say that some skeptical scholars "underestimate the authority that the apostles had as eyewitnesses of Christ and the office and influence that they wielded in the primitive community, while on the other hand they overestimate the creative capacity of the community itself" (V.1).

Written Notes and Oral Tradition   10.9.3.4

The view that the oral stage of passing down Jesus tradition was completely oral is inaccurate. Some of the Twelve were surely able to write—most obviously Matthew the tax collector (Matt 10:3). Gerhardsson has shown the important role that written notes played in the **rabbinic** oral tradition; by analogy, there is no reason to doubt that unofficial written collections of Jesus' sayings and key points of the tradition were written down by the early Christian preachers for use in their own preaching and teaching.[49] In my own studies, I have found much evidence of written collections of Old Testament texts that early Christians used as "proofs" (*testimonia*) for their beliefs about Jesus and the Church.[50]

Flexibility in the Tradition   10.10

The PBC's *Instruction*, while arguing for the historical accuracy of the Gospels, does not claim that they are *verbatim* accounts. The apostles of Jesus took "into account the circumstances of their hearers" and "interpreted his words and deeds according to the needs of their hearers" (VIII.2); *Dei Verbum* also agrees that the apostles selected certain elements of the Jesus tradition, while "others they synthesized or explained with an eye to the situations of the churches" (V 19).

As a concrete example of how the apostles (or possibly the Gospel writers) passed on tradition with "an eye to the situation of the churches," let's compare two versions of Jesus' teaching on divorce: Matthew 19:1–12 and Mark 10:1–12. Both accounts preserve essentially the same teachings, with Jesus using Genesis 2:24 ("That is why a man leaves his father and mother and clings to his wife, and the two of them become one body") to show that divorce and remarriage contradict God's original plan for marriage: "Therefore what God has joined together, no human being must separate" (Matt 19:6; Mark 10:9). But versions of Jesus' further explanation of the teaching differ:

> I say to you, whoever divorces his wife (unless the marriage is unlawful) and marries another commits adultery. (Matt 19:9)

> Whoever divorces his wife and marries another commits adultery against her; and if she divorces her husband and marries another, she commits adultery. (Mark 10:11–12)

First, notice that Matthew applies the teaching only to the case of a man divorcing his wife. This is most likely Jesus' original teaching, since in first-century Jewish society, women had little or no right to initiate a divorce against their husbands. Mark, who most scholars agree was writing for a Greco-Roman audience (many think his Gospel was written in Rome), adjusts Jesus' teaching to include the possibility of a woman initiating the divorce, since such a scenario was more common in Greco-Roman society.

Notice too that Matthew includes an exception to Jesus' teaching: "unless the marriage is unlawful."[51] While it is possible that Matthew is using another version of Jesus' teaching, it is more likely that Matthew added this phrase to adjust Jesus' teaching to the needs of his own audience since only Matthew has this exception; versions of Jesus' teaching in Luke, Mark, and 1 Corinthians do not. In early Christianity, many Gentiles joined the Christian communities; some had marriages to relatives that were in violation of the rules in the Torah (for example, the rules in Lev 18:6–18). Such marriages would have been considered a kind of sexual sin and thus unlawful. It seems that Matthew therefore adjusted Jesus' basic teaching to apply to a situation that did not exist in Jesus' own lifetime.[52]

This example of Jesus' teaching on divorce supports Gerhardsson's view that the Jesus tradition was passed down in fixed sayings that allowed for flexible interpretation.

Remembering with Fuller Understanding

10.11

The PBC writes further,

> Yet it need not be denied that the apostles, when handing on to their hearers the things which in actual fact the Lord had said and done, did so in the light of that fuller understanding which they enjoyed as a result of being schooled by the glorious things accomplished in Christ and of being illumined by the Spirit of truth. (VIII)

The PBC cites some texts from the Gospel of John that suggest that the events of the Resurrection influenced the disciples' memories of historical events. "His disciples did not understand this at first, but when Jesus had been glorified they remembered that these things were written about him and that they had done this for him" (John 12:16; cf. 2:22).

The point was reiterated in *Dei Verbum* (no. 19), "For after the ascension of the Lord, the apostles handed on to their hearers what he had said and done, but with that fuller understanding which they, instructed by the glorious events of Christ and enlightened by the Spirit of truth, now enjoyed."

Again, let's turn to a concrete example of how that "fuller understanding" might have been expressed.

In John 6:22–59 the evangelist records an exchange between a crowd and Jesus at the village of Capernaum in Galilee. Several indications show us that this is not a strictly historical record.

First, Jesus makes explicit claims about himself that are not found in the Synoptic Gospels: "I am the bread of life; whoever comes to me will never hunger" (v. 35); "Everyone who sees the Son and believes in him may have eternal life" (v. 40); "Whoever eats my flesh and drinks my blood has eternal life, and I will raise him up on the last day" (v. 54).

Second, Jesus' words are in the form of a lengthy discourse, not in the short sayings that characterize the Synoptic Gospels and that, as Gerhardsson has shown, were characteristic of the historical Jesus.

Third, the narrative refers to the crowd as "the Jews" (v. 41, 52), and Jesus accordingly tells the crowd, "Your ancestors ate the manna in the desert" (v. 49). Historically, Jesus was of course a Jew, his followers were all Jews, and the crowds to whom he spoke would have been almost exclusively Jewish. The narrative is written from a perspective (decades after the death of Jesus) in which there is a sharp distinction between "the Jews" and Jesus and his followers (now known as "Christians")—such a sharp distinction would have been incomprehensible for the historical Jesus. The text thus clearly describes Jesus' interaction from a later perspective.

Fourth, it seems clear that references to eating the body and drinking the blood of Jesus are influenced by later reflection on the Christian practice of the Lord's Supper. It is historically incomprehensible that Jesus would have publicly discussed the intimate meaning of the Last Supper with a crowd long before the actual Last Supper with his disciples had taken place. Curiously, John does not record the words of Jesus ("This is my body . . . [given] for you") found in the Synoptic Gospels and in Paul's Letter to the Corinthians (11:24–25), but his knowledge of Last Supper traditions and later Christian practice of the Lord's Supper clearly has influenced his writing of the narrative in John 6.

John, then, is not writing strict history, in the sense of recording events as they actually occurred. His portrait of Jesus is colored by later perspectives, as the Gospel itself (12:16) plainly states. The unique character of John has long been recognized; Clement of Alexandria wrote that "John, perceiving that the external facts had been made plain in the Gospel [of Mark], being urged by his friends, and inspired by the Spirit, composed a spiritual Gospel" (quoted in Eusebius's *Ecclesiastical History*, 6.14.7). Clement's remarks seem to be a fair assessment of John's writing: John is not concerned so much with chronological order or strict historical accuracy, as with bringing out the full sacramental and Christological meaning of historical events—a meaning that, historically, did not develop fully until after Jesus' time. This is not to imply, of course, that all development was positive: John's later perspective on the Jews is harsh and stereotyping.

Writing History with Scripture   10.12

A special topic within the larger theme of the historical accuracy of the Gospels is the influence of Scripture (meaning, of course, what Christians now call the Old Testament) on the writing of the Gospels. The

Gospel writers and their sources were convinced that Jesus' life was the fulfillment of Old Testament prophecies. In cases where they did not have eyewitness information, is it possible that the writers might have filled in their narratives with references to Scripture?

John Dominic Crossan writes that the canonical narratives of Jesus' passion and crucifixion are "not history remembered, but prophecy historicized."[53] By "prophecy historicized" Crossan envisions a process in which an author takes an event from Scripture and creates a narrative from it. Crossan estimates, in fact, that 20 percent of the passion narrative is history remembered and 80 percent is prophecy historicized.

We can agree with Crossan that the Gospel writers were surely influenced by Scripture in their writing of history. The question is whether this influence negates the historical reliability of the Gospels. Some examples will demonstrate what particular shape that influence took.

Rereading and Rewriting Scripture   10.12.1

Dei Verbum reiterates the point made by the Pontifical Biblical Commission and by Pius XII that the interpreter must understand the particular literary forms used by the Gospel writers, since "truth is differently presented and expressed" in different types of literary expressions (*DV* no. 12). To understand the way in which the Gospel writers sometimes use Scripture in their writing, we must briefly review the common ancient Jewish techniques of "rereading Scripture" and "rewriting Scripture."

The PBC's *Interpretation of the Bible in the Church*, discusses the importance of the principle of "rereading" (French: *relecture*) within the Bible (III A. 1). Thus the prophecy of Nathan that promised David an heir to his throne (2 Sam 7:12–16) is rephrased in later writings (1 Kgs 2:4; 1 Chr 17:11–14); it is alluded to in prophecies about later kings (Isa 7:13–14); it is applied in different historical situations (Jer 30:9); and later the promised kingdom becomes universalized (Ps 2:8; Dan 2:35). The New Testament writers then reread these texts in light of the life of Jesus.

Prophecies were also "reread." The prophet Daniel (Dan 9:2, 24–27) "rereads" the prophecies of Jeremiah that had applied to the Babylonian Exile (Jer 25:11–12; 29:10) and applies them to a new historical situation in which the Jews were oppressed by Greek rulers. The prophet John in turn "rereads" Daniel's prophecies: Daniel's vision of beasts arising from the sea (Dan 7), originally applied to four kingdoms in Daniel's time (Dan 7:17; cf. Dan 8:20–21), is applied by John to the Roman Empire (Rev 13:–2).

One type of "rereading" Scripture is what Devorah Dimant has called the "compositional" use of Scripture, in which "biblical elements are woven into the work without external formal markers."[54] Thus the biblical character of Tobit is modeled on the earlier biblical character of Job—the author deliberately reuses details from Job's life (his prosperity, his loss of possessions, his nagging wife, his prayer asking to die) in his portrait of Tobit.[55]

Dimant suggests that this same process occurs in a more strictly historical narration. Dimant argues that the description of how Judas Maccabeus was denied safe passage through the city of Ephron during the rebellion against the Greek ruler Antiochus Epiphanes (1 Macc 5:48) is modeled on an account in Numbers 20–21 where the Israelites were denied safe passage through Edom and the land of the Amorites. Dimant suggests that the words of Judas are a conflated quotation of Numbers 21:22, Deuteronomy 2:26–29, and Judges 11:19, three versions of the Israelites' request for safe passage to King Sihon of the Amorites. By employing this technique, "the author of 1 Maccabees implies that Judas was enacting the patterns of biblical history."[56]

In studying this process of "rereading" and "rewriting," we see that the biblical sense of history cannot be separated from Scripture. Historical events reveal God's plan found in Scripture. That is, God works through historical events in the same recurring patterns recorded in Scripture.

The interpreter of the Gospels, then, must understand that the Gospel writers often wrote in this same way—weaving the paradigms, patterns, and even details of Scripture into their telling of the story of Jesus. From a historical-critical perspective, then, we must distinguish between events that are clearly historical and events that reflect a compositional use of Scripture (weaving in Scripture as part of composing a narrative).

Matthew's Infancy Narrative 10.12.2

The infancy narratives of the canonical Gospels (Matt 1–2 and Luke 1–2) are distinct from the rest of the Gospel narratives. They record events that were not part of Jesus' public ministry and thus were likely not passed down in the same way as those later public events.[57]

Many scholars have recognized the compositional use of Scripture in these chapters.

Most scholars agree that Matthew and Luke did not know one another's Gospels, and so they represent two independent witnesses to the historical events. When one compares their two accounts, they agree in basic details:

1. Mary and Joseph are Jesus' parents; Jesus is conceived through the intervention of the Holy Spirit while Mary was still a virgin.

2. An angel announces the birth of the child, directs that he should be named "Jesus," and identifies him as the Savior.

3. The birth occurs in Bethlehem, but Jesus is raised in Nazareth.

4. Joseph is a descendant of King David.[58]

Brown argues in some detail that there is reasonable historical evidence for events narrated by both Gospels: Jesus' descent from the line of King David, Jesus' birth at Bethlehem, and Jesus' birth from Mary while she remained a virgin.[59]

If there is historical evidence for these core details, however, other details in the infancy narratives are much more questionable.[60] We will limit our discussion to Matthew's second chapter, which narrates the story of magi (wise men) from the East visiting Jesus, King Herod's plot to kill Jesus, the resulting massacre of all infants two years old and under in Bethlehem, and Jesus' family's escape into Egypt and eventual return to Nazareth (Matt 2:1–18).

First, these details cannot be reconciled with Luke's account. Luke records that after Jesus' birth, the family completed some religious rituals and returned to Nazareth (Luke 2:21–40). Luke writes nothing of the events recorded in Matthew 2; in fact, within the time frame of Luke's narrative, there would have been no time for these events to occur before a return to Nazareth.

Second, had the events recorded in Matthew been historical, we would expect other historical sources to have recorded them. But we have no record from any source independent of Matthew that Herod and "all Jerusalem" were disturbed by news of the birth of the "King of the Jews" in Bethlehem (Matt 2:3) or that Herod's soldiers carried out a massacre of infants in Bethlehem (Matt 2:16–18). The silence of Josephus, who wrote detailed accounts of King Herod's activities, is especially striking.

Third, the behavior of the star in Matthew's story is inexplicable in a historical or scientific sense. While we have insisted that it is reasonable to accept the possibility of supernatural events (chapter 5), we have also seen that generally biblical miracles are in overall harmony with the workings of nature—they are a supernatural fulfillment of natural powers (see 5.17). In Matthew, the star "preceded" the magi, "until it came and stopped over the place where the child was" (Matt 2:9). It's not clear how a star, even with supernatural assistance, could stop over a house.

Matthew's account in chapter 2, then, does not make sense as strict history. But Brown and other scholars have demonstrated that the account *does* make perfect sense as an example of the compositional use of Scripture or, more simply, "writing with Scripture."[61] In particular, Matthew's account may be seen as a compositional use of the biblical story of Moses' early life (Exod 1–4). Brown has shown that Matthew's chapter makes use not only of the Bible itself, but of other biblical "rewritings" that were known to the Jewish historian Josephus and the Jewish philosopher Philo, both of whom were contemporaries with New Testament authors.

The following table shows some of the parallels:[62]

Matthew 2	Scripture and Scriptural rewritings
Matt 2:13–14: Herod seeks to kill the child Jesus.	Exod 2:15: Pharaoh seeks to kill Moses.
Matt 2:1–6: Herod finds out from the magi and the chief priests and scribes that the "king of the Jews" is to be born in Bethlehem.	Josephus reports that scribes warn Pharaoh that a Hebrew will be born who will threaten his kingdom.
Matt 2:1–3: The magi tell Herod of the future "king of the Jews."	Later sources say that Pharoah's warning dream was interpreted by his magicians (magi).
Matt 2:3 Herod and all Jerusalem are disturbed at the news of Jesus' birth.	Josephus reports that Pharoah and the Egyptians are filled with dread at the news of the birth of a Hebrew savior.
Matt 2:16: Herod orders the massacre of all boys two years of age and under.	Exod 1:22: Pharaoh orders that every Hebrew male baby be thrown into the Nile.

continued

Matthew 2	rewritings *continued*
Matt 2:19: Herod dies.	Exod 2:23: Pharaoh dies.
Matt 2:19 – 20: The angel of the Lord tells Joseph in Egypt, "go to the land of Israel, for those who sought the child's life are dead."	Exod 4:19: The Lord tells Moses in Midian, "go back to Egypt, for all the men who sought your life are dead."
Matt 2:21: Joseph returns to Israel with his wife and son.	Exod 4:20: Moses returns to Egypt with his wife and sons.
Matt 1:20 – 21: God appears to Joseph in a dream and tells him that Mary's baby will "save his people from their sins."	Josephus reports that God appears to Moses' father in a dream and assures him that Moses will escape from Pharaoh and "deliver the Hebrew race from their bondage in Egypt."

The implicit purpose of this section in Matthew is clearly to compare Jesus to Moses. Scholars have shown that this comparison is a constant literary theme in Matthew: Jesus is portrayed as the new Moses, a figure greater than the legendary giver of the Torah.[63]

Other Compositional Uses of Scripture   10.12.3

As Crossan has pointed out, the compositional use of Scripture is prevalent in the passion narratives. For example, in his account of Jesus' crucifixion, Mark relates, "Then they crucified him and divided his garments by casting lots for them" (Mark 15:24; cf. Matt 27:35; Luke 23:34). This appears to be an allusion to Psalm 22:19: "They divide my garments among them; for my clothing they cast lots." The Gospel of John expands the narrative of this incident and ends it with a quotation of Psalm 22:19, prefaced with "in order that the passage of scripture might be fulfilled" (John 19:24).

It is historically certain that Jesus was crucified. A further historical fact is that victims of crucifixion were generally crucified naked and so the dividing of Jesus' clothes is historically plausible. Brown suggests that the original tradition of Jesus' crucifixion that was passed down included "the customary stripping of the prisoner but doing so in the language of a psalm about the suffering just one."[64] In other words, the Gospel writers employed a compositional use of Scripture to fill out some historical details.

Psalm 22 is used compositionally in other places in the Gospel description of the crucifixion. For example, Jesus' words from the cross, "*Eloi, Eloi, lema sabachthani?*" ("My God, my God, why have you forsaken me?" Mark 15:34) is a quotation of Psalm 22:2. It is certainly possible that Jesus did cry out these words before his death. This historical event may then have prompted the Scripture writers (or their sources) to use Psalm 22 compositionally to fill out other details.

Yet if we have a worldview open to the transcendent, we might very well ask, "Why isn't it possible that every event in Mark's passion narrative is historical, and is in fact a fulfillment of prophecy?" Two factors suggest that such a conclusion is unreasonable.

1. Our study of Matthew 2 shows that this chapter is plainly not a strictly historical account, even allowing for the possibility of supernatural events. It is thus fair to assume that Gospel writers might weave scriptural details into their overall historically reliable accounts in other places as well.

2. This literary technique of "writing with Scripture" was a common and culturally acceptable way of narrating historical events among ancient Jewish writers. There is no reason why the Gospel writers would not have used such a common technique in their own writing.

The Passing Down
of the Jesus Traditions   10.13

We have just considered reasons for concluding that the canonical Gospels do not always contain a completely historical account of Jesus' actual words and deeds: Jesus' teachings were adjusted to the needs of the audience of the Gospel writers; the event of Jesus' Resurrection influenced the way in which the writers (especially John) recorded their material; and the Gospel writers at times employed a compositional use of Scripture to fill in details of historical events.

Granted that we cannot expect complete historical accuracy, it is nonetheless apparent that none of these points challenges the *essential* historical reliability of the Gospels. In every case, we are dealing with adjustments or embellishments of detail made to an underlying historical tradition. The one exception seems to be Matthew's narrative of the magi and the flight into Egypt, where the whole narrative seems to lack a historical basis. This record of events before Jesus' public ministry, however, does not challenge the essential historical reliability of the record of Jesus' public ministry (events witnessed by Jesus' closest disciples and other eyewitnesses). In any case, even this narrative is written within an overall framework of historical events passed down in the tradition.

We have seen that scholars such as Mack and Crossan, who argue for a radical difference between the Jesus of history and the Jesus of the canonical Gospels, must rely heavily on speculation regarding hypothetical documents, hypothetical layers of those documents, and hypothetical communities treating these hypothetical documents as Gospels.

When we turn to more solid historical evidence, however, a different picture emerges: a solid line of historical continuity between Jesus, his twelve apostles, Paul, and the Gospel tradition. Jesus is a teacher with an intimate group of followers. These followers, in turn, preserved, studied, and passed on traditions about him in a systematic way.

In the next chapter, we focus specifically on the question of what a reasonable historical study of Jesus can tell us and the implications that such a historical study has for the Christian theological understanding of Jesus.

Questions about the Text

1. Why is the "particularity" of Jesus as the Savior a "shock and offense" to many?

2. How is the view of God expressed in the doctrine of the Incarnation a shock and offense?

3. What was the Christological issue behind the debate at the Council of Ephesus on whether Mary could be called "Mother of God"?

4. How did the Nestorians and the Monophysites view the relationship of the human and the divine in Jesus?

5. What does it mean to say that Christ is the "new Adam"?

6. How did Teilhard de Chardin reconcile a biblical belief in Christ with the theory of evolution?

7. What is the doctrine of the atonement, and why do some contemporary theologians object to it? How do traditional Christians answer these objections?

8. What are the basic positions in the debate about whether the "quest for the historical Jesus" is relevant for Christian faith?

9. Name some ancient noncanonical writings about Jesus. How historically reliable are these sources?

10. What are some reasons for questioning the historical reliability of the canonical Gospels?

11. What are some reasons for thinking that the oral tradition about Jesus was historically accurate? In this regard, what is the importance of Jesus as a teacher, the role of eyewitnesses, the evidence of Paul, written accounts, and the role of the Jerusalem Church?

12. What are some examples of how the traditions about Jesus were adjusted as they were passed down? How have the traditions possibly been influenced by the needs of specific audiences, the later experiences of the disciples, and the Jewish practice of "rewriting Scripture"?

Discussion Questions

1. Have you ever found the Christian beliefs about Jesus to be "shocking" or "offensive"? Explain.

2. To what extent do you personally feel a need to "makeup" or atone for a wrong that you have done?

3. What recent books or films assume differences between the "Jesus of history" and the "Christ of faith"?

4. Do you think historical-critical conclusions about the Gospels should influence the faith of Christians one way or another?

5. What is your overall assessment of how historically accurate the Gospels are?

Endnotes

1. Henri de Lubac gives many references to this teaching, especially from the ancient Greek Fathers. See de Lubac, *Catholicism: Christ and the Common Destiny of Man* (San Francisco: Ignatius, 1988; orig. pub. 1947), 37–39.

2. Joseph Ratzinger, *Introduction to Christianity* (San Francisco: Ignatius Press, 2000; orig. pub. 1968), 234–43.

3. Christoph Schönborn, *Chance or Purpose: Creation, Evolution, and a Rational Faith* (San Francisco: Ignatius Press, 2007), 141.

4. Henri De Lubac, *Teilhard Explained* (New York: Paulist Press, 1968; orig. pub. 1966), 54.
5. Ratzinger, *Introduction to Christianity*, 155.
6. Schönborn, *Chance or Purpose*, 142; De Lubac, *Teilhard Explained*, 54.
7. See Schönborn, *Chance or Purpose*, 142.
8. Ratzinger, *Introduction to Christianity*, 236.
9. Karl Rahner, *Foundations of Christian Faith: An Introduction to the Idea of Christianity* (New York: Crossroad, 1978), 192.
10. Rahner, *Foundations of Christian Faith*, 224–25.
11. De Lubac, *Catholicism*, 39.
12. Hans Urs von Balthasar, *Theo-Drama: Theological Dramatic Theory*, vol. 3, *The Dramatis Personae: The Persons of Christ* (San Francisco: Ignatius Press, 1992), 203.
13. C. S. Lewis, *Mere Christianity* (London: HarperCollins, 2001; orig. pub. 1952), 53–59.
14. Ibid., 57.
15. Ibid., 58.
16. See the summary in S. Mark Heim, *Saved from Sacrifice: A Theology of the Cross* (Grand Rapids, MI: Eerdmans, 2006), 26.
17. Von Balthasar, *Persons in Christ*, 242.
18. Ibid., 256.
19. For a history of the various stages of the so-called quest for the historical Jesus, see N. T. Wright, *Jesus and the Victory of God* (Minneapolis: Fortress, 1996), 13–124.
20. For a discussion of these sources, see John P. Meier, *A Marginal Jew: Rethinking the Historical Jesus*, vol. 1, *The Roots of the Problem and the Person* (New York: Doubleday, 1991), 56–92, and Paul R. Eddy and Gregory A. Boyd, *The Jesus Legend: A Case for the Historical Reliability of the Synoptic Jesus Tradition* (Grand Rapids, MI: Baker Academic, 2007), 165–99.
21. Luke Timothy Johnson, *The Real Jesus: The Misguided Quest for the Historical Jesus and the Truth of the Traditional Gospels* (San Francisco: HarperSanFrancisco, 1996).
22. Ibid., 167.
23. Ibid., 81–104.
24. Avery Dulles, *The Craft of Theology: From Symbol to System* (New York: Crossroad, 1995), 224.
25. On the dating of these documents, see John Dominic Crossan, *The Historical Jesus: The Life of a Mediterranean Jewish Peasant* (San Francisco: HarperSanFrancisco, 1991), 427–29.
26. Burton Mack's two key books are *A Myth of Innocence: Mark and Christian Origins* (Philadelphia: Fortress, 1988) and *The Lost Gospel: The Book of Q and Christian Origins* (San Francisco: HarperCollins, 1993); John Dominic Crossan's classic book on the topic is *The Historical Jesus: The Life of a Mediterranean Jewish Peasant* (New York: HarperSanFrancisco, 1991). See Wright's summary of their work (*Victory of God*, 35–65).
27. Robert W. Funk, Roy W. Hoover, and the Jesus Seminar, *The Five Gospels: The Search for the Authentic Words of Jesus* (New York: Macmillan, Polebridge Press, 1993), 7.
28. See Wright, *Victory of God*, 40–44.
29. On the date of these documents, see Bart D. Ehrman, *Lost Christianities: The Battles for Scripture and the Faiths We Never Knew* (Oxford: Oxford University Press, 2003), xi–xii.
30. For this conclusion, see Meier, *Marginal Jew*, 139–41.
31. In saying, "I AM," Jesus is claiming the divine title of God from Exod 3:14.
32. Approximate dates are from Raymond E. Brown, *An Introduction to the New Testament*, Anchor Bible Reference Library (New York: Doubleday, 1997).

33. For an overview of form-critical assumptions, see Eddy and Boyd, *Jesus Legend*, 239–41; Richard Bauckham, *Jesus and the Eyewitnesses: The Gospels as Eyewitness Testimony* (Grand Rapids, MI: Eerdmans, 2006), 241–46.

34. Bauckham, *Jesus and the Eyewitnesses*, 47–55.

35. Ibid., 39–84.

36. Papias's account is quoted by the ancient church historian Eusebius (*Ecclesiastical History* 3.39.15). For literary evidence in Mark that supports this link to Peter, see Bauckham, *Jesus and the Eyewitnesses*, 155–80; see also Bauckham's analysis of the account (ibid., 202–21).

37. See Bauckham, *Jesus and the Eyewitnesses*, 212–13.

38. Birger Gerhardsson, *The Reliability of the Gospel Tradition* (Peabody, MA: Hendrickson, 2001), 42–46, 120.

39. Ibid., 27–29.

40. Birger Gerhardsson, *Memory and Manuscript: Oral Tradition and Written Transmission in Rabbinic Judaism and Early Christianity*, The Biblical Resource Series (Grand Rapids, MI: Eerdmans; Livonia, MI: Dove Booksellers, 1998; orig. pub. 1961), 280.

41. Gerhardsson, *Memory and Manuscript*, 295. On Paul's recognition of the authority of the Jerusalem church, see also ibid., 274–80.

42. Gerhardsson, *Gospel Tradition*, 22.

43. Gerhardsson, *Memory and Manuscript*, 299–300; *Gospel Tradition*, 21–22.

44. See Eddy and Boyd, *Jesus Legend*, 273.

45. Bauckham, *Jesus and the Eyewitnesses*, 30–38. Papias's statement is preserved in Eusebius, *Ecclesiastical History* 3.39.3–4.

46. Bauckham, *Jesus and the Eyewitnesses*, 94.

47. See Gerhardsson, *Memory and Manuscript*, 220–61, 274–80.

48. See Eddy and Boyd, *Jesus Legend*, 264–66.

49. See Gerhardsson, *Gospel Tradition*, 12–13; Eddy and Boyd, *Jesus Legend*, 241–52.

50. Martin Albl, *"And Scripture Cannot Be Broken": The Form and Function of the Early Christian Testimonia Collections*, Novum Testamentum Supplements 96 (Leiden: Brill, 1999).

51. This "exception" clause can be translated in different ways: the NIV, for example, translates "except for marital unfaithfulness."

52. See the notes to Matthew 5:32 in *Saint Mary's Press College Study Bible New American Bible* (Winona, MN: Saint Mary's Press, 2007).

53. John Dominic Crossan, *Who Killed Jesus? Exposing the Roots of Anti-Semitism in the Gospel Story of the Death of Jesus* (San Francisco: HarperSanFrancisco, 1995), 10.

54. Devorah Dimant, "Use and Interpretation of Mikra in the Apocrypha and Pseudepigrapha," in *Mikra: Text, Translation, Reading and Interpretation of the Hebrew Bible in Ancient Judaism and Early Christianity*, ed. M. J. Mulder; repr. (Peabody, MA: Hendrickson, 2004), 382.

55. Dimant, "Mikra in the Apocrypha," 418.

56. Ibid., 407.

57. See Raymond E. Brown, *The Birth of the Messiah: A Commentary on the Infancy Narratives in the Gospels of Matthew and Luke*, rev. ed., the Anchor Bible Reference Library (New York: Doubleday, 1993), 32–33.

58. Ibid., 34.

59. Ibid., 505–33. The historicity of the last event, of course, presumes a worldview open to the possibility of the supernatural.

60. Ibid., 36.

61. Scholars debate the proper term to use for this type of literary genre. Some have used the term *midrash*, but the basic sense of midrash is a search for the deeper meanings of scriptural texts (for example, a midrash on Genesis). The goal of midrash is to explain Scripture, while the goal of compositional use of Scripture,

or "writing with Scripture," is to reveal the deeper meaning of an event by weaving Scriptural patterns and allusions into the narrative of the event (see Dimant, "Mikra in the Apocrypha," 382). We will therefore use the more generic term, "writing with Scripture."

62. See Brown, *Birth of the Messiah*, 113–15.

63. See, for example, Dale C. Allison, *The New Moses: A Matthean Typology* (Minneapolis: Fortress Press, 1993).

64. Raymond E. Brown, *The Death of the Messiah: From Gethsemane to the Grave*, 2 vols., Anchor Bible Reference Library (New York: Doubleday, 1994), 2:954.

11

The Historical Jesus

The Incarnation: Jesus as a First-Century Jew

The search for the historical Jesus has helped many people to appreciate more deeply the truth of the Incarnation — that God truly did become a specific human being. To understand the human Jesus, we must understand him as we would any other human: within the context of the time and culture in which he lives (see sec. 10.1.2). For Jesus, this time and culture was first-century Judaism.

Contrary to the claims of some Christians, it is historically highly unlikely that Jesus went about "talking as if He was God," claiming that "He has always existed."[1] Passages such as "Before Abraham was, I AM" (John 8:58) are found only in the Gospel of John, which tends to develop the claims of the historical Jesus in the light of later theological reflection (see sec. 10.11). We must therefore analyze the Gospel records critically if we wish to attain a more historically

BACKGROUND IMAGES ROYALTY FREE FROM ISTOCK AND SHUTTERSTOCK

accurate portrait of the words and actions of the first-century Jew named Jesus of Nazareth.

The Third Quest and Traditional Christology 11.2

A recent scholarly trend in historical Jesus studies is sometimes called the "Third Quest."[2] N. T. Wright lists some of the major concerns of this group of scholars.[3]

1. How does Jesus fit into first-century Judaism? Often even orthodox Christians picture Jesus as a divine person who is "above" any particular time and place. Third Quest historians take seriously the likelihood that first-century Judaism shaped Jesus' worldview and actions.

2. What were Jesus' aims in the context of first-century Judaism? An aim is "the fundamental direction of a person's life," a direction shaped by a particular worldview. Assessing the aims of a historical character is not a claim to understand the inner psychology of a person, but rather an attempt to discern the pattern and consistency of a person's words and actions.[4] For example, can it make historical sense to claim that one aim of the first-century Jewish rabbi Jesus was to die for the sins of the world?

3. Why was Jesus executed? Was it because he claimed to be God? All historical scholars agree that Jesus truly was executed; understanding the historical reasons behind this event sheds light on his life as a whole.

4. How and why did the early Church begin? It is historically certain that Jesus lived and died as an ethnic and religious Jew, but the movement he began developed into the religion of Christianity. Was it one of Jesus' aims to begin a new religion? Or are later figures such as Paul the true founders of the Christian religion?

Wright's final question is, "How does the Jesus we discover by doing 'history' relate to the contemporary church and world?"[5] As we look at some of the results of the Third Quest, together with some other historical investigations, we also shall keep this question in mind.

Who Did Jesus Think He Was? 11.3

Did Jesus think he was God, or God's Son, or the Messiah? Some would conclude that such questions are impossible to answer because we cannot "get into the head" of someone who lived thousands of years ago. Others would say these questions are impossible to answer historically because they are questions of faith.

But the historians of the Third Quest believe that if we place Jesus in his historical context and study the overall patterns of his life, reasonable answers will emerge: we can discern Jesus' basic aims.

A common beginning point is the attempt to understand historically what Jesus meant when he preached about the **kingdom of God**. The kingdom of God is a central theme in Jesus' teaching in the Gospels, beginning with his first words recorded in Mark's Gospel (considered by many scholars the earliest Gospel): "This is the time of fulfillment. The kingdom of God is at hand. Repent, and believe in the gospel" (Mark 1:15).

Our first task, then, is to understand the "kingdom of God" in its first-century Jewish context.

Jesus and the Kingdom of God 11.4

On the face of it, the meaning of the term *kingdom of God* (often *kingdom of Heaven* in Matthew), is clear enough: it is a place or a condition in which God is king, where God rules. Such a situation is in stark contrast to the Roman rule of Jesus' day. While many modern Christians tend to assume that the kingdom is the same as heaven, the actual sayings in the Gospels are more complex. At least three distinct understandings emerge:

1. The kingdom is in heaven. Jesus taught, "And if your eye causes you to sin, pluck it out. Better for you to enter in the kingdom of God with one eye than with two eyes to be thrown into Gehenna [hell]" (Mark 9:47).

2. God's kingdom will come to earth in the near future. Jesus taught his disciples to pray to the heavenly Father, "Your kingdom come, your will be done, on earth as in heaven" (Matt 6:10). Jesus seems to believe the kingdom will come very soon: the kingdom is "at hand" (Mark 1:15); Jesus asserts that "some standing

here . . . will not taste death until they see that the kingdom of God has come in power" (Mark 9:1).

3. A few sayings suggest that the kingdom has already come. "But if it is by the Spirit of God that I drive out demons, then the kingdom of God has come upon you" (Matt 12:28).

The kingdom is also associated with final judgment. Jesus compares the kingdom of heaven with a field that has both wheat and weeds: "At the end of the age" the "Son of Man will send his angels, and they will collect out of his kingdom all who cause others to sin and all evildoers. They will throw them into the fiery furnace" (Matt 13:40–42).

In historical Jesus scholarship, there is a debate between those who see Jesus' message about the kingdom as "eschatological" (events or language involving final judgment) and "apocalyptic" (events and language involving the direct and definitive intervention of God in history) and those who see it more along the lines of a "wisdom" teaching (see sec. 10.7.4). The Third Quest understands Jesus within the eschatological framework. As E. P. Sanders points out, the Gospels begin with Jesus being baptized by John the Baptist (who warns that God's final judgment is coming soon). After his death and Resurrection, Jesus' followers expected that he would return soon to establish his kingdom. Paul, in the earliest New Testament document (1 Thessalonians), expects that Jesus will return within his lifetime to gather all his followers up to heaven (1 Thess 4:14–17). "It is almost impossible to explain these historical facts on the assumption that Jesus himself did not expect the imminent end or transformation of the present world order. He thought that in the new age God (or his viceroy) would reign supreme, without opposition."[6]

The Kingdom in Jewish Context   11.4.1

In its first-century Jewish context, the kingdom was not understood simply as God reigning throughout the whole world. Jews believed that God had a special relationship with them as the chosen people. The kingdom thus referred primarily to God's direct action concerning Israel.

According to Scripture, Israel was composed of twelve tribes, descendants of the sons of Jacob. Ten tribes constituted the northern kingdom, but they had been scattered after the eighth-century BCE conquest by the Assyrians. In the "new age" of the kingdom, God would restore the twelve tribes; Meyer writes of "the tie between the reign of God and the restoration of Israel."[7] For Wright too, the establishment of the kingdom meant "that Torah would be fulfilled at last, that the Temple will be rebuilt and the Land cleansed."[8]

What would happen to the Gentiles? Many texts imagine a final battle (for example, the *War Scroll* from the Qumran community, the *Psalms of Solomon*, or Zech 14) in which the Gentile nations are defeated. In some texts, at the end time, the nations would come to Jerusalem to worship God in the Temple:

> The mountain of the LORD's house shall be established as the highest mountain and raised above the hills. All nations shall stream toward it; many peoples shall come and say: "Come, let us climb the LORD's mountain, to the house of the God of Jacob, that he may instruct us in his ways, and we may walk in his paths." (Isa 2:2–3; see also Zech 14:16–19)

These are all *eschatological* or "end time events." But as Wright correctly points out, first-century Jewish images of the "end times" do not necessarily envision an end to the natural world: "There is virtually no evidence that Jews were expecting the end of the space-time universe." For example, when Jesus uses imagery such as "the stars will be falling from the sky, and the powers of the heavens will be shaken" (Mark 13:25), Wright argues that first-century Jews would have recognized these passages as metaphors "to bring out the full theological significance of cataclysmic socio-political events."[9] Sanders also thinks that "Jesus did not expect the end of the world in the sense of destruction of the cosmos."[10] Eschatological events are historical, political events, but they are also events that reveal God's "fulfillment of history."

The Kingdom and the Messiah 11.4.2

How would the kingdom of God be established? A commonly accepted idea in Second Temple Judaism was that God would act through an intermediary, whether a human figure such as a king or a "divine intermediary figure" (see 6.9.5), in order to establish the kingdom on earth. Although this eschatological intermediary was called by various names (such as "Son of Man"), the scholarly discussion often centers on the term *Messiah* or *messianic figure*.

Within first-century Judaism, there was no one fixed concept of the Messiah.[11] The term itself simply means "one who is anointed" and thus has the metaphorical sense of one who has been chosen by God. As such, the term was typically applied to priests, prophets, and kings. The community at Qumran that produced the Dead Sea Scrolls, for example, believed in two Messiahs: a priestly Messiah and a royal Messiah.

Nevertheless, the term in first-century Judaism typically referred to a king: a royal Messiah descended from King David. The term itself did not necessarily imply divine status, however.[12]

From early on in Hebrew history, the king, as leader of the chosen people and as chosen by God himself, was understood to have a unique relationship with God. In Psalm 2, for example, God calls the king "my son" (Ps 2:7). God's promises are also associated with this relationship: God had promised David, the greatest Hebrew king, that "your house and your kingdom shall endure forever" (2 Sam 7:16).

A major role of the Hebrew king, as God's representative, was to establish God's values of peace and justice in society: "You love justice and hate wrongdoing; therefore God, your God, has anointed you with the oil of gladness above your fellow kings" (Ps 45:8). The prophet Isaiah describes a future king ("Messiah") thus, "But he shall judge the poor with justice, and decide aright for the land's afflicted. . . . With the breath of his lips he shall slay the wicked" (Isa 11:2–4).

Closely associated with God, the king at times is described as having God-like characteristics. The same psalm that identifies him as "God's son" (Ps 2:7) also claims that God will make his "possession the ends of the earth" (Ps 2:8). Another passage even refers to him as a "god": "Your throne, O god, stands forever, your royal scepter is a scepter for justice" (Ps 45:7).

The historical reality, of course, never matched this ideal. Many Israelite kings were in fact weak, corrupt, and worshipped other gods. Nor did the rule of the kings literally last forever: with the Babylonian conquest of Jerusalem in 587 BCE, the line of kings descending from David ceased. The Jewish people, however, never lost the hope that one day God would again anoint a king who would restore God's justice not only in Israel but throughout the world.

The Ideal Age of the Messiah   11.4.3

The kingdom of God is thus sometimes identified with the "age of the Messiah." The Bible devotes many passages to this ideal future reign of peace and justice under God's Messiah. "See your king shall come to you. . . . The warrior's bow shall be banished, and he shall proclaim peace to the nations" (Zech 9:9–10). This messianic peace and justice would be so complete that nature itself would be swept up into it:

> Then the wolf shall be a guest of the lamb,
> and the leopard shall lie down with the kid;
> The calf and the young lion shall browse together,
> with a little child to guide them. (Isa 11:6)

In other visions of this future kingdom of peace and justice, God himself reigns as king, not the Messiah: "He [the Lord] shall judge between the nations. . . . They shall beat their swords into plowshares and their spears into pruning hooks; one nation shall not raise the sword against another, nor shall they train for war again" (Isa 2:4).

Again, the ancient Jewish mind did not always associate this ideal future age specifically with a figure called the "Messiah." The figure known as the "Son of Man" was also understood as playing a key role in bringing about the eschatological kingdom of God. In Daniel we read that "one like a son of man" (7:13) "received dominion, glory, and kingship; nations and peoples of every language serve him" (7:14). It is significant that Daniel later identifies this "Son of Man" with the people of Israel: "Then the kingship and dominion and majesty of all the kingdoms under the heavens shall be given to the holy people of the Most High" (7:27). So just as the king could represent his people Israel, so too could the Son of Man represent Israel. This "Son of Man" is portrayed as an eschatological judge in Second Temple literature such as *4 Ezra 13* and *1 Enoch. 1 Enoch* is especially significant in that it combines several different images in its description of the eschatological ruler: the Messiah, the Son of Man, and God's Servant (described in Isa 42–53).

In the following discussion about Jesus' self-identity, then, we will use the term *Messiah* to refer to the eschatological ruler who would act for God in bringing about the final age. But keep in mind that terms such as *Son of Man* were also used by first-century Jews in their speculation about eschatological figures of the final age.

Did Jesus Think He Was the Messiah?   11.4.4

According to scholars such as Rufolf Bultmann, Jesus himself never claimed to be the Messiah; he was only given that role by the Church after his Resurrection.[13] We have seen that more recent scholars such as Crossan and Mack also reject the idea that Jesus thought in these eschatological terms (sec. 10.7.4). In contrast, members of the Third

Quest insist that Jesus must have understood his words and actions in this eschatological, messianic framework.

Several historical considerations support the Third Quest approach:

1. In the earliest writings of the New Testament (Paul's letters), Paul refers so constantly and naturally to "Jesus Christ" (*Christ* is Greek for "Messiah") that the title "Messiah" seems almost part of Jesus' name. It is hard to explain how this title could have become so firmly established so soon after Jesus' death unless it had been used by Jesus' followers already within Jesus' lifetime.

2. The Gospels record that Jesus was crucified as "King of the Jews" (Mark 15:26); it is historically probable that the Romans executed Jesus as a threat to their rule or the rule of their clients (such as Herod). In first-century Judaism, *Messiah* primarily meant "king," a claim that would have captured the Romans' attention in a way that internal Jewish religious debates would not.

3. Non-Christian authors called Jesus "Christ": the Roman historians Tacitus (born 55 CE) and Suetonius (writing in the years 117–138, Suetonius mistakenly writes "Chrestus") and the Jewish historian Josephus (c. 37–100).

4. If Jesus had not been thought of as the Messiah before his death and Resurrection, it is virtually impossible that he would have been called "Messiah" after the fact. First, to refer to any Jew as "Messiah" (king) would have invited trouble from Roman and Jewish authorities. Second, the belief that Jesus rose from the dead could not have convinced anyone that Jesus was the Messiah if they had not believed it previously. We have no first-century evidence that Jews expected the Messiah to rise from the dead. The belief that Jesus rose from the dead could only have been understood as God's confirmation of the messianic beliefs that the followers of Jesus had when he was alive.[14]

Jesus' Actions, the Kingdom, and the Messiah   11.5

The Synoptic Gospels portray Jesus as secretive about his identity as the Messiah. In a scene regarded by many critics as the literary center of the Gospel of Mark, Peter responds to Jesus' question, "Who do you say I am?" with, "You are the Messiah." Jesus then warns the disciples not to tell anyone (Mark 8:29 – 30).

Much has been written about the possible reasons for this "messianic secret." Some argue that it reflects the historical Jesus' actual reticence about the title, and others attribute it to Mark's literary creativity. Without getting into the details of the debate, we can note that, historically, it would have been highly dangerous, even suicidal, for a popular religious leader to claim to be the true king (Messiah) of Israel. Neither the Jewish nor the Roman rulers would have hesitated to respond violently to such a perceived threat to their authority. Thus the Jewish ruler Herod Antipas executed John the Baptist "in part because he proclaimed the coming judgment," and a Roman procurator killed a certain Theudas, a self-proclaimed prophet who claimed that he would divide the Jordan River (see Acts 5:36).[15]

Historically speaking, then, it is highly likely that if Jesus did indeed regard himself as the Messiah, he would have kept his claim quiet to avoid immediate arrest or execution.

Kingdom of God as Defeat of Evil Spiritual Powers   11.5.1

Members of the Third Quest have shown that Jesus' self-understanding as the Messiah of Israel can be discerned not only in his words but also in his actions.

Sanders concludes that the many references to exorcism in the Synoptics "makes it extremely likely that Jesus actually had a reputation as an exorcist."[16] Jesus seems to have understood his power to perform exorcisms as a sign that the kingdom of God was being established through him: "But if it is by the Spirit of God that I drive out demons, then the kingdom of God has come upon you"(Matt 12:28).

A quick look at various New Testament passages demonstrates the ancient Jewish conviction that this current world is dominated by evil spirits. The Gospel of John refers to the devil as the ruler of this world (12:31; cf. 14:30; 16:11); Paul calls the devil the "god of this age" (2 Cor 4:4) and characterizes the current time as the "present evil age" (Gal 1:4). The Gospel of Matthew shares this perspective; in the account of Jesus' temptation, the devil offers Jesus "all the kingdoms of the world" (Matt 4:8-9) — presupposing, of course, that they are his to give. Obviously, such ruling demonic forces would need to be defeated in order for God's kingdom to be established.

Ancient Jewish culture understood illness and demon possession as manifestations of the power of evil in the world. At times illness is said to be directly caused by demons: Jesus explains that a crippled woman had been "bound" by Satan "for eighteen years" (Luke 13:10–16). In other cases, illness is associated with sin: when four men bring a paralyzed man to Jesus for physical healing, Jesus' first response is, "Child, your sins are forgiven" (Mark 2:5). Jesus does deny that a tragedy such as a falling tower killing a group of people was a direct result of their sins, but at the same time he makes it clear that suffering and death are inevitable consequences of sin and evil: "If you do not repent, you will all perish as they did!" (Luke 13:1–5).

Thus when Jesus heals a person, or when Jesus casts out a demon, this action is an assault on the demonic dominance of the world and the beginning of the establishment of the kingdom of God. When Jesus' disciples report that even the demons are subject to them because of Jesus' name (authority), Jesus responds, "I have observed Satan fall like lightning from the sky" (Luke 10:18).

Demonic powers and spirits were associated not only with illness and possession but also with political powers. In the Book of Revelation, for example, a dragon (representing Satan) gives "its own power and throne" to a beast (representing the Roman political power); the beast is further given "authority over every tribe, people, tongue, and nation" (Rev 13:2, 7). This language parallels the passage in Daniel 7, where the "son of man" is given this same authority.

So the establishment of the kingdom of God also refers to Christ taking away the power of these earthly rulers and the spiritual powers that support them, "despoiling the principalities and the powers" (Col 2:15). One of the exorcism stories in Mark may hint at this political connection when it identifies the name of the demon possessing a man as "Legion," Latin for a group of five thousand soldiers (Mark 5:9). Some scholars have seen this as an indirect reference to Jesus' ability to free people from the demonic power of the Roman Empire.

The Kingdom of God and the New Israel 11.5.2

According to the Gospels, Jesus chose twelve men (Mark 3:13–19; see also 1 Cor 15:5) to be his closest followers. At times Jesus taught a public message to the crowds, but privately explained the deeper meaning only to the Twelve (e.g., Mark 4:10–20; 10:10–12; see sec. 10.9.1).

Jesus the Messiah began to establish the kingdom through his preaching, his exorcisms, and his healings; at the same time, he gave his disciples authority to accomplish these same actions and aid him in bringing about the kingdom. Mark relates how Jesus "summoned the Twelve and began to send them out two by two and gave them authority over unclean spirits. . . . So they went off and preached repentance. They drove out many demons, and they anointed with oil many who were sick and cured them" (Mark 6:7–13).

Now for an ancient Jew, the number twelve is not arbitrary. It symbolizes the twelve tribes of Israel, the totality of the chosen people. Jesus' action thus signifies the beginning of the eschatological age: the gathering of the twelve tribes (see 11.4.1).

The place of the Twelve in the eschatological vision of Jesus is striking: "You who have followed me, in the new age, when the Son of Man is seated on his throne of glory, will yourselves sit on twelve thrones, judging the twelve tribes of Israel" (Matt 19:28).

The Authority of the Messianic Teacher   11.5.3

In the last chapter, we considered Jesus as a teacher (see sec. 10.9.2). The people of Jesus' time recognized that he taught with more than ordinary authority. "When Jesus finished these words, the crowds were astonished at his teaching, for he taught them as one having authority, and not as their scribes" (Matt 7:28 – 29). As the Messiah, the Chosen One of God who was establishing the kingdom, Jesus had full authority to interpret the Torah. In the so-called Sermon on the Mount (Matthew 5 – 7), Jesus strikingly contrasts his authority with that of the Torah.

You have heard that it was said, "You shall not commit adultery." *But I say to you*, everyone who looks at a woman with lust has already committed adultery with her in his heart. (Matt 5:27 – 28; emphasis added)

Jesus appeals to no other authority: his interpretation is based on his personal authority as the Messiah.

Indeed, Jesus claims to know God's original intention when he goes beyond the Law of Moses and teaches his followers that they should not divorce: "Because of the hardness of your hearts he [Moses] wrote you this command" (Mark 10:5). ●

We must understand the implications of Jesus' action. Recall that in Jewish eschatological thought, Israel was the key to the renewal of the world. It was only through joining with Israel and submitting to Israel's God that the Gentile nations could be saved. In establishing the Twelve as the leaders of eschatological Israel, Jesus was also claiming that he and his disciples were the key to the ultimate destiny of the world.

Jesus' Relationship with the Father   11.5.4

Jesus' supreme self-assurance as the messianic intermediary is clearly founded on his conviction that he has a unique relationship with God the Father:

- "All things have been handed over to me by my Father. No one knows the Son except the Father, and no one knows the Father except the Son and anyone to whom the Son wishes to reveal him." (Matt 11:27)

- "Everyone who acknowledges me before others I will acknowledge before my heavenly Father. But whoever denies me before others, I will deny before my heavenly Father." (Matt 10:32–33)

- "Whoever receives you receives me, and whoever receives me receives the one who sent me." (Matt 10:40)

Jesus' sense of an intimate relationship with the Father is often expressed (as in the last example) in terms of being "sent."

- "To the other towns also I must proclaim the good news of the kingdom of God, because for this purpose I have been sent." (Luke 4:43)

- "I was sent only to the lost sheep of the house of Israel." (Matt 15:24)

Several other sayings illustrate the same consciousness of being sent by God, but are expressed in terms of "coming":

- "Do not think that I have come to abolish the law or the prophets. I have come not to abolish but to fulfill." (Matt 5:17)

- "Just so, the Son of Man did not come to be served but to serve and to give his life as a ransom for many." (Matt 20:28)

- "I did not come to call the righteous but sinners," (Matt 9:13)

- "Do not think that I have come to bring peace upon the earth. I have come to bring not peace but the sword." (Matt 10:34)

- "For the Son of Man has come to seek and to save what was lost." (Luke 19:10)[17]

The theme of the Father sending the Son is characteristic of the Gospel of John: "These works that I perform testify on my behalf that the Father has sent me" (John 5:36); "This is the work of God, that you believe in the one he sent" (John 6:29). John is simply emphasizing a theme already clear in the Synoptic Gospels.[18]

Theological Implications of "Sending"   11.5.5

We have already noted that in the Gospel of John, Jesus makes unusually explicit claims about his equality with the Father: "The Father and I are one" (John 10:30). But when we look at Jesus' self-understanding from the perspective of being "sent" by the Father, the differences between John and the Synoptics do not appear to be great.

Von Balthasar makes no hard and fast distinction: all four Gospels present Jesus claiming to have a unique relationship to the Father who sent him to establish the eschatological kingdom. Indeed, viewed historically, even Matthew's "I was sent only to the lost sheep of the house of Israel" (Matt 15:24) is not necessarily a limited statement, given the Jewish belief that "the Gentiles would find salvation by assimilation to saved Israel at the judgment bringing history to an end."[19] All four Gospels, then, portray Jesus as convinced that he, as the Messiah, was the central actor in a drama that would determine the destiny of the entire earth.

Von Balthasar believes that the theme of "sending" or "mission" provides the link between the historical understanding of Jesus and traditional Christological beliefs. The Father's sending Jesus into the world parallels the eternal procession of the Son from the Father, in keeping with Rahner's thesis that the economic Trinity is the immanent Trinity (sec. 6.15).

Just as there is a profound unity between Son and Father in the Trinity, so too is there a profound unity between the Father and the incarnate Jesus. Von Balthasar does not claim that Jesus "remembered," in a human way, his time with the Father before the creation of the world. Rather we can say that Jesus' total confidence that the Father has given him the divine mission of establishing the kingdom is analogous to the eternal Son's complete love and acceptance of the

Father within the Trinity. So in this sense, "Jesus' certainty regarding the universality and finality of his mission suffices to allow us to take everything said in the Prologue of the St. John's Gospel [in the beginning was the Word, and the Word was with God] and trace it back to his earthly consciousness."[20]

With this point, von Balthasar does complete justice to Jesus' humanity. Just as all humans can only know the divine by analogical language (see sec. 5.8.3), so too in his human consciousness, Jesus knows the Father in a way analogous to the relationship of Father and Son within the immanent Trinity.

Jesus' Entry into Jerusalem   11.5.6

According to all four Gospels, when Jesus entered Jerusalem, he rode on a donkey (see Mark 11:1–11 par.). This seemingly insignificant detail, however, is quite possibly a deliberate "sign" that Jesus was the Messiah. As John explicitly points out, it fulfilled a prophecy announcing the arrival of Israel's king: "See, your king comes, seated upon an ass's colt" (John 12:15; cf. Zech 9:9). Certainly the crowd's reaction indicates that they understood it as a messianic sign: they welcomed Jesus with cries of "Blessed is the kingdom of our father David that is to come!" (Mark 11:9).

Jesus apparently intended to evoke the entire prophecy of Zechariah 9:9: "Rejoice heartily, O daughter Zion, shout for joy, O daughter Jerusalem! See, your king shall come to you; a just savior is he, meek, and riding on an ass, on a colt, the foal of an ass." In contrast to a militant Messiah who would smash the Gentiles (as in *Psalms of Solomon* 17, for example), Jesus symbolically claims to be a humble Messiah riding on a donkey. As Sanders summarizes, "It is by no means inconceivable that Jesus' ride was a deliberate signal: 'king' yes, of a sort; military conqueror 'no.'"[21]

In acting out a prophecy, Jesus would be following in a long prophetic tradition: the prophet Isaiah walked naked to symbolize the condition of the captives taken by the Assyrians (Isa 20:2–4); the prophet Jeremiah smashed a clay jar as a symbol of the coming destruction of Jerusalem by the Babylonians (Jer 19:10–11).[22]

Replacing the Temple with the New Israel   11.5.7

Many historical Jesus scholars agree that Jesus' action at the Jerusalem Temple is key in understanding his intentions. The Gospel accounts report that Jesus drove out people buying and selling and overturned the tables of the money changers (see Mark 11:15–17 par.). Although a common interpretation is that Jesus was protesting economic exploitation or corruption in the Temple, his intention seems to have gone much deeper than that.

The symbolic significance of the Temple in Second Temple Judaism is hard to overestimate. In Jewish understanding, the Temple was nothing less than the sacred site at which the divine met the earthly (see sec. 1.3).[23] The Temple was built on the "cosmic rock" that held together and gave meaning to the universe; the rabbis speculated that this very spot was

> the site of creation, of Paradise and the tree of life, source of the rivers of the world, proof against the Deluge. Here was the altar on which Abraham was ready to sacrifice Isaac; here, too, was the altar of Melchizedek; here, the house and the throne of God and the destined locale of the judgment of the world.[24]

In the eschatological vision delivered to his disciples, Jesus had predicted that the Temple would be destroyed (Mark 13:1–2); at his trial he was accused of threatening to destroy the Temple (Mark 14:58; see also Acts 6:14 and John 2:19). Picking up on these hints, Meyer, Sanders, and Wright all conclude that Jesus' action was intended not merely as a sign that the practices in the Temple should be reformed, but as a sign of the Temple's imminent destruction. Again, Jesus' intention makes sense within some ancient Jewish eschatological expectations: in the new age of the Messiah, the Temple would be destroyed so that a new and better one could be built.[25]

Wright agrees that the action symbolized the destruction of the Temple, but takes the implications further. For Wright, the action also symbolizes Jesus' attack on the whole Temple system of forgiveness of sin through sacrifices and the associated authority of the priesthood. During his ministry, Jesus had announced to people that their sins were forgiven (for example, Mark 2:1–12; Luke 7:36–50).[26] He had a reputation for associating with, and especially for eating with, the outcasts of society such as the tax collectors and "sinners" (for example, Mark 2:15); his meals with his followers were often understood as "signs" of the "messianic banquet" in the kingdom of God: "Many will come from the east and the west, and will recline with Abraham, Isaac, and Jacob at the banquet in the kingdom of heaven" (Matt 8:11).

The thrust of all of these actions, then, was that "Jesus was replacing adherence or allegiance to the Temple and Torah with allegiance to himself. . . . The point about Jesus' welcome to 'sinners' was that he was declaring, on his own authority, that anyone who trusted in him and his kingdom-announcement was within the kingdom."[27] People would be saved from their sins by belonging to the new, eschatological Israel, and Jesus was the Messiah who was establishing that kingdom.

Meyer's work emphasizes a further key dimension of Jesus' intention: that Jesus intended to replace the Temple not only with his own authority, but more concretely with the community of his followers, centered on the Twelve.

First, Meyer demonstrates the connection between the Messiah and the eschatological Temple in Second Temple thought. A prophecy about a descendant of King David found in 2 Samuel 7:13 ("It is he who shall build a house for my name. And I will make his royal throne firm forever") was interpreted by many to mean that the Messiah would build an eschatological Temple.[28]

For Meyer, Jesus' response to Peter's confession that he (Jesus) was the Messiah (Matt 16:16) is a key to Jesus' intention. Jesus says, "You are Peter, and upon this rock I will build my church, and the gates of the netherworld shall not prevail against it" (Matt 16:18). Jesus here plays on the name *Peter*: in Greek, *Petros* is related to the word *petra*, meaning rock, especially solid rock. Peter's name in Aramaic, *Cephas* (or *Kephas*), is related to the word *kepha*, equivalent to the Greek *petra*.

When Jesus says to Peter, "Upon this rock I will build my church, and the gates of the netherworld shall not prevail against it," he is tapping into the cosmic imagery of the Temple. Meyer explains,

> The text's operative presupposition is that the task of "the Messiah, Son of the living God" (Matt 16:16) is precisely to build the eschatological temple. Here temple is translated by "church," the community of restored Israel, or rather by "my church," for the restored community of Israel is messianic.[29]

The basic meaning of the Greek word *ekklesia*, translated as "church" here, does not correspond exactly to modern ideas of a Christian church. But ancient and modern meanings both point to a people "called out" to form a community.

From his words and actions, interpreted within a Second Temple context, Meyer and others rightly conclude that Jesus' intention was to replace the old system of worship (based on the Temple) with a new system centered on Jesus himself and his eschatological community—the new Temple.

Did Jesus Think He Would Die for the Sins of the World?   11.6

In understanding the historical Jesus, the modern interpreter is challenged by such seemingly unhistorical statements as, "Christ died for our sins in accordance with the scripture" (1 Cor 15:3), or John the Baptist's description of Christ in the Gospel of John as "the Lamb of God, who takes away the sin of the world" (John 1:29).

Must we not conclude that these ideas are later theological additions to Jesus' story? How can one person's death take away another's sins? And even if someone's death could have an influence, how could Jesus die for the sins of the whole world?

Again we must immerse ourselves in the worldview of ancient Judaism, attempting to fuse our modern horizons with the horizons of that far-away time, if wish to achieve true understanding (see sec. 1.11).

Forgiveness and the Kingdom   11.6.1

First, we must recognize that our modern concept of sin is much more individualistic than that of the ancient Jews. We have seen that Scripture itself has a dialectic between a group or "corporate" sense of sin and the concept of individual responsibility (sec. 8.13.1). From a biblical view, we must try to hold onto the truth of both perspectives.

Contrary to some modern interpretations, first-century Jews did not believe that they could "earn" God's forgiveness by their good deeds. As authors such as Sanders and Wright have shown, the whole concept of sin and forgiveness was inseparable from the belief that the individual was part of the community of Israel, the people who had a covenant with God. By remaining faithful (as an individual) to this covenant (made by the group) an individual was saved.[30]

From the eschatological perspective of Jesus, then, forgiveness of sin was tied to the *renewed* covenant that God would make with Israel in the last days:

> The days are coming, says the LORD, when I will make a new covenant with the house of Israel and the house of Judah. . . . I will place my law within them, and write it upon their hearts; I will be their God, and they shall be my people. . . . For *I will forgive their evildoing and remember their sin no more.* (Jer 31:31–34; emphasis added)

Wright sums up, "Forgiveness of sin is another way of saying 'return from exile': the eschatological gathering of the twelve tribes."[31]

If, as we have argued throughout this chapter, Jesus understood himself as the Messiah who would restore Israel, it follows that he would expect to play a key role in this eschatological forgiveness of sins.

Dying for the Sins of Others   11.6.2

Before looking at the ancient evidence, we can first recall the point we made in chapter 10: the general concept of atoning, making up for sins, is by no means merely a primitive or outdated way of thinking; rather, we can argue that it is a deeply held belief that is known across the spectrum of human cultures (see sec. 10.6.1.1).

The belief that one person could die to atone for the sins of another was well known in the ancient Greco-Roman world. The Roman poet Lucan, a contemporary of the apostle Paul, records the speech of the statesman Cato: "This my blood will ransom all the people; this my death will achieve atonement for all the [punishment] Romans have deserved through their moral decline."[32]

More relevant for the Jewish context of Jesus are examples taken from Fourth Maccabees, composed around the time of Jesus' death in the middle of the first century CE. The work describes the Jewish resistance to Antiochus IV Epiphanes' attempt to force the Jews to convert to Greek religion. In the following passage, the author narrates how the aged priest Eleazar is tortured to death for refusing to eat pork. Just before dying, Eleazar proclaims,

> You know, O God, that though I could have saved myself I am dying in these fiery torments for the sake of the Law. Be merciful to your people and let our punishment be a satisfaction on their behalf. Make my blood their purification and take my life as a ransom for theirs. (4 Macc 6:27–29)

In his reflections on the death of Eleazar and other martyrs for the Jewish faith, the author concludes, "Through them our enemies did not prevail against our nation, and the tyrant was punished and our land purified, since they became, as it were, a ransom for the sin of our nation" (4 Macc 17:21).

Further examples of atonement are found in Scripture itself. In Isaiah, the "Servant" of God atones for the sins of the people:

> Yet it was our infirmities that he bore, our sufferings that he
> endured, while we thought of him as stricken, as one smitten by
> God and afflicted. But he was pierced for our offenses, crushed for
> our sins, upon him was the chastisement that makes us whole, by
> his stripes we were healed. (Isa 53:4–5)

> He gives his life as an offering for sin. . . . Through his suffer-
> ing, my servant shall justify many, and their guilt he shall bear. (Isa
> 53:10–11)

Finally, consider a passage from the prophet Ezekiel:

> Then you shall lie on your left side, while I place the sins of the
> house of Israel upon you. As many days as you lie thus, you shall
> bear their sins. . . . When you finish this, you are to lie down
> again, but on your right side, and bear the sins of the house of Judah
> forty days; one day for each year I have allotted you. (Ezek 4:4–6)

Jewish tradition, then, provides several clear examples of the
belief that one person's suffering or death could atone for the sins of
the people. If Jesus understood himself as the Messiah, the royal representative of his people, he could well have imagined the possibility
of suffering or dying on behalf of his people.[33] Historically it is likely
that Jesus was influenced by the example of the Servant of the Lord in
Isaiah—a figure who (like the Messiah) is especially chosen by God
(Isa 42:1) and who, like the Messiah, represents his people Israel. The
Second Temple writing, *1 Enoch*, had already identified Isaiah's Servant
with the Messiah.

Did Jesus Know He Would Die?   11.6.3

The Gospels portray Jesus as predicting his death and Resurrection.
For example, directly after narrating Peter's confession of Jesus as the
Messiah and Jesus' warning not to tell anyone, Mark adds, "He began
to teach them that the Son of Man must suffer greatly and be rejected
by the elders, the chief priests, and the scribes, and be killed, and rise
after three days" (Mark 8:31).

Is this a classic case of what John Dominic Crossan calls "prophecy historicized"? Writing years after Jesus' death, has Mark simply
added these "prophecies" to embellish the supernatural nature of his
main character Jesus?

These reasonable questions can best be answered historically. Jesus
led a messianic movement that proclaimed the kingdom of God—in

other words, he implicitly proclaimed a challenge to the ruling authorities, both Jewish and Roman. During his public ministry, the Gospels show Jesus playing down the revolutionary character of his movement, warning his disciples, for example, not to tell anyone that he was the Messiah (e.g., Mark 8:30 par.).

But at a certain point, it seems clear that Jesus intended to provoke a confrontation. He traveled from his own home base of Galilee to Jerusalem, center of Jewish priestly power and Roman military and political authority, and—most importantly—the site of the Temple. He entered Jerusalem as a king (in fulfillment of Zech 9:9) and he performed an action that symbolized the destruction of the Temple. He was claiming, if still symbolically, that he was the messianic king sent by God to destroy the current Temple and replace it with an eschatological one.

Jesus would have known that by radically challenging the authority of either Jewish or Roman authorities he was virtually assuring himself of a death sentence. He was well aware of what happened to prophets such as John the Baptist (notice Jesus' reaction to the news of the Baptist's death in Matt 14:13) and Theudas who challenged the authorities (see sec. 11.5).

Jesus' words to his disciples at the Last Supper, then, make historical sense, drawing together many of the threads we have been discussing. Breaking the bread, Jesus said, "Take it; this is my body." After drinking from the cup, Jesus said, "This is my blood of the covenant, which will be shed for many" (Mark 14:22–24 par.).

In speaking of the covenant, Jesus refers to the coming of the kingdom and Israel's renewed covenant with God. In case anyone should miss the point, he adds, "I say to you, I shall not drink again the fruit of the vine until the day when I drink it new in the kingdom of God" (Mark 14:25). The breaking of the bread and the drinking of the wine are completely consistent with Jesus' practice of performing symbolic actions. Both bread and wine were rich symbols in first-century Judaism: both were dietary staples and thus symbols of life, both were associated with the Temple and thus with sacrifice. The two as a meal symbolized the eschatological banquet in the kingdom of God.

Simply at the practical, human level of knowledge, Jesus knew that because of his more direct challenge to the religious and political authorities his death was imminent. Given first-century Jewish thought on the atoning death of martyrs, Jesus' self-understanding as the Messiah, representative of Israel, and his likely identification of himself with the Servant of the Lord, Jesus very reasonably believed that he was laying down his life as a sacrifice for the sins of his people, the renewed Israel.[34]

Jesus thus seems to have thought of his own imminent suffering and death as the final showdown between the powers of evil (represented by the ruling authorities) and the power of God's kingdom (represented by himself and his disciples). This final struggle was the beginning of the "final test" that Jesus referred to in the Lord's Prayer (Matt 6:13).[35]

We have seen that the salvation of the Gentiles was associated with the salvation of Israel in the eschatological age in much Second Temple thought. Given evidence of Jesus' openness to Gentiles in the Gospel record (for example, healing a Roman officer's slave in Luke 7:1–10), it is likely that Jesus thought along these lines as well.[36] In this sense it is no exaggeration to say that Jesus thought of his death as a sacrifice for the sins of the world. Such a claim is perfectly understandable in the context of first-century Jewish eschatology.

The historical probability that Jesus himself believed in the atoning value of his death also is the best historical explanation for the very early traditions that were taught to the apostle Paul. Quoting traditions that go back to the first Jerusalem community (within a few years of Jesus' death), Paul asserts that "Christ died for our sins" (1 Cor 15:3) and that on the night he was betrayed, Jesus took bread, gave thanks, broke it, and said, "This is my body that is for you" (1 Cor 11:24).

Did Jesus Expect to Rise on the Third Day?   11.6.4

If, historically speaking, it is plausible that Jesus understood his own death as a sacrifice for renewed Israel, what can we say about the claim that he knew he would "rise on the third day"? Once again, this at first sounds suspiciously like a later belief placed back into the mouth of the historical Jesus as a prophecy.

Recall Jesus' words: "He began to teach them that the Son of Man must suffer greatly and be rejected by the elders, the chief priests, and the scribes, and be killed, and rise after three days" (Mark 8:31). One key to interpreting the passage would be to identify exactly what Jesus meant by the title "Son of Man."

For this purpose, let's consider the exchange between the high priest Caiphas and Jesus at his trial:

"Are you the Messiah, the son of the Blessed One?" Then Jesus answered, "I am; and 'you will see the Son of Man seated at the right hand of the Power and coming with the clouds of heaven.'" (Mark 14:61–62; Mark writes "Power" as a substitute for "Lord")

Jesus' answer is a conflation of two Old Testament texts, "I saw one like a son of man coming, on the clouds of heaven" (Dan 7:13) and "The LORD says to you, my lord: 'Take your throne at my right hand'" (Ps 110:1).

Both Meyer and Wright think that Jesus identified himself with this "Son of Man" from Daniel 7 who would establish the kingdom. Second Temple writings such as *1 Enoch* (48:10 and 52:4) and *4 Ezra* identify the Danielic "Son of Man" with the Messiah, and we have good evidence that the historical Jesus thought of himself both as the Messiah and as the Son of Man.[37] An especially significant section of 1 Enoch known as the *Similitudes* speaks of a human being, Enoch (see Gen 5:21–24), being raised up into heavenly glory as the Son of Man who will judge all humans in the eschatological age (1 Enoch 71:14 and 69:27).[38]

Jesus' vision, then, is of a time after his death when he would be raised to heaven and enthroned with God: God's vindication of Jesus as the true representative of Israel.[39] This belief is consistent with Jesus' overall eschatological and apocalyptic outlook. Historically speaking, however, such a vision of vindication in heaven does not indicate whether Jesus thought of himself as rising bodily from the dead—the vision itself may simply refer to a "spiritual" vindication.

Finally we should note that the phrase "on the third day" does not necessarily refer to three calendar days. Biblically, it can mean simply "a short time," but it also has a symbolic sense of the time one must wait for God's salvation. Thus Jonah remained in the belly of the fish for three days and three nights (Jon 2:1); Hosea records the people's hope, "He will revive us after two days; on the third day he will raise us up" (Hos 6:2).[40]

Did Jesus Rise from the Dead?   11.7

Does the central Christian belief in Jesus' Resurrection make rational sense? Before trying to answer the question directly, we need to address two preliminary concerns: (1) What exactly do we mean by "rise from the dead"? (2) Is Jesus' Resurrection something that can be studied historically?

Defining *Resurrection* 11.7.1

Not only do scholars disagree about *whether* Jesus rose from the dead, but also about *what* the claim entails.

Luke Timothy Johnson, for example, defines the Resurrection as "the passage of the human Jesus into the power of God."[41] In his definition of "Easter faith," John Dominic Crossan writes that after his death, "Jesus' presence was still experienced as empowerment. . . . It started among those first followers of Jesus in Lower Galilee long before his death, and precisely because it was faith as empowerment rather than faith as domination, it could survive and, in fact, negate the execution of Jesus himself. . . . An empty tomb or a risen body susceptible to food and touch were dramatic ways of expressing that faith."[42] Still other scholars trace the Resurrection back to visionary or psychological experiences of Jesus' followers.[43] From such perspectives, then, the early Christians may have spoken of Jesus' Resurrection as a "spiritual" or visionary event.

N. T. Wright argues, however, that as historians we should pay close attention to the words the earliest followers of Jesus used to describe their experience and then seek to understand the meaning of those words within a first-century Jewish context. When early Christians speak of Jesus' Resurrection, they use such Greek words as *anastasis* ("resurrection"; "rising"), *anistemi* ("to raise or rise up") and *egeiro* ("to raise"). The reference was *not* simply to a person entering a spiritual afterlife, but rather to a person coming back to earthly life after a period of being dead.[44] "God raised (*egeiro*) him from the dead; of this we are witnesses" (Acts 3:15).

At the same time, early Christian records are clear in their belief that Jesus was not simply a resuscitated corpse, a dead body come back to normal human life. Both the Gospel stories of Jesus' risen body and Paul's description (a "spiritual body"; 1 Cor 15) show that they are *not* speaking of a spirit or ghost, on the one hand, or of a corpse come back to life on the other. They are speaking of a deceased person raised to a transformed, bodily type of life after a period of being dead (see sec. 7.8–9).

But is this early Christian claim true?

Resurrection in the Context of Ancient Belief 11.7.2

This Christian belief in the resurrection of the body shows both similarities to and differences from other ancient beliefs. Following Wright's account we briefly summarize the major points:

1. The belief in a resurrection of the body differentiated Jewish belief from Greco-Roman belief. In general, Greco-Roman ideas pictured some kind of shadowy postdeath existence in Hades or perhaps the Isles of the Blessed or Tartarus, while the Platonic tradition emphasized the immortality of the soul.

2. Ancient Jewish tradition held a variety of beliefs: Sadducees denied the resurrection of the body; the Jewish philosopher Philo believed in continued existence of the soul without a body; the author of 2 Maccabees plainly believed in a bodily resurrection, as did the Pharisees.

3. The early Christian view of resurrection, however, differed even from those Jews who accepted bodily resurrection in two ways: (1) against the Jewish view that there would be a general resurrection of the dead on the Day of Judgment, the early followers of Jesus insisted that Jesus had *already* risen as a kind of prototype or model for the resurrection of his followers (1 Cor 15:20); and (2) the resurrected body was described as a transformed physical body.[45]

4. Beliefs about Jesus' Resurrection are remarkably consistent across a wide range of New Testament and early Christian writings.

Can the Resurrection Be Studied Historically? 11.7.3

Starting from his definition of Jesus' Resurrection as "the passage of the human Jesus into the power of God," Luke Timothy Johnson concludes that since Jesus "is no longer defined by time and space" the event lies beyond "history's limited mode of knowing." "The Christian claim concerning the resurrection in the strong sense is simply *not* historical." The only sense in which it can be considered historical is "as an experience and claim of human beings, then and today, that organizes their lives and generates their activities."[46]

But Johnson's definition of resurrection is clearly at odds with the early Christian definition of resurrection as the raising of a physically transformed body. The early Christians, moreover, made two claims about Jesus' Resurrection that are in fact open to historical investigation: (1) Jesus' tomb was empty, and (2) Jesus appeared to many eyewitnesses in a transformed bodily state. These in fact are historical claims that can be checked using the usual historical tools.

History and Jesus' Resurrection   11.7.4

Wright agrees that, in the strictest sense, the actual moment of Jesus' Resurrection cannot be studied historically. No one claims to have witnessed the moment when Jesus (allegedly) rose up and walked out of the tomb.[47]

What can be studied, however, are the early Christian beliefs and accounts about the Resurrection: the claim that Jesus was raised bodily from the dead. To study these claims about a supernatural event, however, we must practice what Eddy and Boyd have called an "open historical-critical method" (see sec. 5.16). Recall two key elements of this approach:

1. It is open to the possibility of a transcendent, supernatural cause of an event within history (sec.s 5.15–16).

2. The method will only prefer a supernatural explanation if no plausible natural explanations are available.

Focusing on the main witnesses to Jesus' Resurrection, the Gospel accounts, we begin with the claim that Jesus' tomb was found empty. In assessing this claim, we are faced with two general options: (a) the accounts are historically accurate, or (b) the accounts were fabricated. If we accept option (b), however, several historical difficulties arise:

1. Historically speaking, there was no reason for Jesus' followers to fabricate a story that Jesus had risen bodily from the tomb. As we have seen, ancient Greco-Roman society and many first-century Jews did not believe in a bodily resurrection. Those groups (like the Pharisees) who did believe in bodily resurrection, believed in a general eschatological resurrection, not in the resurrection of a single individual. We have, moreover, no evidence that any first-century Jewish group thought the Messiah in particular would rise from the dead, much less that he would rise as an individual before the general eschatological resurrection.

2. All four Gospels indicate that women were the main witnesses to the empty tomb. If the accounts were fabricated to persuade people that Jesus had risen from the dead, why would the followers of Jesus have invented women witnesses? In ancient Jewish society in particular, "women were simply not acceptable as legal witnesses."[48]

It is thus simply inconceivable, from a historical point of view, that the earliest followers of Jesus would have invented a story that made no sense within any first-century worldview, and then supported their story by fabricating women eyewitnesses. The only reasonable conclusion is that the stories relate an actual supernatural event—option (a).

We will now consider the other Gospel accounts: the appearances of the risen Jesus in a transformed body. In this case, the options are more complex: (a) the accounts record actual historical events; (b) the accounts were fabricated; or (c) the followers of Jesus experienced some kind of visions or hallucinations of Jesus.

Option (c) is highly implausible, since the Gospel accounts are plainly designed to rule out the explanation that these events were merely visions or appearances of Jesus' spirit. Luke records Jesus telling his disciples, "Touch me and see, because a ghost does not have flesh and bones as you can see I have" (Luke 24:39). The orthodox Christian tradition is unified in its insistence that Jesus was raised in a transformed body: they explicitly rule out the possibility that the appearances were visions.[49] The first-century Jewish mind was more than capable of distinguishing between claims of seeing ghosts and visions and claims that Jesus was seen in a transformed bodily state. When his disciples saw Jesus walking on water, "they thought it was a ghost" (Mark 6:49); when Rhoda, a member of the Jerusalem community, claimed that she had seen the imprisoned Peter, her fellow believers insisted, "You are out of your mind. . . . It is his angel" (Acts 12:13–15).[50]

We are left with the first two options: the encounters with the risen Jesus in his transformed body are either (a) historical accounts of actual events, or (b) fabrications of the early Christians. Once again option (b) raises serious historical problems.

1. If the early followers of Jesus had intended to persuade others that Jesus had risen from the dead, they did a remarkably poor job.

   First, the claim that Jesus' body was a transformed physical body fits into no first-century worldview. While some first-century groups such as the Pharisees did believe in a resurrection of the body, we have no evidence that they expected it in the odd way that it is described in the Gospels.

   Second, if the account was supposed to persuade those like the Pharisees, one might have expected a glorious figure in blinding white robes instead of the strange Gospel descriptions where

Jesus is mistaken for a gardener (John 20:15; cf. Luke 24:16), still bears the marks of his crucifixion (John 20:27), and eats fish (Luke 24:43).

2. The Resurrection appearances cannot be interpreted as attempts to portray the heavenly vindication or exaltation of Jesus. If this were the case, the Christians would have reported visions of Jesus in heaven (along the lines of Mark 14:62).

The historical problems with option (b) are so serious that unless one had already ruled out *a priori* the possibility of a supernatural explanation, one would have to consider option (a), that the Gospels record historical events.

Consider also two final points.

The accounts of the Gospels receive striking, independent confirmation in Paul's description of the body in the Resurrection as a "spiritual body." The correspondence between Paul and the Gospels emphasizes the uniqueness of the Christian claim over against all other ancient worldviews.

It is true that the Gospel accounts of the empty tomb are inconsistent in some details; for example, the four accounts differ in exactly which women were at the tomb.

- Matthew reports Mary Magdalene and the "other Mary" (28:1)

- Mark reports Mary Magdalene, Mary the mother of James, and Salome (16:1)

- Luke reports Mary Magdalene, Joanna, Mary the mother of James and "others" (24:10)

- John reports Mary of Magdala alone (20:1; although in verse 2 Mary says, "We don't know . . .")

But these discrepancies in detail are hardly evidence that the stories were fabricated. If anything, they support the conclusion that the empty tomb is historical, since such minor discrepancies in detail are exactly what the historian expects from oral traditions passed down over several years. If the details of all four accounts were precisely the same, this would have raised suspicions that the early Christians had agreed to fabricate an account that was then repeated.

The explanation that best fits the available evidence in the Gospels is that Jesus' tomb was found empty and that Jesus actually appeared to many witnesses in a transformed bodily form. All alternative explanations must create hypothetical scenarios that fit badly within the historical context of first-century Judaism.

Conclusions   11.8

The purpose of the original quest for the historical Jesus was to demonstrate the discrepancy between the actual Jesus of history and the portrait of Jesus found in the Gospels and in the Church. It is ironic, then, that many of the results of the Third Quest for the historical Jesus support the plausibility of traditional Christological beliefs.

Within the context of first-century Jewish eschatology, we have found solid historical evidence to support the conclusion that Jesus believed he was God's Messiah, whose work was to establish the eschatological reign of God on earth. We found it historically plausible that Jesus believed that his death would atone for the sins of his people (and, by extension, the sins of the world), and that God would raise him in vindication. Finally, we found solid historical evidence for Jesus' Resurrection from the dead in a transformed physical body.

The efforts of the Third Quest are a decisive vindication of the Catholic and Christian principle that reason (in this case a reasoned study of history) can never contradict faith. On the contrary, the use of an open historical-critical method lends convincing support to traditional belief. In fact, to the extent that the Third Quest has allowed believers to gain a more concrete sense of Jesus as a first-century Jew, historical study has deepened believers' understanding of the Incarnation.

Questions about the Text

1. What are some characteristics of the Third Quest for the historical Jesus?

2. How was the kingdom of God understood in first-century Judaism? What was the role of Israel in that kingdom? What was the role of the royal Messiah in establishing the kingdom?

3. What is the historical evidence that Jesus considered himself to be the Messiah?

4. How do Jesus' exorcisms fit within the first-century Jewish understanding of the kingdom?

5. How does Jesus' selection of twelve disciples fit into the first-century Jewish view of the kingdom?

6. How does von Balthasar relate the relationship between the Father and the Son within the Trinity to the relationship between the Father and the incarnate Jesus? Consider especially the significance of Jesus' self-consciousness of being "sent" by the Father.

7. How do members of the Third Quest interpret Jesus' action at the Temple? How does this action fit into first-century Jewish eschatological expectations of the Messiah and the Temple?

8. How does Meyer relate Jesus' Temple action with Jesus' interaction with Peter in Matthew 16:16–18?

9. In what ways is it historically plausible that Jesus thought his death would atone for the sins of the world? Consider especially Jesus' self-consciousness as the Messiah and first-century Jewish concepts of eschatological salvation.

10. How did early Christian beliefs about Jesus' Resurrection compare with ancient Greco-Roman and Jewish views of life after death?

11. What are the arguments for concluding that Christian claims about Jesus' Resurrection are open to historical investigation?

12. What is the historical evidence for and against Christian claims that Jesus' tomb was found empty? What is the historical evidence for and against Christian claims that Jesus appeared to his followers in a transformed physical body?

Discussion Questions

1. Do you picture the historical Jesus more as an eschatological Messiah or a teacher of wisdom? Could he have been both?

2. Do you agree with Wright that claims about whether Jesus rose from the dead can be studied historically? What about claims that Jesus died for the sins of the world?

3. Discuss popular films or books that relate to the study of the "historical Jesus."

Endnotes

1. C. S. Lewis, *Mere Christianity* (London: HarperCollins, 2001; orig. pub. 1952), 51.

2. In this understanding, the rationalist studies of the life of Jesus (such as the works of Strauss and Renan in the nineteenth century) are labeled the "First Quest," and the studies of scholars, beginning in the 1950s, reacting against Bultmann's historical skepticism about writing a life of Jesus, are labeled the "New Quest." Scholars whom Wright identifies with the Third Quest include Ben Meyer and E. P. Sanders; Wright himself is a leading scholar of the Third Quest. See N. T. Wright, *Jesus and the Victory of God* (Minneapolis: Fortress, 1996), 16–82.

3. Ibid., 89–116.

4. Ibid., 110–12; see also Ben F. Meyer, *The Aims of Jesus* (San Jose, CA: Pickwick Publications, 2002; orig. pub. London: SCM, 1979).

5. Wright, *Victory of God*, 117.

6. E. P. Sanders, *The Historical Figure of Jesus* (New York: Penguin Books, 1993), 183.

7. Meyer, *Aims of Jesus*, 133.

8. N. T. Wright, *The New Testament and the People of God* (Minneapolis: Fortress Press, 1992), 302.

9. Ibid., 333.

10. Sanders, *Historical Figure of Jesus*, 183.

11. See Wright, *People of God*, 307–20.

12. See Wright, *Victory of God*, 477.

13. See the discussion in Meyer, *Aims of Jesus*, 177.

14. On these points, see Wright, *Victory of God*, 487–88; Martin Hengel, *The Atonement: The Origins of the Doctrine in the New Testament* (Philadelphia: Fortress, 1981), 41, 49; Meyer, *Aims of Jesus*, 175–79.

15. See Sanders, *Historical Figure of Jesus*, 29–30.

16. Ibid., 149. Sanders lists the evidence from the Synoptics (149–50); interestingly, John does not record any exorcisms.

17. On the "sent" and "coming" sayings, see also Meyer, *Aims of Jesus*, 166–68.

18. See this point in Hans Urs von Balthasar, *Theo-Drama: Theological Dramatic Theory*, vol. 3, *The Dramatis Personae: The Persons in Christ* (San Francisco: Ignatius Press, 1992), 152.

19. Meyer, *Aims of Jesus*, 168.

20. Von Balthasar, *Persons in Christ*, 255.

21. Sanders, *Historical Figure*, 241–42. See also Wright, *Victory of God*, 490–91; Meyer, *Aims of Jesus*, 199.

22. See Wright, *Victory of God*, 415; Sanders, *Historical Figure of Jesus*, 253.

23. In his discussion on the significance of Jesus' Temple action, Sanders says, "Some readers may think that I have made too much of the issue. I think that it is almost impossible to make too much of the Temple in first-century Jewish Palestine" (*Historical Figure of Jesus*, 262).

24. Meyer, *Aims of Jesus*, 185–86.

25. Sanders, *Historical Figure of Jesus*, 254–62.

26. Wright, *Victory of God*, 272–74.

27. Ibid., 274.

28. Meyer, *Aims of Jesus*, 179–80.

29. Ibid., 186.

30. See Wright, *Victory of God*, 268–74, and E. P. Sanders, *Paul and Palestinian Judaism: A Comparison of Patterns of Religion* (Philadelphia: Fortress, 1977), 236; 426–28.

31. Wright, *Victory of God*, 268.

32. *Pharsalia* 2.304–9; quoted in Hengel, *The Atonement*, 23–24.

33. For these examples and further discussion, see Wright, *Victory of God*, 579–91.

34. On the above points, see Hengel, *The Atonement*, 65–75; Wright, *Victory of God*, 540–611; Meyer, *Aims of Jesus*, 216–19.

35. Meyer, *Aims of Jesus*, 208–9.

36. Ibid., 217–18.

37. On Second Temple literature, see John J. Collins, *The Scepter and the Star: The Messiahs of the Dead Sea Scrolls and Other Ancient Literature* (New York: Doubleday, 1995), 181–87; Meyer, *Aims of Jesus*, 202–9; Wright, *Victory of God*, 510–19.

38. On the complex relationship between the "Son of Man" and the human Enoch, see Collins, *Scepter and Star*, 178–81.

39. Wright, *Victory of God*, 524–28; Meyer, *Aims of Jesus*, 209.

40. See other references in Meyer, *Aims of Jesus*, 182.

41. Luke Timothy Johnson, *The Real Jesus: The Misguided Quest for the Historical Jesus and the Truth of the Traditional Gospels* (San Francisco: HarperSanFrancisco, 1996), 136.

42. John Dominic Crossan, *Who Killed Jesus? Exposing the Roots of Anti-Semitism in the Gospel Story of the Death of Jesus* (San Francisco: HarperSanFrancisco, 1995), 209–10.

43. See the discussion in N. T. Wright, *The Resurrection of the Son of God* (Minneapolis: Fortress, 2003), 20; Johnson, *Real Jesus*, 137.

44. Wright, *Resurrection*, 31.

45. We should keep in mind, of course, that the term *Christian* was not applied to the followers of Jesus until years after Jesus' death and Resurrection. The Book of Acts reports that the disciples were first called "Christians" at Antioch (11:26).

46. Johnson, *Real Jesus*, 136.

47. The *Gospel of Peter* does record that the Roman soldiers saw three men emerge from the tomb (apparently Christ and two angels) followed by a cross.

48. Wright, *Resurrection*, 607.

49. See the evidence in ibid., 480–552.

50. See ibid., 134.

12

Ecclesiology
The Church of Christ and the Catholic Church

"Called Out" to Form a Community

The branch of theology that reflects on the meaning of the Church—the body of the followers of Christ—is known as *ecclesiology*. The English word derives from the Greek *ekklesia*—the standard Greek term for *church* (literally those who are "called out" to form a community). In this chapter, we begin by considering the various meanings of the word *Church*. We then consider why the Christian tradition teaches that belonging to a social group, the Church, is considered necessary for a person's salvation. We then turn to a more specific discussion of the relationship between the Roman Catholic Church and other Christian churches. We conclude with some reflections on the relationship between the Christian Church and non-Christian religions.

Once again, we must ask whether traditional teachings on ecclesiology are reasonable in the modern world. With our modern appreciation of freedom and individuality, does it make sense that a person would have to join a group in order to worship or have a relationship with God? Isn't that something persons can do on their own?

When we consider specifically Roman Catholic claims, further questions arise. With our modern appreciation of pluralism and tolerance, can it make sense for one institution to claim that "it is through Christ's Catholic Church alone, which is the universal help towards salvation, that the fullness of the means of salvation can be obtained" (*UR* no. 3)?

We begin our study by clarifying the meaning of Church and then discussing reasons why the Christian tradition teaches that the Church is necessary for salvation.

Is the Church Necessary for Salvation? 12.1

Church can have a variety of meanings. It can mean the building, or the local congregation of faithful who gather in it. *Church* can also refer to larger branches or "denominations" of Christianity: thus we speak of the Lutheran Church or the Russian Orthodox Church. Vatican II documents typically refer to the Roman Catholic Church simply as "the Church." Finally, Christians speak of the "Church" in the sense described in the Nicene Creed: "one, holy, catholic, and apostolic," the community of all Christians who follow the tradition handed down from the apostles, regardless of denomination.

The purpose of any religion is to lead people to salvation: the overcoming of sin, weakness, and suffering and the fulfillment of human destiny in union with the divine or transcendent. The Catholic Church teaches plainly that the Church "is necessary for salvation" (*LG* 14). But even if we accept that people are too weak to free themselves from their sinful nature, and thus need the help of Christ, why would the Church be necessary? Couldn't people obtain Christ's help on their own, apart from the Church?

The Social Character of Salvation 12.2

"Are you saved?" On any busy downtown street, we might find a Christian handing out tracts asking (and answering) this question. Such a tract generally instructs a person that to be saved he must confess that he is a sinner, ask Christ to come into his life, and accept Christ as his personal Lord and Savior.

As we have seen, the Roman Catholic Tradition would agree that God offers salvation through Christ, and that it is realized in persons' lives when they respond in faith. Catholic Tradition would insist, however, that salvation is not to be understood as individualistically as the above formulation suggests. Rather,

> [God] has . . . willed to make men holy and save them, not as individuals without any bond or link between them, but rather to make them into a people who might acknowledge him and serve him in holiness. (*LG* 9)

Consider some biblical examples. God called Abraham (Gen. 12:2) not to save him as an individual, but so that he could become father of a community, Israel. In the desert, God established a covenant not with Moses as an individual, but with the people as a whole: "The LORD, our God, made a covenant with us at Horeb; not with our fathers did he make this covenant, but with us, all of us who are alive here this day" (Deut 5:2–3). Jesus, from the beginning, preached about a communal concept of salvation (the kingdom of God) and took concrete steps to establish a new community around himself, led by the Twelve. Salvation would come by joining his community, the renewed Israel.

Why Communal Salvation?   12.3

Recall that "salvation" means that persons overcome all that is dark or wrong in their lives and begin to live fully and completely as God intended. An essential ingredient in making our lives full and meaningful is precisely our relationships with other people. Our capacity to make friends, communicate with, love, and care for others, is essential to true happiness and thus ultimately salvation.

The root of sin, on the other hand, can be see as the tendency to isolate ourselves, to treat others as less than human, to be antisocial, anticommunity. Pope Benedict XVI teaches that sin "is understood by the Fathers as the destruction of the unity of the human race, as fragmentation and division."[1] The original unity of all humanity, based on the premise that all people have God as Father and are created in God's image, "was shattered into a thousand pieces" by sin.[2] Salvation, then, is "the recovery of supernatural unity of man with God, but equally of the unity of men among themselves."[3]

In the Christian imagination, judgment and final destiny are pictured in social terms. On the Day of Judgment, *all people* will be raised. The kingdom of God is pictured as a banquet (Matt 8:11) and heaven as a city (Heb 11:10).[4] Eternal life is participation in the community of love within the Trinity. Aquinas taught that the final destiny of humans is "to attain to beatitude, and that can only consist in the kingdom of God, which in its turn is nothing else than the well-ordered society of those who enjoy the vision of God."[5]

Only hell, the loss of God and salvation, is without community.

For these reasons, Catholic tradition teaches that people are not saved as isolated individuals, but rather as a social gathering of the faithful: the Church.

This does not imply that an individual Christian has no personal responsibility. On the contrary, the individual's free personal choice is essential for salvation. The Catholic teaching, however, is that this personal choice can only occur within the larger context of the social gathering of the Church.

Why Does God "Choose" Certain Groups?   12.4

If salvation is essentially social, something an individual achieves as part of a community, we must ask: Why does the Judeo-Christian tradition seem to define salvation as joining oneself to an *exclusive* group? Why does Scripture speak of the Hebrews as the "chosen people," seemingly implying that all other peoples are ignored or even rejected by God? Why have traditional Christians proclaimed that only followers of Christ are "saved," implying (or explicitly stating) that non-Christians are *not* saved?

In discussing the idea of Incarnation, we pointed out the Christian belief that the only way in which the divine could truly come into concrete contact with the human is to be united to a specific individual (see sec. 10.1.2). In an analogous way, the Judeo-Christian tradition tells us that God chooses to work through a specific group — the Jewish people, the Christian Church — with the ultimate goal of drawing all of humanity back to himself.

We also discussed earlier (sec. 11.4.1) that this was precisely how many ancient Jews understood salvation: all the nations would be saved through Israel. "The mountain of the LORD's house shall be established as the highest mountain and raised above the hills. All nations shall stream toward it" (Isa 2:2).

Yves Congar concludes, "The biblical idea of election is always that of setting someone aside to carry out a plan in the world. . . . It is not set apart in order to remain separated, but rather to serve God in the fulfillment of his universal plan of salvation."[6]

"Preparation" for the Church   12.5

Christian theology has always had a problem with time. If Christ is the Savior of all humanity, why was he born thousands of years after humans first evolved? Similarly, if the Church is so important for salvation, why was it not established until many millennia had passed?

We have already noted that the effects of the Incarnation are not limited by time (sec. 10.6.1.3). In a similar way, the Christian Church began at a certain place and time but is not strictly limited by those boundaries.

The *Catechism*, in fact, traces the origin of the Church to the beginning of human history:

> The gathering together of the People of God began at the moment when sin destroyed the communion of men with God, and that of men among themselves. The gathering together of the Church is, as it were, God's reaction to the chaos provoked by sin. This reunification is achieved secretly in the heart of all peoples: "In every nation anyone who fears him and does what is right is acceptable" to God. (*CCC* no. 761)

Congar writes, "Salvation was there, and hence, in ways and in a mode that theologians must strive to define, there was faith and charity, grace and the presence of Christ during the ten thousand centuries that preceded the eighteen centuries reaching from Abraham to Jesus."[7]

The history of the people of Israel, however, is the primary prerequisite for the establishment of Christ's Church. God's calling of the people of Israel is "a preparation and figure of that new and perfect covenant which was ratified in Christ" (*LG* no. 9). Of course, Israel continues as a living community after the coming of Christ, and the Catholic Church recognizes that a special relationship still exists between the Church and Israel (see sec. 12.28.3).

Did Jesus intend to begin a new religion different from Judaism? The question is probably anachronistic. We saw (chapter 11) that Jesus thought in eschatological terms: he believed that he was establishing the kingdom of God, eschatological Israel. He took concrete steps to establish a structured community, led by the Twelve, around himself. In the Catholic understanding, Jesus' eschatological community is the concrete beginning of the Church.

Of course there was development: Jesus and his first followers considered themselves to be Jews, and a clear distinction between Jews and Christians did not arise until after Jesus' time. Nor did Jesus clearly and directly establish all the beliefs and practices of the Christian Church. Nevertheless, in the Catholic view, all essential Christian beliefs and practices (the leadership structure, the sacramental system) developed naturally from Jesus and his first apostles.

The Church as the Body of Christ   12.6

One of the earliest Christian reflections on the Church is Paul's conception of the Church as the "Body of Christ." "Now you are Christ's body, and individually parts of it" (1 Cor. 12:27). Paul compares the individual parts of the human body (eye, hand) with the individual members of the Corinthian church: all the parts/members must work together so that the whole body can function properly.

Paul's conception of the Body of Christ is closely tied to two rituals that later came to be called "sacraments" (see sec. 9.18.1). A person joins the Body of Christ through the ritual of baptism: "For in one Spirit we were all baptized into one body" (1 Cor. 12:13); "For all of you who were baptized into Christ have clothed yourselves with Christ" (Gal. 3:27). The Body of Christ understood as the Church community is also tightly connected to the Body of Christ understood as the Lord's Supper (Eucharist): "Because the loaf of bread is one, we, though many, are one body, for we all partake of the one loaf" (1 Cor 10:17).

By joining the Body of Christ, the Church, a person unites with Christ in a mystical way: "Or are you unaware that we who were baptized into Christ Jesus were baptized into his death?" (Rom 6:3). As we saw (sec. 10.6.1.2), the idea that the believer is united with Christ in his death is one way to understand how Jesus' atoning death can bring about forgiveness for the sins of the individual person: "We know that our old self was crucified with him, so that our sinful body might be done away with, that we might no longer be in slavery to sin" (Rom 6:6).

Paul's thought thus draws out a specific reason why the Church is necessary for salvation: it is only through joining oneself to Christ's Body, the Church, that a person's sinful way of life can "die with Christ" and the person is freed to live a life not dominated by sin.

The Church as Sacrament   12.7

Aquinas defined a sacrament as the "sign of a holy thing so far as it makes men holy" (*ST* 3.60.2) and thus leads a person toward salvation (*ST* 3.60.4). The "signs" are physical, since it "is part of man's nature to acquire knowledge of the intelligible from the sensible" (*ST* 3.60.4): we learn things through our senses. A sacrament, however, is not simply an external symbol of a spiritual reality, it is rather "efficacious"—it brings about the reality of the thing signified. "Celebrated worthily in faith, the sacraments confer the grace that they signify. They are efficacious because in them Christ himself is at work" (*CCC* no. 1127). Thus in the sacrament of baptism, according to Catholic belief, the spiritual grace of Christ works through the physical means of water to cleanse sins. The water, then, is not a symbolic extra—it is essential, because God has chosen (to speak analogically) to work through the physical.

The sacraments (seven, in the Catholic Church), as Newman saw, are related to the Incarnation.[8] The *Logos* of God became incarnate in a human body so as to bring the opportunity of salvation to humanity. In the same way, God chooses to continue to communicate supernatural benefits ("grace") through the physical means of the sacraments. Both the Incarnation and the sacramental system are radical affirmations of the Christian belief in the goodness of God's creation (see Gen 1).

Logically prior to the seven sacraments, however, the Church itself is a sacrament. The Christian Church, as a visible, physical institution, continues to offer the spiritual grace of Christ long after Christ himself is no longer physically in the world.

In the Incarnation the divine *Logos* was revealed in the human man Jesus. If the divine teaching, authority, and power of the *Logos* can be communicated through the human nature of Jesus, it is consistent to suppose that his divine teaching, authority, and power could continue to be expressed through a human institution such as the Church.

De Lubac writes,

> If Christ is the sacrament of God, the Church is for us the sacrament of Christ; she represents him, in the full and ancient meaning of the term, she really makes him present. She not only carries on his work, but she is his very continuation, in a sense far more real than that in which it can be said that any human institution is its founder's continuation.[9]

The Church Is One   12.8

In the Nicene Creed, the Church is described as "one, holy, catholic, and apostolic." This "oneness," the unity of the Church, is emphasized in Scripture. When Paul tells his community in Corinth that they are members of the Body of Christ, he does not mean the Corinthian church alone. "As a body is one though it has many parts, and all the parts of the body, though many, are one body, so also Christ. For in one Spirit we were all baptized into one body, whether Jews or Greeks, slaves or free persons, and we were all given to drink of one Spirit" (1 Cor 12:12–13; see also Rom 12:5). The Letter to the Ephesians also speaks of "one body, one Spirit . . . one Lord, one faith, one baptism; one God and Father of all" (Eph 4:4–6). This unity of the followers of Christ was also stressed in Jesus' prayer in the Gospel of John before his death, "that they may all be one, as you, Father, are in me and I in you, that they also may be in us, that the world may believe that you sent me" (John 17:21). As the Vatican Council stated, "Christ the Lord founded one Church and one Church only" (*UR* no. 1).

The Visible, Hierarchical Church and the Mystical Body of Christ   12.9

How does the Catholic tradition understand this one Church? *Lumen Gentium* compares the Church to the incarnate *Logos*, since the Church is "one complex reality which comes together from a human and a divine element." The Church is hierarchical, visible, and earthly; at the same time, it is the "mystical body of Christ," "a spiritual community," and a "Church endowed with heavenly riches." The visible structure of the Church serves the "Spirit of Christ" who gives life to it in a way similar to how the assumed human nature of Jesus "serves the divine Word as a living organ of salvation." The visible, hierarchical structure of the Church and the mystical body are not to be thought of as two realities; rather they form together "one complex reality" (*LG* no. 8).

The Church is "mystical" or "spiritual" in a variety of ways. We see this aspect first in the belief that the Church existed in some way before Jesus established his eschatological community, above all in the community of Israel (see sec. 12.5). The continuing presence of Christ in the "Body of Christ" transcends strictly rational explanation. So too the precise way in which believers are united to Christ through the sacraments of baptism and the Eucharist is mysterious. There is a close relationship between the concepts of mystery and sacrament: in Latin, *sacramentum* means the sign of a hidden reality [a *mysterium*] of salvation. The Orthodox churches in fact call the sacraments "the holy mysteries." The way in which the Church is related to the rest of the world is described in terms of a sacramental mystery: "The Church is the sacrament of the unity of the human race" (*CCC* no. 775).

By "visible structure," *Lumen Gentium* means especially the hierarchical structure of the Catholic Church: the pope is the head, governing the Church in union with the bishops. At this point, then, we need to turn specifically to the Roman Catholic understanding of its role in the mystical Body of Christ.

The One, Holy, Catholic, and Apostolic Church and the Roman Catholic Church 12.10

Many passages in the Vatican II documents are complimentary toward and open to dialogue with other Christian and non-Christian faiths. But in the clear words of the Council's *Decree on Ecumenism*, "it is through Christ's Catholic Church alone, which is the universal help towards salvation, that the fullness of the means of salvation can be obtained" (*UR* no. 3).

Referring to the "one, holy, catholic, and apostolic" Church described in the Nicene Creed, the Vatican II Council taught,

> This Church, constituted and organized as a society in the present world, *subsists* in the Catholic Church, which is governed by the successor of Peter and by the bishops in communion with him. Nevertheless, many elements of sanctification and of truth are found outside its visible confines. (*LG* no. 8)

The visible structure of the one Church, then, is identified with the Roman Catholic Church. The Vatican's *Congregation for the Doctrine of the Faith (CDF)* comments that there is "an essential identity between the Church of Christ and the Catholic Church. . . . We encounter the Church of Jesus Christ as a concrete historical subject in the Catholic Church."[10] The *Congregation's* 2000 document, *Dominus Iesus*, taught that "the Church of Christ . . . continues to exist fully only in the Catholic Church" and that "there is an historical continuity—rooted in the apostolic succession—between the Church founded by Christ and the Catholic Church"(no. 16).

The claim may appear arrogant: one out of the hundreds of Christian denominations claiming to be the only one in which the Church of Christ exists fully. Why does the Catholic Church insist on this point?

To answer this question, we must refer once again to the doctrine of the Incarnation and its particularity. In Christian belief, the divine truly was reconciled with the human in the one man Jesus at a particular time and place in history. Jesus, in turn, established a specific, visible community headed by twelve apostles, passing on to them his teaching and sharing with them his authority (see sec. 10.9.1–2). The twelve apostles and their close associates, in their own turn, passed down this teaching and authority to their successors (see sec. 12.13).

In the Catholic understanding, only certain churches (that is, churches within the Catholic and the Orthodox traditions) can show in a specifically concrete and historical way that they are in continuity with this apostolic tradition. Only the Catholic Church, in its continuity with the role and authority of the apostle Peter and his successors as the visible head of the Church, is in full continuity with this apostolic tradition.

We will consider these Catholic claims in more detail below. For the present, however, it is enough to point out that this Catholic insistence on visible, historical continuity is consistent with the great Christian principles of the Incarnation and the sacramental nature of the Church. The common threads are the convictions that God works through the concrete, the spiritual flows through the physical, and the human can be reconciled with the divine.

The Visible and the Invisible Church 12.11

The Catholic insistence on the visible and historical nature of the one Church may become clearer if we briefly consider one alternative to it. Avery Dulles sums up the thought of the influential Protestant theologian Paul Tillich:

> Tillich made a sharp distinction between the "Spiritual Community," which he viewed as one and undivided, and the "churches," which he regarded as mutually disunited human organizations. He

refused even to use the term "Church" with a capital "c," for he looked upon the "Spiritual Community" not as an organized body but as a mystical reality latent in and behind the visible churches.[11]

In the Catholic view, however, conceptions such as Tillich's come dangerously close to a Gnostic separation of the spiritual from the earthly, bodily, and historical realm. As *Lumen Gentium* (no. 8) taught, one cannot separate the "spiritual community" from the concrete, physical structures of church hierarchy, just as the body and the soul cannot naturally be separated from each other.

In the Catholic understanding, this is also the only way to safeguard the "oneness" of the Church. If a central Christian belief is that the Church is "one" (sec. 12.8), then it is essential to have a clear, visible sign of that "oneness" in the visible structure of the Roman Catholic Church. Otherwise, how could we describe the "oneness" of the Church? Would it be a vague idea of the sum total of all churches that call themselves Christian? If so, in what sense are they "one," since their beliefs and practices are often quite different? How could such a vague concept of unity make a real, practical difference in the lives of the individual churches?

The concern to identify the visible structure and unity of the Church is not solely a Catholic one. The great Protestant theologian Karl Barth wrote, "If we seek to solve the question of the unity of the Church by appealing to an invisible church, we speculate as Platonists instead of listening to Christ."[12] Ola Tjørhom shows that the Reformers themselves were concerned to maintain visible structures of the Church, including visible sacraments and an ordained ministry.[13]

A Sociological Perspective on Institutional Structure   12.12

From a sociological perspective, all groups need some kind of organized structure and authority. A business organization, for example, needs to have its supervisors and executives. If a business has no hierarchical organization, it is unlikely to be efficient and productive, and won't last long.

The earliest groups of followers of Jesus were no exception. True, the descriptions of early church services (such as 1 Cor 14:26–33) sound quite spontaneous, as if the members were led by the Holy Spirit with no structured order. But notice that even here the apostle Paul is concerned for structure and order: "If anyone speak in a tongue, let it be two or at most three, and each in turn. . . . He is not the God of disorder but of peace. . . . But everything must be done properly and in order" (1 Cor. 14:27–40). This same letter also refers to a hierarchical structure of authority: "Some people God has designated in the church to be, first, apostles; second, prophets; third, teachers" (1 Cor. 12:28).

If the followers of Jesus had not organized themselves into structured communities with a clear leadership, Jesus' teaching would have been forgotten and lost within a few generations. The whole process of writing and canonizing the New Testament could only have been accomplished through organized communities (see sec. 8.15.2).

We now turn to a consideration of a particular group of the earliest Christian community leaders—the apostles, and the Catholic notion of apostolic succession.

Visible Structure of the Church and Apostolic Succession 12.13

We have already noted the concept of apostolic succession in our discussion of tradition (sec. 9.14.1). "Apostolic tradition" and "apostolic succession" are closely related, since the reliability of the tradition (what is taught) cannot be separated from the reliability of the teachers.[14]

Lumen Gentium teaches that Jesus appointed the Twelve, whom "he constituted in the form of a college or permanent assembly, at the head of which he placed Peter." The apostles were "preaching everywhere the Gospel" and would "gather together the universal Church" (*LG* no. 19).

Bishops are seen as the successors to the apostles, the "transmitters of the apostolic line" (*LG* no. 20). "In order that the full and living Gospel might always be preserved in the Church the apostles left bishops as their successors. They gave them their own position of teaching authority" (*DV* no. 7).

The "apostolic succession" also includes a spiritual authority expressed through sacraments; this authority is understood as a specific gift of the Holy Spirit. The apostles, having received the Holy Spirit from Jesus, passed on the gift of the Spirit to their "auxiliaries" (see 1 Tim 4:14; 2 Tim 1:6–7). This transmission of spiritual authority occurs within the sacramental ritual of ordination. In the Catholic understanding, this spiritual authority, the "gift of the Spirit" that the apostles received from Jesus, is passed down in the sacrament of Holy Orders, where a bishop ordains a priest or deacon with the laying on of hands (*CCC* no. 1576). Vatican Council II teaches that this gift of the Spirit "is transmitted down to our day through Episcopal consecration" (*LG* no. 21).

As an example of this spiritual authority that Jesus gave the apostles, consider the authority to forgive sins. According to the Gospel of John, the risen Jesus appeared to his disciples.

> [Jesus] said to them again, "Peace be with you. As the Father has sent me, so I send you." And when he had said this, he breathed on them and said to them, "Receive the holy Spirit. Whose sins you forgive are forgiven them, and whose sins you retain are retained." (John 20:21–23)

This authority is also seen in Jesus' words to Peter, "I will give you the keys to the kingdom of heaven. Whatever you bind on earth shall be bound in heaven; and whatever you loose on earth shall be loosed in heaven" (Matt. 16:19). Jesus gives a similar authority of binding and losing to all the disciples in Matthew 18:18.

This apostolic authority to forgive sins, in the Catholic understanding, is then passed down within the Church, "who through the bishops and his priests forgives sins in the name of Jesus Christ" (*CCC* no. 1448).

Early Church Witnesses to the Apostolic Tradition   12.14

Since apostolic succession is crucial in the Catholic understanding of the Church, let's consider the historical evidence for the process more carefully. Clement of Rome (writing c. 96) says that the apostles appointed bishops and deacons and instructed them to appoint successors (1 Cor 42–44). Ignatius of Antioch (martyred c. 107) speaks of the presbyters who take the place of the apostles (*Magnesians* 6.1; *Trallians* 2:1-3; 3.1). Both (especially Ignatius) stress the authority of the office of the bishop: "So too let everyone respect the deacons like Jesus Christ, and also the bishop, who is the image of the Father; and let them respect the presbyters like the council of God and the band of the apostles. Apart from these a gathering cannot be called a church" (*Trallians* 3:1).

Irenaeus (c. 130–c. 200), bishop of Lyon, claims that orthodox Christians of his time were able to trace the line of bishops in their churches back to the apostles. As an example, Irenaeus describes the apostolic succession at Rome: the church was founded by the apostles Peter and Paul, they appointed a certain Linus, who was succeeded by Anacletus. Irenaeus then names each bishop in succession down to his day (*Against Heresies* 3.3.1–3).

Irenaeus had a specific purpose for citing this unbroken chain of authority. Opposing the claims of Gnostic Christians that Jesus had passed down a secret tradition though disciples such as Thomas, Irenaeus insists that the tradition passed down by Jesus' followers is a public, open record that can be traced. Irenaeus himself says that he remembers, as a boy, seeing Polycarp, who had been appointed a bishop by apostles in Asia (*Against Heresies* 3.3.4).

Tertullian (c. 155–c. 222) follows the essentials of Irenaeus's argument: the apostle John appointed Polycarp at Smyrna, and Peter appointed Clement at Rome. Tertullian's description is somewhat more nuanced, however, arguing that the teaching must be transmitted from "apostles or apostolic men." Tertullian also knows of other churches that "although they derive not their founder from apostles or apostolic men (as being of much later date, for they are in fact being founded daily), yet, since they agree in the same faith, they are accounted as not less apostolic because they are akin in doctrine" (*Proscription against Heresies*, 32).

Historical Challenges to Apostolic Succession 12.15

Vatican II's general paradigm is that Jesus taught the twelve apostles, that the apostles handed on the tradition to bishops they had appointed, and that the bishops in turn handed down the tradition to their successors in an unbroken line of apostolic succession until modern times. Historical and critical studies show, however, that this paradigm is overly simplistic.

We should note first that although the Council tends toward identifying the apostles only with the Twelve (see *LG* no. 19), it admits that the apostles had "various helpers in their ministry" (for example, the "Hellenists" [Acts 6:2–6] and presbyters [Acts 15:2]) and that the apostles appointed people not only to the office of bishop but also to "various offices," the "chief place" held by the bishops (*LG* no. 20).

Despite these nuances, several historical criticisms of the Council's position still can be raised.[15]

1. By tending to identify the apostles with the Twelve, the Council is ambiguous about the role of other apostles, such as Paul and Barnabas.

2. Within the New Testament, there is little evidence that the Twelve were missionaries who appointed bishops in various locations. They are described more as the leaders within the Jerusalem church, although reference is made to the missionary activity of Peter.

3. In the New Testament, presbyters (*presbyteroi*) are not clearly distinct from bishops (*episkopoi*). Paul, for example, refers to the Ephesian presbyters as "bishops" (Acts 20:28).[16] In addition, the exact role of an *episkopos* in the New Testament is not at all clear: the model of a single bishop governing a church (a "monarchical bishop") seems to be a later development (first clearly witnessed in the letters of Ignatius of Antioch). *Episkopoi* is thus often better translated as "overseers" instead of "bishops" in such passages as Philippians 1:1.

4. The Acts of the Apostles portrays the apostles Paul and Barnabas as appointing presbyters in their churches (14:23), but Paul himself does not mention doing this in his letters. In the "Pastoral Epistles" (1 and 2 Timothy and Titus), Paul does have his associates Timothy and Titus appoint presbyters (e.g., Titus 1:5); many scholars, however, believe that these letters were written by Paul's followers and not Paul himself.[17]

Raymond Brown concludes his survey of the New Testament evidence thus: "The affirmation that all the bishops of the early Christian church could trace their appointments to the apostles is simply without proof — it is impossible to trace with assurance any of the presbyter-bishops to the Twelve and it is possible to trace only some of them to apostles like Paul." For Brown, however, the Catholic teaching that Christ established the order of bishops "can be defended in the nuanced sense that the episcopate gradually emerged in a Church that stemmed from Christ and that this emergence was (in the eyes of faith) guided by the Holy Spirit."[18]

A Nuanced View 12.16

The whole question of apostolic succession requires careful historical study. Though the model of the Twelve appointing an unbroken succession of bishops has little concrete evidence, a strong historical case can be made that the Jerusalem church (led by the Twelve, and later by James, brother of Jesus) was the central authority in formulating and passing down the traditions about Jesus (see sec. 10.9.3.2). Even if the office of a single bishop as head of individual churches did not develop until after New Testament times, there is no reason to doubt that the presbyters, teachers, and other leaders of orthodox churches consciously traced their authority back to the apostles and the apostolic teaching centered in the Jerusalem Church led by the Twelve.

As Tertullian noted, even churches not directly founded by an apostle could be considered apostolic, if they were "akin in doctrine" to the known apostolic churches (see sec. 12.14).

In his discussion of apostolic succession, Joseph Ratzinger focuses on the authority of certain churches connected with the apostles. He points out that in his debate with "heretics," Tertullian emphasizes the authority of churches connected with the apostle Paul: Corinth, Philippi, and Ephesus. Above all he stresses the authority of the church at Rome, since it is connected with two apostles, Peter and Paul, both of whom were martyred there (*Proscription against Heretics*, 32). Irenaeus also writes of the Roman church, "For it is a matter of necessity that every church should agree with this church, on account of its preeminent authority" (*Against Heresies* 3.3.2).

Thus a church could be considered apostolic if it was in union with one of the great apostolic churches, especially with Rome. The authority of the Roman church as a defender of the orthodox faith developed gradually (especially in the West) during the early centuries of Christianity; the Roman church often served to settle disputes between Western churches.[19] The Eastern churches recognized the Roman church as important, but tended to see it as only one of several centers of teaching authority; the "patriarchal sees" of Alexandria, Antioch, Constantinople, and Jerusalem also held special authority.

The importance of the apostolic succession is valued differently by different Christian churches today. Many churches no longer have an episcopal structure (a structure based on the office of the bishops) and tend to focus more on the Bible as the guarantee that the faith has been passed down accurately.

In 1982, the World Council of Churches, an alliance of 349 churches from around the world (including most Orthodox churches and many churches with roots in the Reformation), issued "Baptism, Eucharist, and Ministry," a statement that recognized "episcopal succession as a sign of the apostolicity of the life of the whole Church."[20] A dialogue between Anglican churches in Great Britain and Ireland with Lutheran churches in Scandinavia produced the *Porvoo Common Statement* (1992), a document focusing on ways of understanding apostolic continuity in the various churches today.[21]

The Indefectability and Infallibility of the Church 12.17

Irenaeus and Tertullian emphasize the apostolic succession in opposition to Gnostic claims. They exemplify the orthodox Christian concern to ensure the integrity and trustworthiness of the Christian faith by stressing the need for visible church leaders who could trace both their doctrine and their spiritual authority back to Jesus' apostles. Jesus had established the eschatological community of the Church, and it is therefore reasonable that the Church and its leaders would have received a share of Jesus' authority to ensure that the tradition was passed down without error and corruption.

Newman draws out this point well. Christianity claims to be a supernatural revelation of a particular doctrine. For Newman, the nature of any doctrine is to develop as its implications are drawn out, obscure points are clarified, new situations are addressed, outside challenges are answered, or the doctrine is compared with other systems of thought. Development is what naturally happens to living ideas (see sec. 9.18).[22]

If this is the case, however, it is to be expected that God would give an *external authority* along with the revelation, an authority that could judge which of the inevitable developments of thought and practice are legitimate, and which apparent developments are actually corruptions.[23] Newman's point is that if we take seriously the belief that the transcendent God has revealed a true teaching, a true way of life, then a logical extension of that belief is that God would also provide a completely reliable ("infallible") means of protecting that revelation from corruption and misinterpretation. If a revelation of divine truth can be corrupted and lost, what is the point of giving it in the first place? The Church, the eschatological community established by Jesus, then, must have some kind of divine authority to ensure that the revelation remains trustworthy. In Catholic theology, God has given the Church the gift of **infallibility**.

Non-Catholic Christians also accept the general concept of an absolutely trustworthy authority as a protection from false teaching. This concern to ensure the integrity of faith is expressed in the Lutheran tradition as the belief in the Church's "indefectibility": that is, a divine guarantee of "the continued existence of the Church in all its essential aspects, including its faith."[24] The idea that God protects the Church "from falling away from the truth of the gospel" has been widely held by Christians throughout the centuries, including the Reformers Luther, Calvin, Melancthon, and Zwingli.[25] In a modern Lutheran-Catholic theological dialogue, both parties agreed that "because of the promises given in the Scriptures and because of the continued assistance of the risen Christ through the Holy Spirit, the Church will remain to the end of time" and will persevere "in the truth of the gospel."[26]

Infallibility of the Bishops and the Pope   12.18

In the Catholic understanding, the worldwide group ("college") of Roman Catholic bishops, in union with the bishop of Rome (the pope), possesses the divine gift of infallibility. As the primary teachers and pastors of the Church, it is their responsibility to pass down the faith accurately. "In order to preserve the Church in the purity of the faith handed on by the apostles, Christ who is Truth willed to confer on her a share in his own infallibility" (*CCC* no. 889).

The gift of infallibility is expressed by the bishops when they agree, in union with the pope, that a certain teaching on faith and morals is to be held "definitively and absolutely" (*LG* no. 25). This authority is especially clear when the bishops teach in an ecumenical council, such as the great councils of Niceae, Constantinople, Ephesus, and Chalcedon (see sec. 10.1.5).[27] In the great Christological controversies the need for an absolute, decisive authority became apparent: Christians were divided and all parties believed that their position was supported by scriptural evidence. There would have been continuous conflict and confusion unless a single, authoritative, absolute voice had spoken.

The authority of the bishops, in the Catholic view, however, is not independent of the authority of the pope: "The college or body of bishops has for all that no authority unless united with the Roman Pontiff" (*LG* no. 22).

The pope thus has a unique authority: "The Roman Pontiff, head of the college of bishops, enjoys this infallibility in virtue of his office, when, as supreme pastor and teacher of all the faithful—who confirms his brethren in the faith—he proclaims by a definitive act a doctrine pertaining to faith or morals" (*LG* no. 25).

Papal Infallibility   12.19

Once again, we are confronted with a Catholic doctrine that, at first glance, seems completely unreasonable. How is it possible that a limited human being could be considered infallible, incapable of making a mistake? Isn't this claiming something for the pope that should only be reserved to God? Several points can be made, however, in favor of the reasonableness of this view.

First, papal infallibility is based on, and is only an expression of, the wider infallibility given to the Church. We have just seen that understanding the Church to have some kind of infallibility or indefectibility seems to be a necessary correlate of the belief that a divine revelation was made in Jesus.

Let's consider some specifics of the Catholic understanding of the pope's authority. The pope is considered to be the successor to Peter, who had a unique authority as the head of the apostles:

> [After Peter confesses Jesus as Messiah, Jesus tells Peter]: "And so I say to you, you are Peter, and upon this rock I will build my church, and the gates of the netherworld shall not prevail against it. I will give you the keys to the kingdom of heaven. Whatever you bind on earth shall be bound in heaven; and whatever you loose on earth shall be loosed in heaven." (Matt 16:18)[28]

> [Jesus says to Peter]: "but I have prayed that your own faith may not fail; and once you have turned back, you must strengthen your brothers." (Luke 22:32)

The pope has further authority as bishop of Rome, a church with ancient claims to apostolic authority, which was seen by authors such as Irenaeus (*Against Heresies* 3.3.2) as the model of orthodox belief.

The doctrine of papal infallibility does *not* claim that a pope is perfect and never makes mistakes. Nor does it imply that the pope is without sin. In Catholic theology, the pope is an ordinary, fallible human being who sins and stands in need of Christ's forgiveness along with all other people.

Every teaching of the pope (or the bishops), moreover, must be "in conformity with revelation itself"; a pope cannot proclaim "any new public revelation as pertaining to the divine doctrine of faith" (*LG* no. 25). The pope has no authority to announce a new teaching revealed to him personally: he only has the authority to define more clearly what has already been revealed.

The occasions under which a pope can make an officially recognized infallible statement, moreover, are tightly limited. Generally recognized conditions are the following:

1. The pope must be speaking in his office as "supreme pastor and teacher of all Christians," not as a private person.

2. He must appeal to his authority as successor of Peter, the head of the Church.

3. He must be defining or clarifying a doctrine of faith or morality.

4. He must intend that the doctrine be accepted by the whole Church.[29]

There is some disagreement among Catholics concerning how often this strictly defined papal authority has been used; the doctrine of papal infallibility itself was not officially defined until the First Vatican Council in 1870. The following are undisputed examples: (1) Pope Pius IX's definition (1854) of the Immaculate Conception of Mary (the teaching that Mary, in view of her unique role as Mother of God, was protected from original sin); (2) Pope Pius XII's definition (1950) of the Assumption of Mary (the belief that at the end of her life, Mary was taken body and soul into heaven). In both cases, the Church claimed to be defining officially a belief that had been held though Church tradition for centuries, although the belief is not found in Scripture.[30]

The Pope as Symbol of Christian Unity

12.20

In his 1995 encyclical *Ut Unum Sint (That They May Be One)*, Pope John Paul II reiterated the Catholic tradition's belief that the ministry of the pope is the "perpetual and visible principle and foundation of unity" (referring to *LG* no. 23) and that the pope is "the visible sign and guarantor of unity" (no. 88).

John Paul understood this papal role as a "ministry of unity"—a visible sign of the unity of the one Church (see sec. 12.8). This ministry was not one of power, but of service to other Christians: the visible head of the Church should be the "servant of the servants." He emphasized that he, like Peter, is humanly weak and frail, and therefore must depend completely on God's grace to fulfill this ministry (nos. 4, 91).

The Pope as Visible Representative of Christian Values

12.21

In the Catholic vision, the pope serves as an important symbol of, and spokesman for, Christian values in an increasingly secular world.

In economic and social affairs, for example, popes, especially since Leo XIII (1878-1903), have articulated a new vision of a society and economy based on the transcendent dignity and value of the human person. In developing this vision, the popes have vigorously opposed the collectivist and atheistic elements in socialism and communism, at the same time condemning the abuses of unbridled capitalism.[31]

Popes have also served as prophetic voices unafraid to criticize the values of mainstream societies. Pope John Paul II, for example, incisively analyzed the modern "culture of death" that views abortion and euthanasia as acceptable methods of dealing with social problems, and instead offered the Church's "Gospel of Life" as an alternative vision.[32] In this Christian

continued

continued

vision, the weakest and most defenseless members of society (the unborn, sick, and elderly) are treated with special concern and dignity, not as "social problems" that need to be eliminated.

While Pope Paul VI's encyclical *Humane Vitae* (1968) upholding the Catholic Church's condemnation of artificial birth control was widely criticized as regressive, many are now seeing the pope's warnings about the negative consequences of separating the unitive and procreative purposes of sexual intercourse as prophetic. Many see John Paul II's "Theology of the Body" as a life-giving way of helping modern societies recover a sense of the sacred nature of sexual relations and the lifelong commitment that those relations imply (see sec. 7.6.3).

In his 2008 address to the United Nations, Pope Benedict reminds the world community that moral relativism is a threat to basic human rights: if there are no universal standards of right and wrong, the pope declared, then there is no solid basis for defending human rights (see sec. 5.5.4).

The office of the papacy, then, has served a vital function as a visible, concrete representative of the Christian message to the world on a variety of issues. This is not to deny, of course, that papal teaching on social issues is often controversial, and other Christian and non-Christian leaders often disagree with the popes (especially on issues of human sexuality). ●

The pope notes that many recent ecumenical dialogues, including the Faith and Order Commission of the World Council of Churches, as well as Roman Catholic dialogues with Anglicans, Lutherans, and the Orthodox, have focused on the question of a "universal ministry" that would visibly demonstrate Christian unity (no. 89). In a Lutheran-Catholic dialogue on teaching authority and infallibility, the two churches agreed that "there may appropriately be a Ministry in the universal Church charged with primary responsibility for the unity of the people of God in their mission to the world."[33]

John Paul explicitly asked for help from non-Catholic Christians in finding a way for the pope to exercise his primacy (his unique authority as head of all Christians) over the Church, "which, while in no way renouncing what is essential to its mission, is nonetheless open to a new situation" (nos. 95–96). Several churches have responded to the pope's request.[34]

The Role of the People in the Church's Infallibility 12.22

In the Catholic view, the Church's gift of infallibility is normally expressed through the Magisterium, the teaching authority of the Church embodied in the pope in union with the bishops. At the same time, however, the "ordinary" faithful of the Church also play a role. The Council taught:

> The whole body of the faithful who have an anointing that comes from the holy one (cf. 1 John 2: 20 and 27) cannot err in matters of belief. This characteristic is shown in the supernatural appreciation of the faith (*sensus fidei*) of the whole people, when, "from the bishops to the last of the faithful," they manifest a universal consent in matters of faith and morals. (*LG* no. 12)

One of the primary characteristics of the Vatican II Council was its emphasis on understanding the Church not primarily in terms of its visible hierarchical structure but in terms of the whole community of the faithful. Some key images of the Church in *Lumen Gentium*, the Council's teaching on the Church, are the Church as "The People of God" and as a "Pilgrim Church."[35] The Council stressed that the laity (those who are not ordained or in religious orders) has its own particular "apostolate" or mission in proclaiming the Christian message to the world through their ordinary occupations and activities. Laypersons are also called, in their own way, to a life of holiness.[36]

What is the precise relationship between the official teaching authority and the ordinary faithful Catholic? The Council taught that when the bishops are teaching in communion with the pope, the faithful "are obliged to submit to their bishops' decision, made in the name of Christ, in matters of faith and morals. . . . This loyal submission of the will and intellect must be given, in a special way, to the authentic teaching authority of the Roman Pontiff" (*LG* no. 25).

In this age of widespread challenges to authority, these teachings sound outdated to many and are often ignored. Many in the Church have become "cafeteria Catholics": Catholics who feel free to choose which Church teachings they personally wish to follow. Are they wrong to do so? The issue of obedience to authority and individual freedom of conscience is complex, but we can make a few relevant points.

First, the Catholic Church does indeed teach that persons ultimately must follow their consciences. "A human being must always obey the certain judgment of his conscience" (*CCC* no. 1790). The entire Christian moral system is based on the belief that humans have true freedom and responsibility to make personal decisions on what is right and wrong.

But the Catholic tradition also insists that a person's conscience be an *informed conscience*. Although the Catholic tradition asserts that humans have an inherent sense of the natural law, this sense can easily be led astray. If a child, for example, is raised in an environment where moral values are not clearly defined, then that child will have a warped sense of right and wrong. Thus there is the need to inform one's conscience by studying the teachings of the Church, since the Church as the Body of Christ is the continued visible presence of Christ in the world (*CCC* nos. 1783–85). A Catholic, then, should have a fundamental "hermeneutic of trust" (see sec. 3.4.2.2) in the reliability of the divinely guided Church, and a healthy sense of his or her own individual limitations of understanding.

If a person, after seriously studying and attempting to live out a Catholic teaching, still feels in conscience that the teaching is wrong, then that person is obliged to follow his or her conscience. Depending on the frequency and seriousness of such disagreements, at some point the person would need to think seriously, for the sake of honesty and integrity, about leaving the Catholic Church.

The Sensus Fidelium 12.22.1

In teaching that Catholics should obey the teachings of the Magisterium, the Council did not imply that the faithful should be merely passive. As part of the People of God, they are given the *sensus fidei* (the "sense of faith"), a supernatural "feel" for the rightness of Church teaching.

Newman taught that what he called the *sensus fidelium* ("the sense of the faithful") was one important way in which the apostolic tradition is revealed.

> I think I am right in saying that the tradition of the Apostles . . . manifests itself variously at various times: sometimes by the mouth of the episcopacy, sometimes by the doctors, sometimes by the people, sometimes by liturgies, rites, ceremonies, and customs, by events, disputes, movements, and all those other phenomena which are comprised under the name of history.[37]

Newman's "sense of the people" is related to his "illative sense," the more personal, implicit, and not strictly logical way of knowing that forms the basis of many of our actions and decisions (see sec. 2.5.1.4).

The Tradition is thus preserved in many different ways, and the faith of the people as a whole is an important witness to the Tradition. Before declaring the belief in the Immaculate Conception of Mary an official teaching of the Church (1854), Pope Pius IX asked the bishops of the world to determine the beliefs of the common people. This *sensus fidelium* was an important factor in determining whether the belief should be officially defined.[38] In a similar way, Pope Pius XII wrote to the world's bishops to determine their sense, and the sense of their people, before defining the Assumption of Mary as an official Catholic belief.[39]

In the end, the bishops have the duty of discerning, judging, and teaching the faith, but Newman believed it was important for them to have a good sense of the actual beliefs of the people. In fact, Newman argues, at certain times the faithful sense of the people has been more reliable than the teachings of the bishops as a whole. This was the case during the Arian controversy: while most of bishops were following Arian teaching, the faithful preserved the correct understanding of the fully divine nature of Christ in their worship of him.[40]

The Role of the Faithful: "Reception" of Church Teaching 12.22.2

In Catholic thought, when a teaching is declared infallible by the pope, the assent of the Church is not necessary in order to make it a valid teaching, since the teaching is validated by the Holy Spirit (*LG* no. 25). At the same time, the Council also taught that "the assent of the Church can never be lacking to such definitions on account of the same Holy Spirit's influence" (*LG* no. 25). Contemporary American Catholic theologian Avery Dulles therefore concludes that one expects that an infallible teaching will correspond with the people's sense of faith "and will therefore evoke assent, at least eventually." He writes carefully,

> If in a given instance the assent of the Church were evidently not forthcoming, this could be interpreted as a signal that the pope has perhaps exceeded his competence and that some necessary condition for an infallible act had not been fulfilled.[41]

The role and significance of the faithful in "receiving" Church teaching is an ongoing topic of discussion in Catholic theology.

In closing our study of the concept of infallibility, we reiterate its foundation. If one accepts that God has revealed a truth about human salvation in Jesus Christ, then it follows logically that God would provide a means for that revelation to be passed down without corruption. In traditional Christian (not only Catholic) understanding, the Church was given divine authority to protect the revelation. In the Catholic view, the bishops and pope have the primary task of clarifying that teaching, but the role of the people in preserving the revelation is not simply passive.

The Catholic Church and Other Christian Churches 12.23

Vatican II teaches that members of non-Catholic Christian communities are certainly Christians and are saved through Christ. "All who have been justified by faith in baptism are incorporated into Christ; they therefore have a right to be called Christians, and with good reason are accepted as brothers by the children of the Catholic Church. . . . For the Spirit of Christ has not refrained from using them [non-Catholic Christian churches] as means of salvation" (*UR* no. 3).

Lumen Gentium taught that, "Many elements of sanctification and of truth are found outside its [the Catholic Church's] visible confines; these elements are gifts belonging to the Church of Christ" (*LG* no. 8). These elements include "the written Word of God; the life of grace; faith, hope, and charity, with the other interior gifts of the Holy Spirit, as well as visible elements" (*UR* no. 3).

In his reflections on ecumenism, John Paul II writes the Catholic Church is already in a "real but imperfect communion" with non-Catholic Christians. Thinking of those Catholic and non-Catholic Christians who have been willing to give their lives as martyrs, however, the pope goes further, "I now add that this communion is already perfect in what we all consider the highest point of the life of grace, *martyria* unto death, the truest communion possible with Christ who shed his Blood, and by that sacrifice brings near those who once were far off" (cf. Eph 2:13).[42] This common "witness" (the basic meaning of the Greek word *martyria*) of those who have been willing to die for their faith is a foreshadowing of the end of time when the Church will achieve its full measure of unity.

Dietrich Bonhoeffer: Martyr for the Faith 12.24

In referring to those who were willing to shed their blood for their faith in Christ, John Paul may well have had in mind people such as Dietrich Bonhoeffer (1906–1945), a German Lutheran pastor and theologian. Bonhoeffer was involved in the ecumenical movement, studied at Union Seminary in New York, and pastored German churches in London.

From the beginning he opposed the Nazi regime. Lecturing in the United States shortly before World War II, Bonhoeffer had the opportunity to stay in America, but chose to return to Germany to share the fate of his people. At first believing that the Nazis could be resisted nonviolently, he eventually became convinced that the Nazi evil could only be stopped by force and became involved in a failed attempt to assassinate Hitler.

He was arrested and spent two years in prison, where he ministered as well as he could to the emotional and spiritual needs of his fellow prisoners. On the day of his execution, he was seen praying fervently. His last recorded words were, "This is the end – for me, the beginning of life." He was hanged by the Nazis on April 9, 1945.

At Westminster Abbey in London, Bonhoeffer is honored, along with nine other witnesses to the faith (including the Baptist Martin Luther King, the Catholic Archbishop Oscar Romero, the Orthodox Grand Duchess Elizabeth of Russia, and the Anglican Lucian Tapiedi) as a twentieth-century martyr. This monument to the martyrs is a visible symbol of John Paul's vision of the perfect unity among Christian denominations already achieved by those who shed their blood for their faith. ●

The Catholic Church and Orthodox and Protestant Christians 12.25

The Council made some clear distinctions in discussing Catholic relationships with other Christians. Because of their ancient roots in the apostolic traditions of the earliest centuries, the Orthodox churches have an especially close relationship with the Catholic Church. "These Churches, although separated from us, yet possess true sacraments, above all — by apostolic succession — the priesthood and the Eucharist, whereby they are still joined to us in closest intimacy" (*UR* no. 15).

Catholics consider the Orthodox to be "sister Churches."[43] A key issue that continues to separate Catholics and Orthodox, however, is that the Orthodox do not accept the primacy of the pope as the visible head of all Christians. Because the Orthodox lack this communion with the pope, the Vatican teaches that "these venerable Christian communities lack something in their condition as particular churches."[44]

The Catholic tradition fully recognizes the members of non-Orthodox churches (including Anglican, Protestant, and evangelical communities) as Christians who are in "some, though imperfect communion with the Catholic Church" (*UR* no. 3). Speaking of all non-Catholic Christians, *Lumen Gentium* holds that "these Christians are in some real way joined with us in the Holy Spirit for, by his gifts and graces, his sanctifying power is also active in them and that has strengthened some of them even to the shedding of their blood" (*LG* no. 15). These communities are especially linked to Catholics through the sacrament of baptism, "whenever it is properly conferred in the way the Lord determined and received with the proper dispositions of soul." In baptism, "man becomes truly incorporated into the crucified and glorified Christ" (*UR* no. 22).

The Council did not explicitly state that non-Catholic Christians are members of the one Church. But by stating that non-Catholic Christians are incorporated into the Body of Christ (*UR* no. 3), the Council clearly implied that all baptized Christians are members of the one Church.[45]

A key difference between the Catholic Church and the churches originating at the time of the Reformation, however, involves the understanding of sacraments: "We believe they have not preserved the proper reality of the Eucharistic mystery in its fullness, especially because of the absence of the sacrament of Orders" (*UR* no. 22). The Vatican's Congregation for the Doctrine of the Faith explains specifically that these Protestant communities "do not enjoy apostolic succession in the sacrament of Orders," and thus "have not preserved the genuine and integral substance of the Eucharistic Mystery."[46] Because they "have not preserved the apostolic succession or the valid celebration of the Eucharist," they are "not Churches in the proper sense of the word," but rather "ecclesial Communities."[47]

The insistence that Protestant communities should not be called "Churches" but rather "ecclesial communities" has, naturally enough, offended many, especially those in Protestant and evangelical communities with historical ties to the Reformation. The main

Catholic concern is sacramental — in order to preserve the full mystery of Christ's Real Presence in the Eucharist, Catholic teaching insists that the ministers of the sacrament must belong to the visible apostolic succession. While Catholic pronouncements legitimately insist on not glossing over significant differences between Anglican, Protestant, evangelical, and Roman Catholic understandings of Church and sacrament, we must ask whether it is really necessary to deny the title "Church" to such communities. If the Catholic tradition recognizes these communities as Christian bodies that preach the word of God, legitimately baptize their members, and offer them salvation, it seems inconsistent to deny these communities the title of "Church."

These issues involving differing understandings of apostolic succession, ordination, and sacraments (especially the Eucharist) raise some crucial topics for further ecumenical discussion. One aspect of the discussion might focus on the understanding of apostolic succession, especially in light of historical criticisms of the concept of the bishops as direct successors to the apostles (see 12.15–16).

One helpful step in the dialogue, it seems to me, would be for the Catholic Church to state clearly that baptized non-Catholics are members of the one Church. Further clarification is also needed on the concept that the one Church "subsists" in the Catholic Church. In some of its expressions, the 2007 CDF document identifies the two, speaking of "an essential identity between the Church of Christ and the Catholic Church." But if a non-Catholic Christian is a member of the Church of Christ through baptism (*UR* no. 22), it seems clear that the Church of Christ must be broader than the visible Catholic Church. Thus expressions such as "the 'fullness' of the Church of Christ is in the Catholic Church" seem to capture the Catholic belief more accurately.

The Pilgrim Church   12.26

A key image in the Council's teaching is that of the "Pilgrim Church" (*LG* chapter 7). The image envisions a community made up of fallible humans, but aided with the gift of infallible divine assistance, on its way toward the ultimate goal of history. In the words of the Council, the Church currently is "at once holy and always in need of purification, follows constantly the path of penance and renewal" (*LG* no. 9). The Church will remain incomplete until it is perfected, along with all of nature, at the end of time, in the fully realized kingdom of God (*LG* no. 48).

Pope John Paul II speaks explicitly of the sinfulness of the members of the Catholic Church:

> The experiences of these years have made the Church even more profoundly aware of her identity and her mission in history. The Catholic Church acknowledges and confesses *the weaknesses of her members*, conscious that their sins are so many betrayals of and obstacles to the accomplishment of the Saviour's plan. (*Ut Unum Sint* no. 3, emphasis original)

In recent years, no one can be unaware of the sinfulness and failings of the Catholic Church as evidenced in the widespread scandals of priests sexually abusing children and some bishops covering up this abuse. In his remarks to American bishops, Pope Benedict minced no words, calling the scandal an "evil" and a "sin," and admitting that the scandal was "sometimes very badly handled" by Church authorities. The pope expressed the hope, however, that in the long run this shameful experience might purify the Church. He quoted the words of John Paul II, "We must be confident that this time of trial will bring a purification of the entire Catholic community," leading to "a holier priesthood, a holier episcopate and a holier Church."[48]

When the Nicene Creed speaks of the one Church as "holy," this clearly does not mean that all its members are perfectly holy. As Ratzinger says, "the word 'holy' does not apply in the first place to the holiness of human persons but refers to the divine gift that bestows holiness in the midst of human unholiness."[49] In the Catholic view, the fact that God entrusted the divine mission of the Church to fallible humans is a sign of God's great confidence in human goodness and the great human potential to attain salvation.

Catholic Commitment to the Ecumenical Movement 12.27

In his encyclical *Ut Unum Sint*, Pope John Paul II declared that at "the Second Vatican Council, the Catholic Church committed herself *irrevocably* to following the path of the ecumenical venture" (no. 3, emphasis original).

The ecumenical dialogue has already produced some concrete results.

At the end of the Vatican II Council, Pope Paul VI and the Orthodox Patriarch of Constantinople Athenagoras declared that both the Catholic and Orthodox Church "regret and wish to erase from the memory and midst of the Church" the mutual excommunications that marked the split between Eastern and Western Christianity in 1054.[50]

In 1999, the Lutheran World Federation and the Catholic Church issued a *Joint Declaration on the Doctrine of Justification* (see sec. 7.17.4). This remarkable document achieves a theological consensus on an issue that once divided the churches.

Pope John Paul II (*Ut Unum Sint* no. 79) outlines some key areas for continued ecumenical dialogue:

1. The relationship between sacred Scripture and sacred Tradition

2. The sacramental understanding of the Eucharist

3. Ordination as a sacrament

4. The role of the Magisterium of the Church as an authority for "teaching and safeguarding the faith"

5. The theological understanding of the Virgin Mary

The goal of ecumenical dialogue, from the Catholic perspective, is not merely better relationships or better understanding between Christian churches (although these certainly may be considered as legitimate intermediate goals). As John Paul II wrote, the Catholic Church asks "the Lord to increase the unity of all Christians until they reach full communion."[51] This also mirrors the goal of the World Council of Churches, whose members believe that "they are called to the goal of visible unity in one faith and one eucharistic fellowship."[52] Full unity, then, would be expressed through a full sharing of beliefs and of sacraments in worship.

For John Paul II, Christian unity is to be a reflection of the unity of the Trinity: "Christian unity . . . has its divine source in the Trinitarian unity of the Father, the Son and the Holy Spirit. . . . The faithful are *one* because, in the Spirit, they are in *communion* with the Son and, in him, share in his *communion* with the Father."[53]

Christianity and Non-Christian Religions 12.28

Having considered the relations between Catholics and other Christians, we now turn to the Catholic understanding of the relationship between the Church and non-Christian religions—a central issue in today's pluralistic world. We will consider in turn: (1) Karl Rahner's influential theory that members of other religions are "anonymous Christians," (2) Vatican II teaching on the topic, and (3) some recent considerations of Joseph Ratzinger, the current Pope Benedict.

Rahner's Theory of Anonymous Christians 12.28.1

Rahner argues that God's grace must work through non-Christian religions, based on the following points.[54]

1. The logical conclusion of Christian belief is that Christianity is the one true religion. If one believes that humans cannot free themselves from sin, and therefore are only saved through the union of the human and divine in Jesus, then it follows that Christianity is the one path to salvation.

2. Millions of people, however, have lived either before the Incarnation of Christ or have never heard the Christian message.

3. It is impossible that God would simply allow these millions of non-Christians no chance at salvation, since God created them out of a free act of love and because "God our savior . . . wills everyone to be saved" (1 Tim 2:3–4). Therefore God must have presented to them, in some way, the offer of supernatural grace through Christ.

4. This kind of supernatural offer, however, cannot have been made solely to each isolated individual, since religion and salvation are essentially social (see sec. 12.2). Therefore the offer of God's supernatural grace must have been made through every non-Christian's cultural and religious traditions.

5. The number of non-Christians who accept God's supernatural offer of salvation cannot be slight. Each person is of course free to accept or reject the offer, but it seems to contradict God's loving plan of creation and redemption to think that only a tiny percentage of the billions of non-Christians would actually be saved.

6. Since salvation can come only through Christ, and God makes offers of salvation through non-Christian religions, those who accept the offer can justifiably be called "anonymous Christians." They are saved through accepting God's supernatural offer of grace through Christ, even though they are not explicitly aware of Christ.

In support of his theory, Rahner refers to the account of Paul's preaching in Athens. Speaking to the polytheistic Athenians, Paul declares:

> You Athenians, I see that in every respect you are very religious. For as I walked around looking carefully at your shrines, I even discovered an altar inscribed, "To an Unknown God." What therefore you *unknowingly worship*, I proclaim to you. (Acts 17:22–23, emphasis added)

The belief that non-Christians can attain salvation, Rahner insists, does not imply that Christians should give up all missionary efforts. All other things being equal, a person's chances at salvation are better if that person has a clear and explicit understanding of the Christian offer of grace, rather than an "anonymous" understanding, and so evangelization is and remains a Christian priority.

Rahner's thesis of the "anonymous Christian" has been criticized from many directions. Some see it as arrogant and condescending: How would Christians like to be called "anonymous Buddhists"? Others conclude that, despite Rahner's protestations, accepting the theory would have the practical effect of stifling Christian missionary activity. Why convert to Christianity if one is already an "anonymous Christian"?

Vatican II on Salvation and Non-Christian Religions   12.28.2

Nevertheless, many of Rahner's points remain valid. If God truly chose to save humanity through the Incarnation and atonement of Jesus Christ, then every person's salvation must in some way be connected with Jesus. Further, it is indeed inconceivable to one who believes that God is love to conclude that God would allow millions of non-Christians no reasonable opportunity for salvation. The conclusion seems inescapable that many people who have never heard of Jesus explicitly may still be saved through Jesus in some "anonymous" way.

This "anonymous" connection with Jesus, then, would most plausibly be through a connection with the Christian Church, since the Church is Christ's continuing presence in the world, and people are saved through joining themselves to Christ's Body (see sec. 10.6.1.2). Such a notion, moreover, is consistent with the understanding of the Church as a sacrament that works for the salvation of the whole world (*LG* no. 48).

Chapter 16 of *Lumen Gentium* closely connects salvation and a person's relationship to the Church. The Council teaches that "those who have not yet received the Gospel are related to the People of God in various ways." This relationship has taken on various historical forms: Christians have an especially close relationship with Jews and Muslims. The Church is also related to

> Those who, through no fault of their own, do not know the Gospel of Christ or his Church, but who nevertheless seek God with a sincere heart, and, moved by grace, try in their actions to do his will as they know it through the dictates of their conscience — *those too may achieve eternal salvation*" (*LG* no. 16, emphasis added).

John Paul II also echoes the teaching of the Council. For those who are not Christian, John Paul says,

> Salvation in Christ is accessible by virtue of a grace which, while having a mysterious relationship to the Church, does not make them formally part of the Church, but enlightens them in a way which is accommodated to their spiritual and material situation. This grace comes from Christ; it is the result of his Sacrifice and is communicated by the Holy Spirit.[55]

But exactly how is the non-Christian in relationship to the Church? The Council was content to say that God does this "in ways known to himself."[56] The CDF's *Dominus Iesus* taught that theologians are free to explore specific ways in which this relationship could be conceived, while insisting that it was against Catholic teaching to say that the Church was only "*one* way [among many] of salvation" (no. 21, emphasis original).

The Council, then, clearly agrees with Rahner that salvation is possible for members of non-Christian religions. *Lumen Gentium*'s discussion of the point ends, however, by citing Paul's criticism of those who knew God through the creation, but "became vain in their reasoning" and "exchanged the truth of God for a lie" (Rom 1:18–25). The Church therefore "takes zealous care to foster the missions" (*LG* no. 16).

Vatican II's *Declaration on Non-Christian Religions* 12.28.3

Vatican II also devotes a specific document to this question. The *Declaration on the Relation of the Church to Non-Christian Religions (Nostra Aetate)* presents a quite positive view of non-Christian religions and encourages interreligious dialogue. Special attention is given to the Church's relationship with Muslims and, above all, with the Jewish people. "It is true that the Church is the new people of God, yet the Jews should not be spoken of as rejected or accursed. . . . God does not take back the gifts he bestowed or the choice he made" (*NA* no. 4).

In a central paragraph, the Council again balances a respect for non-Christian religions with a sense of the Church's unique role and the centrality of Christ. The language parallels the image used in describing the relationship of the Catholic Church with other Christians: the Church contains the "fullness" of religious life; other religions contain elements of truth.

> The Catholic Church rejects nothing of what is true and holy in these religions. She has a high regard for the manner of life and conduct, the precepts and doctrines which, although differing in many ways from her own teaching, nevertheless often reflect a ray of that truth which enlightens all men. Yet she proclaims and is duty bound to proclaim without fail, Christ who is the way, the truth and the life (John 14:6). In him, in whom God reconciled all things to himself (2 Cor 5:18–19), men find the fullness of their religious life. (*NA* no. 2)

Ratzinger and World Religions 12.28.4

Ratzinger disagrees with Rahner's "anonymous Christian" solution. He argues that Rahner's theory was based on two misleading presuppositions: (1) from the start it frames the questions from the Christian point of view, asking if non-Christian religions can lead to salvation, and (2) it lumps all non-Christian religions together.[57] Ratzinger offers a contrasting approach: (1) starting from a more neutral perspective, seeking first to analyze the various forms of world religions and looking for common patterns, thus allowing (2) the development of a more sophisticated appreciation of the similarities and differences between religions.

Ratzinger also describes a "pluralist" position associated with theologians John Hick and Paul Knitter. This position rejects the idea that salvation can be based on Christ and the Church alone, whether explicitly or "anonymously." In this view all religions can be paths to salvation; Christ is an important figure, but by no means the only savior.[58]

A view related to the pluralist position is that of the Indian writer Radhakrishnan, who taught that one cannot differentiate between religions: they are all equal attempts to understand a spiritual reality that is, in the end, beyond description.[59] This view is in turn related to a widespread modern assumption that all religions are equal paths to God, and that it is intolerant and narrow-minded to claim that one religion is "better" or "truer" than another.

Ratzinger believes that this modern assumption, however, is often tied to a further, unstated assumption: religious beliefs are merely subjective opinions, and thus it is meaningless to ask whether any one of them is closer to the truth than the others. Religious faith, since it is in the realm of feeling and emotion, cannot be measured by objective, scientific standards. Therefore the question of truth does not arise. If one religion claims to be "truer" than another, this is only a sign of its unreasonable intolerance of other opinions.

We are familiar with these assumptions from our discussion in chapter 2. There we considered in detail reasons for concluding that religious faith is not based on opinion alone, but rather is compatible with reasonable analysis. Ratzinger too rejects the idea that faith is completely subjective, and thus begins his reflections with a reasoned analysis of the variety of religious traditions. Naturally no person can conduct a completely objective study of all religions, but an attempt can be made to understand the "horizons" of other religions on their own terms and to look for overall patterns (see secs. 1.11; 3.5.1).

An Analysis of World Religions 12.28.5

At the beginning of all religions, Ratzinger finds what he calls "primitive experience," the encounter with the numinous (sec. 1.3). This experience then gives rise to myths — stories of the gods and goddesses, often envisioned as personified forces of nature. Ratzinger believes that humans have developed three basic ways of moving beyond this common mythical stage.

1. **Mysticism.** Religions such as Hinduism and Buddhism understand myths as symbols for the religious experience of the transcendent. These religions regard this inexpressible transcendent experience as the highest religious value.

2. **Monotheism.** Judaism, Christianity, and Islam reject the myths of the gods and goddesses as false. Their highest religious value is revelation, the call of the transcendent God received by a prophet.

3. **Enlightenment.** In this tradition myth is rejected as precritical thinking and rational thought is set up as the highest value, moving

its followers beyond all traditional religions. This tradition prevailed in the Enlightenment and remains strongly influential today.

Ratzinger thus sees two religious options available in the modern world: mysticism or monotheism. Yet many moderns see the monotheistic religions as intolerant when they make the absolute claim that their revelation from God is the highest truth, in contrast to a thinker such as Radhakrishna (within the tradition of mysticism), who seems much more tolerant.

But Ratzinger argues that Radhakrishna's claim that mystical spiritual experience is the highest value in religion is just as absolute as the monotheistic claims regarding their revealed truths. How does Radhakrishna *know* that a mystical experience of the transcendent is more important, or healthier, or more helpful for the progress of humanity, than one of the monotheistic revelations?

Ratzinger further analyzes the differences between the two main religious options. The following table combines Ratzinger's comments with a few of my own.

Mystical religions	Monotheistic religions
Salvation is defined as merging the individual "self" with the Absolute; "the Divinity and the depths of the soul are identical"[60]	Salvation is defined as becoming one's true self within a community of other true selves, all within the community of the Trinity
The Absolute does not act—the relationship between humans and the Absolute can only involve the human moving toward union with God (for example, through the practice of meditation)	God calls humans through revelation; humans can only respond to the divine call
Tends to see time as an endless cycle of death and rebirth	Tends to see history moving toward a final eschatological goal
Believes in reincarnation	Believes in one life and final judgment

Such differences are not minor, and they have practical consequences.

In Hinduism, for example, it is not clear that there is a solid basis for the dignity of the individual person, since a person's ultimate destiny is to be reincarnated for endless ages, ultimately to be absorbed into the Absolute. Ratzinger quotes H. Burkle's claim that modern Hindu reform movements based on individual rights and dignity could arise only when the Hindu reformers borrowed the Christian concept of person.[61]

Ratzinger also notes, "In the mysticism of identity there is in the end no distinction between good and evil."[62] C. S. Lewis saw this point as well.[63] But if there is no true good and evil, then any action can be justified. Ratzinger argues that when such a view of the Absolute is made part of a political system, it can have tragic results. For example, Marxist philosophy also denies any real distinction between good and evil, and thus has allowed Marxist regimes to justify killing thousands of people "as a necessary part of the world's dialectical process."[64]

In the modern worldview where tolerance is the highest value, all religions are assigned equal value. Ratzinger's response to such a position is blunt:

> But that is by no means the case. There are in fact sick and degenerate forms of religion, which do not edify people but alienate them. . . . And even religions whose moral value we must recognize, and which are on their way toward the truth, may become diseased here and there. . . . In Hinduism . . . there are some marvelous elements — but there are also negative aspects: involvement with the caste system; suttee [self-immolation] for widows. . . . Even Islam, with all the greatness it represents, is always in danger of losing balance, of letting violence have a place and letting religion slide away into mere outward observance and ritualism. And there are of course, as we all know but too well, diseased forms of Christianity — such as when the crusaders, on capturing the holy city of Jerusalem, where Christ died for all men, for their part indulged in a bloodbath of Moslems and Jews.[65]

Brief comments of course cannot do justice to the complex reality of religions like Hinduism, as Ratzinger himself acknowledges.[66] Yet his reflections are enough to suggest that it is quite misleading and naïve to claim that all religions are fundamentally the same. There are in fact profound differences between them, and these differences in turn have profound effects on how people live their daily lives.

Finally, Ratzinger reminds us that the question of the world religions raises the question of truth. If we have a relativist worldview, then of course the question of which religion is true does not arise — since there is no such thing as truth. But true dialogue between the religions is impossible on the basis of a relativistic concept of truth. How could the dialogue partners make an honest analysis of healthy and diseased elements in their own religious traditions if they have no objective standards of what is healthy?

World Religions and Salvation   12.28.6

As noted, Ratzinger downplays the question of salvation in his analysis of the world religions. He is of course aware of the tension between (1) Catholic teaching that all salvation is through Christ and his Church alone, and (2) Catholic teaching that those who have never heard of Christ still have the opportunity for salvation (see sec. 12.28.2).

But in contrast with Rahner's assumption that salvation must also come through non-Christian religions, Ratzinger simply asks, "How do we know that the theme of salvation should only be tied to religions? . . . Do we necessarily have to invent a theory about how God can save people without abandoning the uniqueness of Christ?"[67] Ratzinger is content to leave the question of salvation to God, since God alone is judge of the world.[68] For Ratzinger, Christian theologians have the more humble task of patiently seeking the truth by means of their own tradition, while remaining open to dialogue with other worldviews.

Questions about the Text

1. In the Christian understanding, what is the distinction between "churches" and the one "Church"?

2. What does it mean to say that "salvation is social"? What are some biblical examples that illustrate this belief?

3. In the Judeo-Christian tradition, what is the relationship between the "chosen people" (Israel, the Church) and the rest of humanity?

4. What is the relationship between Jesus' eschatological community and the Christian Church?

5. In what sense can the Church be called "sacramental"?

6. What is the biblical evidence that the Church should be "one"?

7. What does it mean to say that the Church is a "Mystical Body"?

8. Why does the Catholic Church insist that the Mystical Body must also have a "visible structure"? In the Catholic view, what is this visible structure?

9. What is "apostolic succession"? In the Catholic view, why is it necessary? What are some historical questions raised by this belief?

10. What does it mean to say that the Church has the divine gifts of "indefectabililty" or "infallibility"? Why would such gifts be considered necessary?

11. What is the Catholic understanding of the roles of the pope, the bishops, and the people in relation to the infallibility of the Church?

12. What does it mean to say that the one Church "subsists" in the Catholic Church?

13. How does the Catholic Church describe its relationship with the Orthodox churches and the churches of the Reformation?

14. What is Rahner's theory of the "anonymous Christian," and what are some criticisms of it?

15. How would you summarize Vatican II's teaching on the relationship between the Church and non-Christian religions?

16. In what ways does Ratzinger's approach to world religions differ from Rahner's?

17. What distinctions does Ratzinger make between religions based on mysticism and monotheistic religions? What are some practical implications of their different beliefs?

18. How does Ratzinger describe the task of the Christian theologian in addressing non-Christian religions?

Discussion Questions

1. Do you think a person needs to belong to an organized church in order to have a relationship with God?

2. What is your personal experience of the relationship between Catholics and non-Catholic Christians, and between Christians and non-Christians?

3. Do you believe that the ecumenical goal of one Christian Church, sharing beliefs and sacraments, is realistic?

Endnotes

1. Pope Benedict XVI, *Saved in Hope: Encyclical Letter (Spe Salvi)* (San Francisco: Ignatius Press, 2007), no. 14.
2. Quotation from Maximus the Confessor (c. 580–662) in Henri de Lubac, *Catholicism: Christ and the Common Destiny of Man* (San Francisco: Ignatius, 1988), 33.
3. De Lubac, *Catholicism*, 35.
4. On the social understanding of eternal salvation, see de Lubac, *Catholicism*, 51–63.
5. SCG 4.50; quoted in de Lubac, *Catholicism*, 60.
6. Yves Congar, "The People of God," in *Vatican II: An Interfaith Appraisal*, ed. J. H. Miller (Notre Dame: University of Notre Dame Press, 1966), 200.
7. Ibid., 201.
8. John Henry Newman, *An Essay on the Development of Christian Doctrine* (Westminster, MD: Christian Classics, 1968), 93–94.
9. De Lubac, *Catholicism*, 29.
10. CDF, *Commentary on the Document "Responses to Some Questions Regarding Certain Aspects of the Doctrine of the Church."* Accessed October 10, 2008, at http://www.vatican.va/roman_curia/congregations/cfaith/documents/rc_con_cfaith_doc_20070629_commento-responsa_en.html.
11. Avery Dulles, *Models of the Church*, expanded ed. (Garden City, NY: Image Books, 1987), 144–45.
12. Quoted in de Lubac, *Catholicism*, 25.
13. Ola Tjørhom, *Visible Church, Visible Unity: Ecumenical Ecclesiology and the "Great Tradition of the Church,"* Unitas Books (Collegeville, MN: Liturgical Press, 2004), 3–4, 11.
14. On this connection, see Joseph Ratzinger, *God's Word: Scripture, Tradition, Office* (San Francisco: Ignatius Press, 2008), 28.
15. On this question, see also Raymond E. Brown, *Priest and Bishop: Biblical Reflections* (New York: Paulist, 1970), 47–86.
16. Ibid., 65.
17. See Catherine Cory, "Introduction to 1 Timothy," in *Saint Mary's Press College Study Bible.* (Winona, MN: Saint Mary's Press, 2007), 1832.
18. Brown, *Priest and Bishop*, 73.
19. See Robert B. Eno, "Some Elements in the Pre-History of Papal Infallibility," in *Teaching Authority and Infallibility in the Church*, eds. P. C. Empie et. al., Lutherans and Catholics in Dialogue 6 (Minneapolis: Augsburg Publishing House, 1980), 238–58.
20. See "Apostolic Succession," in *Oxford Dictionary of the Christian Church*, eds. F. L. Cross and E. A. Livingstone, 3rd ed. (Oxford: Oxford University Press, 2005), 92.
21. Tjørhom, *Visible Church, Visible Unity*.
22. Newman, *Development of Christian Doctrine*, 55–75.
23. Ibid., 75–92.
24. "Teaching Authority and Infallibility in the Church: Common Statement," in Empie, *Authority and Infallibility*, 25.
25. Avery Dulles, "Infallibility: The Terminology," in Empie, *Authority and Infallibility*, 75–76.
26. "Common Statement," in Empie, *Authority and Infallibility*, 31.
27. The authority of seven ecumenical Councils is accepted by both Eastern and Western churches: Nicaea I (325), Constantinople I (381), Ephesus (431), Chalcedon (451), Constantinople II (553), Constantinople III (680–681), and Nicaea II (787). The Roman Catholic Church recognizes the ecumenical authority of fourteen further Councils, up to and including Vatican Council II.

28. There are critical questions about this passage, but Ben Meyer has made a strong case for its historicity (see sec. 11.5.7).

29. See Avery Dulles, "Moderate Infallibilism," in Empie, *Authority and Infallibility*, 85–87.

30. See "Teaching Authority and Infallibility in the Church: Roman Catholic Reflections," in Empie, *Infallibility in the Church*, 52.

31. See the summary of papal teaching in the Pontifical Council for Justice and Peace's *Compendium of the Social Doctrine of the Church* (Vatican: Libreria Editrice Vaticana, 2004).

32. See, for example, John Paul's encyclical, *The Gospel of Life: On the Value and Inviolability of Human Life (Evangelium Vitae)* (Vatican City: Libreria Editrice Vaticana; Washington, DC: USCC, 1995).

33. See "Common Statement," in Empie, *Infallibility in the Church*, 31.

34. For example: *"Ut Unum Sint*: a response from Faith and Order," *The Ecumenical Review* (April 1998). Accessed October 8, 2008, at *http://findarticles.com/p/articles/mi_m2065/is_n2_v50/ai_20881099*, and Walter Kaspar, ed., *The Petrine Ministry: Orthodox and Catholics in Dialogue* (New York: Newman Press, 2006).

35. See further, Yves Congar, "The People of God," in Miller, *Interfaith Appraisal*, 200.

36. See *LG*, chapters 4 and 5.

37. John Henry Newman, *On Consulting the Faithful in Matters of Doctrine* (New York: Sheed and Ward, 1962), 63.

38. See Michael Sharkey, "Newman on the Laity," *Gregorianum* 68 1–2 (1986): 339–46. Accessed October 8, 2008, at *http://www.ewtn.com/library/Theology/new mnlay.htm*.

39. Pius XII, *Munificentissimus Deus*, no. 11–12. Accessed October 8, 2008, at *http://www.ewtn.com/library/papaldoc/p12munif.htm*.

40. See John Henry Newman, *The Arians of the Fourth Century* (London: Longmans, Green, and Co., 1908), 445–68.

41. Avery Dulles, "Moderate Infallibilism," in Empie, *Authority and Infallibility*, 88–89.

42. John Paul II, *On Commitment to Ecumenism (Ut Unum Sint)* (1995) no. 84. Accessed October 8, 2008, at: *http://www.vatican.va/holy_father/john_paul_ii/encyclicals/documents/hf_jp-ii_enc_25051995_ut-unum-sint_en.html*.

43. John Paul II, *Ut Unum Sint*, no. 52.

44. CDF, *Commentary on the Document "Responses to Some Questions"*; *Dominus Iesus*, no. 17.

45. See T. F. Stransky, "The Decree on Ecumenism," in Miller, *Interfaith Appraisal*, 380; Yves Congar, "People of God," in Miller, *Interfaith Appraisal*, 204.

46. CDF, *Reponses to Some Questions Regarding Certain Aspects of the Doctrine of the Church. Response to Question 5.*

47. CDF, *Commentary on the Document "Responses to Some Questions"*; *UR* no. 22.

48. Benedict XVI, address to U.S. bishops, April 16, 2008. Accessed October 8, 2008, at *http://www.vatican.va/holy_father/benedict_xvi/speeches/2008/april/documents/hf_ben-xvi_spe_20080416_bishops-usa_en.html*.

49. Joseph Ratzinger, *Introduction to Christianity* (San Francisco: Ignatius Press, 2000; orig. pub. 1968), 340.

50. "The Common Declaration of Pope Paul VI and Patriarch Athenagoras," in *Vatican Council II*, vol. 1, *The Conciliar and Postconciliar Documents*, ed. A. Flannery; rev. ed. (Northport, NY: Costello Publishing Co., 1975), 471–72.

51. John Paul II, *Ut Unum Sint*, no. 79.

52. "What Is the World Council of Churches?" Accessed October 8, 2008, at *http://www.oikoumene.org/en/who-are-we.html*.

53. John Paul II, *Ut Unum Sint*, nos. 8–9. Emphases original.

54. Rahner, "Christianity and the Non-Christian Religons," in *Theological Investigations*, vol. 5, *Later Writings* (Baltimore: Helicon; London: Darton, Longman & Todd, 1966), 115–34.

55. John Paul II, *Redemptoris missio* (1990) no. 10. Accessed October 8, 2008, at *http://www. vatican.va/holy_father/john_paul_ii/encyclicals/documents/hf_jp-ii_enc_07121990_ redemptoris-missio_en.html.*

56. *Decree on the Church's Missionary Activity (Ad gentes)* no. 7; see also *GS* no. 22.

57. Joseph Ratzinger, *Truth and Tolerance* (San Francisco: Ignatius Press, 2004), 17–18.

58. See the summary in ibid., 52.

59. Ibid., 24–25.

60. Ibid., 34.

61. Ibid., 47.

62. Ibid., 49.

63. C. S. Lewis, *Mere Christianity* (London: HarperCollins, 2001; orig. pub. 1952), 36–38.

64. Ratzinger, *Truth and Tolerance*, 48.

65. Ibid., 204.

66. Ratzinger (*Truth and Tolerance*, 39) writes that in a dialogue between representatives of monotheism and representatives of mysticism "a great deal of patience, tact, and integrity in their religious seeking will be needed on both sides."

67. Ibid., 53.

68. Ibid., 18.

Glossary

analogy, analogical language: language that describes God using comparisons to natural realities, based on the belief that God and other supernatural realities cannot be described directly.

anthropomorphic: described or thought of as having human characteristics. Applied to God, these characteristics might be either physical ("God's arm") or emotional and psychological ("God's jealousy").

apocalyptic: a type of thinking or writing dealing with end-of-the-world themes; its language is often heavily symbolic and emphasizes God's direct intervention in human affairs.

apophatic approach: applied to theology, the belief that human language cannot describe God directly, but can only say what God is not.

apostolic succession: the handing on of the beliefs, practices, and spiritual authority of Jesus' apostles to their successors the bishops.

argument from design: the argument that evidence of a planned design in nature (animate or inanimate) points toward a mind responsible for the design.

atonement: the belief that Jesus' death in some way "made up for" or "paid for" the sins of all humanity. The Christian tradition has proposed different models of exactly how Jesus' death accomplished this atonement.

Babylonian Exile: the period from approximately 587 to 538 BCE when the Judean people were in exile in Babylon after the destruction of the Jerusalem Temple.

canon, canonical: the basic meaning of *canon* is "a standard or guide." In a Christian context, it refers to the books that the Church has accepted as authoritative Scripture.

canonization: the process by which Israel and the Church discerned which books were authoritative Scripture. (The Roman Catholic

Church also applies the term to the process of discerning whether an individual should be declared a saint.)

Catholic v. catholic: As used in this book, *Catholic* with a capital *C* generally refers to the Roman Catholic Church; *catholic* with a lowercase *c* refers to the broader Christian tradition whose beliefs are expressed by the Apostles' Creed and the Nicene Creed.

Church: As used in this book, *Church* with a capital *C* generally refers to the one, holy, catholic, and apostolic Church to which the Nicene Creed refers, and in a few instances to the Roman Catholic Church. (Many Vatican II documents use *Church* to refer specifically to the Roman Catholic Church.) The term is also capitalized when referring to a particular denomination: e.g., the *Lutheran Church*.

creed: a short summary of basic Christian beliefs. The two most influential Christian creeds are the Apostles' Creed and the Nicene Creed.

Darwinian theory of evolution: the scientific theory of evolution by natural selection; distinct from *evolutionism*, a materialistic, deterministic worldview.

Deist: of or relating to Deism, a view, popular in the Enlightenment, that understands God as the "Divine Watchmaker" who created the universe and its laws but no longer intervenes in the natural order.

determinism: a worldview that denies human free will, believing that all human actions are determined by forces such as genetics and environmental influences.

development of doctrine: the belief that essential Christian teachings (such as the doctrine of the Trinity) and practices (such as confession or infant baptism) have evolved naturally over time without corrupting original Christian beliefs or practices.

Docetism: the view that Jesus was a supernatural being who appeared to be human, but in reality was not.

ecclesiology: the systematic theological study of the nature of the one Christian Church and the various churches.

ecumenical council: the gatherings of Christian bishops from around the world. The authority of seven ecumenical councils is accepted by both Eastern and Western Churches: Nicaea I (325), Constantinople I (381), Ephesus (431), Chalcedon (451), Constantinople II (553), Constantinople III (680–681), Nicaea II (787). The Roman

Catholic Church recognizes the ecumenical authority of fourteen further councils, up to and including Vatican Council II.

ecumenical dialogue, ecumenical movement: the modern movement to establish better mutual understanding and cooperation among various Christian churches. For some, the eventual goal is full visible unity of all Christian churches.

Enlightenment: an influential European philosophical and cultural movement of the eighteenth century that promoted religious toleration and freedom of thought, but also tended toward rationalism and Deism.

eschatological: having to do with the "last times," the fulfillment of earthly history.

ethical relativism: the belief that no fixed standards of right and wrong exist; rather, ethical standards change according to particular circumstances.

fallen human nature, the Fall: the Christian belief that human nature has become corrupted with inherent tendencies toward sin and self-destructive behaviors.

fideism: a belief system founded on religious feeling rather than on a reasoned faith.

Gnostic: a religious and philosophical trend that tended to see the material world as evil and defined salvation as the spirit's escape from the material world. Christian Gnostics thus held a docetic view of Jesus.

grace: a supernatural gift of God that cannot be earned by any human efforts.

Hebrew and Jewish: as ethnic designations, *Hebrew* generally names the tribes of Israel up until the time of the Babylonian captivity; *Jewish* is generally first applied to the Judean captives returning to Jerusalem.

Hellenistic: refers to the Greek culture spread throughout the eastern Mediterranean world after the conquests of Alexander the Great (356–323 BCE).

hermeneutics: guidelines to determine the meaning and valid interpretation of classic texts, especially of the Bible.

historical-critical method: a general approach that applies historical, cultural, and literary analysis to Scripture.

historical Jesus: the understanding of Jesus in his historical and cultural context as a first-century Jew.

Incarnation: the belief that the Second Person of the Trinity became human as Jesus of Nazareth.

inerrancy: the belief that God protected the writers of Scripture from error. *Strict inerrancy* is the belief that God protected the writers from any error, including historical or factual errors. *Limited inerrancy* is the belief that God protected the writers from essential theological or ethical errors related to salvation.

infallibility: the belief that the Church has the divine gift of proclaiming essential truths of faith and morals without error. In the Roman Catholic understanding, the pope and the bishops in union with him have the authority to proclaim infallible teachings.

inspiration: the belief that the Holy Spirit guided the writers of Scripture to record the truths of salvation without error. Some recent theologians locate the gift of inspiration in the community of faith (Israel, the Church) as a whole.

kingdom of God: the eschatological culmination of history in which God's will is established fully. The kingdom began to be established in the person of Jesus and in his founding of the Church.

logos: a Greek philosophical term referring to the rational order in the human mind and in the universe. Christian theology identifies the *Logos* (capital *L*) with the Second Person of the Trinity.

Magisterium: in Roman Catholic understanding, the official teaching authority of the Church, expressed through the bishops and the pope.

materialism: a worldview that understands the physical, tangible universe as the only reality.

metaphysical: of or relating to metaphysics, a branch of philosophy that deals with the ultimate origin and nature of being and reality.

natural law: in ethics, the belief that human reason naturally recognizes true ethical standards that distinguish between right and wrong behavior.

open historical-critical method: a use of the historical-critical method that does not rule out *a priori* the possibility of supernatural intervention in nature.

original sin: the belief that human nature as a whole has fallen from its original condition of harmony with God.

Orthodox and orthodox: *Orthodox* with a capital *O* refers to a group of Eastern churches, such as the Greek and Russian Orthodox churches, who share a common faith expressed in the seven ecumenical councils. *Orthodox* with a lowercase *o* literally means "right belief," referring to Christian belief and practice as expressed in the ecumenical councils.

rabbi, rabbinic Judaism: *Rabbi* is the Hebrew name for "teacher." Rabbinic Judaism is based on the Torah (Law) as interpreted in the Mishnah (c. 200 CE) and the Palestinian and Babylonian Talmuds (c. fourth–sixth centuries CE).

rationalism: a worldview holding that the only valid knowledge is scientifically verifiable knowledge; religious beliefs are seen as subjective opinion only.

Reformation: a movement, beginning in the sixteenth century, in which reformers broke away from the Roman Catholic Church and established such churches as the Lutheran and Reformed churches. Churches with roots in the Reformation are typically called *Protestant.*

sacrament: a physical sign through which God's grace is channeled to humans. All traditional Christian Churches recognize the Lord's Supper and baptism as sacraments; the Catholic Church recognizes seven sacraments.

salvation: the definitive, eschatological fulfillment of a human being; the reunion of humans with God through the overcoming of sin.

Second Temple period: time from the end of the Babylonian Exile until the destruction of the Jerusalem Temple by Rome in 70 CE.

sola scriptura: the Protestant principle that Scripture alone is the basis for Church teaching and practice.

theology: the rational study of faith from the perspective of a particular faith tradition.

Tradition or tradition: *Tradition* with a capital *T* refers to the Christian faith as a whole, including Scripture and essential Christian beliefs and practices, as it has been passed down through the generations. In Catholic theology *Tradition* may also refer to essential teachings and practices that are not explicitly in Scripture.

Tradition with a lowercase *t* may refer to denominational beliefs and practices (e.g., the Lutheran tradition) or to nonessential practices of various churches.

transcendent: supernatural reality beyond the empirical or natural world.

worldview: a particular philosophical paradigm through which all reality is perceived and interpreted.

Index